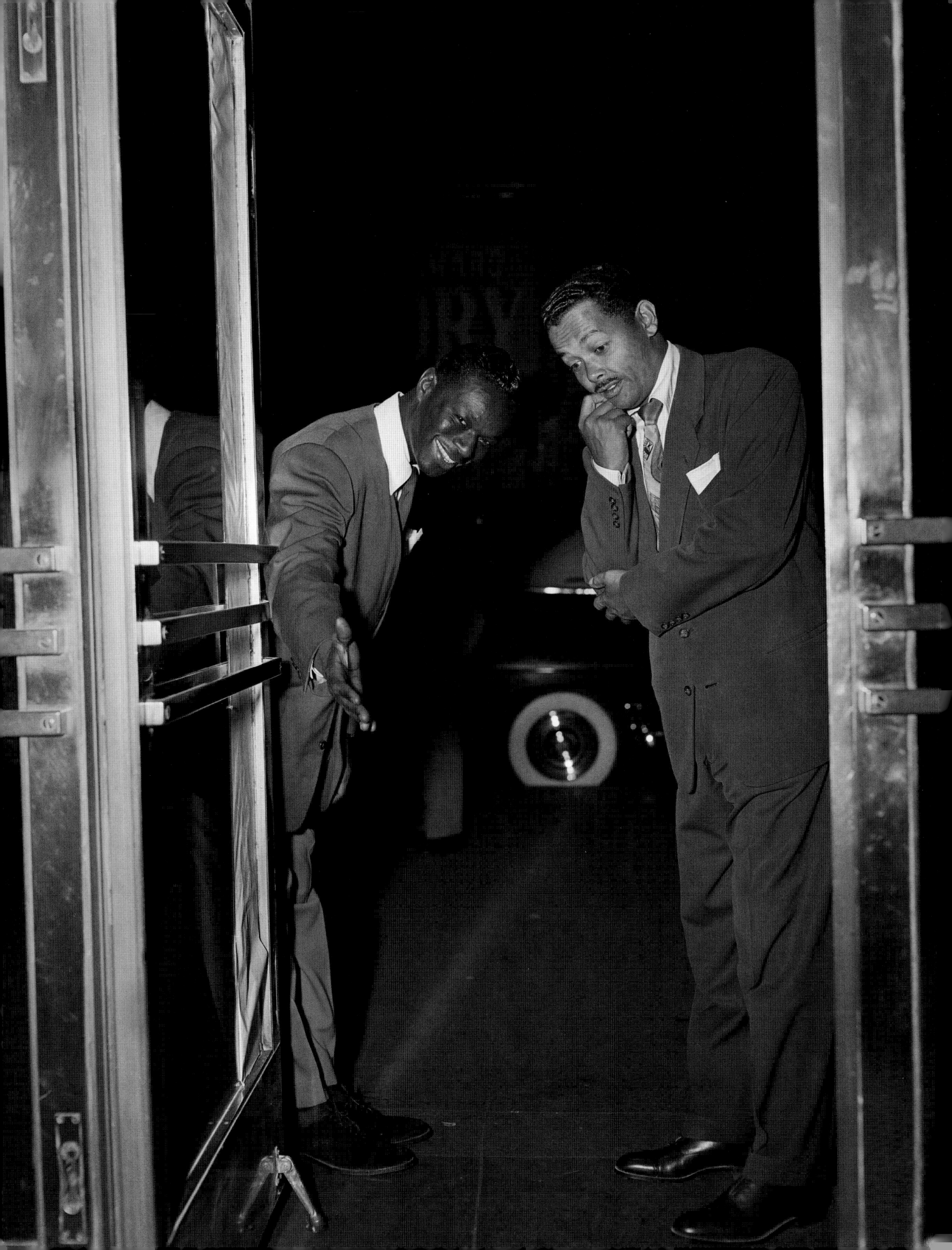

JAZZ, GIANTS, AND JOURNEYS

THE PHOTOGRAPHY OF

Herman Leonard

EDITED BY DAVID HOUSTON AND JENNY BAGERT

FOREWORD BY QUINCY JONES

SCALA

Scans and digital image preparation:
David Guidry and David Leonard, Lakeside Camera Photoworks, New Orleans.

Digital image correction:
David Leonard and Jenny Bagert

Writing consultants:
Brod Bagert and Henry Griffin

Sponsored in part by:
Joshua Mann Pailet, A Gallery for Fine Photography, New Orleans
and
David Guidry, Lakeside Camera Photoworks, New Orleans

Acknowledgments:
Special thanks to Jill Hershorin, Jordan Schulman, Elizabeth Underwood and Allie Verlander for their dedicated work that made much of this book possible.

This book could never have been realized without the total dedication, perseverance, patience, boundless energy, unfailing loyalty and devotion of Jenny Bagert.
Herman Leonard

This book © Scala Publishers Limited 2006
Photography © Herman Leonard Photography LLC 2006
Text © The Ogden Museum of Southern Art 2006

First published in 2006 by
Scala Publishers Limited
Northburgh House
10 Northburgh Street
London EC1V 0AT
UK
www.scalapublishers.com

Distributed in the USA in the booktrade by
Antique Collectors' Club Limited
Eastworks
116 Pleasant Street, Suite 60B
Easthampton, MA 01027
United States of America
ISBN: 978-1-85759-434-8

All rights reserved. No part of this book may be reproduced, stored in a retrieval system or transmitted in any form or by any means, electronic, mechanical, photocopying, recording or otherwise, without the written permission of The Ogden Museum of Southern Art and Scala Publishers Limited.

Every effort has been made to acknowledge copyright of images where applicable. Any errors or omissions are unintentional and should be notified to the Publisher, who will include corrections in any reprinted editions.

Designer: Katy Homans
Project Editor: Oliver Craske
Copy Editors: Sandra Pisano, Julie Pickard
Production Manager: Claudia Varosio
Printed and bound in Singapore

10 9 8 7 6 5 4 3

All photographs by Herman Leonard except as follows:
Jenny Bagert: 27 (top and bottom)
Elizabeth Braunlich: 25 (right)
Quincy Jones: 29
Yousuf Karsh: 12
Joseph A. Rosen: 27 (middle)
Hugh Talman: 28
Photographer unknown: 6, 10 (all), 17, 19, 20, 21 (top and bottom left), 26

Page 2: Billy Eckstine & Nat King Cole, Royal Roost, NYC, 1948

Contents

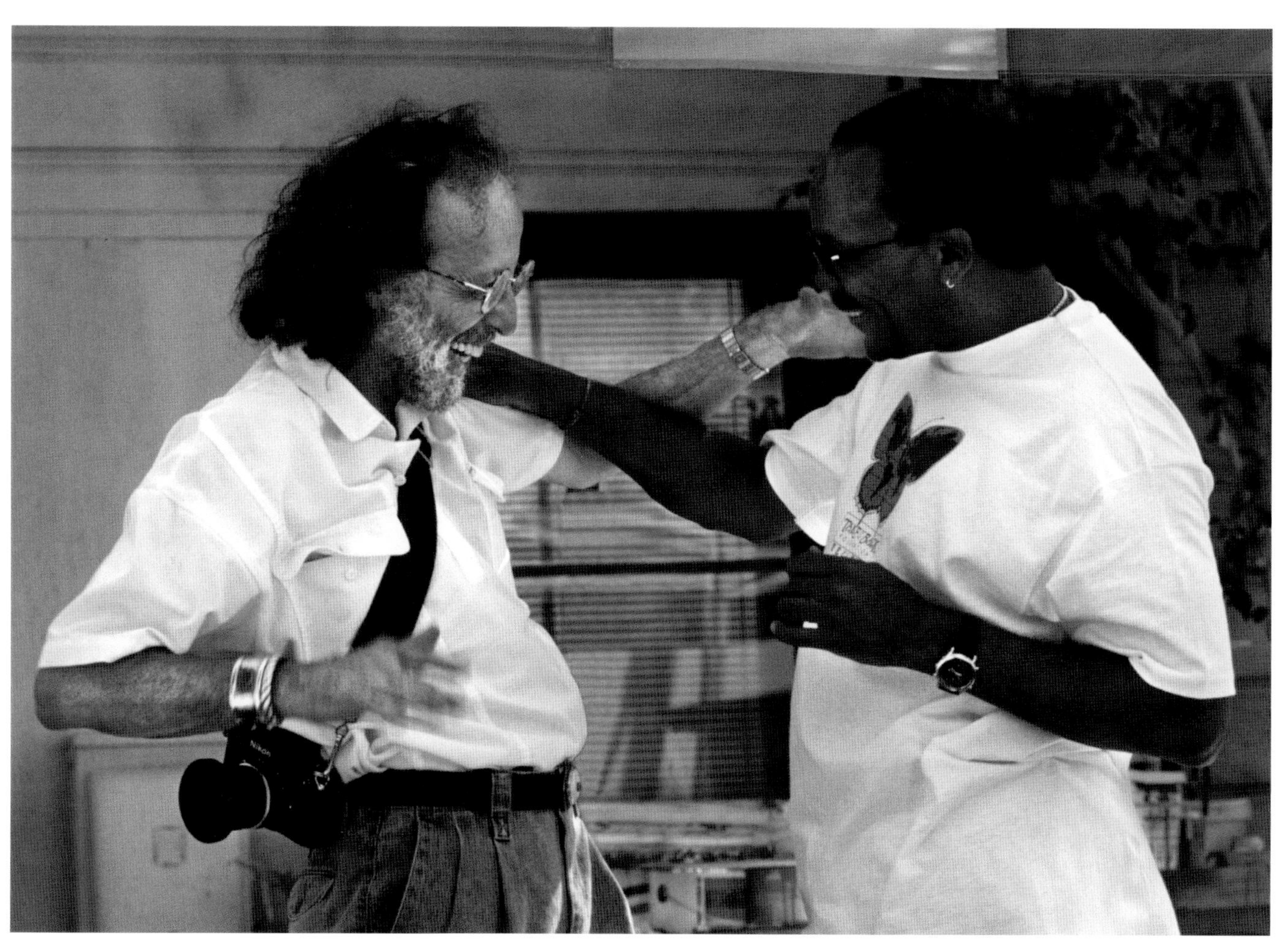

Herman Leonard and Quincy Jones

Foreword

Quincy Jones

Jazz and photography go so well together (and so frequently), that you can't help but see similarities between them. I used to tell cats that Herman Leonard did with his camera what we did with our instruments. Looking back across his career, I'm even more sure of the comparison: Herman's camera tells the truth, and makes it swing.

The biggest challenge for a musician is to dig down and find his own sound. A trumpeter has to shed and shed and shed until he can play 'Cherokee' without reminding folks of Clifford Brown's intimidating solo. Herman found his own style the same way, shooting roll after roll, until he wrote the vernacular of jazz photography. When people think of jazz, their mental picture is likely one of Herman's.

We met in New York in the late Forties, a glorious period that found me playing in Dizzy Gillespie's big band. The Apple was swarming with music at the time, and if you weren't gigging, you were watching somebody else. But wherever you went, there was Herman, holding his Speed Graphic at an angle, like Lester Young.

We stayed friends when we both moved to Paris the next decade. My recording sessions were Herman's, too, to my benefit. Musicians loved to see him around. No surprise, he made us look good. And not just us. Herman used the same eye on a half naked Thai boxer as he did for similarly topless models for *Playboy*.

The life laid out in these pages is the story of a man who was always in the right place at the right time, in more ways than one: he was in the right city at the right vantage for the right moment during the right period. Wherever Herman was, that was where it was at.

Perfect photographs look lucky. But when you see so many in a row, well, there's another, more accurate word for that kind of luck: talent. If there's any luck in the long, illustrious career of Herman Leonard, it belongs to me and all of his other subjects, for his patient diligence, his discriminating eye, and in my case, his enduring friendship. After all these years, his work is still music to my eyes.

Bop City, NYC, 1948 (overleaf)

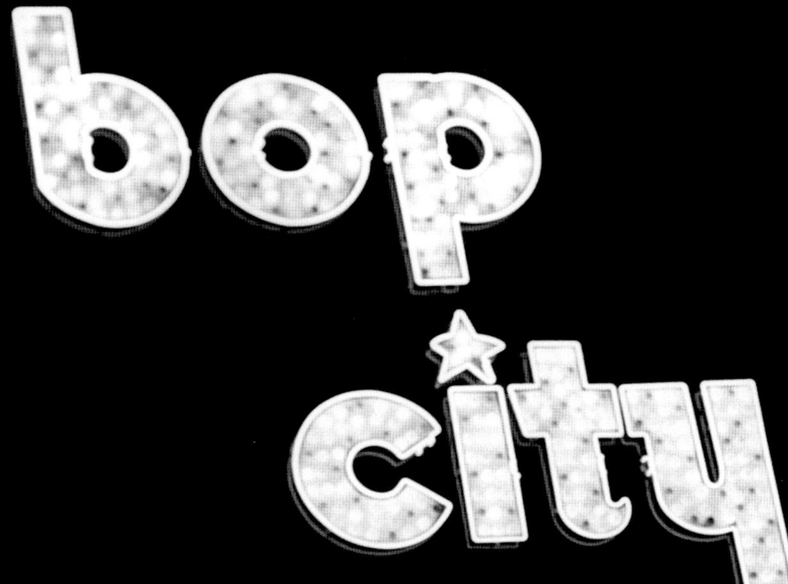
bop city
bop city
ARTIE SHAW
SYMPHONY ORCHESTRA
ELLA FITZGERALD
RAY BROWN KAI WINDING
JAZZ CENTER
OF THE WORLD
TURF
RESTAURANT
BAR

Herman Leonard

David Houston

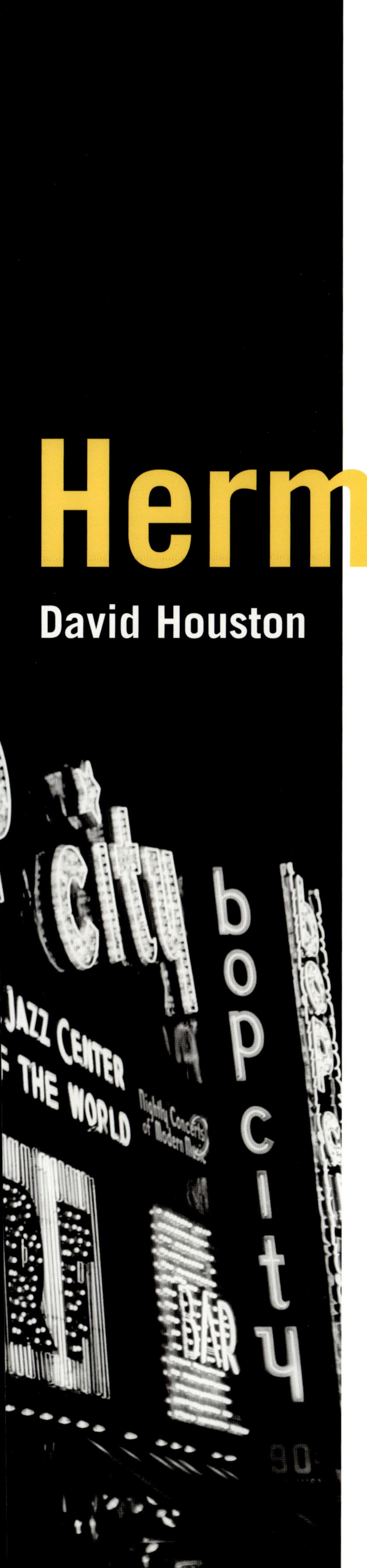

Herman Leonard's camera is his passport to the world. Although best known for his atmospheric images of jazz musicians of the Bebop era, Leonard's work has taken him to Europe, Russia, the Middle East, and Asia. He has photographed musicians from Charlie Parker to Lenny Kravitz, the intellectuals Albert Einstein, Jean-Paul Sartre, and Simone de Beauvoir, and the actors Marlon Brando, Brigitte Bardot, and Marilyn Monroe. His direct, empathetic approach to portraiture has earned him the respect of his peers and the friendship of his subjects. While many of his photographs were taken on assignment, much of his collection is the result of Leonard's unquenchable curiosity about people, music, and the far points of the world, fueled by his friendship with many of the cultural icons of the last six decades. With this volume, we are finally able to see Leonard's iconic jazz photographs within the context of the larger body of his life's work, some of it published here for the first time.

Herman Leonard was born in Allentown, Pennsylvania, in 1923, the third child of Joseph Leonard and Rose Morrison, Jewish immigrants from Yassi, Romania. His father was a prosperous businessman, founder of the Charis Corporation, which manufactured women's foundation garments. Typical of many immigrant families, Leonard's parents valued initiative, hard work and the importance of education, and passed these values on to their children. As a child, Leonard traveled extensively, accompanying his mother on a trip to South America in 1930, and again in 1935, on an extended three-year visit to Palestine, finding time for trips to Egypt and Europe. The lasting impressions of this period planted the seeds for Leonard's later travels, as well as equipping him with a natural fascination for the unknown.

His parents encouraged his early interest in photography, and provided important moral and financial support at key moments in his career. His brother gave Leonard his first camera, and the twelve-year-old quickly discovered that photography was a comfortable way to approach the world and to connect with it. 'The camera wiped away all of my self-consciousness with people,' he recalls. At first, Leonard photographed largely for himself. Later he became his high school's official photographer, shooting social, academic, and sporting events. He particularly enjoyed giving prints to appreciative friends. By his late teens he had already acquired a thorough knowledge of basic photographic skills and a considerable amount of camera and darkroom experience—skills that would soon provide an entrée into a diverse range of social milieus and unexpected friendships. This youthful mastery of photography enabled him to use the medium as a highly personal way to engage with people and to connect with the larger world. This would remain his guiding methodology throughout his career. 'For me,' Leonard says, 'the camera was my open sesame.' While many of his peers were self-taught or learned their craft in the military or on the front lines of photojournalism, Leonard trained for his life's work by earning a college degree in his chosen profession. After graduating from public school in Allentown in 1940, Leonard enrolled at Ohio University at a time when photographic education was in its infancy. With six years of photographic experience behind him, he enrolled on one of America's few Bachelor's programs in photography.

Leonard's college years were interrupted by the Second World War and from 1943 to 1945 he served in the United States Army Medical Corps in Burma. The harsh realities of

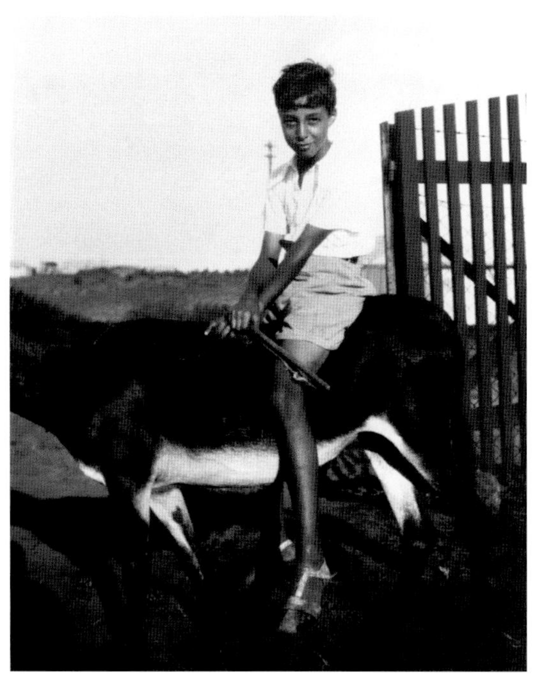

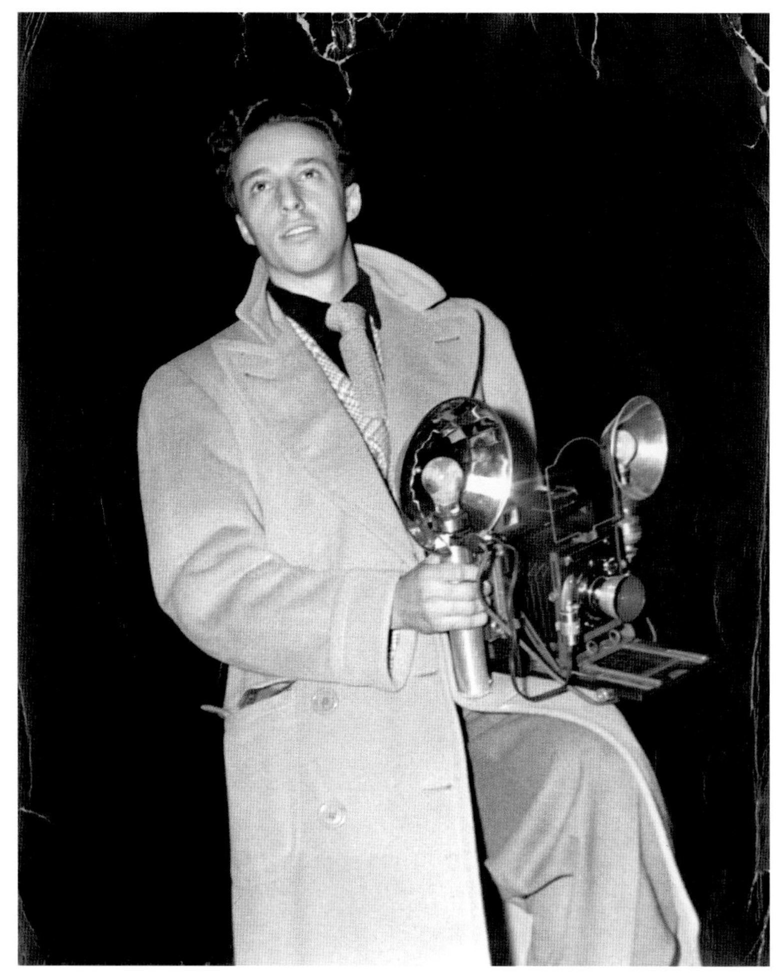

May 17, 1944
This is my
Burma darkroom.
Parachute lining!
blanket covering!
stretcher Table.
Glass from an
ambulance & a
cardboard box.
It works!

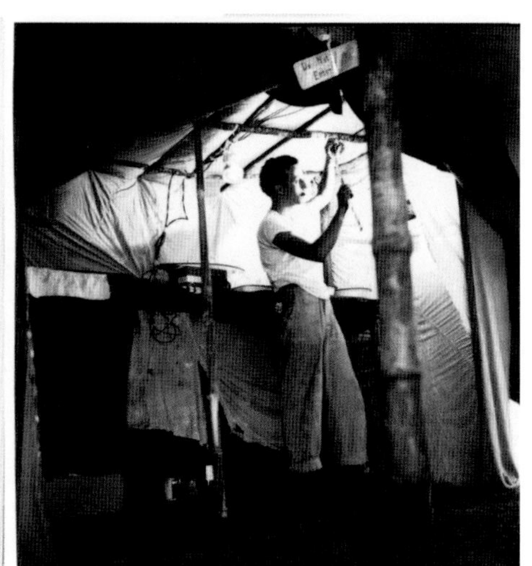

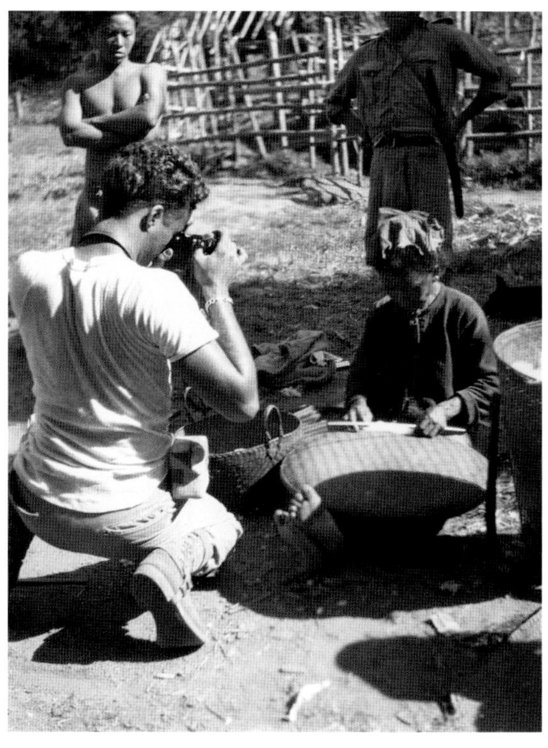

Leonard, Palestine, 1935

Leonard, Ohio University, Athens, Ohio, 1941

Leonard, World War II darkroom, Burma, 1944

Leonard, World War II, Burma, 1945

war provided a monumental experience for the young photographer, one that he sees as 'one of the turning points of my life.' Ironically, he failed in his attempt to become a military photographer because of missing one question on the entrance examination. 'They turned me down because I didn't know the chemical formula for a developer that we used straight out of the package,' a formula he still uses today, remaining unaware of its precise chemical make-up.

During his two years of service as an army medic, he saw constant action on the front lines. Although the intensity of his work as a medic precluded him from photographing regularly, he occasionally found time to shoot, developing his film on moonless nights in chemicals mixed in a combat helmet. Few of his war photographs have survived, and those that have focus on the Burmese people (see page 44). With a few notable exceptions (see page 49), Leonard tended to avoid the dramatic style of photojournalistic war reportage. Instead, he favored a quieter approach, photographing the people he regularly encountered, foreshadowing his later work.

Since his youth, Leonard had been interested in anthropology and the diverse people of the world. Photography was, for him, about people and their circumstances and less about the big story. Unlike many young photographers whose ambition it was to travel the world as reporters for *Look* or *Life* magazines, Leonard found his point of reference in the direct, humanistic approach pioneered by *National Geographic*.

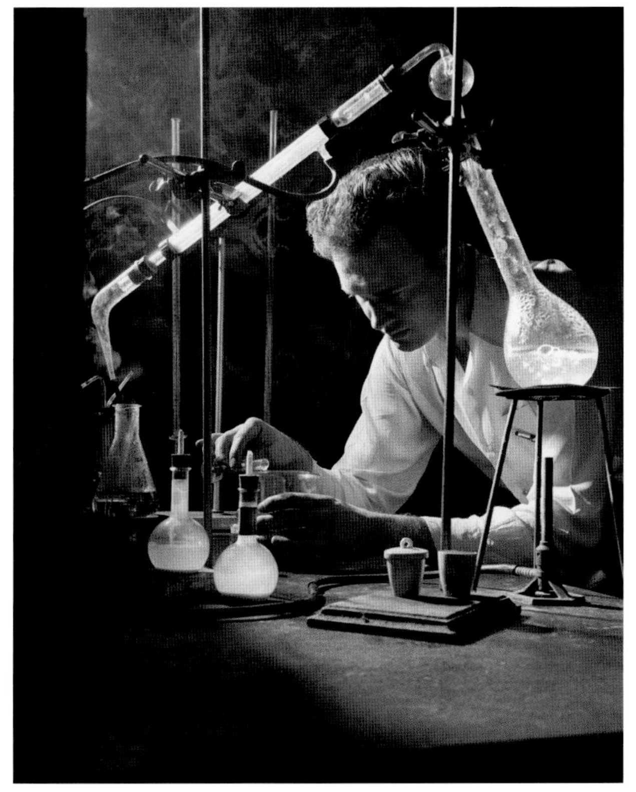

Ohio University, Athens, Ohio, 1946; Leonard's first backlit photograph

After his military service, Leonard returned to Ohio and continued work on his bachelor's degree, shooting regularly for the school yearbook. One of his yearbook photographs would accidentally provide insight into a studio lighting technique that remained important to him throughout his career. While photographing in the chemistry lab, Leonard set up typical studio lighting, utilizing two flash bulbs that would provide a smooth, evenly illuminated scene. In shooting a chemistry experiment, one of the front flashbulbs failed to fire in one exposure. He nevertheless developed that flawed shot, along with those illuminated by two lights, and was immediately intrigued. The negative with the one backlight did not exhibit the flat, consistent light demanded by the school yearbook, but the unintentional backlit effect created an illusion of three-dimensional relief and dramatic separation in the pictorial elements of the composition. Leonard's subsequent experimentation with light—both found and manipulated—to create emotional impact, would remain one of the defining characteristics of his photography.

After completing his Bachelor's degree in 1947, Leonard felt the need for further photographic training and sought an apprenticeship with the renowned Canadian photographer Yousuf Karsh. Leonard traveled to Canada for a lunch meeting to discuss his ambitions. Though Karsh was not known for taking on apprentices, by the end of the day he had offered Leonard the opportunity to work for him as an unpaid assistant. For an entire year, Leonard worked at the side of this established master of portraiture. He absorbed Karsh's lighting techniques and the many tonal ranges and nuances of light that Karsh was able to tease out of the final print in the darkroom. Soon, Leonard himself was printing the well-known images that had inspired him to seek an apprenticeship with Karsh, but Karsh's influence would go far beyond lighting technique.

Early on, Leonard observed that the personal interaction between Karsh and his sitter, as well as his control over mood and situation, often provided the basis of successful portraiture. Leonard recalls that Karsh 'knew how to handle people so as to get what he was after in the photograph.' Karsh had a favourite story that made a particularly lasting impression on the young Leonard. As Karsh prepared to photograph Winston Churchill at the beginning of the Second World War, he knew that the prime minister was a famously difficult subject and that there would be only a few minutes for the shoot. Karsh was prepared when Churchill entered the room, grumpy and sporting his ever-present cigar. While making his final adjustments to the camera, Karsh politely asked Churchill not to smoke, a request the prime minister ignored. Karsh walked across the room and firmly pulled the cigar out of Churchill's mouth, and then squeezed the release bulb. The scowling image he recorded on film that day became one of the iconic images of British resistance to Nazi aggression throughout the Second World War, and remains one of the most important portraits of the twentieth century. The lesson Karsh wished to impress on his young apprentice was clear: the skilled photographer can be an active agent in creating images, rather than a mere passive recorder of them. Undeniably, this memory must have inspired Leonard later, when he came to realize that the only way for him to achieve the results he desired was to control the environment, however foreign.

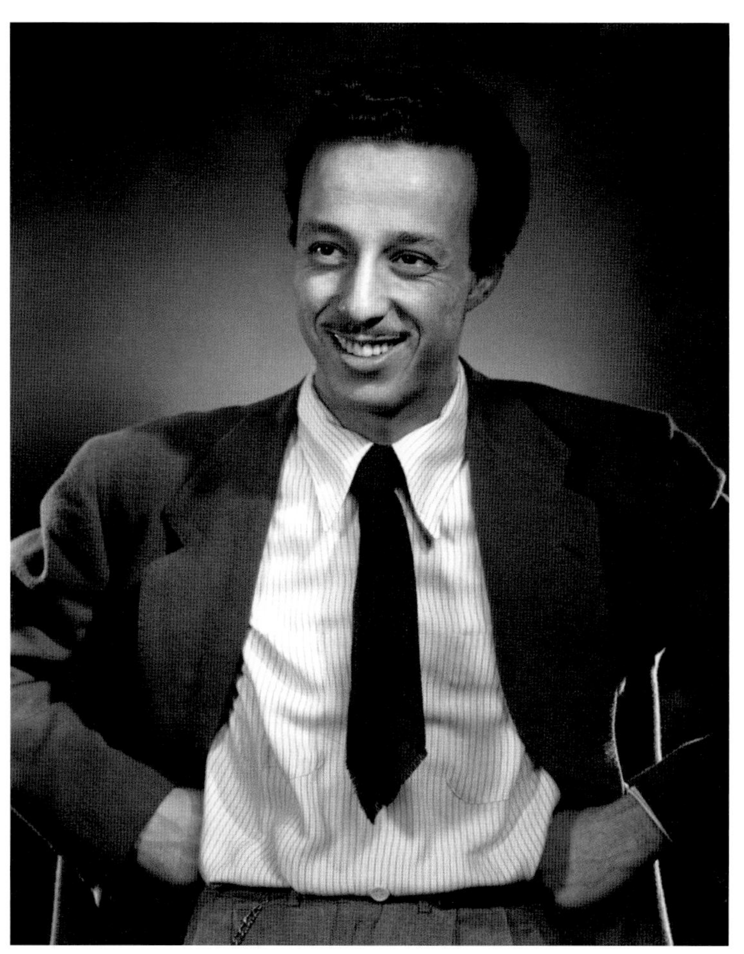

Leonard would later have the opportunity to be present and to assist at another famous session, when Karsh photographed Albert Einstein at The Center for Advanced Study at Princeton University. Leonard was both excited and intimidated by the prospect of meeting Einstein, especially since he had been told by his parents that Einstein 'was the smartest man in the world.' The person he encountered at Princeton was not an intimidating giant, but a gentle, affable man of great charm. Leonard was to capture his own portrait of Einstein that day, shot from the physicist's right, and catching him just as he looked directly into the lens of Karsh's view camera (see page 66).

Leonard came away that day with an important insight into the creative process, from an unexpected source. Finding a disparity between Einstein's innovative work in physics and his passion for the violin, Leonard asked him what physics and playing the violin had in common. Einstein replied that both music and physics are reliant on the art of improvisation, the art of moving beyond the conventions of the standard approaches that often reach only ordinary conclusions. Einstein was the first of many legendary improvisers among Leonard's subjects.

These months of apprenticeship were decisive in Leonard's development. It was Karsh's creative vision, his ability to carry through from the camera to the final print, that

Leonard, Ottowa, Canada, 1948; photograph by Yousuf Karsh

Yousuf Karsh; gift from Karsh, 1947

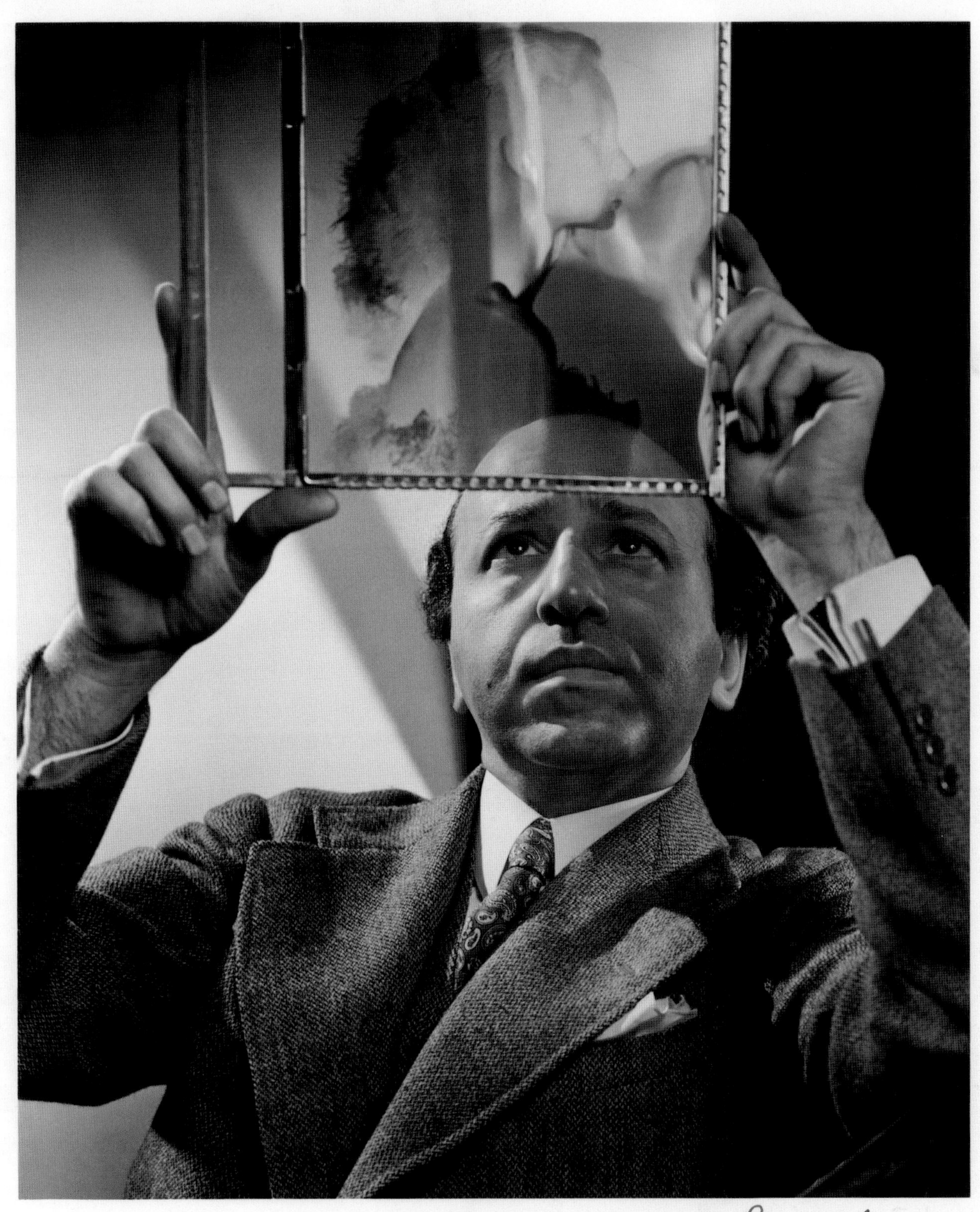
To "Leonard"
I know you have It in You
to be a great Photographer.
"Go ahead and conquer"
Yousuf Karsh.

provided Leonard with a larger framework for pursuing an expressive personal vision through photography. Leonard also credits Karsh with teaching him 'how to visualize the final image and how to pull it out of the negative. Not so much the specifics of how to realize it, but what to work for in a successful print.' A simple statement by Karsh proved an even more profound influence on Leonard, one that would form the ethical core of his work: 'always tell the truth but tell it in terms of beauty.'

After his year with Karsh, Leonard moved to New York City and opened a studio at 220 Sullivan Street in Greenwich Village. He was attracted to the vitality of the city's emergent post-war culture and set out to find his own place within it.

Little of Leonard's early New York work has survived, but in the few extant photos we see him trying out the popular approach of grabbing images in the street photography style popularized by Helen Levitt and others. In these photos, shot on Sullivan Street near his studio, using a medium-format Rolleiflex camera, we see Leonard concentrating on the primacy of the human subject over the larger mood or context, in what might be called an environmental portrait (see pages 39–41). These early New York photographs may be understood as successful experiments or minor flirtations with the most influential photographic trends of the era, trends that Leonard respected but ultimately chose not to pursue. For Leonard, street photography and the photo reportage popularized by *Life* and *Look* magazines were interesting but could not replace his passion for portraiture. For him, the decisive moment was not to be pulled from the chaotic flow of everyday life, but was created by the close-up and purposeful interaction between the photographer and his subject—the approach he had successfully absorbed from his apprenticeship with Karsh.

Leonard, however, was soon to develop a highly personal approach which combined the spontaneity of the action shot with the control of portrait sitting. Rather than relying on the vagaries of available light, Leonard adapted studio lighting techniques to location photography. This novel approach allowed him not only to control the intensity of light, letting him shoot where others dared not, but to control the use of light as a tool for emotional expression. This approach would distinguish his first important body of work of musicians shot in the jazz clubs of New York City in the late 1940s and the early 1950s—the moment when Leonard's passion for photography would merge with his love for music.

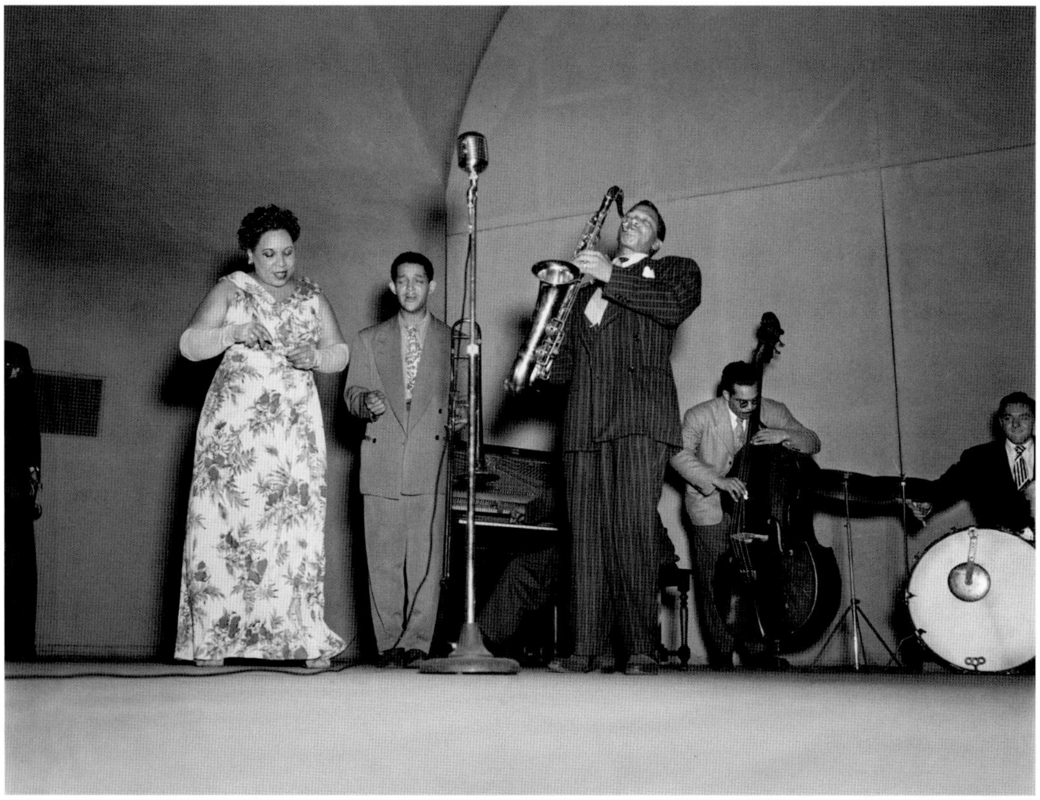

'Jazz at the Philharmonic' concert, Columbus, Ohio; Leonard's first photograph of jazz musicians

Leonard's interest in music first emerged in high school, when he regularly listened to swing and big band music on the radio. 'My parents loved classical music and all my childhood musical experiences had been traditional. Then when I heard jazz, it was a whole new thing, like eating candy for the first time.' His growing love for and knowledge of jazz resulted in his being asked to work as the DJ for a jazz program on his college radio station. Later still he had his first live-on-stage jazz experience. It was during his last year of college when he drove to Columbus, Ohio, to hear one of Norman Granz's 'Jazz at the Philharmonic' concerts in 1947. It was the night he met Granz, an unsung hero of early jazz and the founder of Verve Records. Leonard would later be invited to shoot many of Granz's recording sessions, providing opportunities to photograph a veritable parade of jazz greats. It was also the night Leonard took his first photograph of jazz musicians, marking the beginning of an obsession that would eventually yield some of the music world's most powerful images.

For the next nine years, Herman Leonard frequented the smoky clubs of New York City, obsessively photographing the jazz musicians who were revolutionizing music. Unable to afford regular visits to the New York jazz clubs, Leonard realized he could barter his photographs for unfettered access to this new music. Reviving a practice from his teenage years, he started giving prints to both the musicians and the club owners, and soon found his work being used for promotional fliers and club marquees. Leonard saw photography as a way to get closer to the musicians whose passion and creativity he revered. By photographing them, Leonard felt a kinship with these young lions, a shared sense of creative adventure. 'I didn't always know what I got when I shot. It was a thrill to develop the film and later see what I had captured that night.' With free access to this musical inner sanctum and the respect his work gradually garnered, Leonard had become an integral part of an emerging moment in American history. Reflecting back, Leonard observes, 'I had no idea when I shot those pictures that they would be significant twenty or thirty years later. I just wanted to be near the music and had no idea that it would become a part of history.' The new music was fast, free, and full of complex harmonies. Irreverently labelled 'Bebop,' it immediately drew the ire of the traditionally minded music world—fans and musicians alike. But change was in the air, and Leonard had become a part of it.

New York City in 1948 was becoming the center of the jazz world. Among Leonard's first subjects were Charlie Parker, Ella Fitzgerald, Dizzy Gillespie, Billy Eckstine, and Stan Getz. The list grew to include a veritable catalogue of the musicians and promoters who created America's original art form, many of whom Leonard would ever after count among his lifelong friends. While Leonard's photographs of the founding of modern jazz today constitute a remarkable record of a revolutionary era, interest in the music and the musicians who made it was limited to a small number of hardcore fans. The same could be said of the audience for photography, which was itself limited to serious photographers and connoisseurs. For both jazz and photography, a larger audience and greater media attention would come much later.

The jazz clubs of the late Forties were dark, and film speeds were slow, so musicians usually went to a photographer's studio during the day for a posed studio portrait printed on the typical eight-by-ten glossy paper. So it was both unusual and significant that Leonard was photographing musicians inside the clubs—in the shadowy, smoky, intimate milieu that was as much a part of the experience as the music itself. Leonard rose to the challenge by his successful adaptation of studio lighting techniques to the live stage. He would simply position his strobes to match the stage lights so that, when fired, they lit the subject at precisely the same angles as the existing lighting. In this way his studio strobes could approximate and retain the mood of the club setting while generating enough light to capture the image on film. What resulted were images so vital you could almost hear the music, images so dramatic that seeing them was almost akin to actually being there. His technique was simple but revolutionary.

Leonard would arrive at a club during afternoon rehearsals to set his strobes, shoot a few exposures to check his settings and balance, then return to his studio to develop his test shots before the evening performance. This approach allowed optimal control of the lighting and produced many negatives that would have been impossible to capture on the slow film emulsions available at the time without using additional lighting. This freedom to supplement the photographic limitations of club lighting offered Leonard a greater range of possibilities, including his ongoing use of backlighting for dramatic effect.

The effectiveness of the technique is particularly noticeable in one of Leonard's favorite photographs, his shot of Kenny Clarke playing drums at the Royal Roost (see page 176). His lighting creates the illusion of three dimensions, a technique common in the studio but made possible in the club by Leonard's innovative use of strobes. The sheer joy expressed on Clark's face impresses upon the viewer the full sense of his high-energy performance. Leonard calls it 'painting with light.'

Another example of this is the 1949 photograph of Ella Fitzgerald's birthday celebration at the Downbeat Club (see page 99). Realizing that this event would draw a celebrity audience, Leonard directed one strobe toward the stage and a second one toward the front row of tables in the audience. That night he took a position behind Fitzgerald on stage and waited for her to step into the right position to block the blinding strobe light from his lens. Leonard was shooting with a 4x5 Speed Graphic, had only ten shots for the entire evening, and no idea when Ella would move her head. He recalls that night with a smile. 'I got lucky,' he says, and indeed he did. His strobes capture Duke Ellington and Benny Goodman seated at the same table immediately in front of the stage, completely caught up in Fitzgerald's performance.

Many of Leonard's classic portraits were shot not for professional assignment or for publication, but out of personal interest or friendship. One of these was Leonard's first jazz portrait, a studio sitting with Lena Horne (see page 83). Introduced by a mutual friend, Leonard visited Horne in her dressing room before the evening performance. When he expressed interest in photographing her, she immediately said, 'How about tonight?' and showed up that evening at Leonard's Greenwich Village studio. The resulting image, with Horne's eyes closed and face cupped in her hands, is a photograph of tranquillity and intimacy that hardly looks like the result of a session squeezed in between two evening sets at the Copacabana. This sensitive portrait is evidence that Leonard was quick to adapt the lessons he had learned from Karsh, seen in the mood created by his use of lighting and the darkroom technique he employed to lessen the prominence of the singer's hands in the composition.

In a similarly posed portrait of Art Tatum, Leonard creates the opposite effect, making the hands purposefully prominent. The photograph was shot at the pianist's California

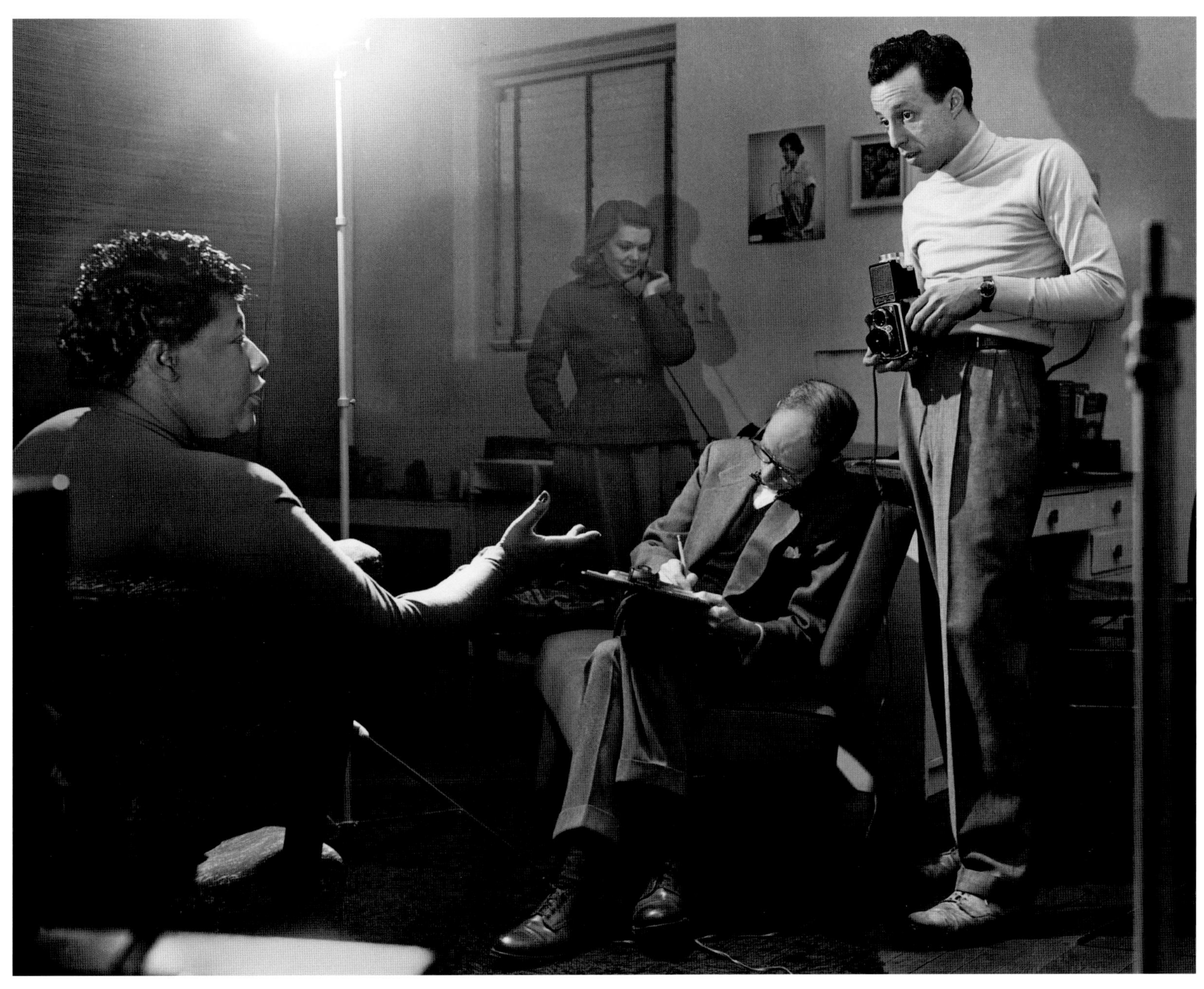

Leonard and Ella Fitzgerald, Sullivan Street studio, NYC, 1949

home on assignment from the great producer Norman Granz (see page 148). Tatum's portrait, capturing him in a light-colored suit, with downcast head and closed eyes, is dominated by the prominence of his long-fingered hands, the medium of the blind pianist's Mephistophelian talent. Leonard says that 'it was one of my few posed portraits and I wanted his wonderful hands, not his eyes, to be the focal point.'

Billie Holiday was the subject of another important studio session shot on assignment for *Ebony* magazine (see image on left of page 91). Leonard was given the assignment in 1949 on Holiday's release from jail on drug charges. He recalls, 'She met me standing in the doorway of her modest apartment wearing an apron over her dress and a smile. You'd never guess this was the great Lady Day just out of jail. She was healthy and beautiful and was cooking a steak for her boxer dog. After taking a few photographs in her apartment, we walked across the street to a small nightclub where she had arranged for me to photograph her in front of a microphone.' This radiantly lit image, featuring Leonard's signature use of smoke, and revealing a cherub lurking in the background, captured Billie Holiday on the ascent, with some of her best work before her (see page 93).

This session stands in sharp contrast to Leonard's last session with the singer six years later in 1955. These photographs were taken during a Norman Granz recording session, with Billie clearly on the decline (see pages 90, 94–95). Leonard recalls that she showed up at the session in both physical and mental distress. He recalls, 'She looked so drawn at this session that I didn't open up my cameras at first. But Norman wisely told me to "get your ass out there and shoot. It may be your last chance," and it was.' Leonard is still pained by his recollection of this last session with Lady Day, a session that put to the test Leonard's desire as an artist to 'always tell the truth but tell it in terms of beauty.' He has always been reluctant to publish these late photos of someone he remembers for her beauty and elegance. Over the years, he has gradually come to appreciate their importance as a historical record of a life that was marked by both accomplishment and tragedy.

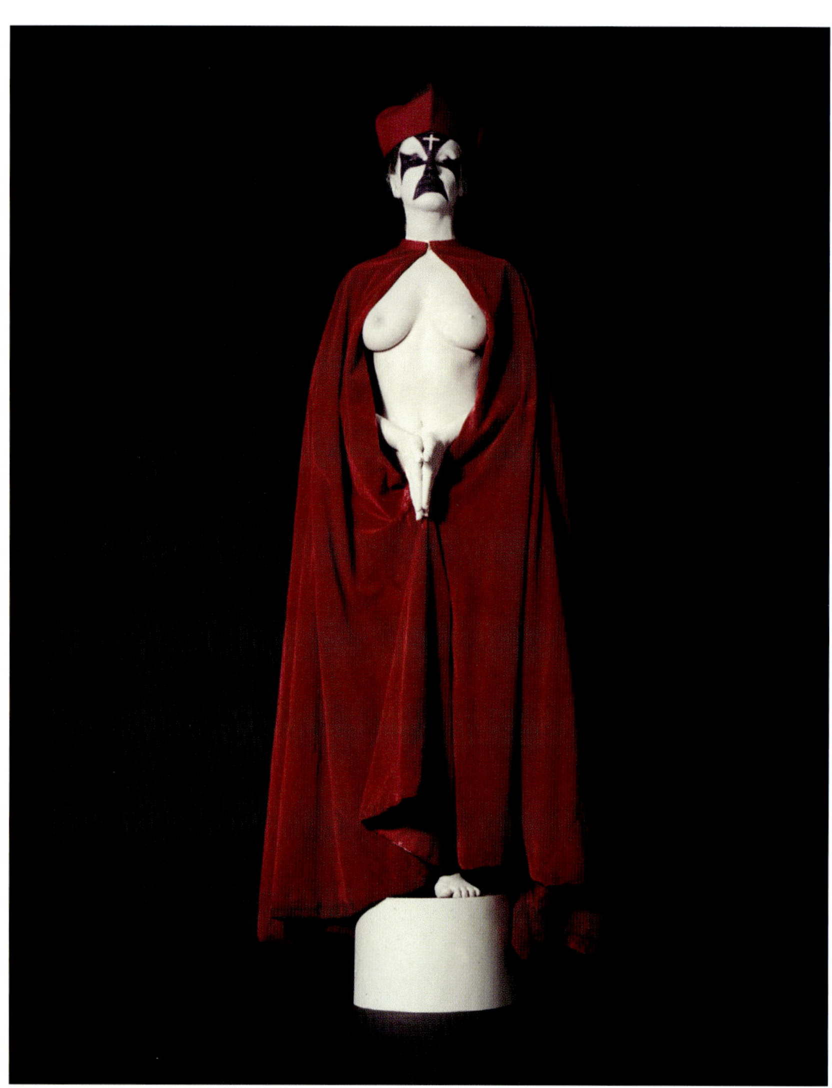

'Bishop', ***Playboy Magazine***, **chess compendium, 1956**

Leonard's connection with the musicians he photographed went far beyond the simple artist-subject relationship. He developed in-depth knowledge of the nuances of their music. He knew their personal quirks, their likes and dislikes, their good and bad habits, as well as their dreams. Early on, long before their genius became a public commodity, Leonard captured the cool of Miles Davis, the intensity of Clifford Brown, the playful antics of Dizzy Gillespie and Charlie Parker, the elegance of Duke Ellington, and the hermetic ecstasy of Bud Powell. His portrait of Thelonious Monk writing at the piano was taken during one of Monk's long engagements at the New York jazz club Minton's. Leonard was particularly delighted because Monk was 'addicted to a myriad of hats, and I finally caught him at Minton's Playhouse in a rare moment without one' (see pages 150–51).

Where Thelonious Monk sported an ever-changing repertoire of hats, the saxophone player Lester Young was known for wearing only one – a thin black porkpie that was at once old-fashioned and elegant. One of Leonard's most unusual photographs is a still life featuring that very black hat (see page 135). On first viewing, the composition looks so perfect that it appears to be posed. The photo was actually shot at a recording session when Leonard looked across the room and discovered this perfect composition waiting for his camera. Lester's hat, hanging on a corner of the saxophone case, sits above an empty Coke bottle with a lit cigarette on top of it. Lying in the saxophone case is the score for the recording session's music.

One musician known as a difficult subject, but who was particularly close to Leonard, was Miles Davis. Their friendship endured throughout the trumpet player's lengthy career. From Leonard's first shot of him, with Charlie Parker at Birdland in 1948, Davis remained one of his favorite subjects. Leonard was present at Davis's last concert at the Montreux

Jazz Festival in 1991. After the customary pre-concert photo session, all of the photographers were asked to leave so the band could make their final plans for the evening performance. Just before the doors closed, Miles walked up to the microphone and, in his inimitable, raspy voice said, 'Herman, let Herman stay.' The shots Leonard took that day were some of the last taken of Davis performing (see page 123). Six weeks later Miles was dead. His career had spanned the evolution of jazz, from the cool jazz Forties and Fifties, through the experimental Sixties and Seventies, and into the emerging era of electronic music and hip-hop. Leonard's photographs reflect that evolution.

It was at this point in his career that Leonard enjoyed a number of confidence-building experiences. In addition to his jazz work, he photographed many aspiring young actresses in New York. These glamour shots earned him a new fan, a young entrepreneur who in 1954 was creating a magazine that would soon be known the world over as *Playboy*. Hugh Hefner asked Leonard to participate, and in its third year of publication, Leonard contributed two featured 'Playmate of the Month' spreads (see pages 193 and 196).

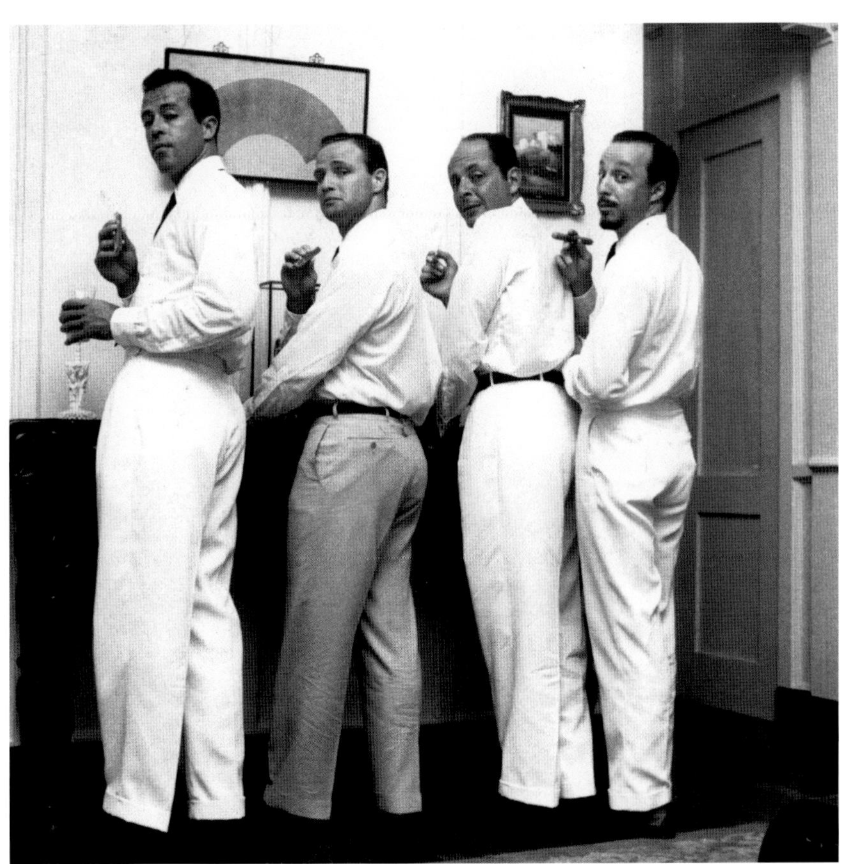

George Englund, Marlon Brando, Stewart Stern and Leonard, Hong Kong, 1956

In the meantime, Leonard had acquired yet another famous fan. Marlon Brando, an enthusiast of both photography and jazz, discovered Leonard's work through the recommendation of a friend. Soon after, Leonard was invited to serve as Brando's personal photographer, accompanying him on a six-week trip that took them from Hawaii, through the Philippines, Hong Kong, Thailand, and Bali (see page 58). It was a turning point in Leonard's career. His travels with Brando had awakened a new sense of adventure and rekindled his youthful desire to see more of the world. 'I always wanted to be Marco Polo,' Leonard says of his wanderlust. When Leonard returned to the States he was restless. There was a big world out there and he wanted to be part of it. The opportunity to do just that came when he received a letter from Eddie and Nicole Barclay in 1956 inviting him to become the staff photographer for their record label, Barclay Records, headquartered in Paris.

After accepting the Barclay job, *Playboy* then offered him a position as their first European correspondent. He accepted this offer as well, and worked for the next three years establishing contacts and eventually setting up a Paris studio of his own. Barclay Records gave him a base of operations, *Playboy* provided the travel assignments, and soon he was photographing for the Paris couture designers Christian Dior, Yves Saint Laurent, Chanel, and Balenciaga. His work appeared regularly in the prominent fashion magazines *Elle*, *Mademoiselle*, and *Marie Claire*. He also shot an extended photo essay on the celebrated designers behind the success of the Parisian couture houses and a photo essay on the personal and intellectual partners Simone de Beauvoir and Jean-Paul Sartre, both for *Playboy* (see page 68).

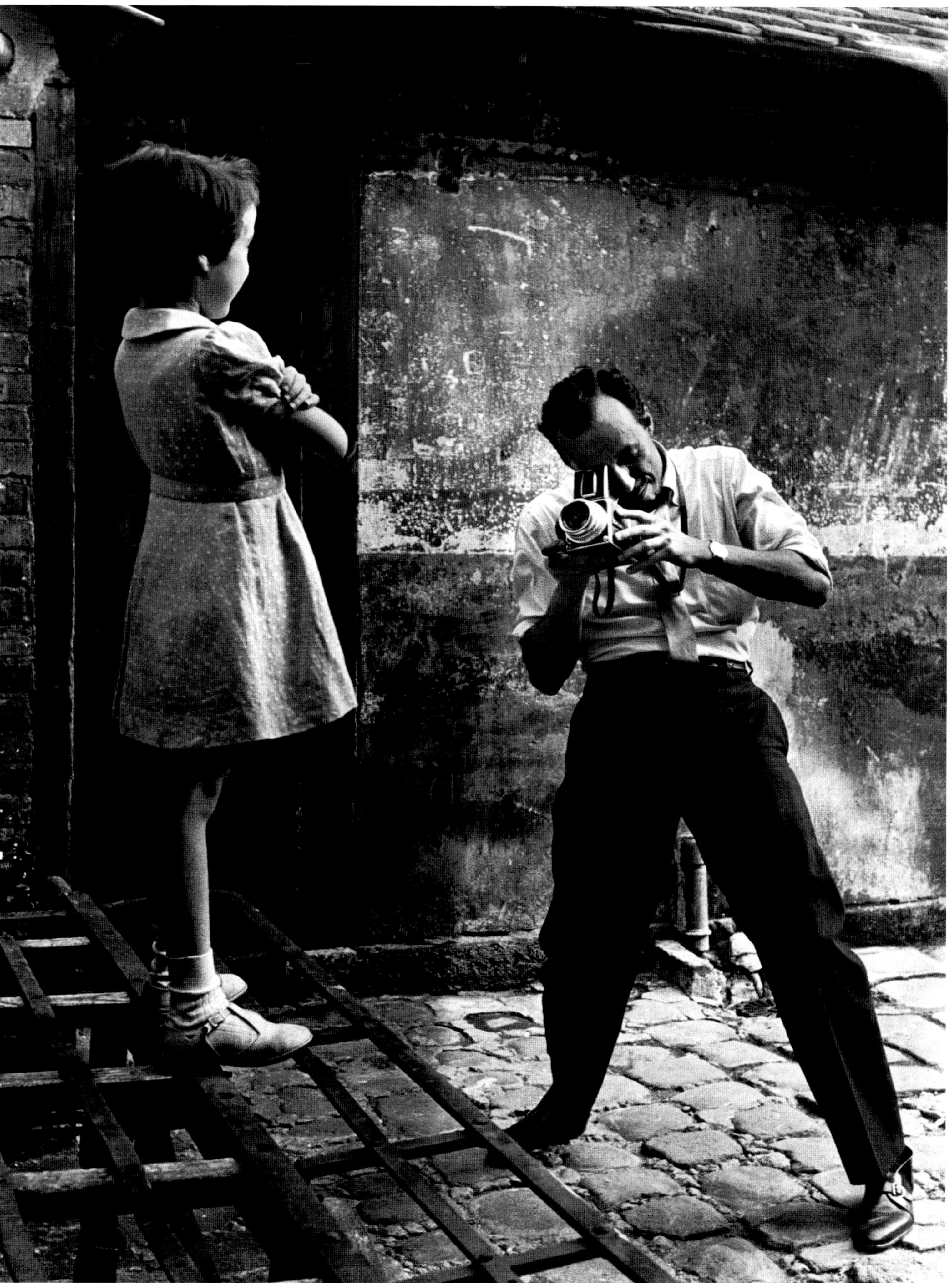

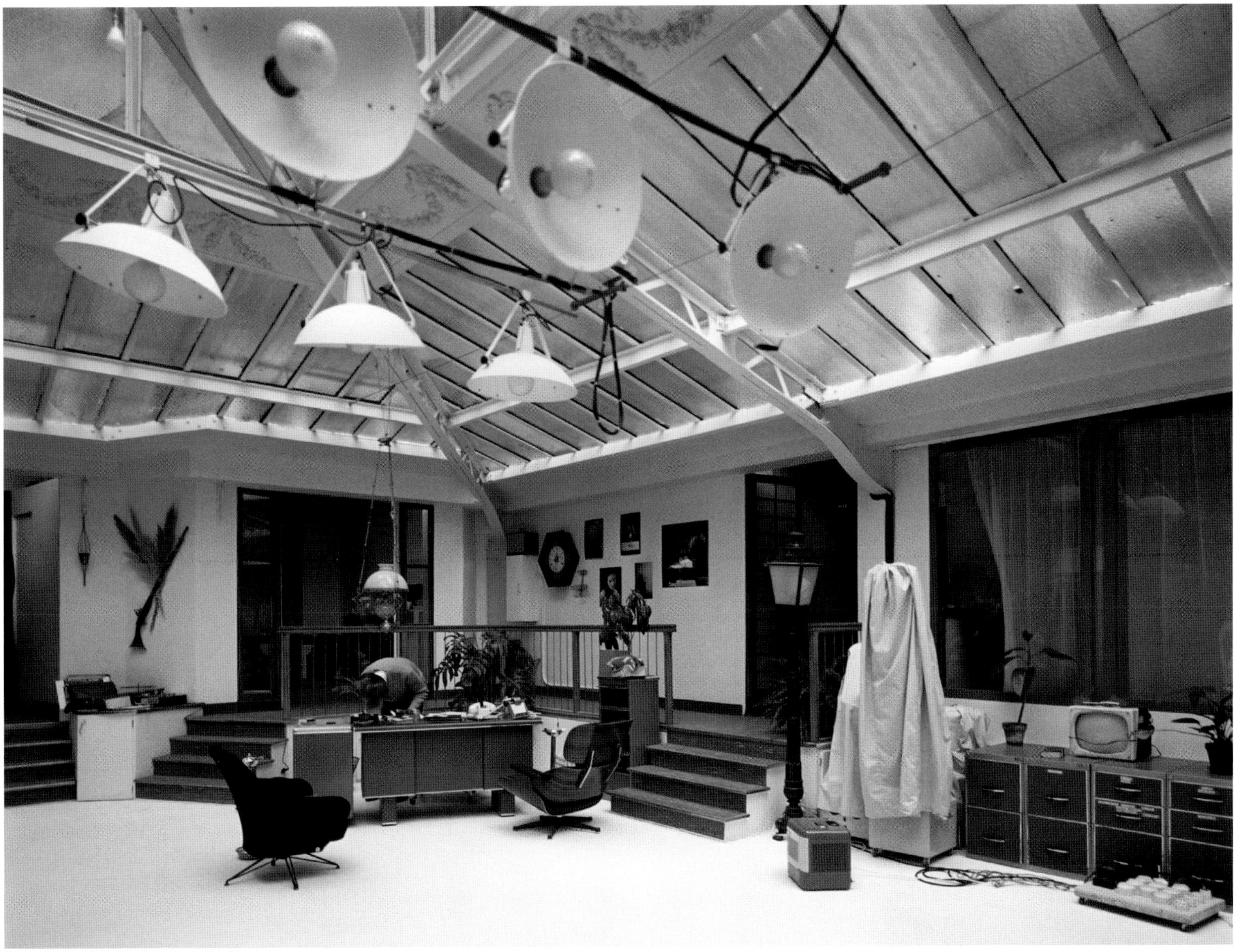

Leonard, Paris, 1958

Leonard's Paris studio, 1961

Leonard and models, Paris, 1963

Yves Saint Laurent advertisement, Paris, 1968

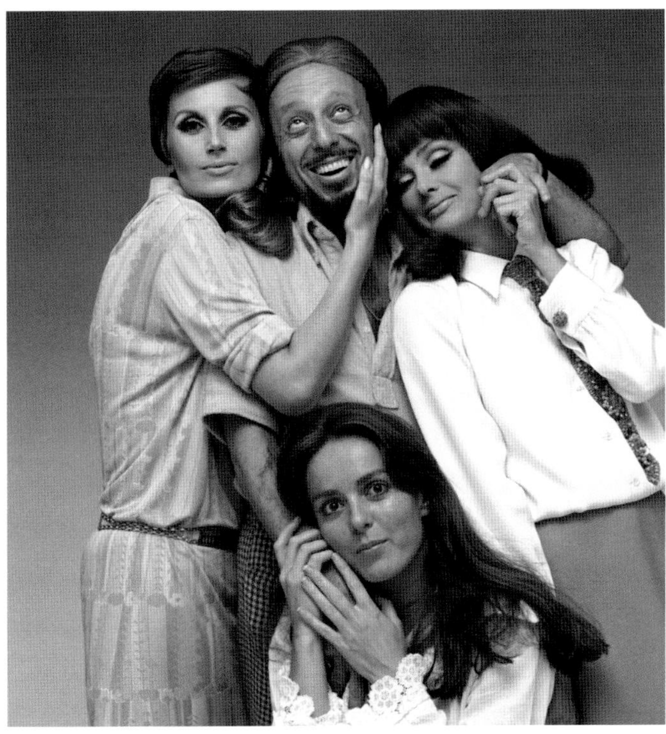

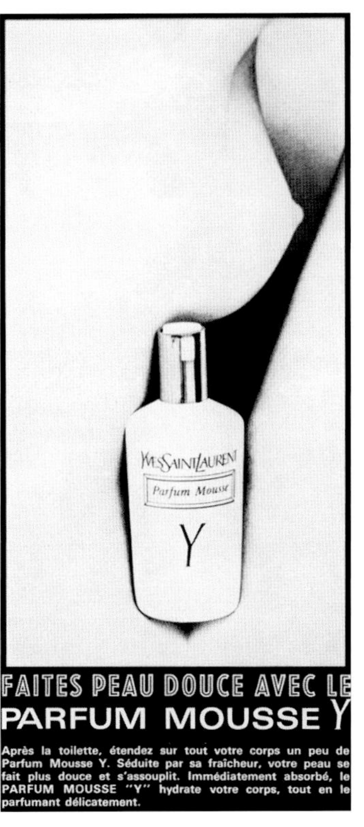

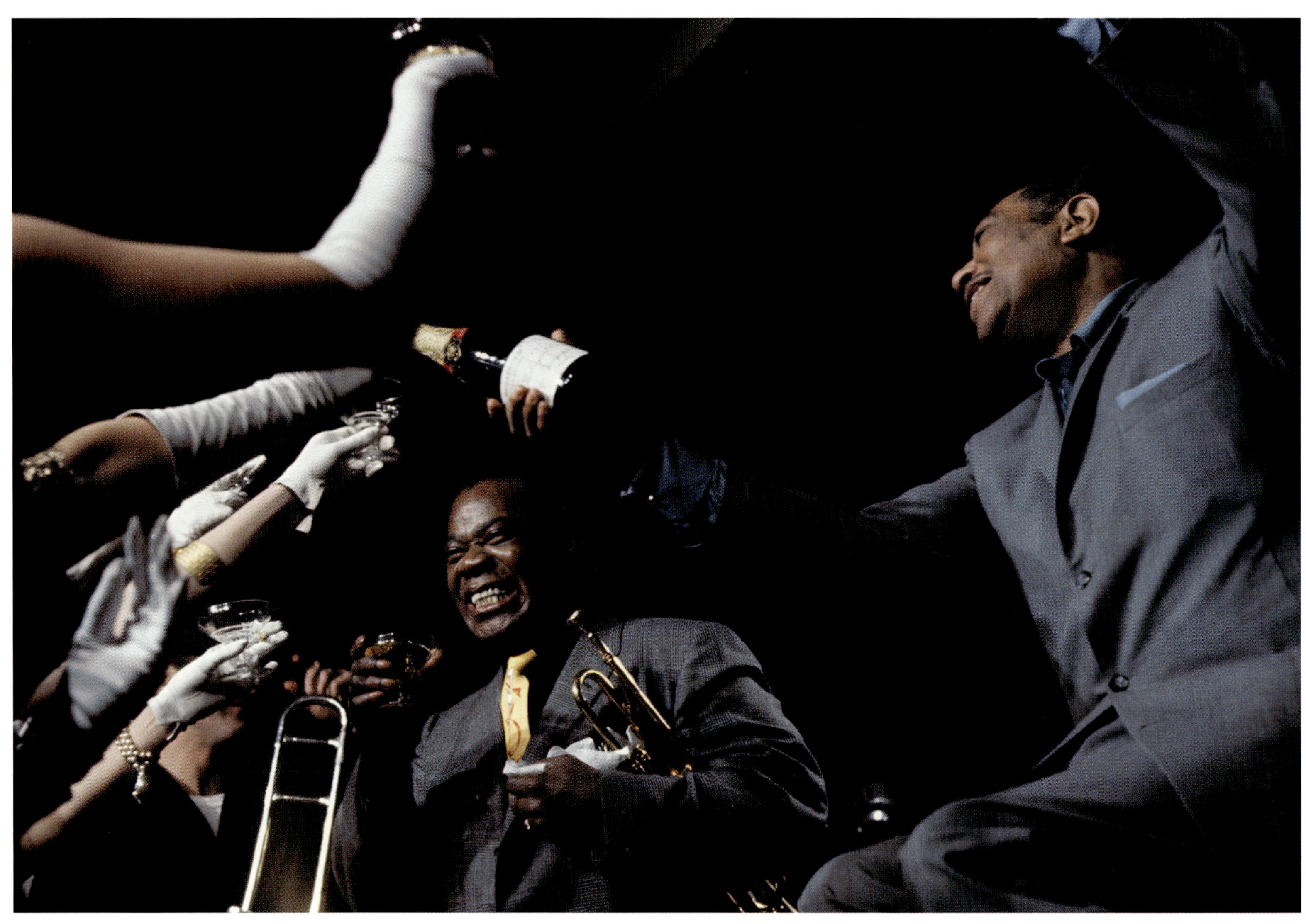

Not all assignments from *Playboy* were so civilized. At the height of the Cold War, Hefner asked Leonard to travel to the USSR, Poland, and Czechoslovakia to shoot 'Girls of Russia and the Iron Curtain Countries.' At that time, the level of social and cultural control in the USSR was absolute, and all foreigners were looked upon with suspicion, especially those wielding cameras. Somehow Leonard was able to break through this, and arranged to meet one of the potential models in the USSR for the shoot. Realizing he was always being followed, he tried to position the young woman so as to be out of view of his official tail in the black sedan. After an unsuccessful session, he came to the correct conclusion that he was in a compromised position with the Soviet officials and possibly in personal danger. A quick call to Hefner confirmed his opinion and he promptly left the country with a new appreciation for the openness of the West.

Leonard's years in Paris also yielded more classic images of jazz musicians. He photographed many of the American musicians who came to Europe, as well as the French musicians Jacques Brel and Stephane Grappelli (see page 186). By the late Fifties and early Sixties many of Leonard's old New York friends were no longer obscure musicians performing for small audiences in a few select clubs. They were the celebrated stars of new American jazz, with real record contracts and an ever-expanding audience. In Paris, they were treated as international celebrities. Many made Paris their European base, and a few made it their home. For African-American musicians, Europe proved to

Louis Armstrong and Duke Ellington, Paris, 1960

The Crazy Horse Saloon club, Paris, 1970

be a haven from the discrimination and social barriers that clouded life back home in the States.

The premier place in Paris for visiting Americans was the tiny Club St Germain, located in an old wine cellar in the seventh arrondissement. This small club with vaulted ceilings booked the most progressive musicians, and was a meeting spot for visiting artists, expatriate musicians, and fans alike. Leonard was delighted to renew old friendships and to photograph these musicians at a different stage of their careers. Many were gone: Charlie Parker, Billie Holiday, Lester Young, and Clifford Brown had all passed away. Others were moving into different phases of their work. In the Sixties, a new, harmonically freer approach pioneered by Ornette Coleman and John Coltrane would signal a new direction in jazz. In the relaxed atmosphere of the Club St Germain, Leonard was able to capture jazz royalty at the pinnacle of their careers. His photos of Miles Davis, Duke Ellington, Sarah Vaughan, Ella Fitzgerald, and Stan Getz share a continuity of approach with his earlier New York jazz photographs, and capture perfectly the twilight mood of the post-war jazz scene.

With Paris as his home base, Leonard's career grew at an accelerated pace. In the Seventies, his commissioned work involved a mix of advertising, catalogue, fashion, and travel photography. From 1970 to 1973, the German magazine *ER* sent Leonard on numerous globetrotting missions, often giving him significant freedom to decide his choice

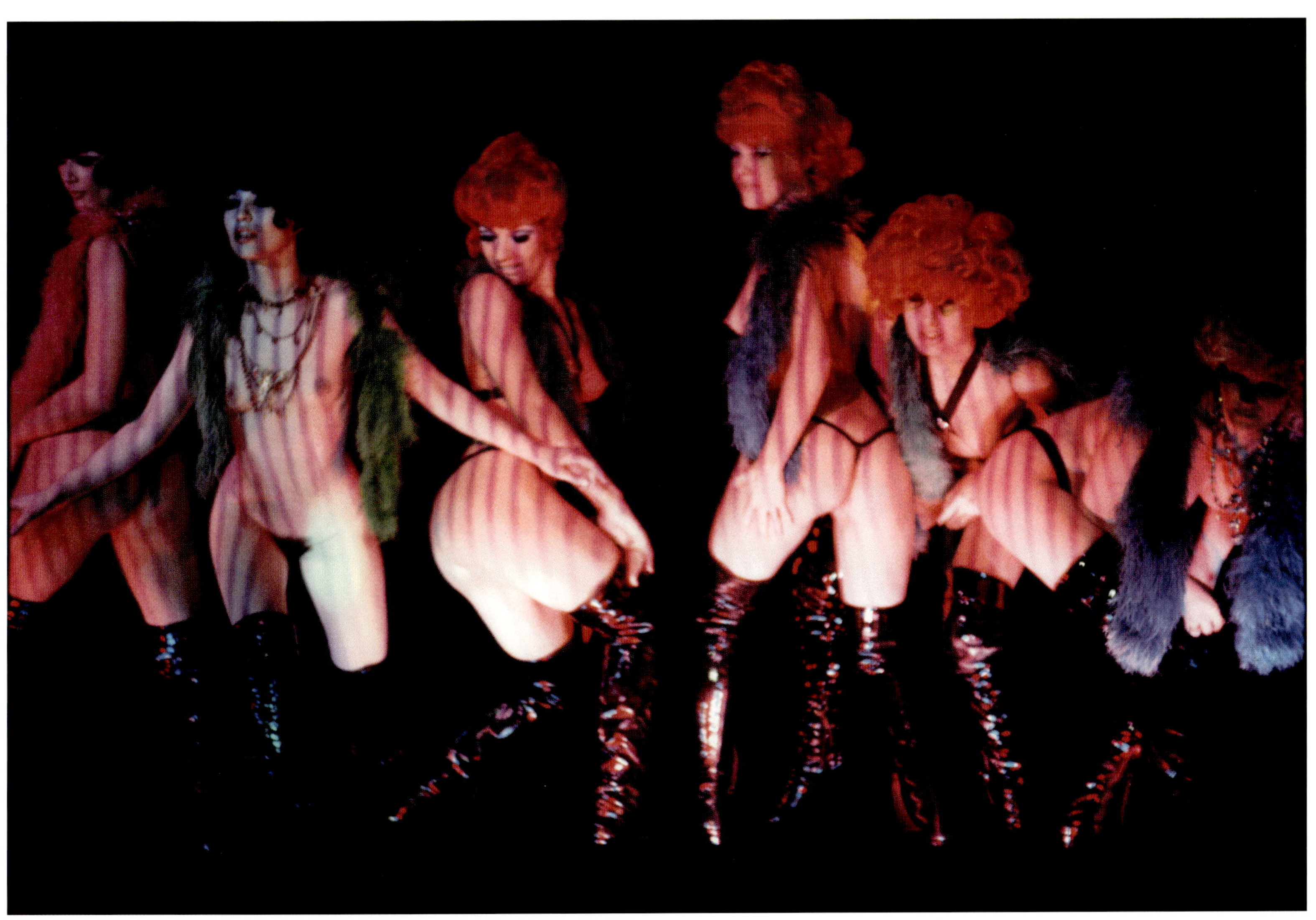

of location. Most associate Leonard exclusively with black and white photography, yet in the Seventies he worked increasingly with color. Particularly significant are his color images of his travels in Afghanistan, Bali, Ethiopia, Hong Kong, India, Kashmir, Malaysia, Singapore, Thailand, and Turkey. He traveled the world, each time returning to Paris. Leonard fulfilled his commissions while simultaneously following his internal artistic imperative, adding to his sizable body of work in the process (see pages 50–59).

It was at this point, and at what seemed like the height of his success, that Leonard began to long for a simpler life. He started looking for a place to 'bring up his children in an unpolluted, non-commercial atmosphere.' He did not have to look far. While living in Europe, Leonard had spent all of his summers on the small Mediterranean island of Ibiza. An as yet undiscovered paradise—isolated, inexpensive, and only a short flight from Paris —Ibiza was becoming home to many of Europe's artists and writers. In 1980, Leonard rented a 300-year-old stone farmhouse near the beach for $40 a month and moved there with his family. There, with no running water, no electricity, and no telephone, he and his wife raised their young children in peaceful isolation. Contact with the outside world was provided by a battery-powered radio.

Leonard had dropped out of the hectic world of Paris, isolating himself from the worlds of fashion and jazz that had provided most of his subject matter for the last four decades. Now his work was predominantly color photographs of his family and his surroundings. It was a new life that served his and his family's needs for nearly a decade, but things change, even in paradise. Ibiza grew in popularity among the international party set, the educational needs of Leonard's children began to outreach the capacity of the island's one-room school, and the need to generate income in the face of dwindling financial resources brought an end to Leonard's Ibiza years.

Herman Leonard was reborn as a photographer in London in 1988, but not without a struggle. It was not an easy task to find a receptive audience for a 65-year-old photographer who had been out of the public eye for a decade. He felt that his most marketable body of work consisted of his photographs of jazz musicians from the Forties and Fifties, which by then were historical documents of celebrated musicians. With this portfolio in hand, Leonard made the rounds of London galleries and was met with rejection after rejection. Finally, the Special Photographers Company, after reviewing his work, agreed to exhibit his photographs, but only if Leonard would bear the cost of space rental and promotional material. Having only a handful of prints at his disposal, Leonard would also have to produce the prints for the show. In the end, Ford sponsored the exhibition and the British firm Ilford provided the paper and chemicals for the prints. Now it was up to the public.

The exhibition ran for one month and was an instant success. Leonard's distinctive images of musicians of the Bebop and cool jazz movements captured a new audience that was fascinated by his work. Hundreds attended on opening night and 10,000 saw the exhibition during its one-month run. London's *Sunday Times Magazine* ran an eight-page spread of Leonard's photographs, and the BBC aired a short story on the photographer and his work. 'They came in like bees,' he recalls. 'These musicians that I knew in New York were now people that everybody knew.' For Leonard it was a gratifying affirmation of his work. He also sold 250 prints. The public response far exceeded his expectations. Leonard

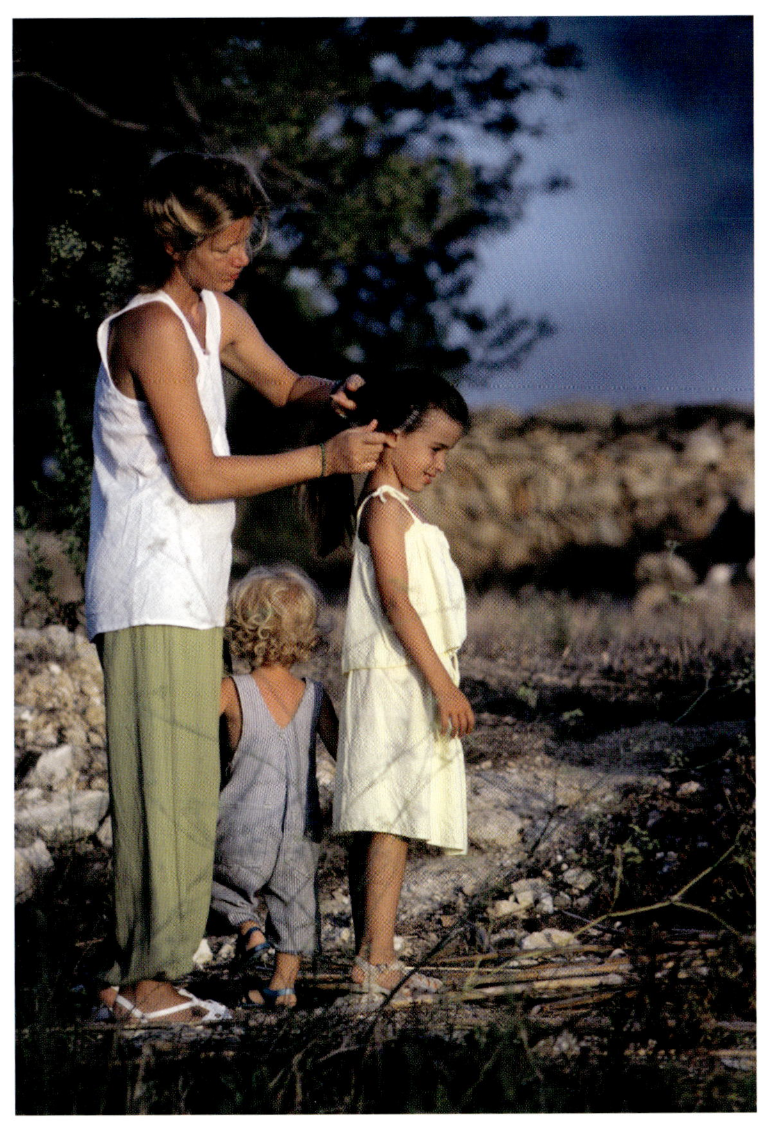

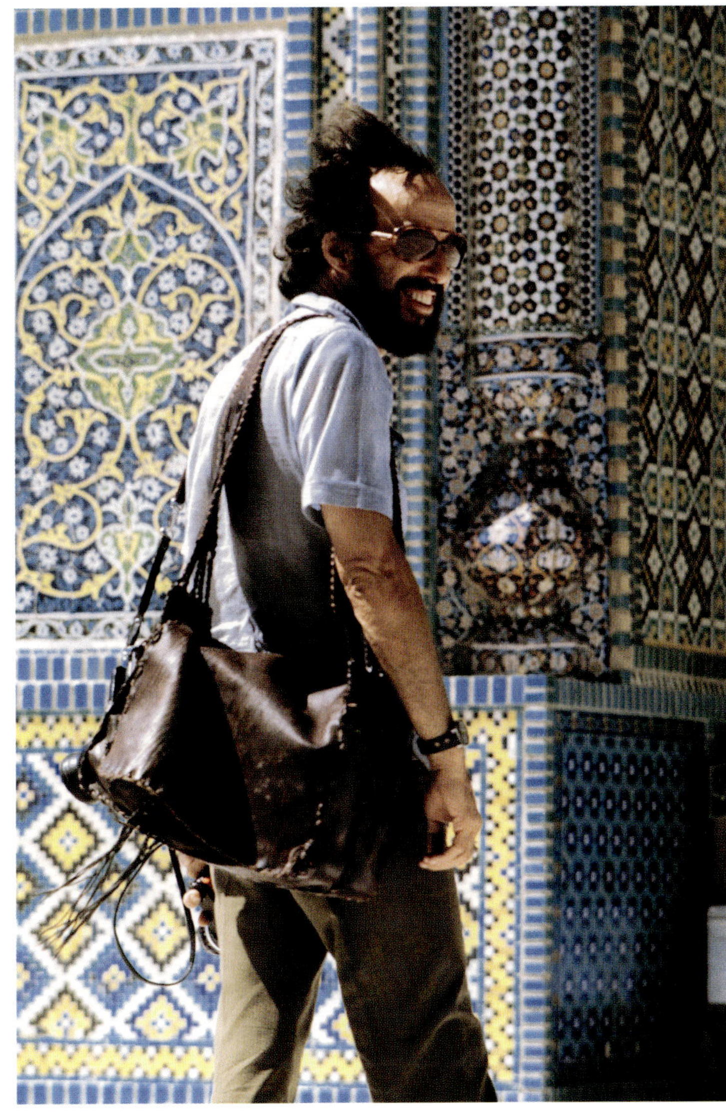

Elisabeth, Shana and David, Ibiza, Spain, 1980

Leonard, Mazar-i-sharif, Afghanistan, 1971

moved to London and enrolled his children in English schools. Less than two years later, having entered England on a tourist visa that had long expired, Leonard packed his bags again, this time headed back to America.

In 1989, Leonard moved to San Francisco. He had always heard that it was America's most European city and hoped he would feel at home there. He did some work on assignment, mainly for the London *Times Magazine* and other British publications that had known him in London. It was on one such assignment that Leonard was able to photograph Miles Davis again, whom he had not photographed since the Club St Germain days in Paris. On this occasion he photographed the trumpet player at his Malibu home on assignment with a reporter for the London *Sunday Times Magazine*. The session produced an unusual photograph of Davis that has become Leonard's favorite. Having completed the shoot for the newspaper, Leonard was asked by Miles to stay for a visit after the British reporter's departure. Later that day, Leonard photographed Miles leaning over one of his paintings in a white outfit in front of a white background (see pages 210–11).

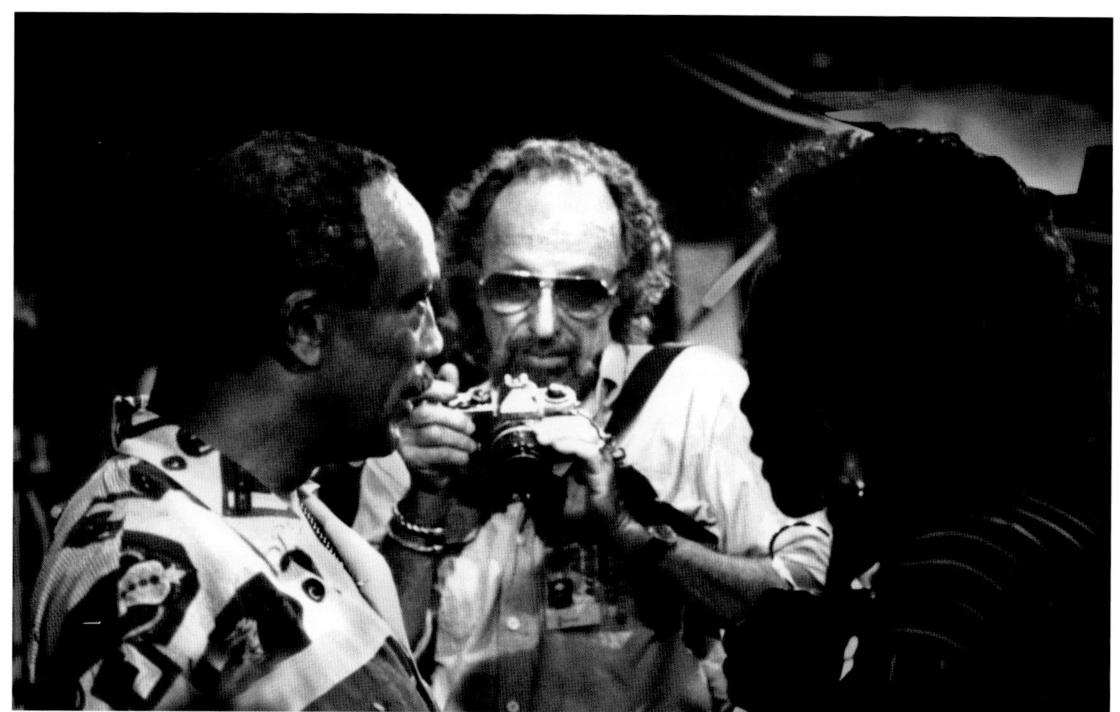

Quincy Jones, Leonard and Miles Davis, Montreux, 1991

At about the same time, a traveling show of Leonard's jazz photographs began touring major cities in the United States. Venues included Santa Monica, San Francisco, Chicago, Boston, New York, Washington DC, Miami, and most importantly for Leonard's future, New Orleans. The show in New Orleans was hosted by A Gallery for Fine Photography, where Leonard traveled to attend the opening reception of his show. His response to the city was immediate. 'It was only shortly after I got out of the cab that I knew I wanted to live here,' he recalls. 'It wasn't just the history or the music that I found so attractive. It was the people, their attitudes, the atmosphere of tolerance I felt there. This truly was the most European city in America.' Years later, on the occasion of his eightieth birthday celebration, Leonard said, 'I have never felt so comfortable in my own skin as I do in New Orleans.'

One of the crossroads of American music, New Orleans was fertile territory for Leonard's later work. The annual New Orleans Jazz and Heritage Festival, 'second line parades', and street musicians offered wonderful opportunities for casual shooting. Leonard's portraiture also emerged during this period as a significant component of his work. Among his favorite subjects were friends, celebrities, and a fascinating flow of marvellously weird, often unique, New Orleans characters.

One poignant photograph that spans the decades of Leonard's career brings together Doc Cheatham, age 91, with New Orleans's own Nicholas Payton, age 23 (see page 224).

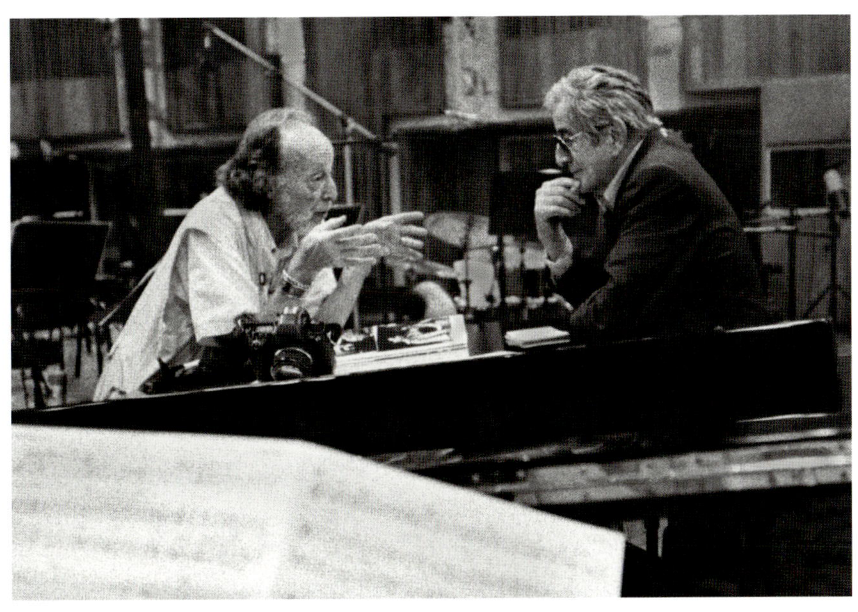

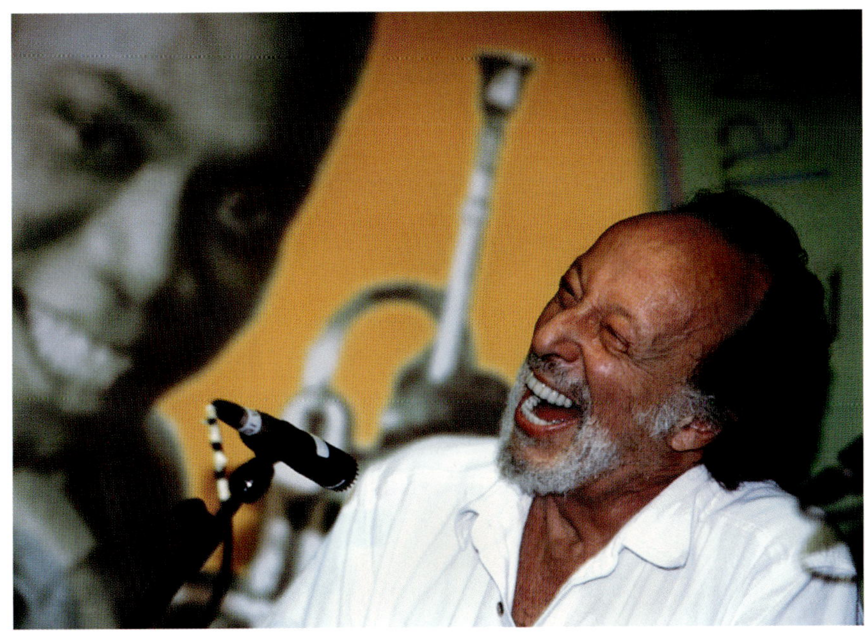

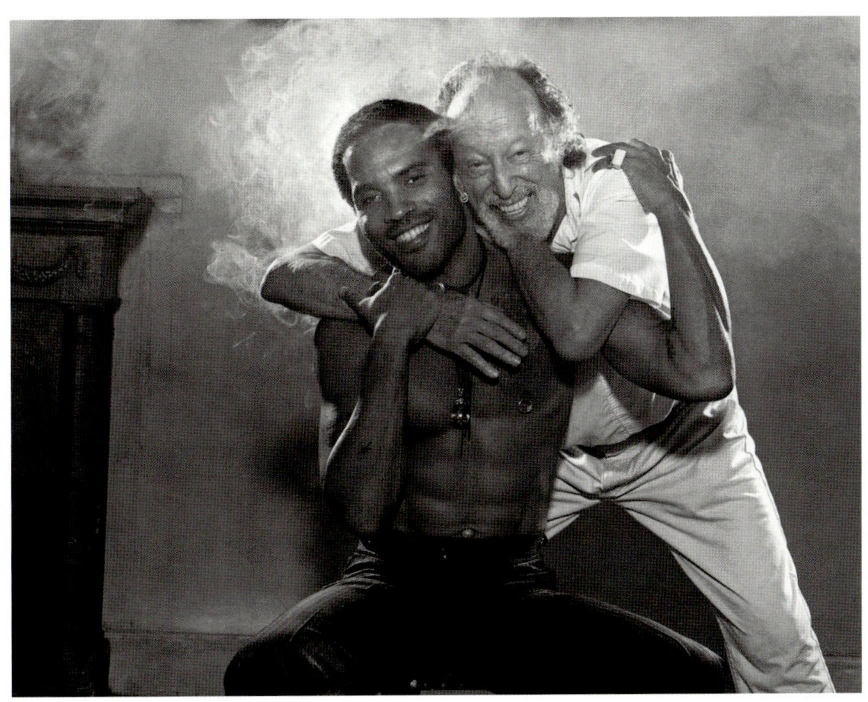

Leonard and Tony Bennett, NYC, 1999

Leonard, New Orleans, 2001

Leonard and Lenny Kravitz, New Orleans, 2004

The two trumpeters, each from a different generation of musicians and each representing a different approach to the instrument, had recently collaborated on a new recording. Leonard captured them in a criss-crossed composition that utilizes his characteristic backlighting.

One of his most distinctively New Orleans photographs was taken at the première of *A Creole Mass*, by Wardell Quezergue, in St Louis Cathedral at Jackson Square (see page 217). The opening sequence of the mass features dancers moving down the nave of the cathedral recalling the famous New Orleans second line parades. Leonard, shooting from the end of a church pew, captures dancer Michelle Gibson in a moment that brings together the formal and the informal, the interior and exterior, and the European and African influences of the city into one ecstatic moment.

The vitality and continuity of Leonard's work may also be seen in two recent photos of Lenny Kravitz shot in New Orleans (see pages 214–15). Leonard, who knew Kravitz through a relative who had been one of the musician's early managers, was an invited guest at a Kravitz recording session. Leonard captured him lost in the flow of the music as he stands in front of a mixing board And years later Leonard again photographed Kravitz in a French Quarter hotel. For aficionados of Leonard's work, these photographs are a joy. Each depicts a decidedly contemporary musician shot with the same dramatic chiaroscuro that characterizes his classic jazz photographs shot a half century earlier.

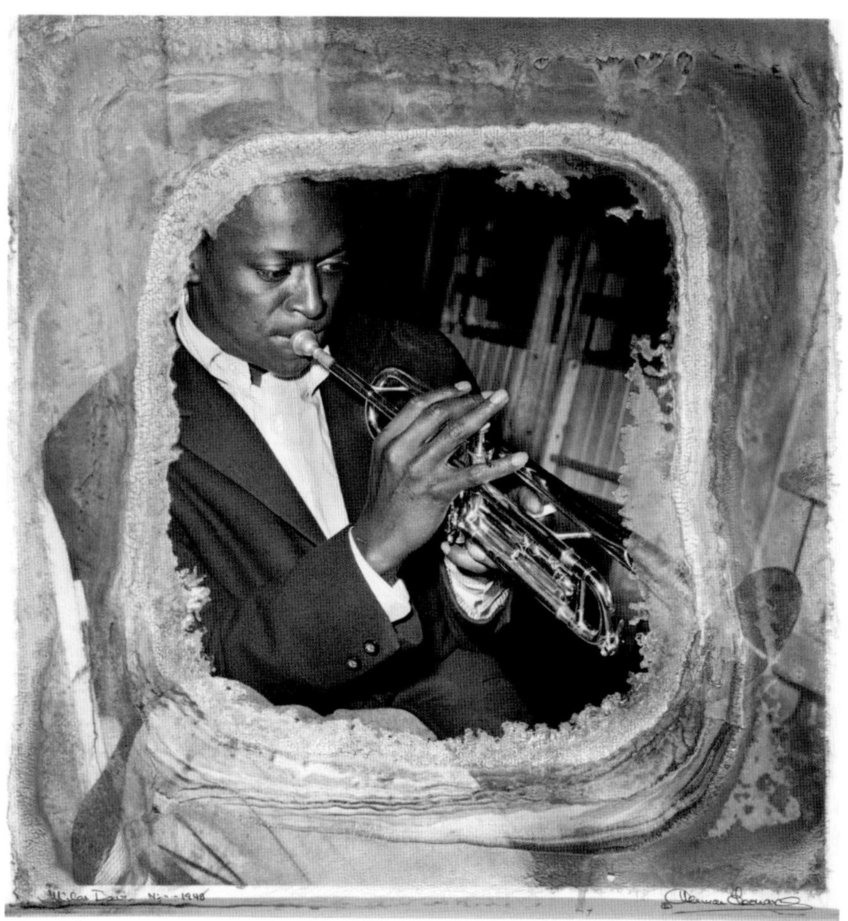

Leonard loved New Orleans and indeed New Orleans loved him back, but as the summer of 2005 drew to a close, fate was to play yet another card. It was the summer when Hurricane Katrina destroyed hundreds of thousands of New Orleans homes and businesses; Leonard's home and studio were among them. Leonard's accomplishments rest largely on his ability to evolve. He had survived the radical changes that reshaped the world several times during the span of his career; he had seen war overseas and political unrest at home; he had embraced photography's digital revolution; and in the spring of 2006, at age 83, and in the wake of unprecedented natural disaster, Leonard was poised to evolve yet again.

Herman Leonard has spent his life doing what he loves; there can perhaps be no greater statement of a person's career, and no greater ingredient to success. His jazz photographs alone would be enough to secure his legacy in photography; his iconic shots of the founding celebrities of music's coolest culture are frequently reproduced and widely collected. Yet Leonard cast his eye to a broader variety of subjects, and throughout his career his work has continually redefined what it is that makes a photograph 'a Herman Leonard.'

Miles Davis photograph salvaged from studio after Hurricane Katrina, 2005

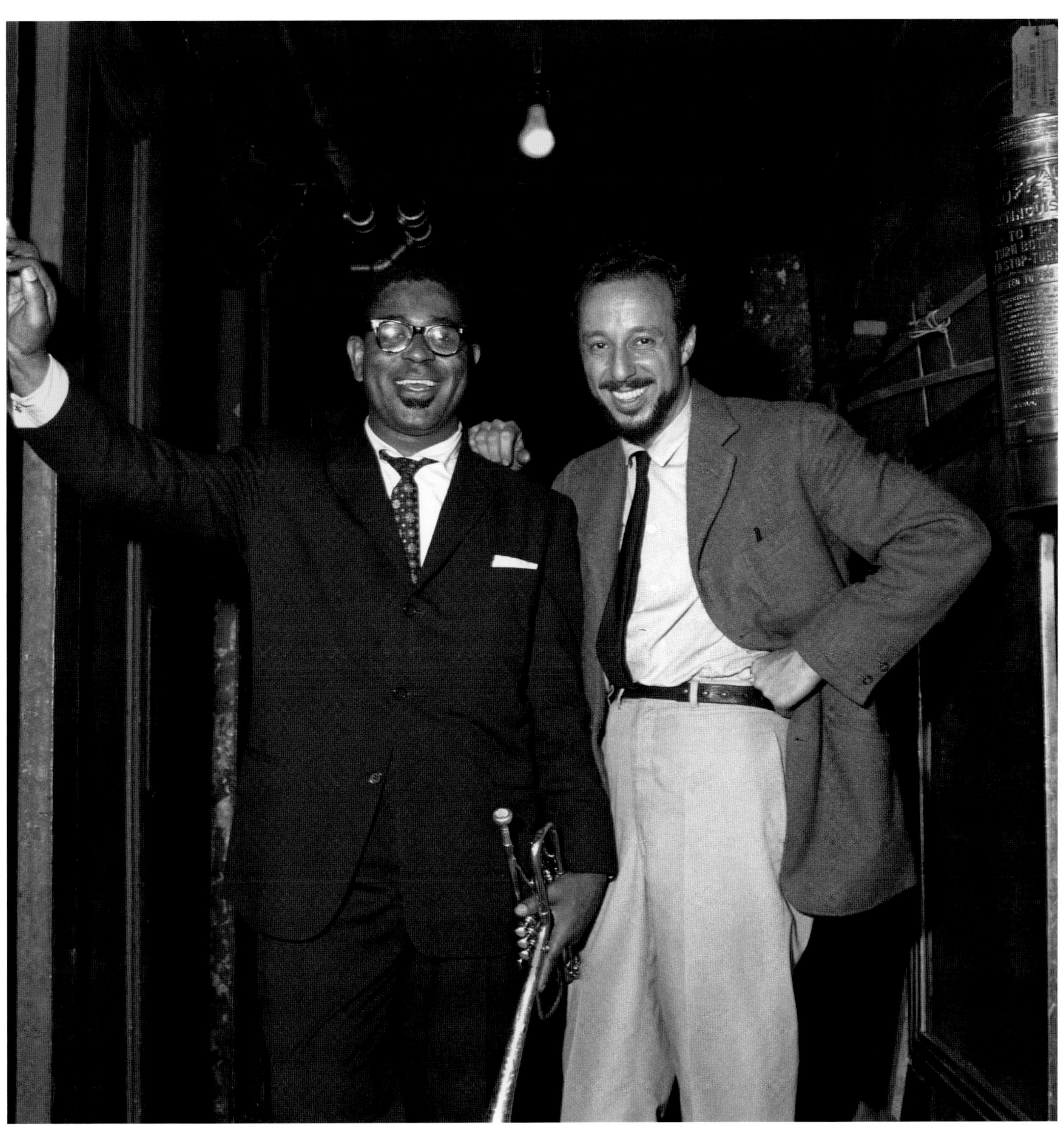

Leonard and Dizzy Gillespie, Birdland, NYC, 1955;
photograph by Quincy Jones

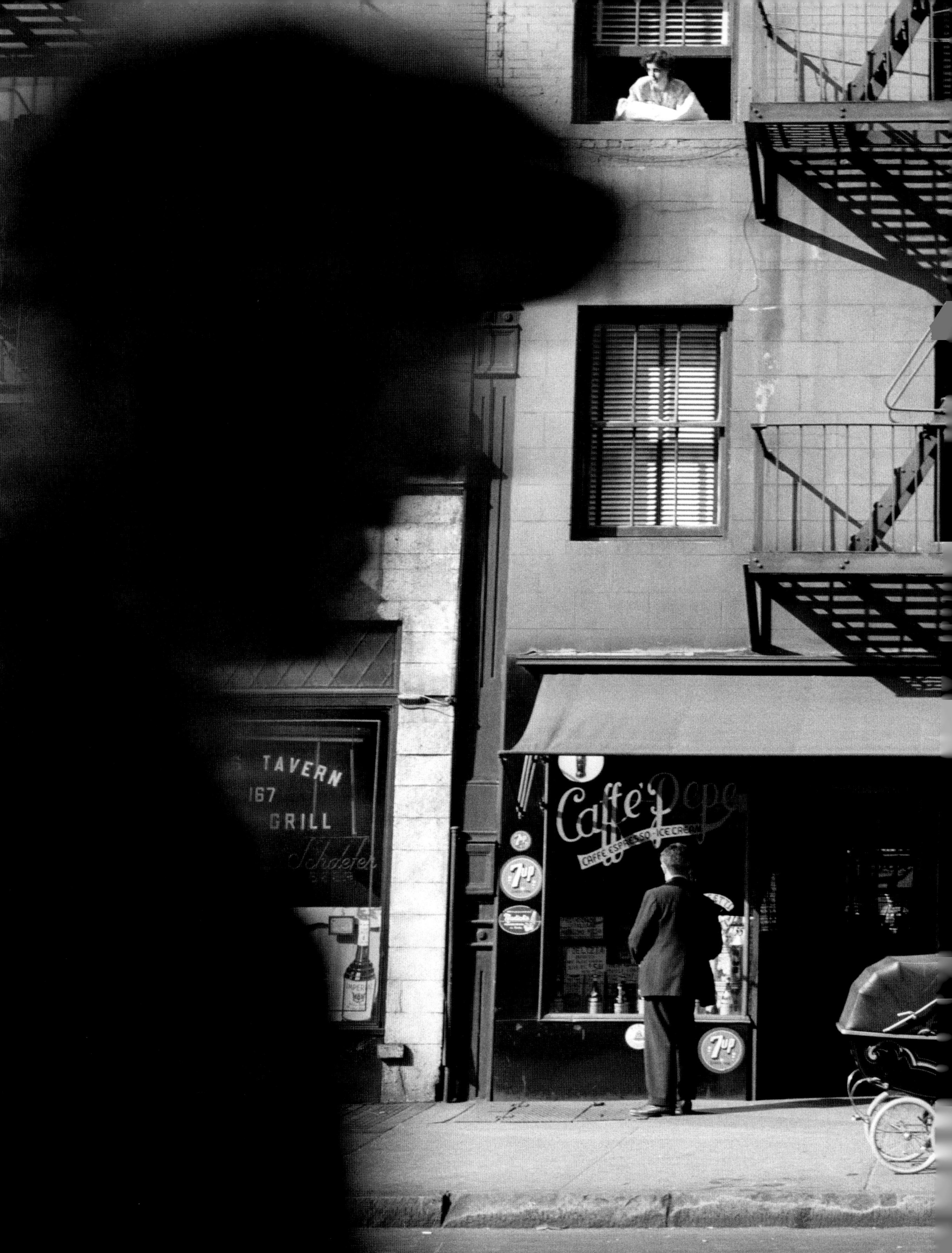
TAVERN
167
GRILL
Schaefer
Caffe' Pepe
CAFFE ESPRESSO - ICE CREAM
7up
7up

Early Work

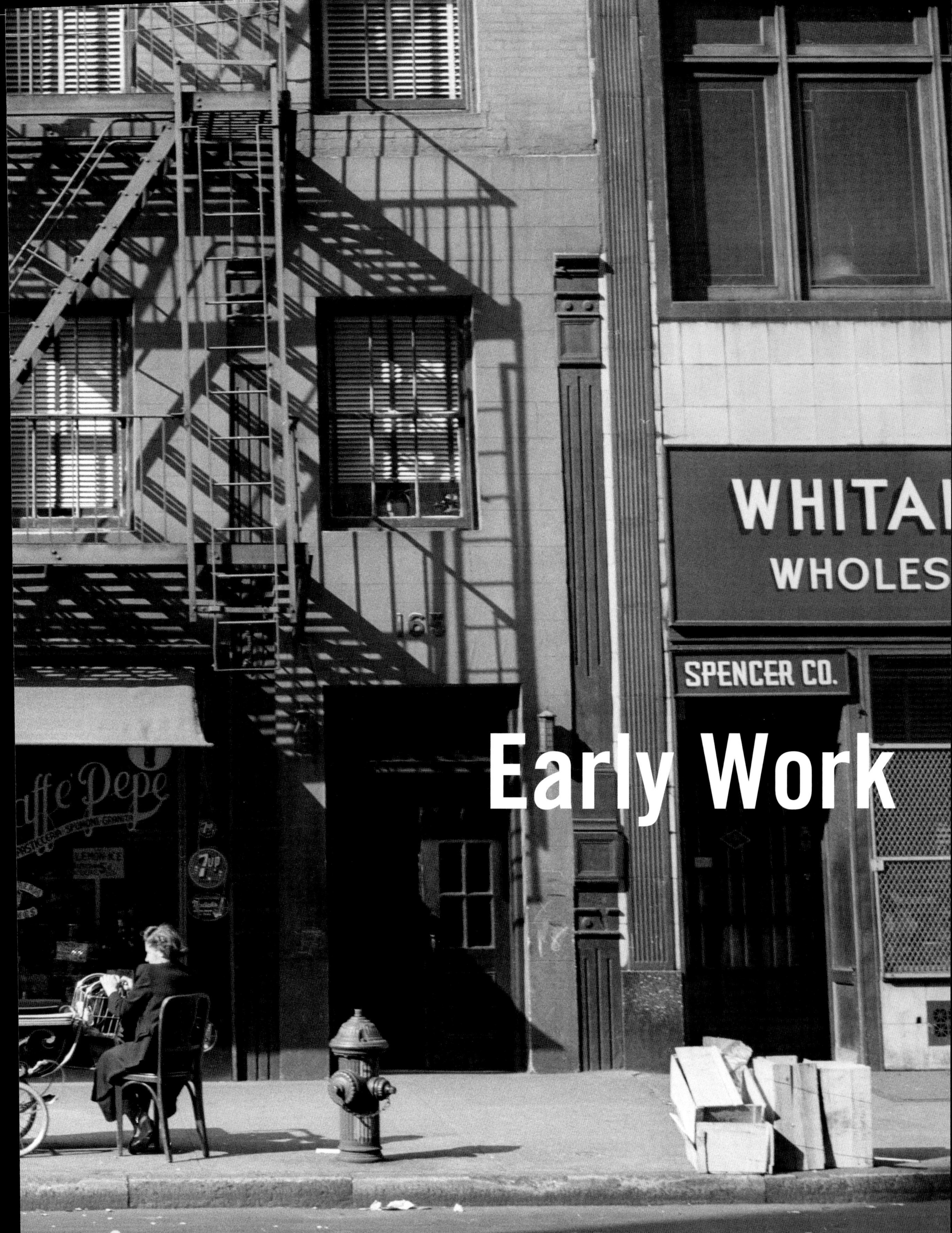

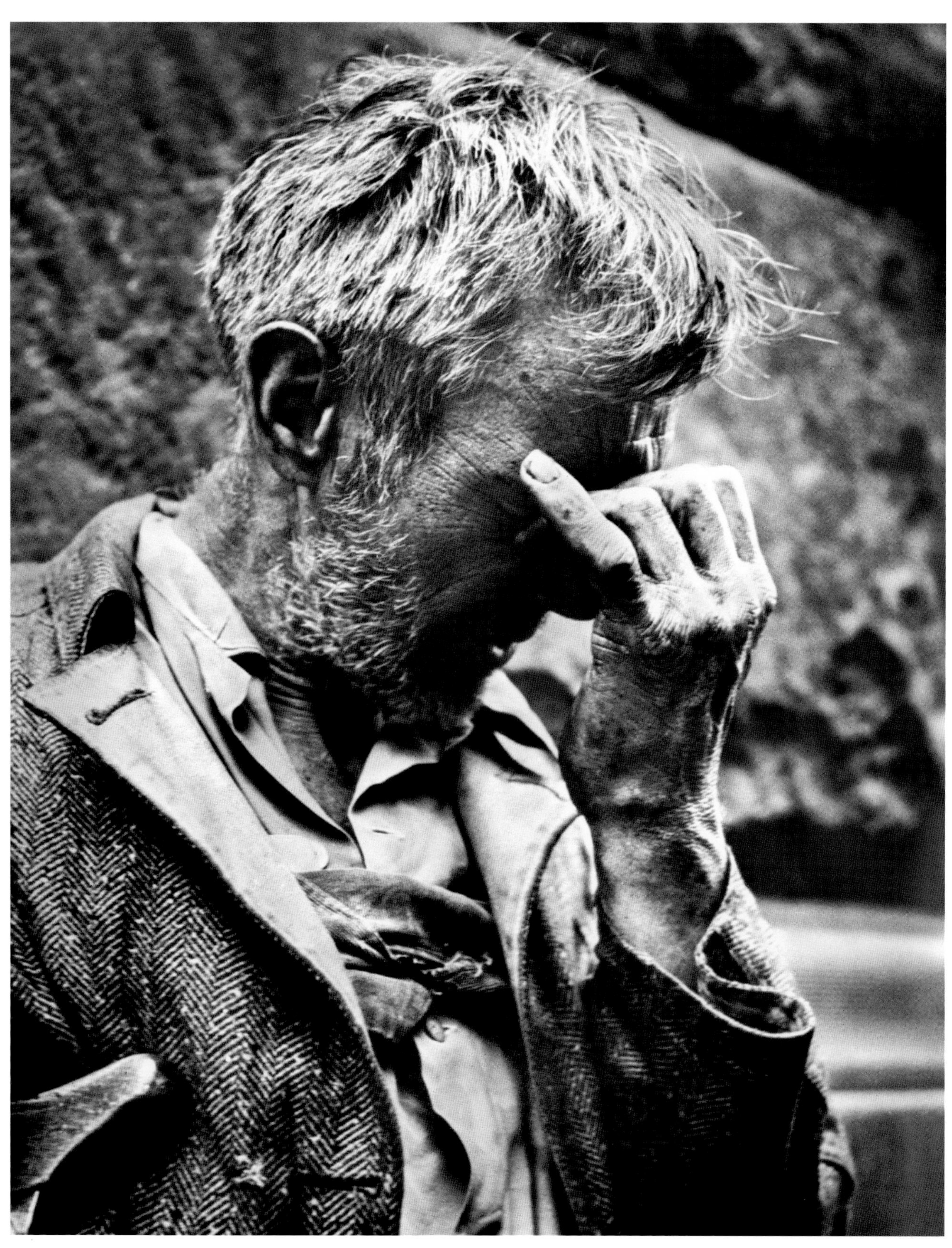

Washington Square, NYC, 1948

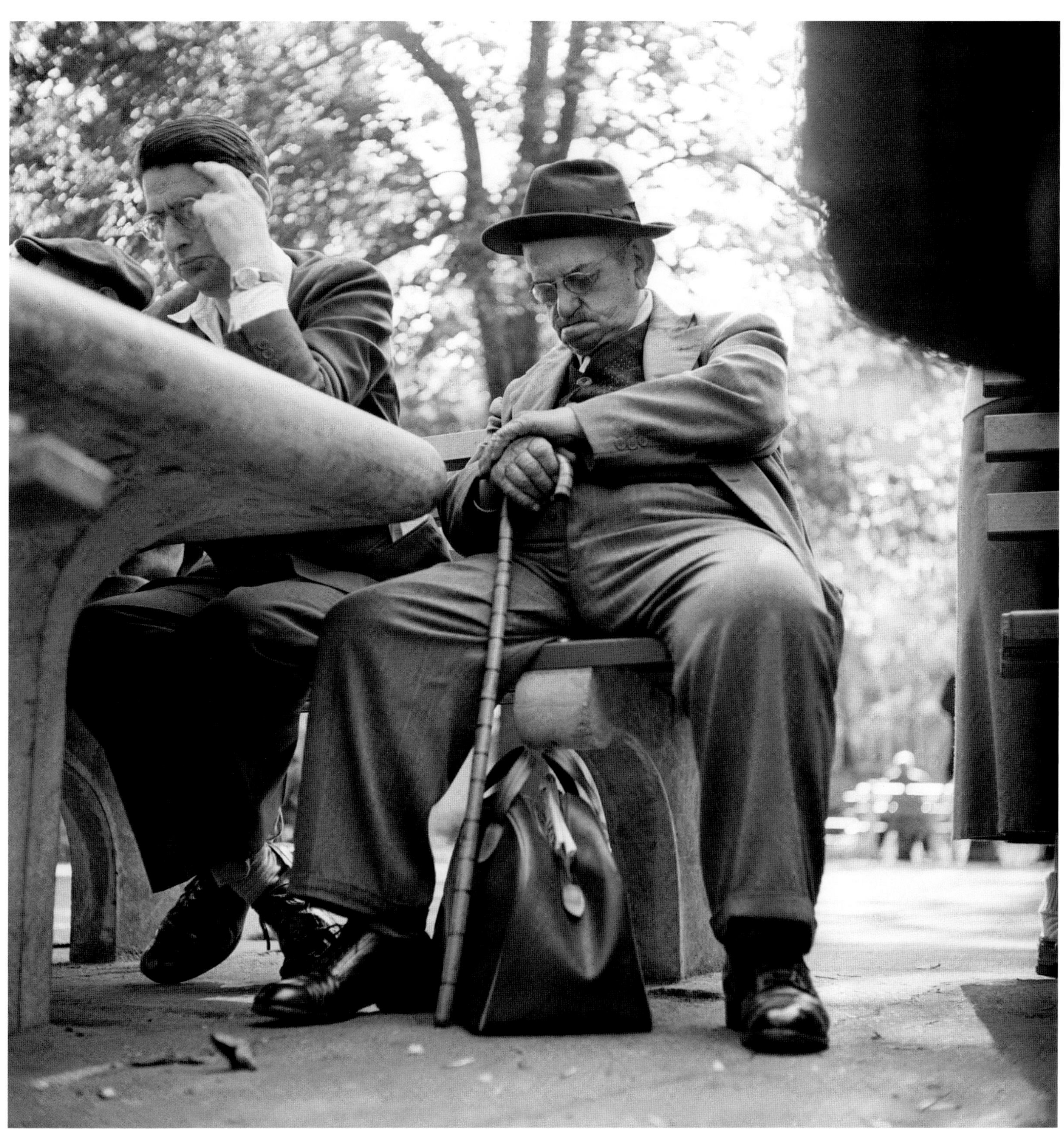

Washington Square, NYC, 1948

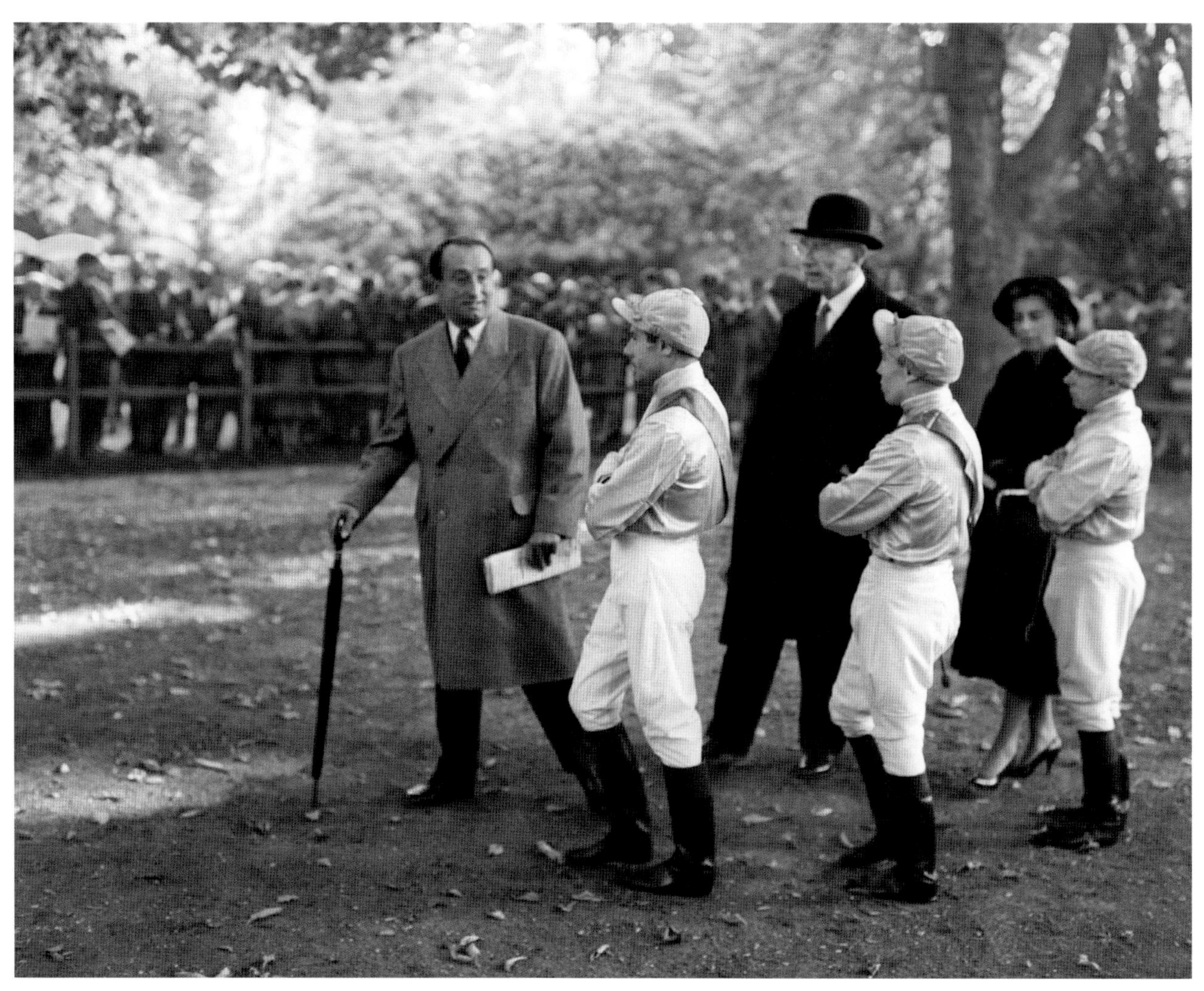

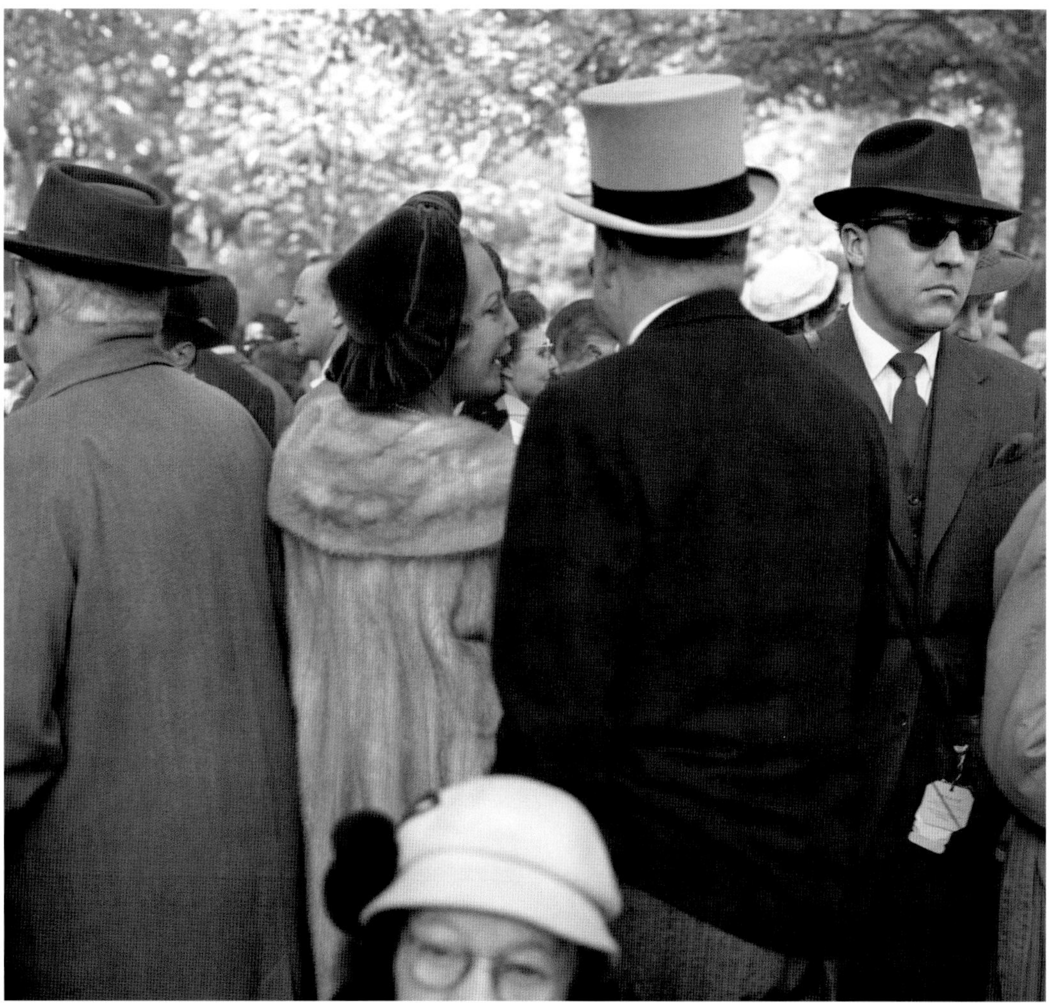

Longchamps Racetrack, Paris, 1957

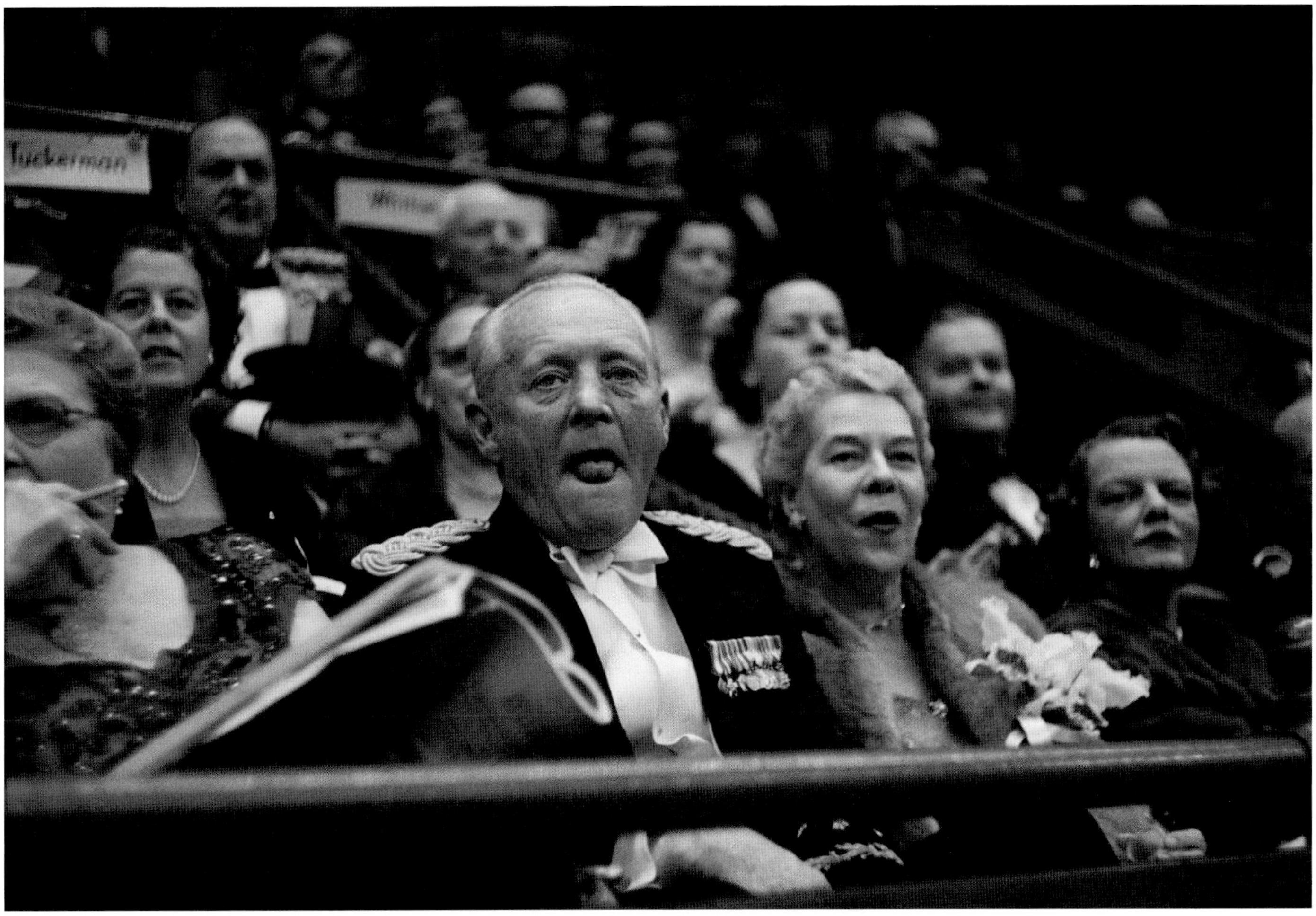

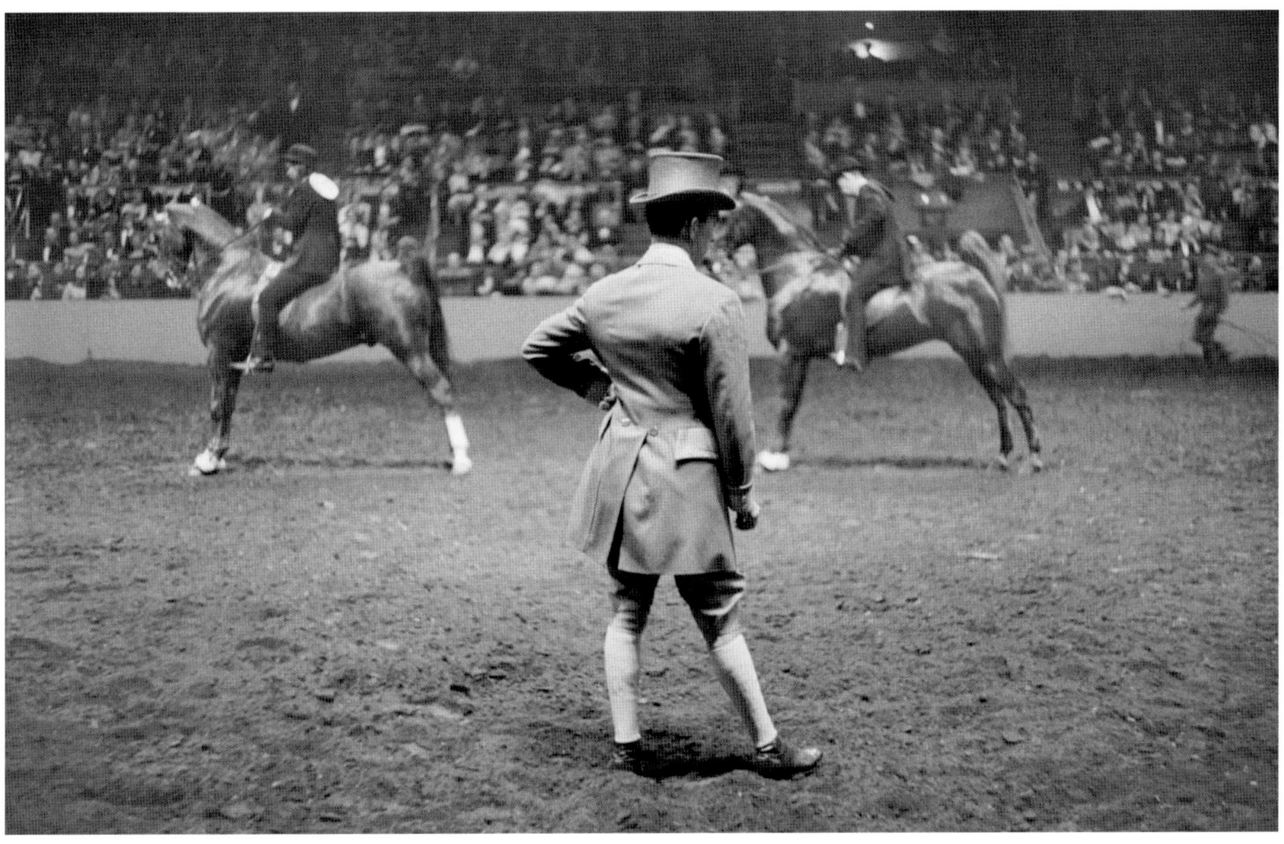

Madison Square Garden, NYC, 1949

Greenwich Village, NYC, 1948

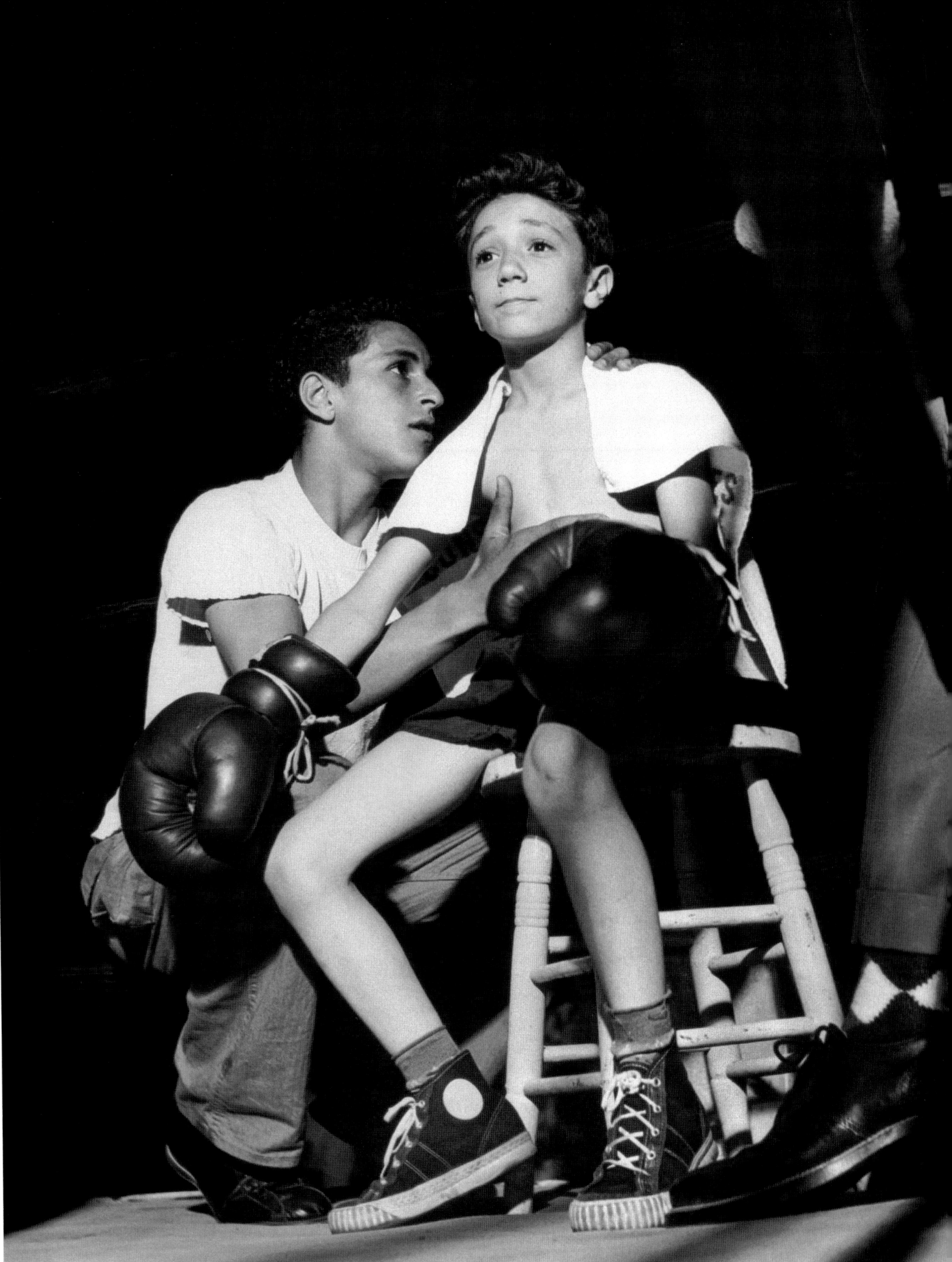

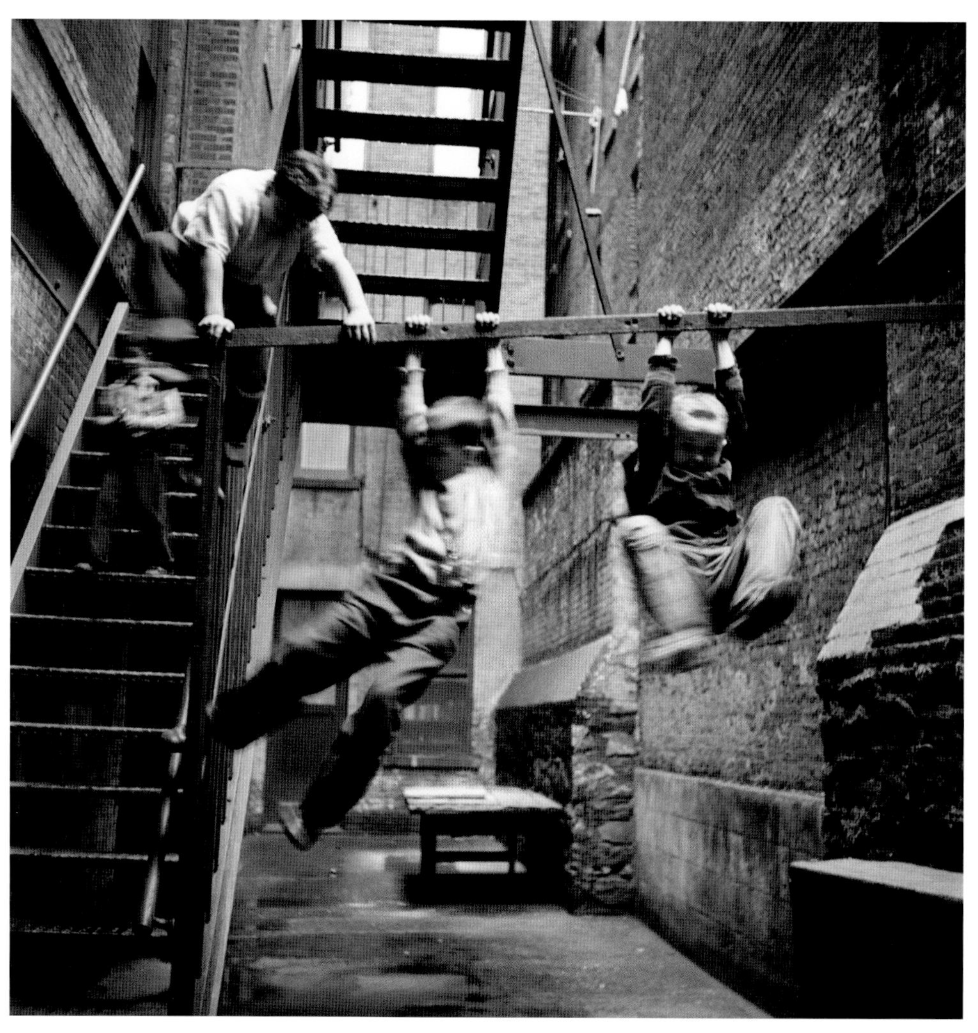

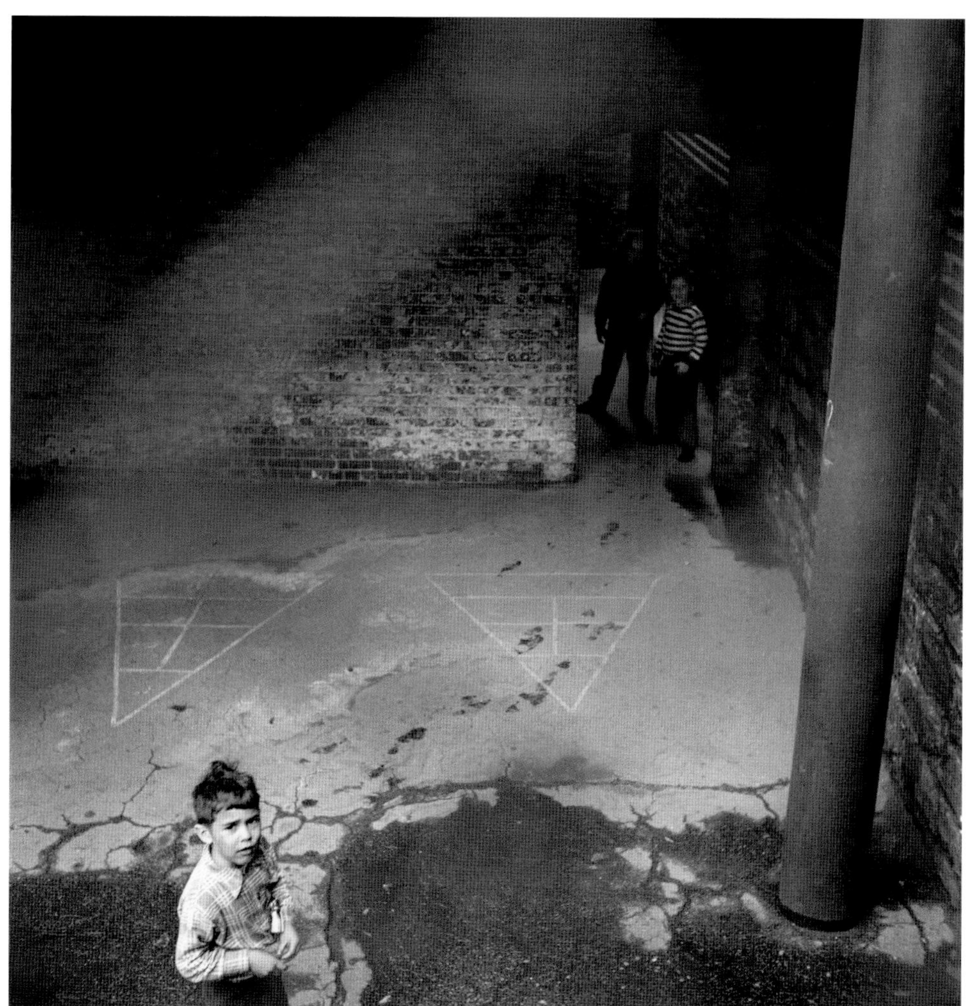

Greenwich Village, NYC, 1948

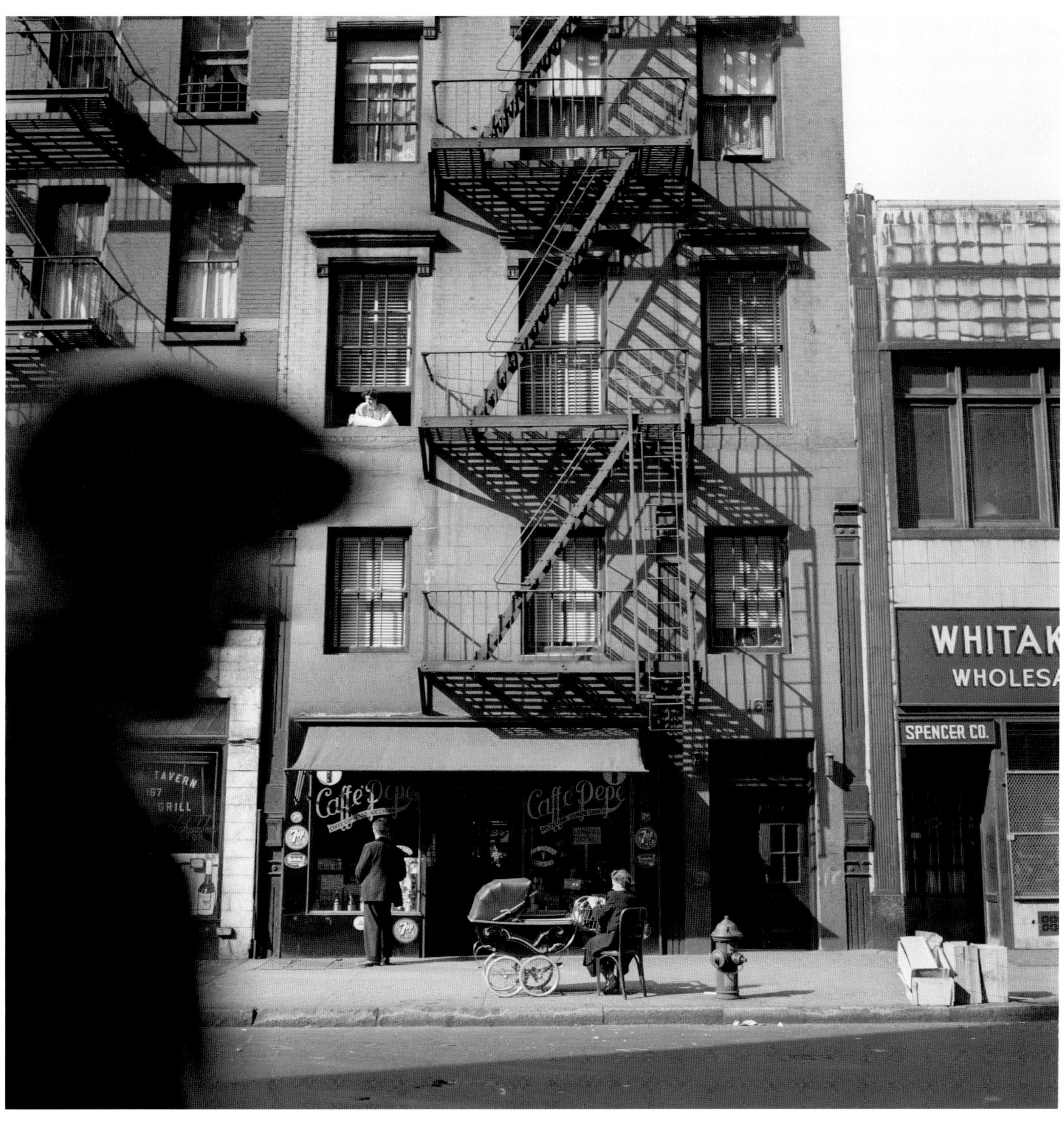

Greenwich Village, NYC, 1948

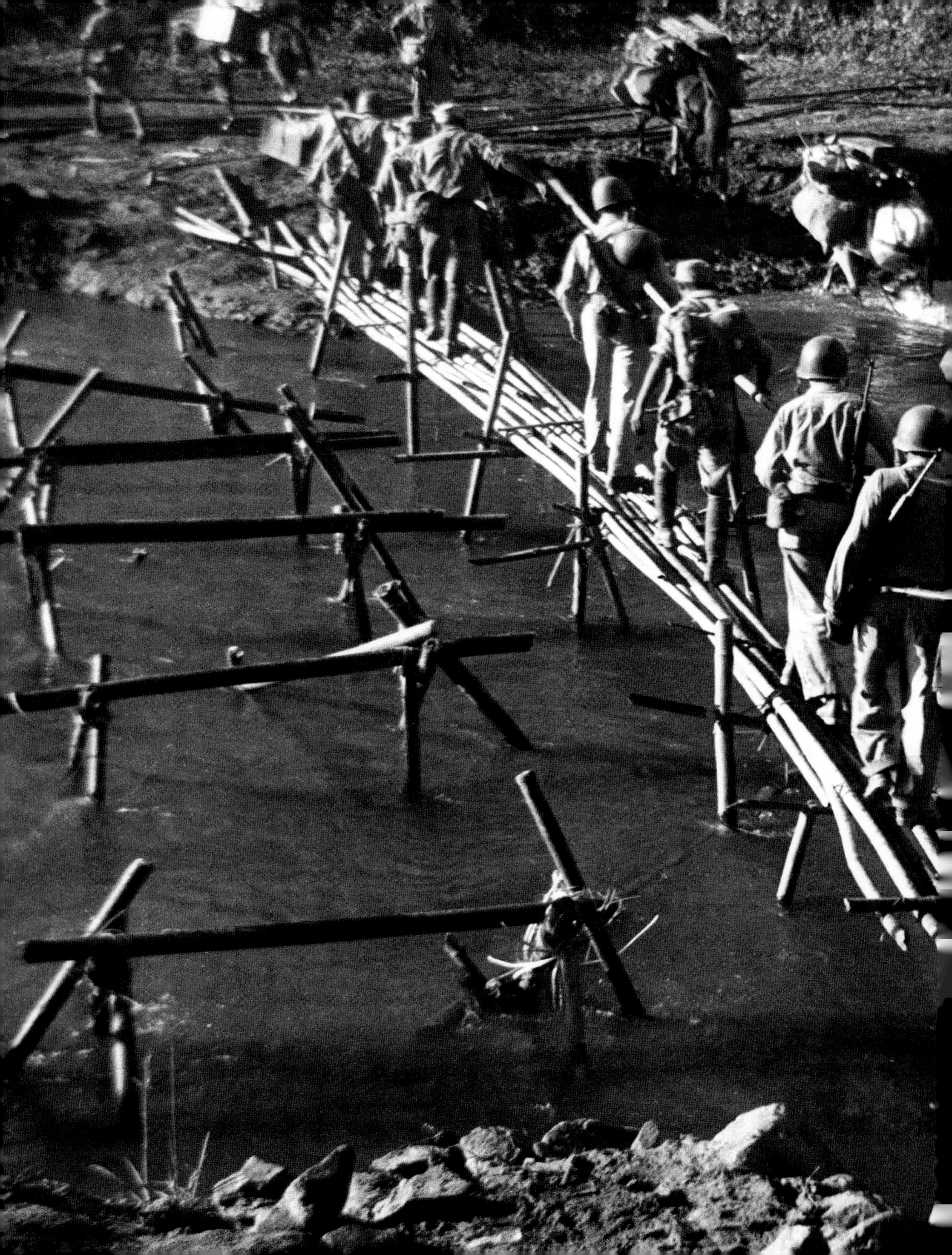

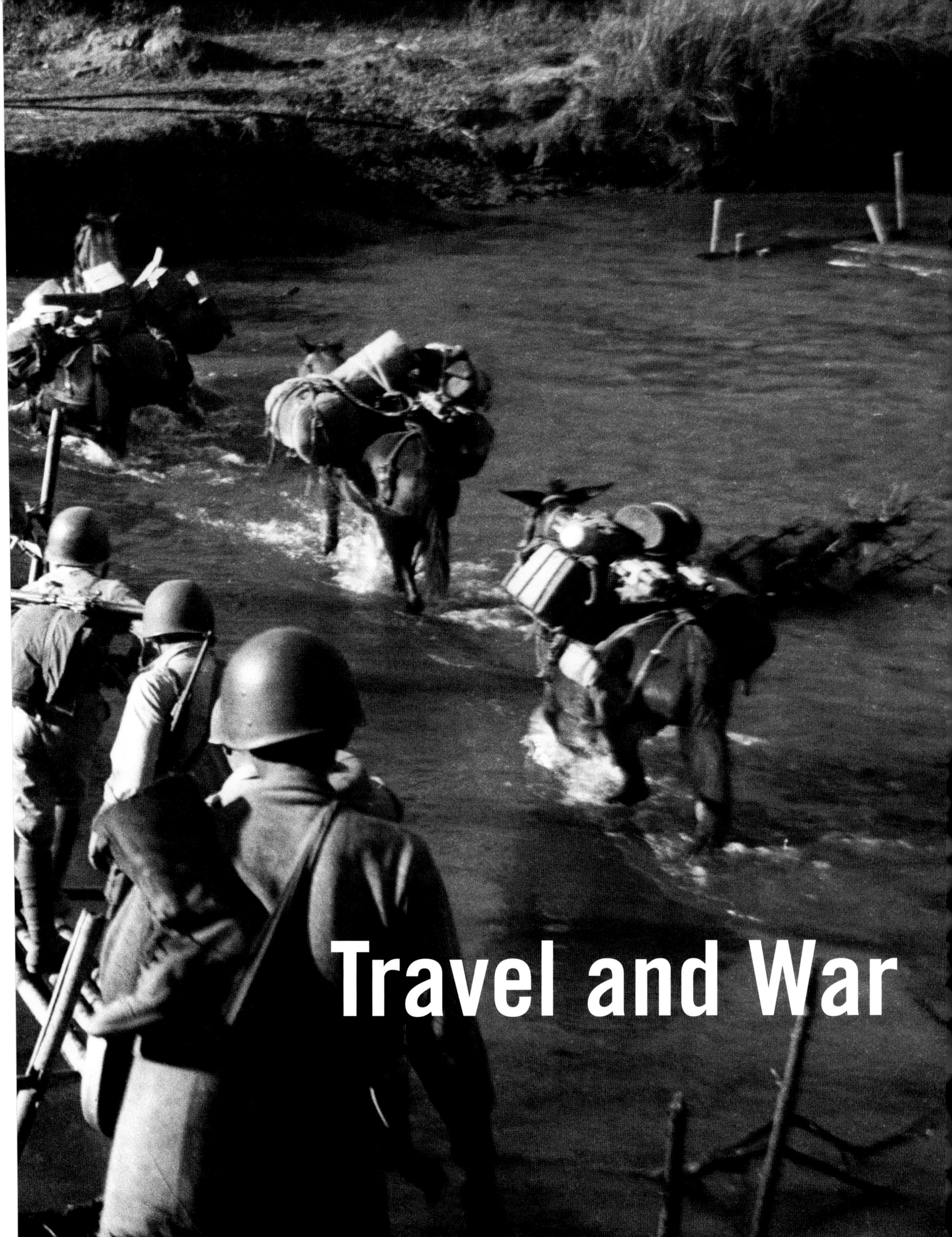

Travel and War

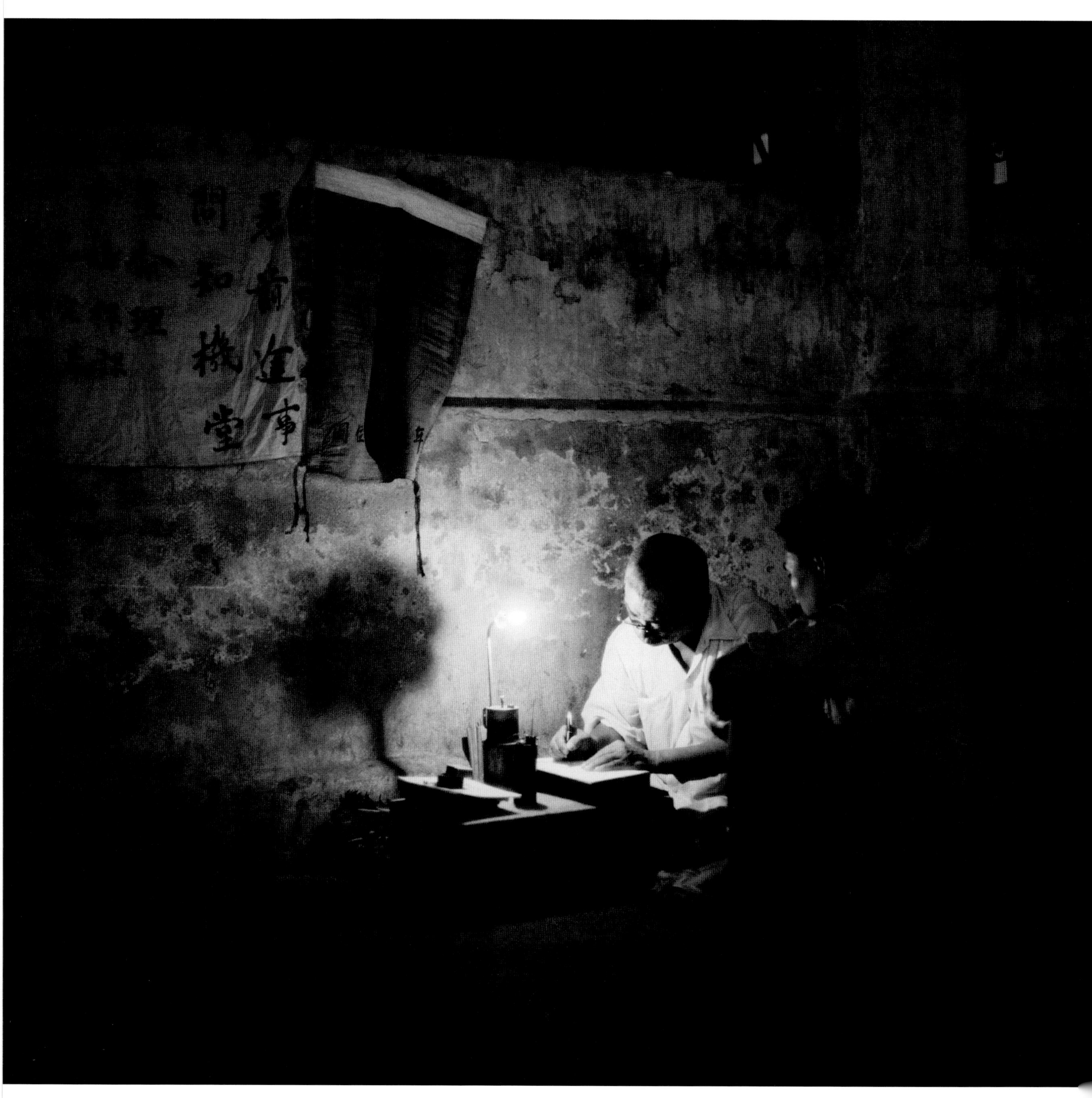

Letter writer, Singapore, 1970

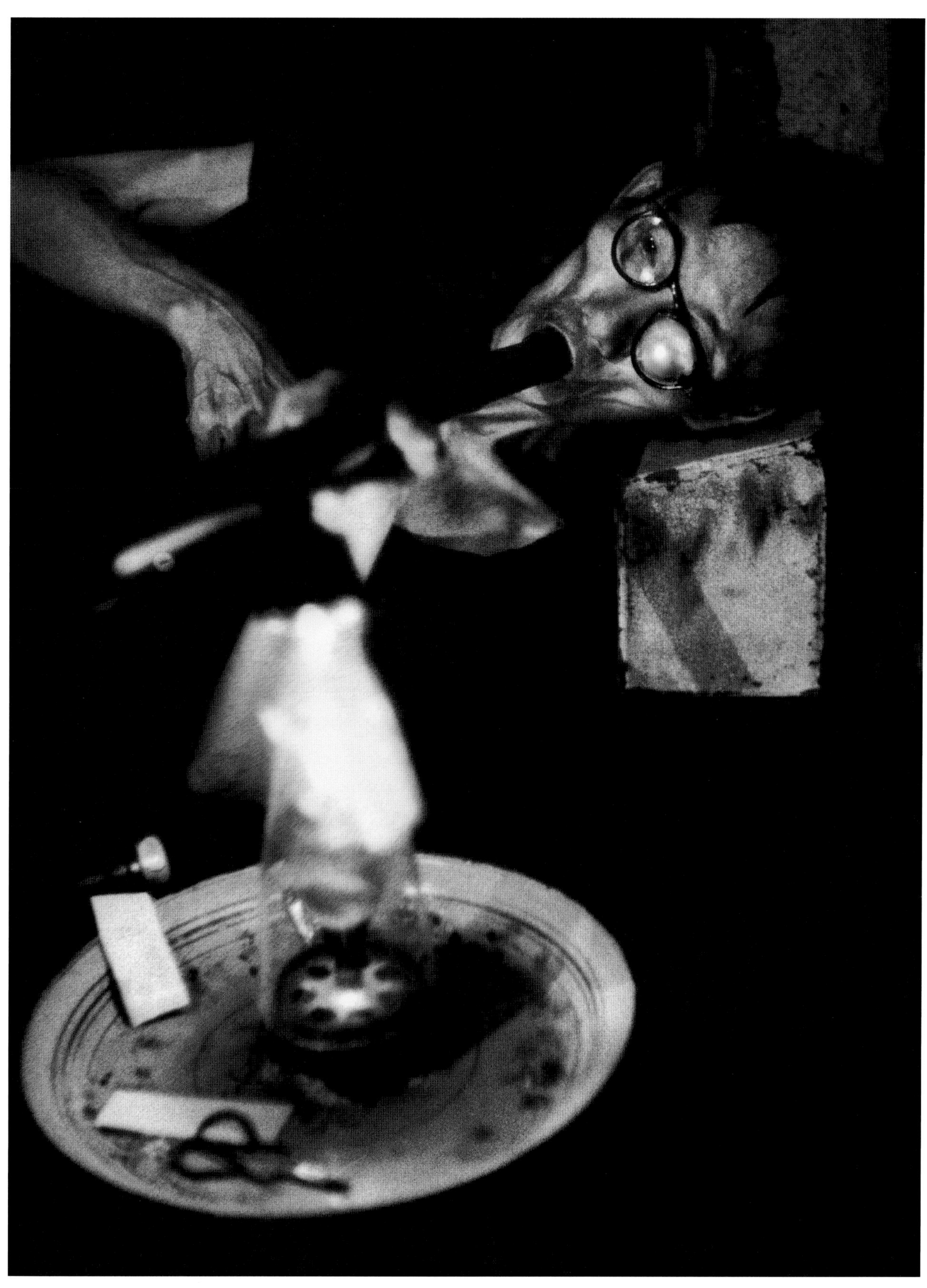

Opium smoker, Bangkok, 1956

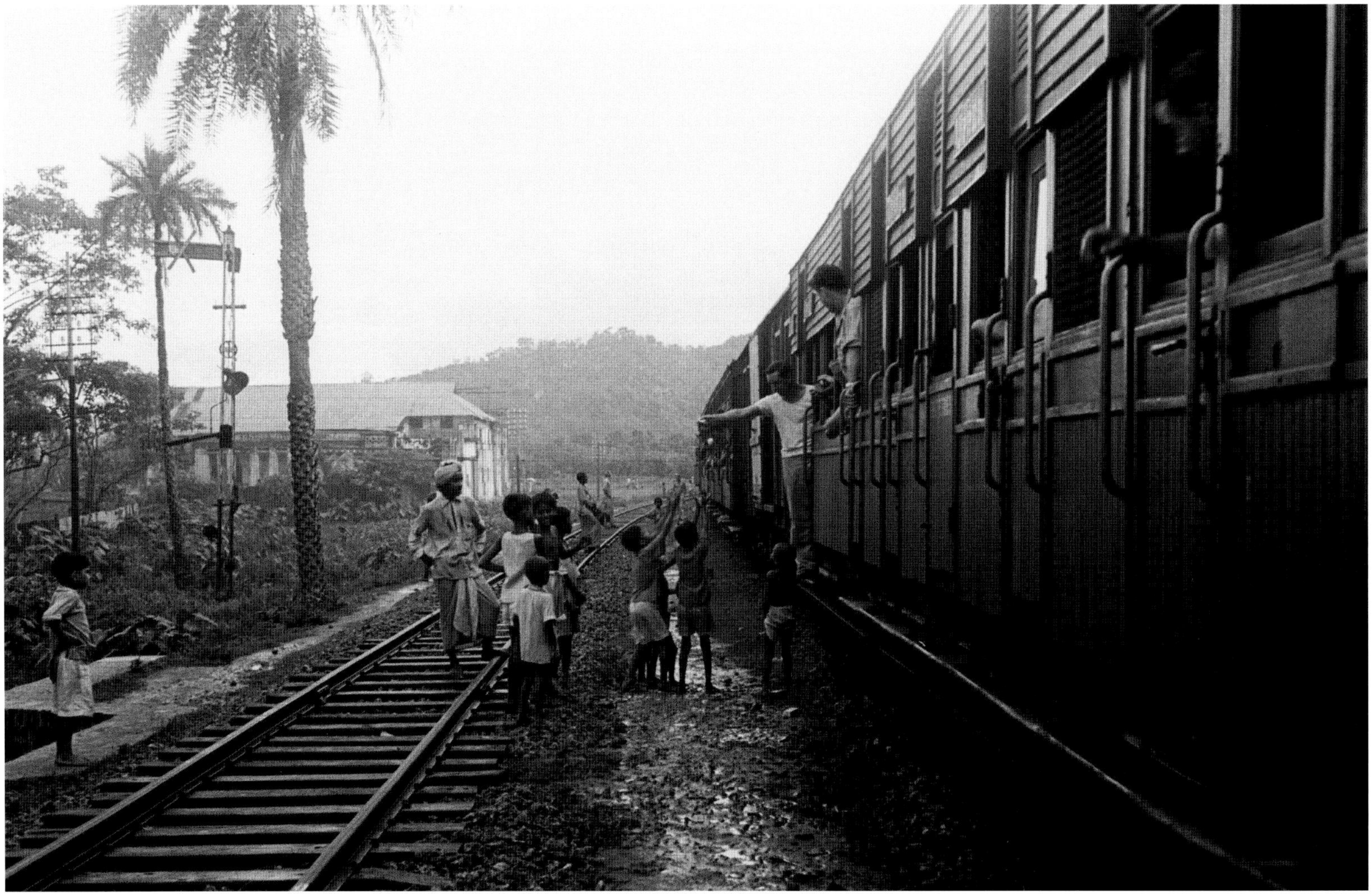

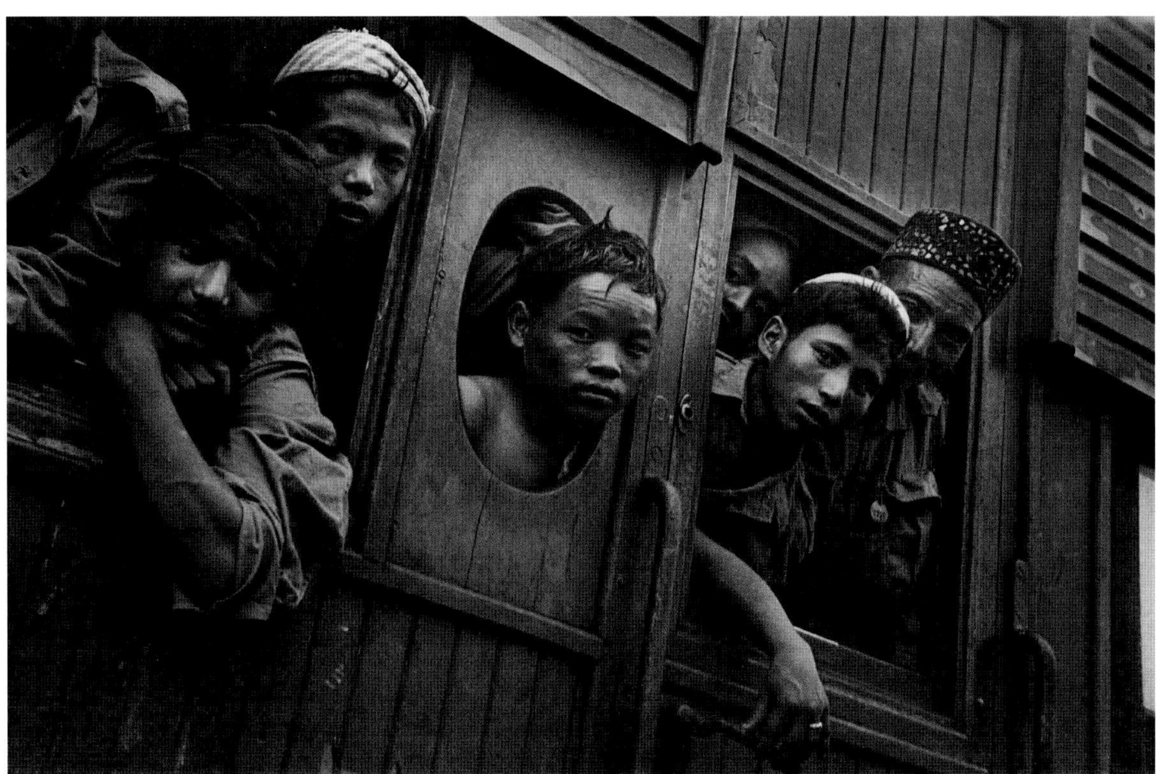

World War II, India, 1943

World War II, Burma, 1944 (opposite)

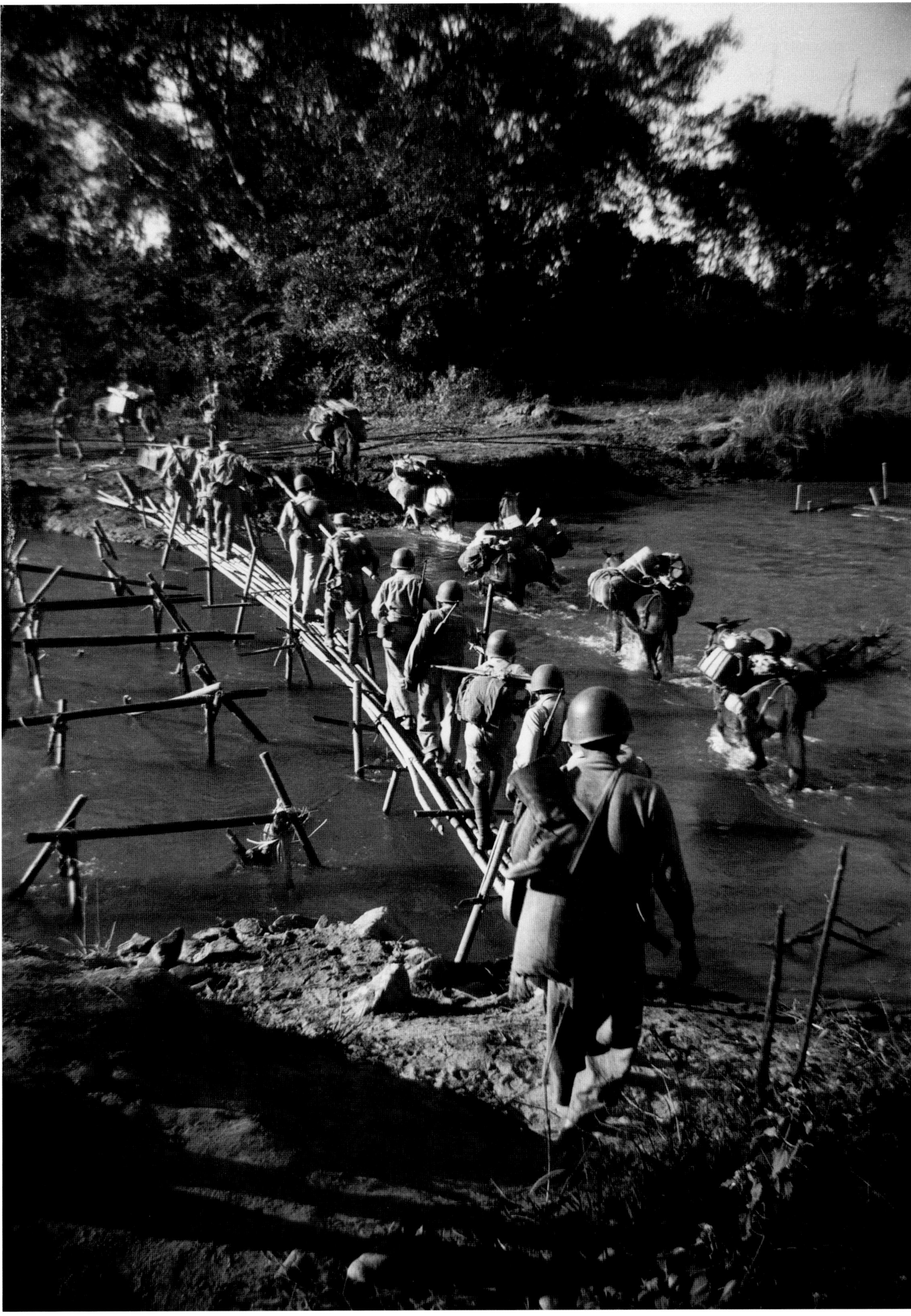

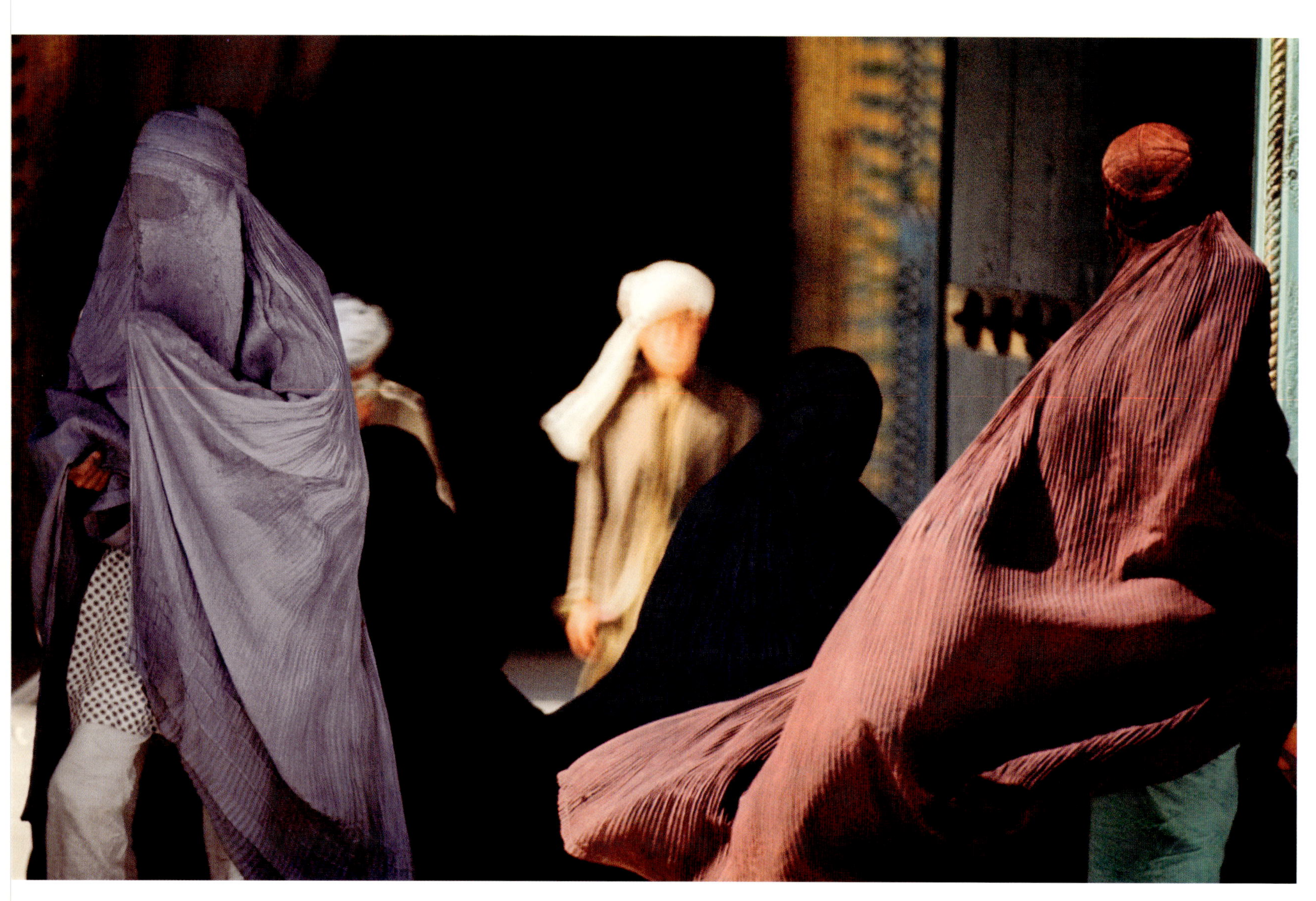

Mazar-i-Sharif, Afghanistan, 1971

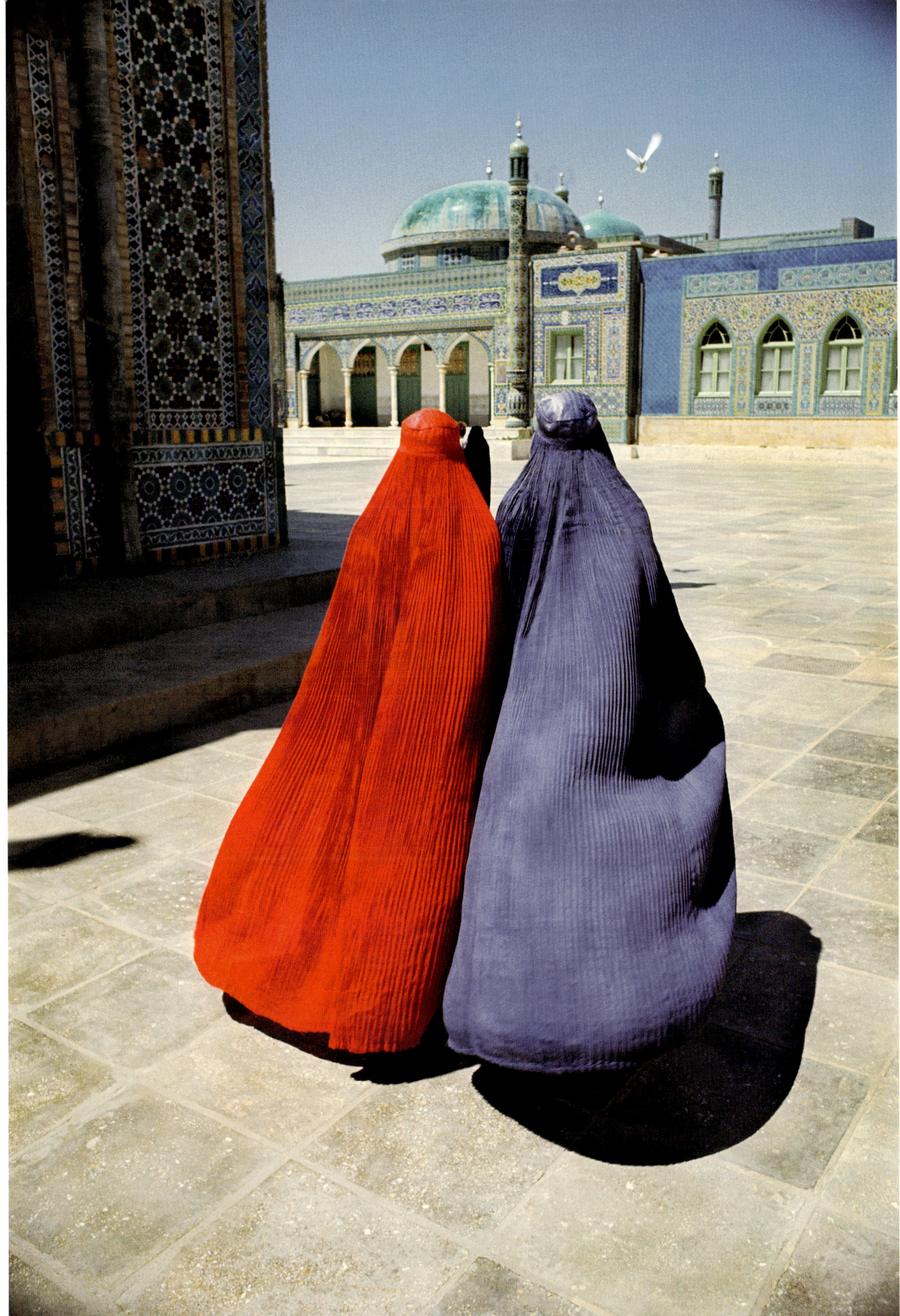

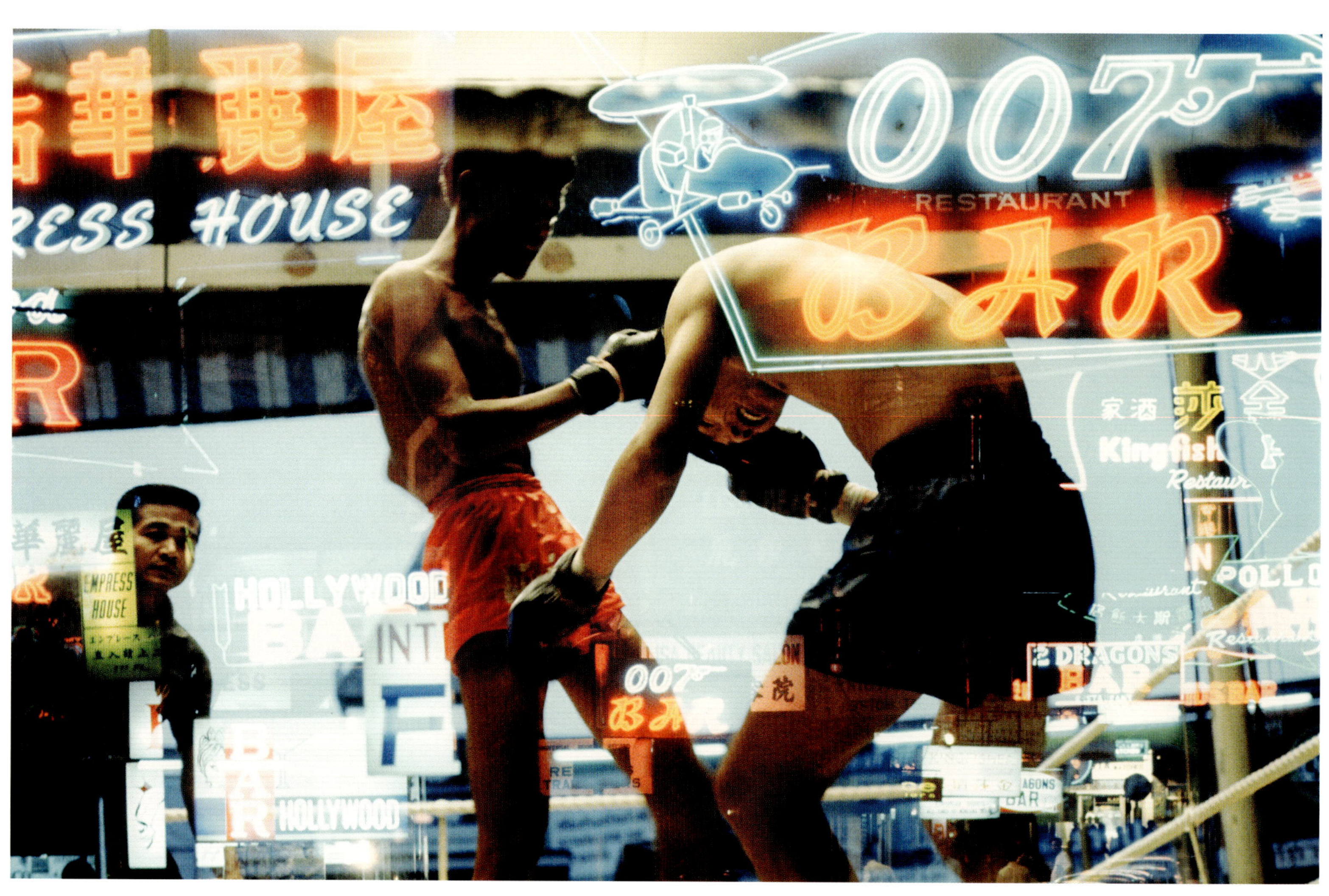

Boxers, Bangkok, 1970

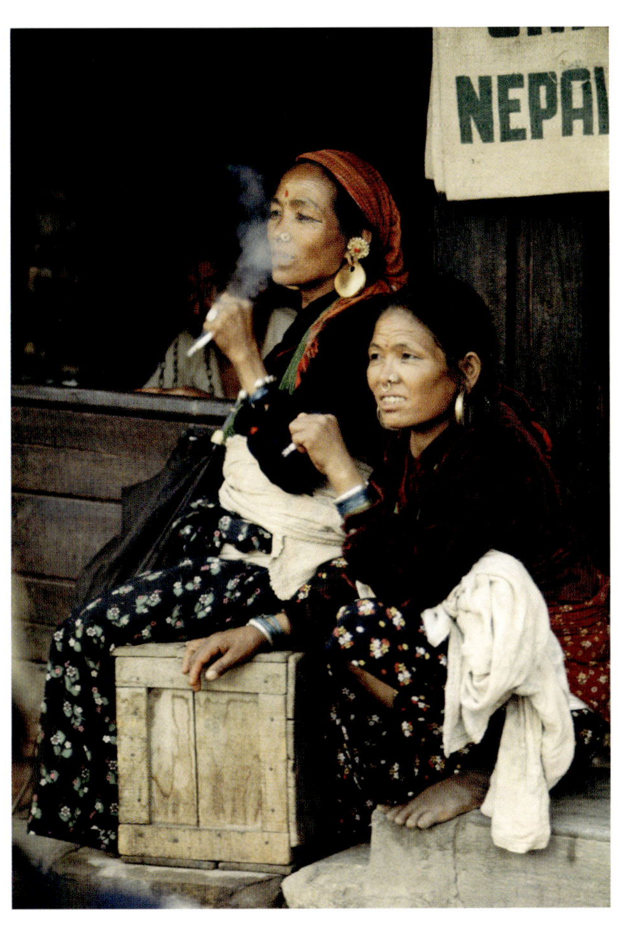

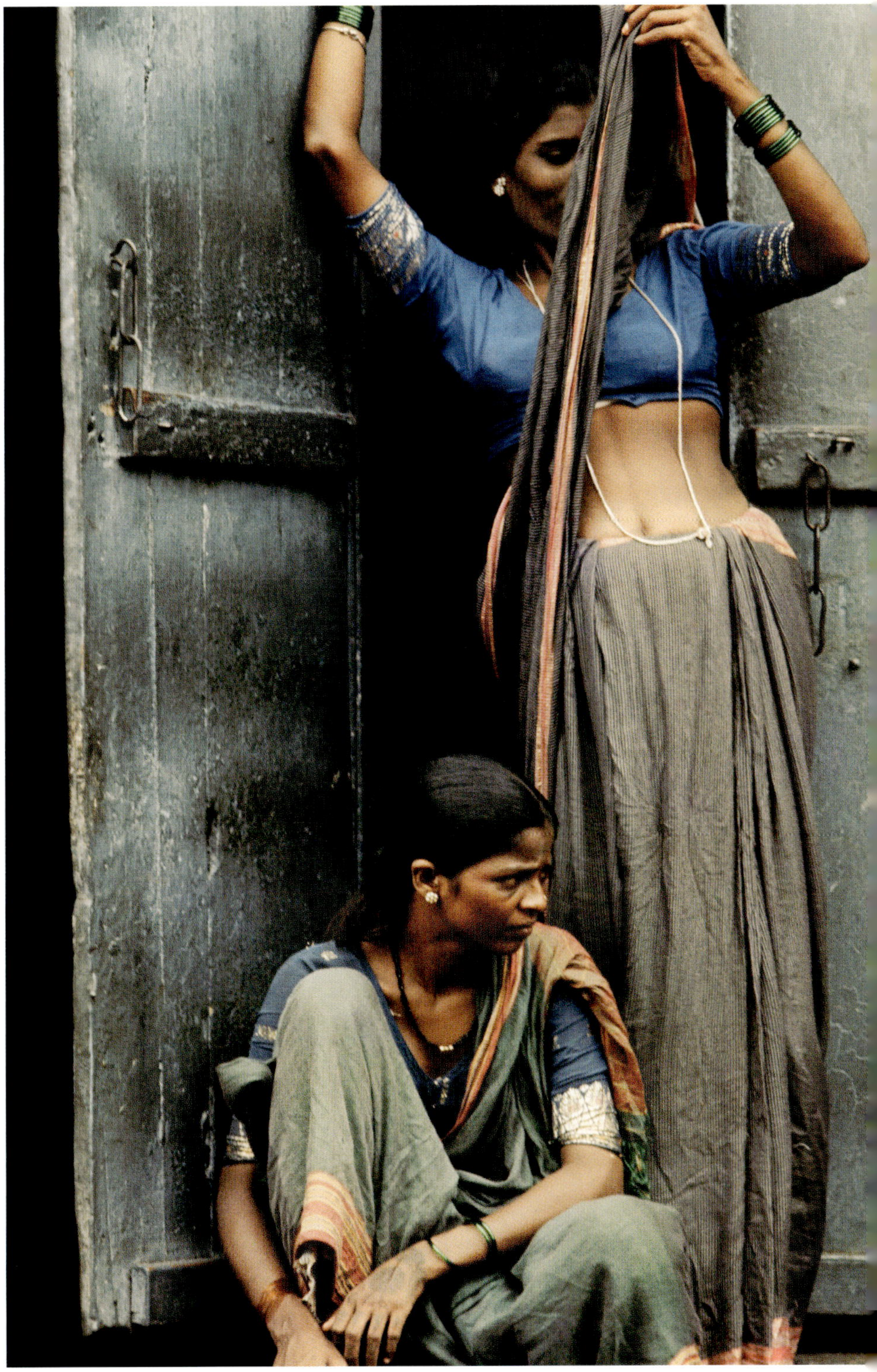

Kathmandu, Nepal, 1972

Prostitutes, Bombay, 1970

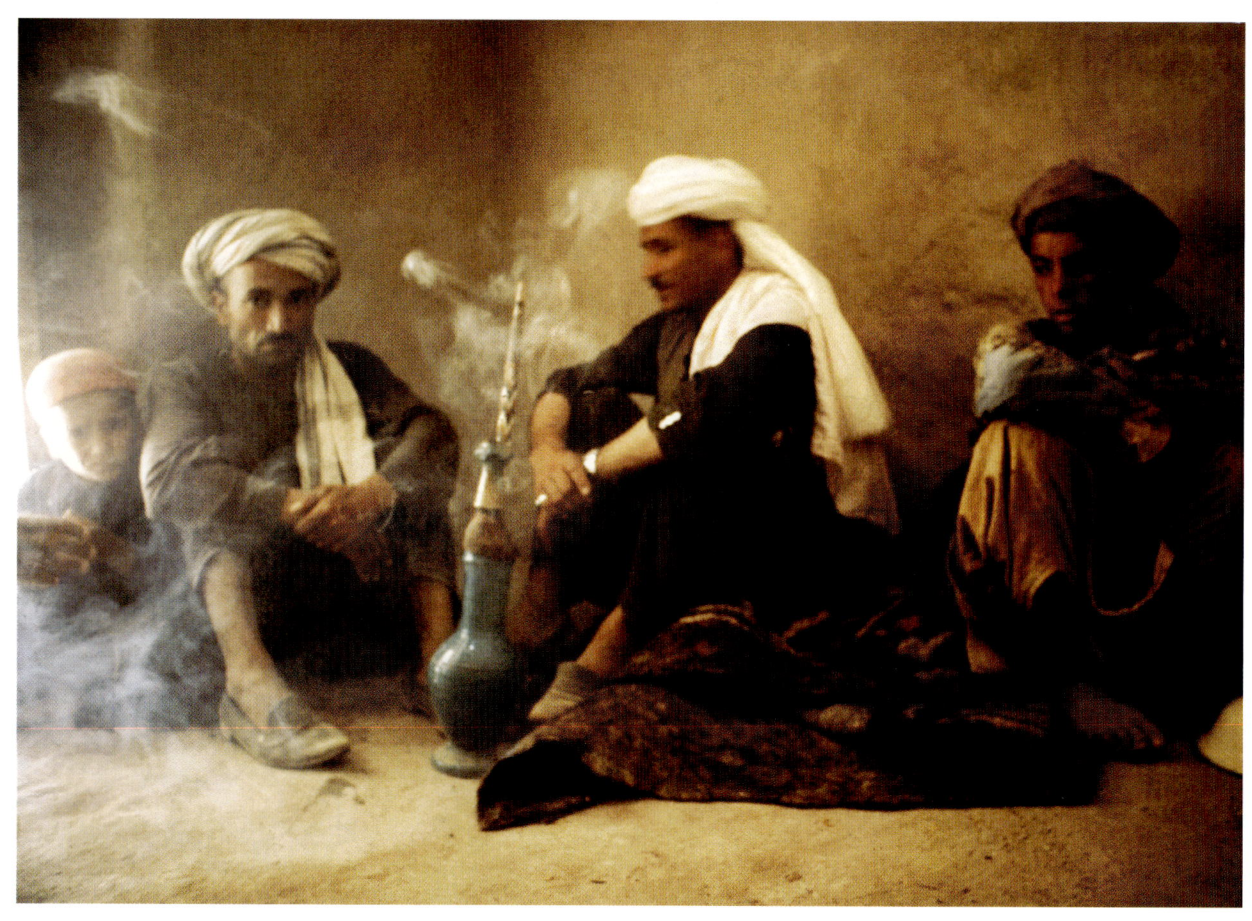

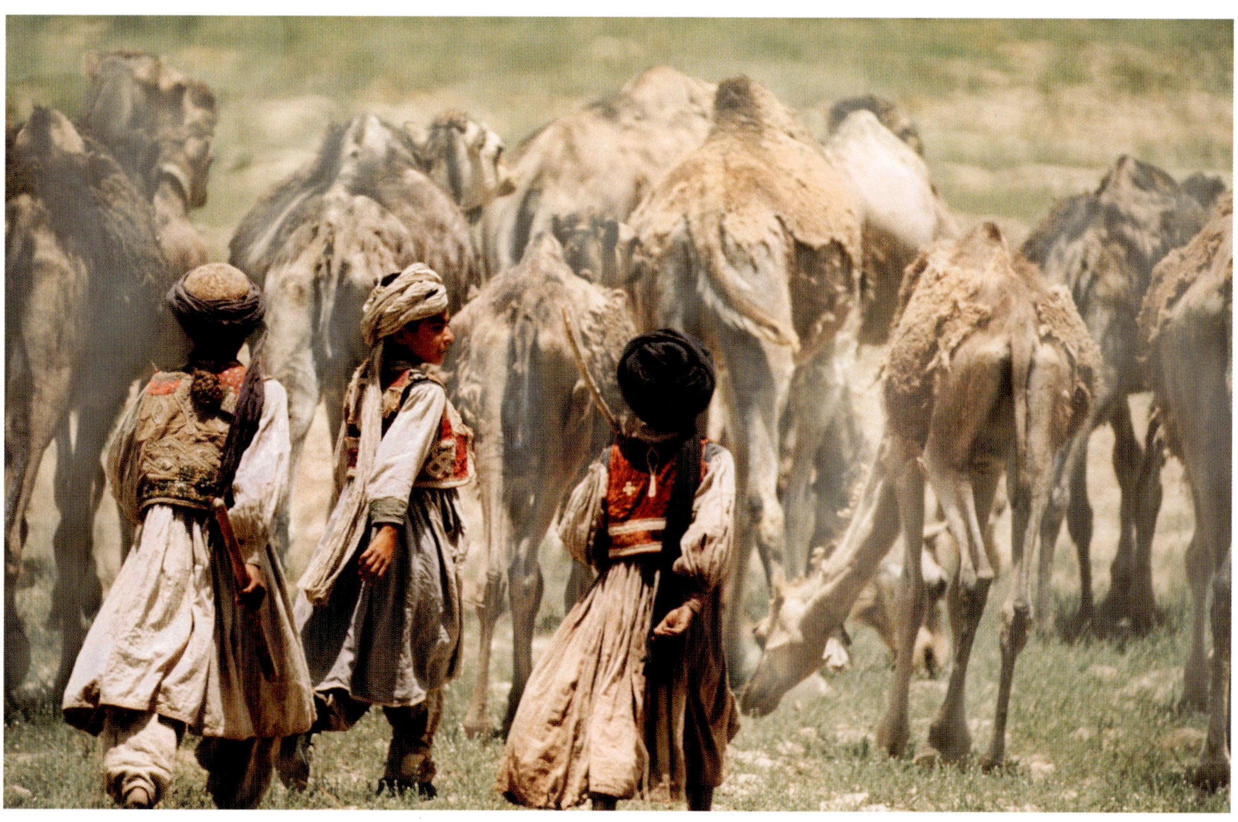

Mazar-i-Sharif, Afghanistan, 1971

Afghanistan, 1971

India, 1970

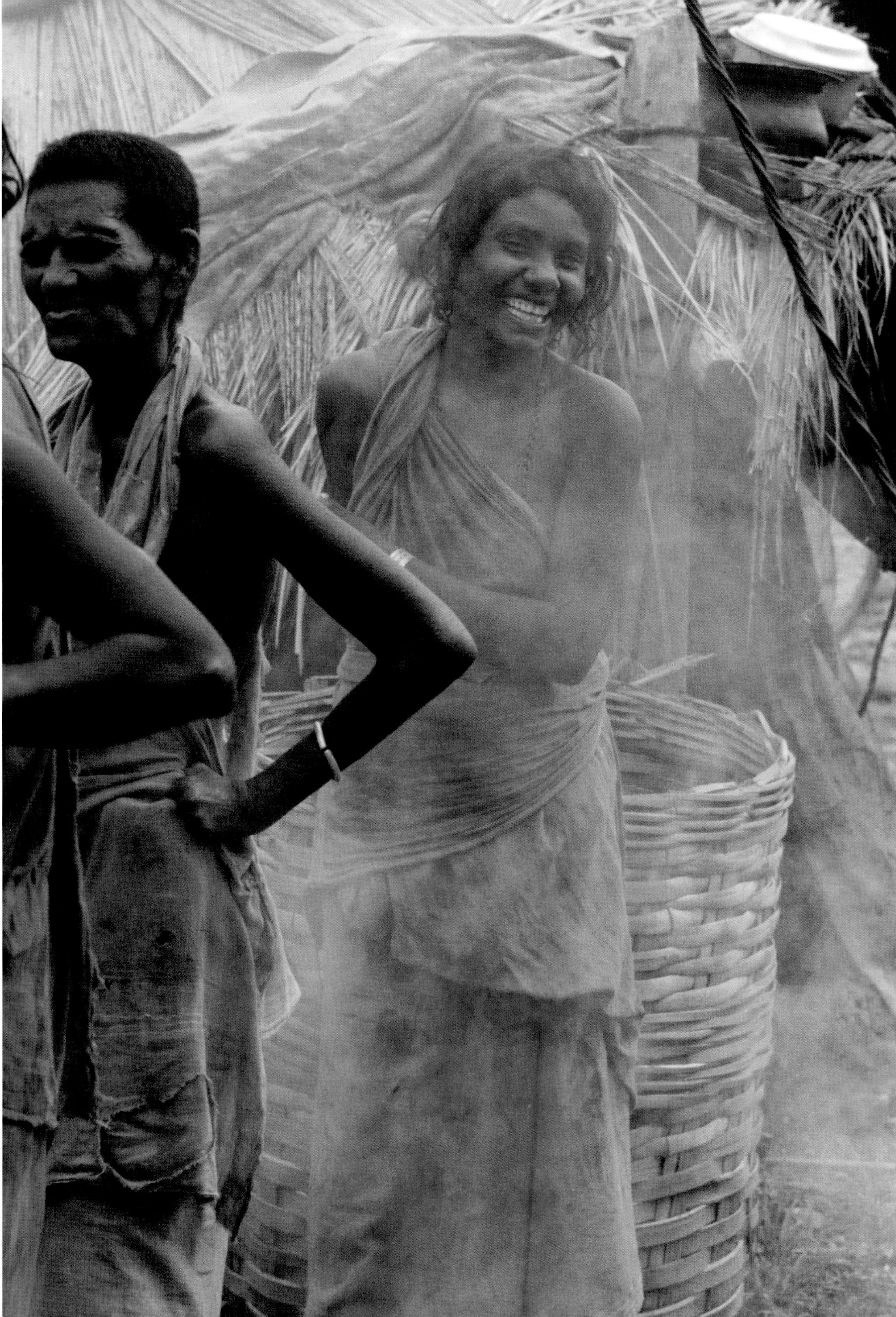

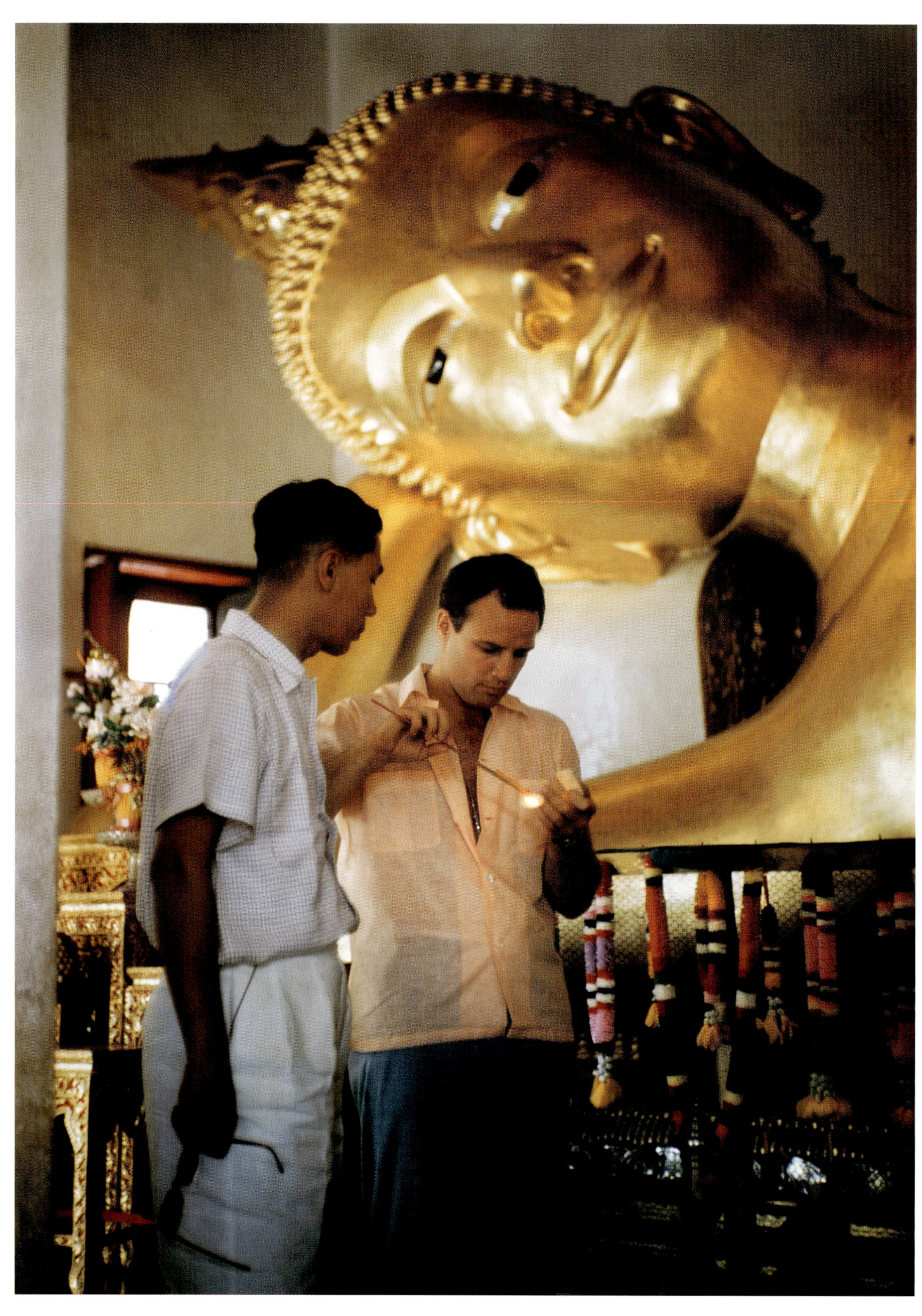

Marlon Brando, Bangkok, 1956

Bamiyan, Afghanistan, 1970

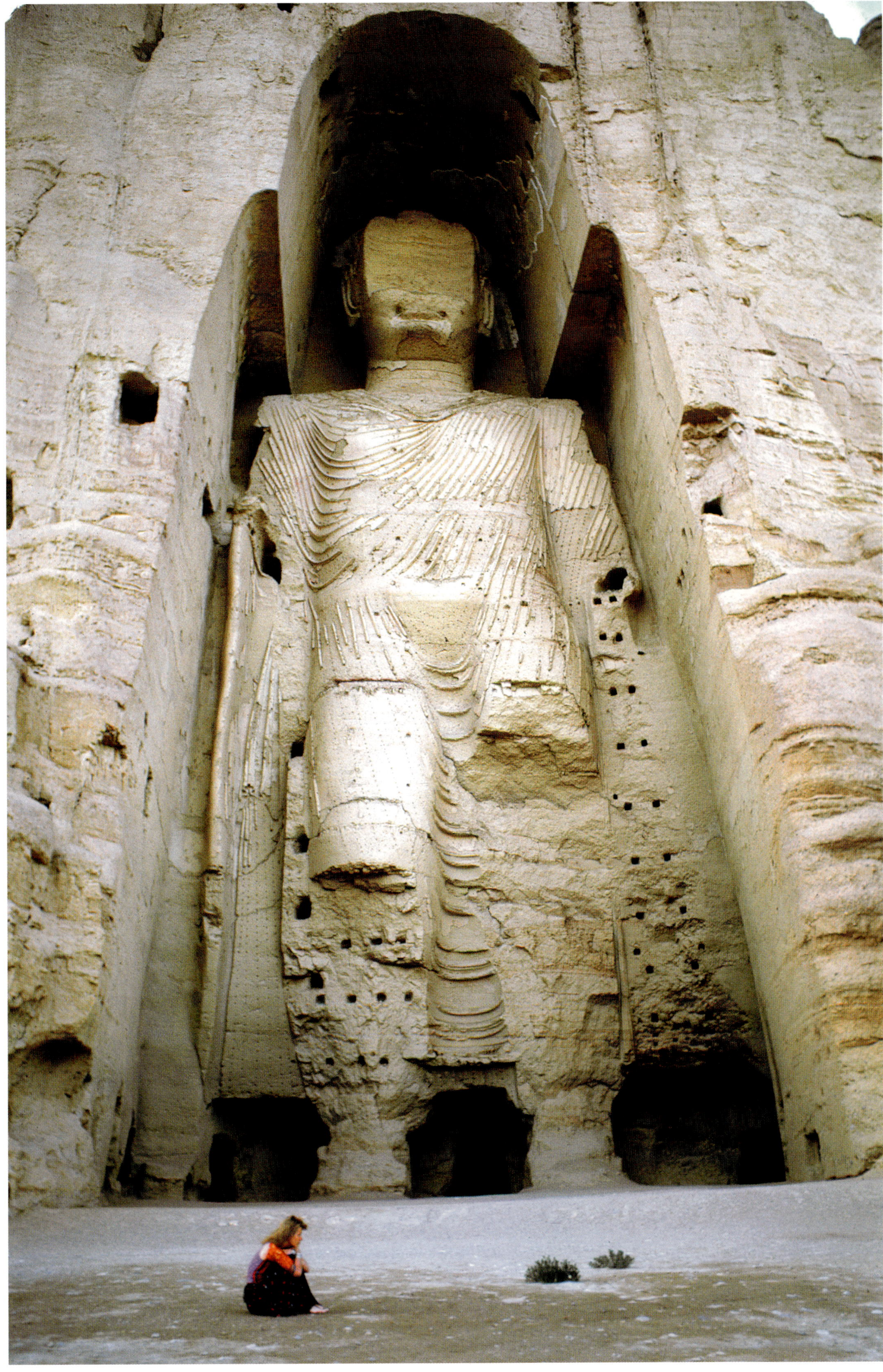

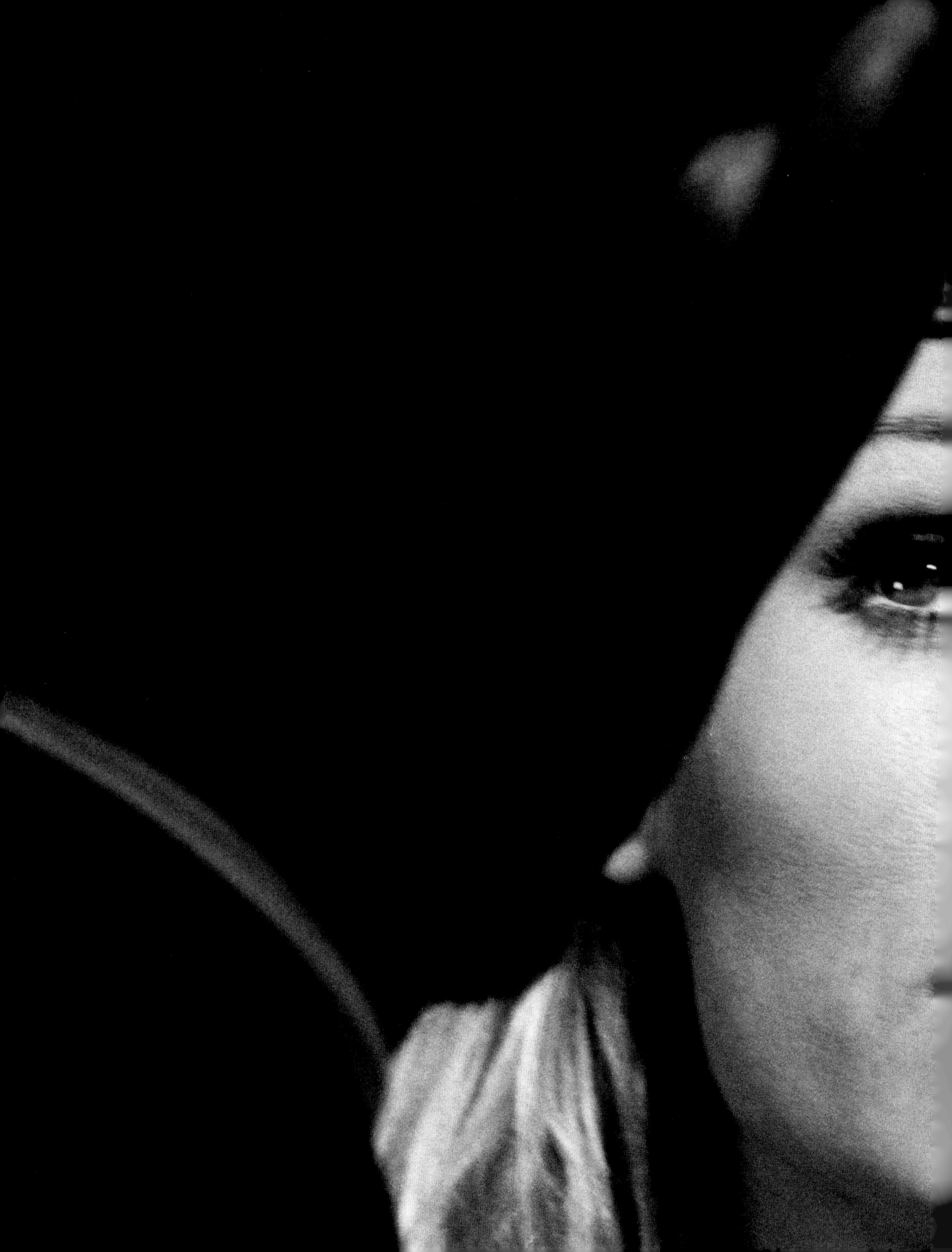

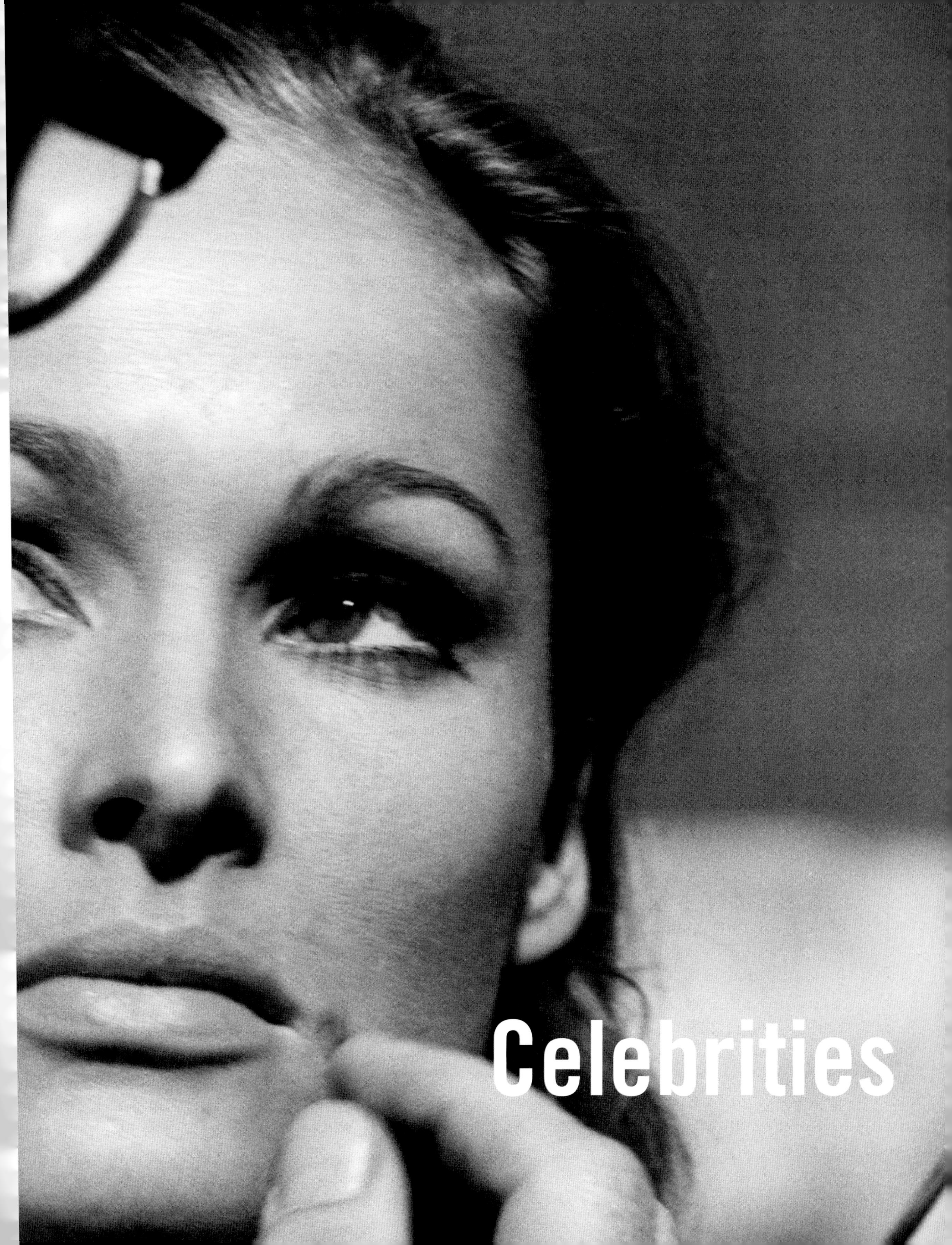

Celebrities

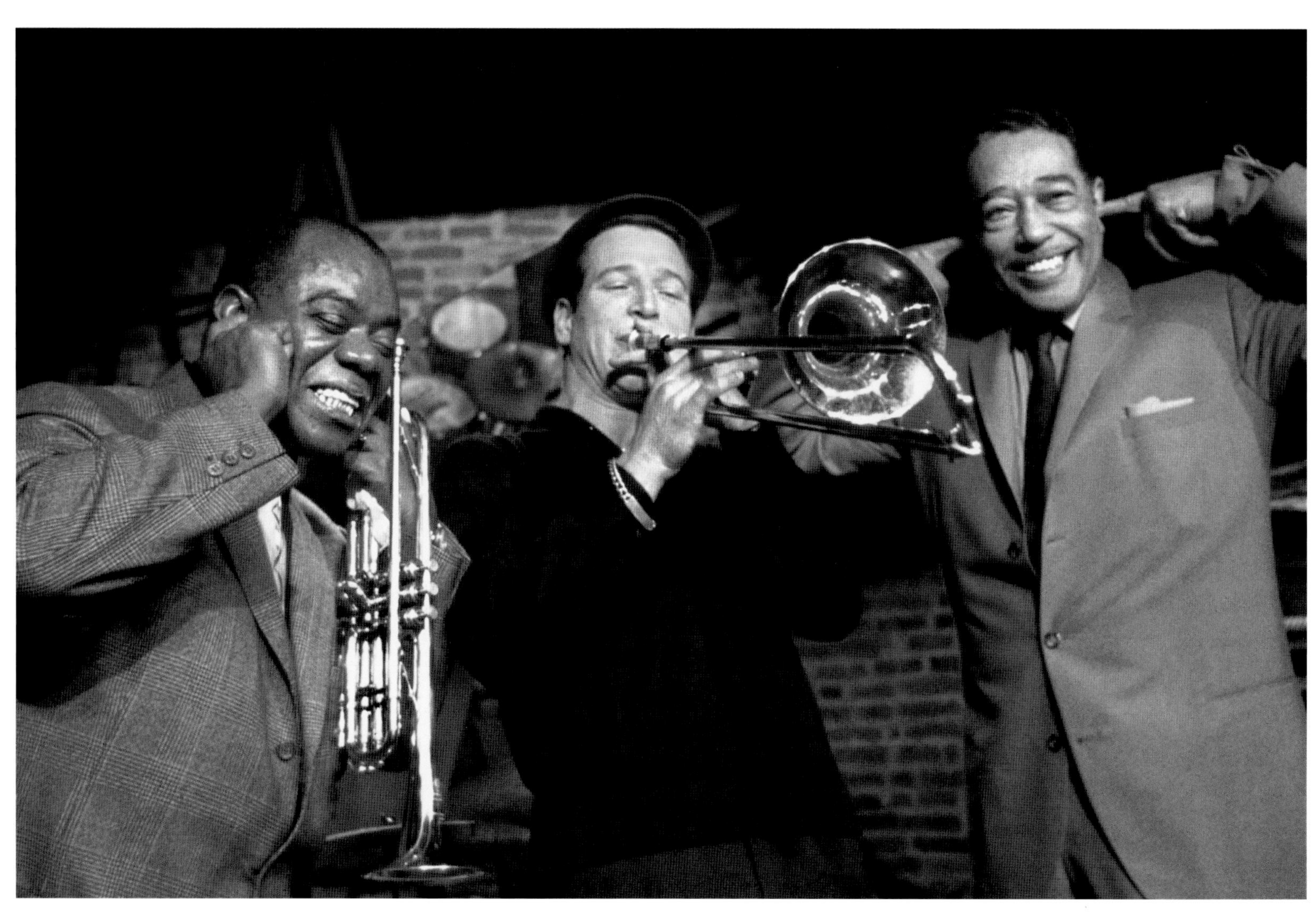

Paul Newman, Louis Armstrong and Duke Ellington on the set of *Paris Blues*, Paris, 1960

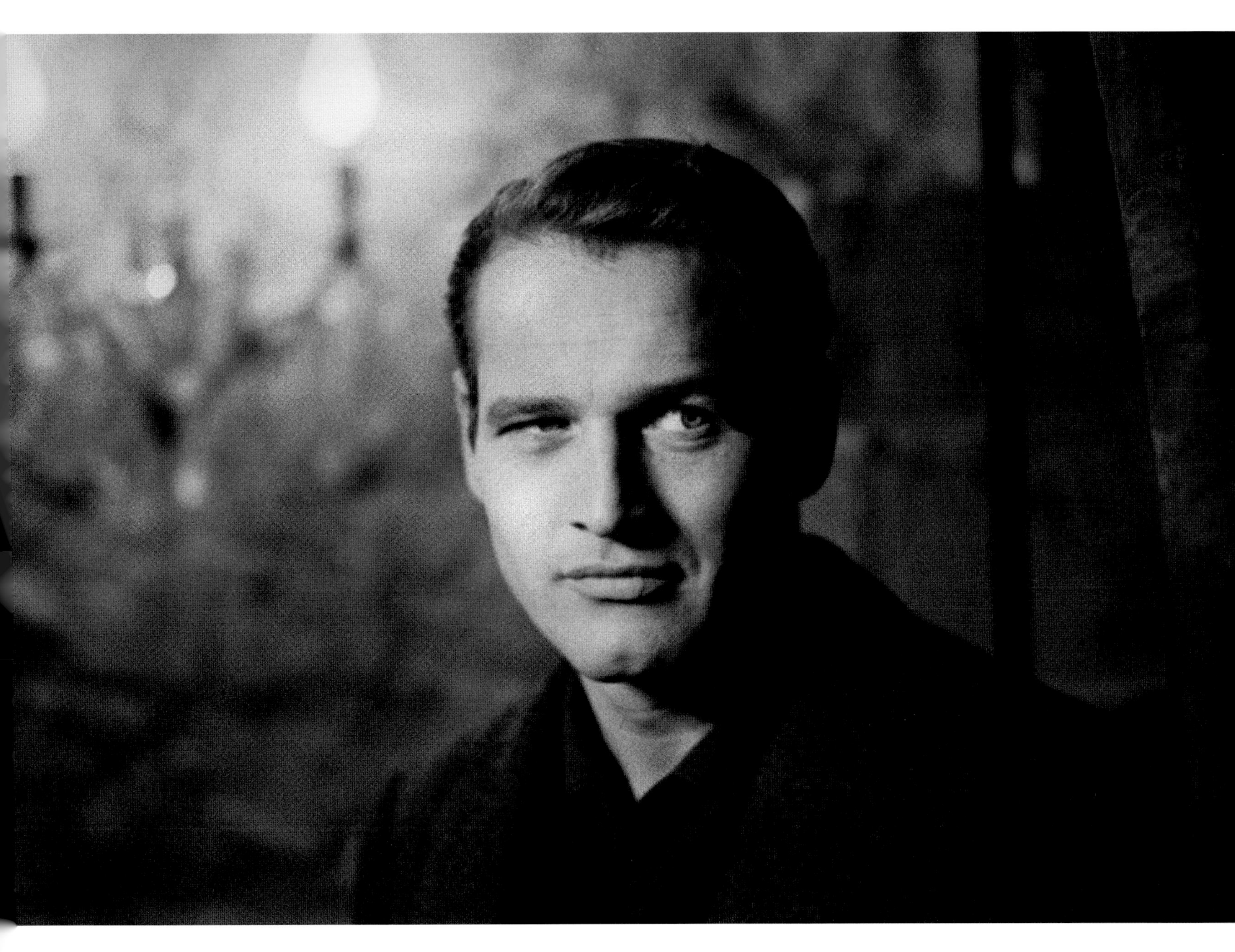

Paul Newman on the set of *Paris Blues*, Paris, 1960

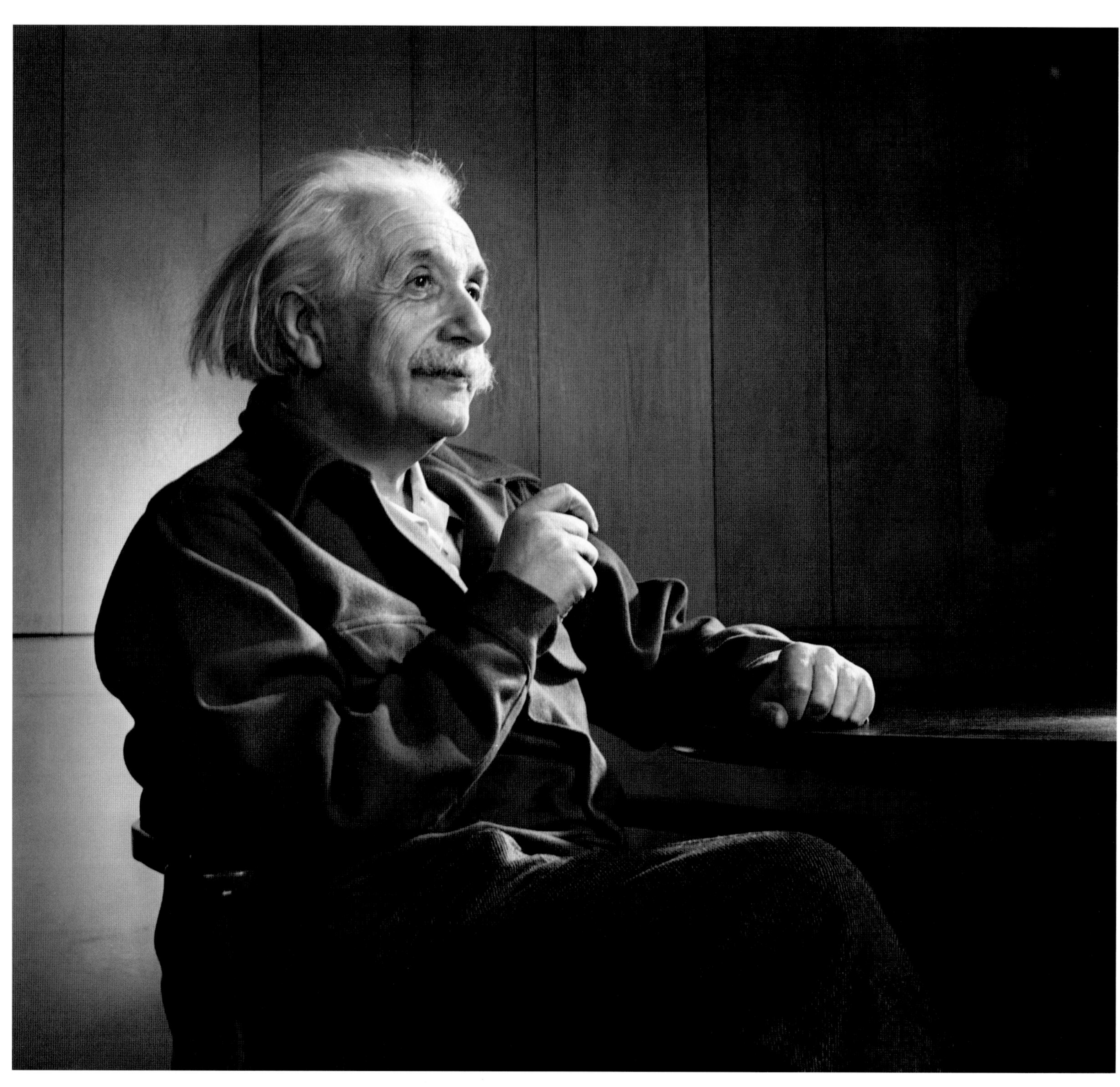

Albert Einstein, Princeton University, New Jersey, 1948 and Martha Graham, NYC, 1948 (both taken during Yousuf Karsh's photo sessions)

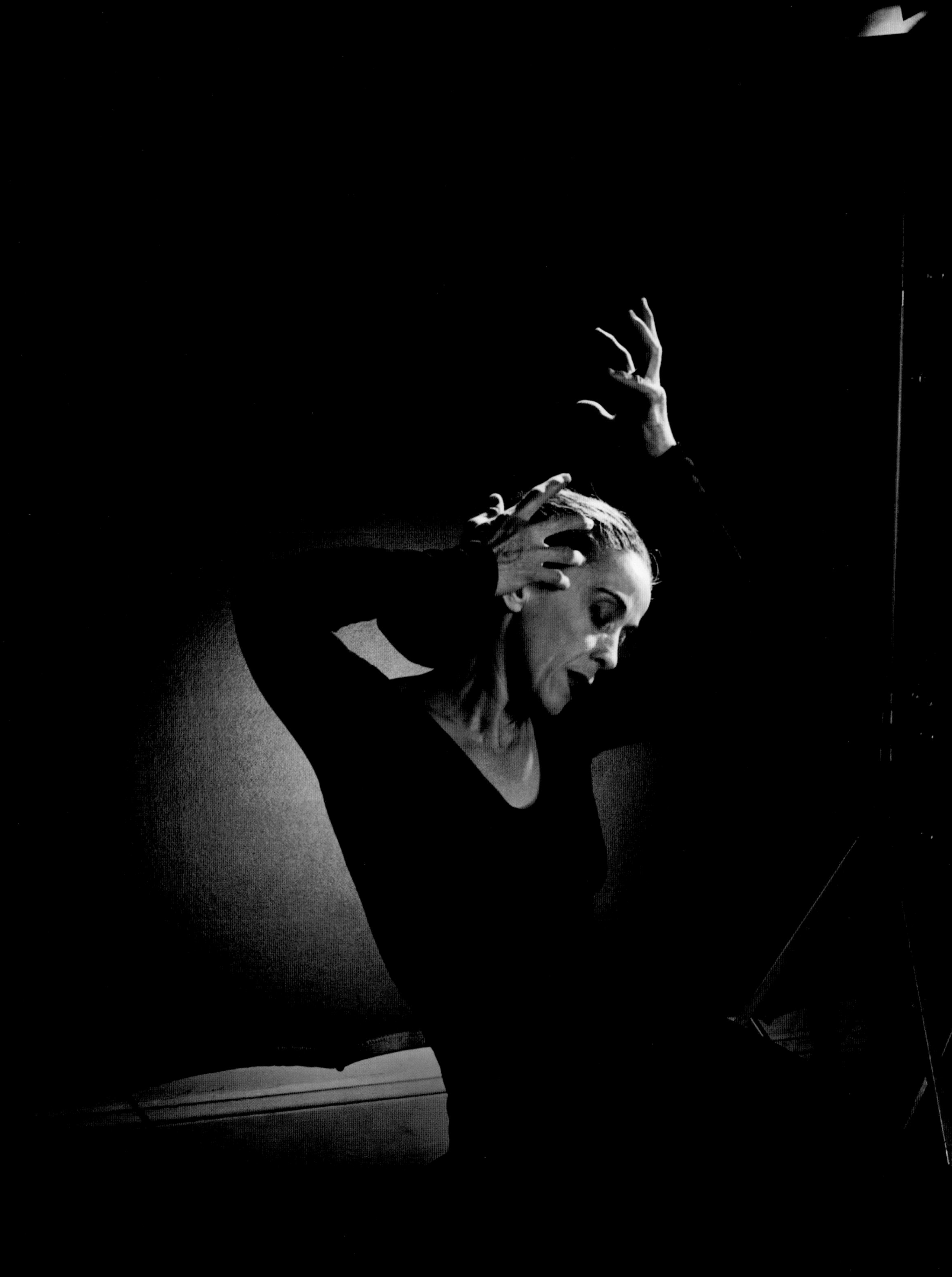

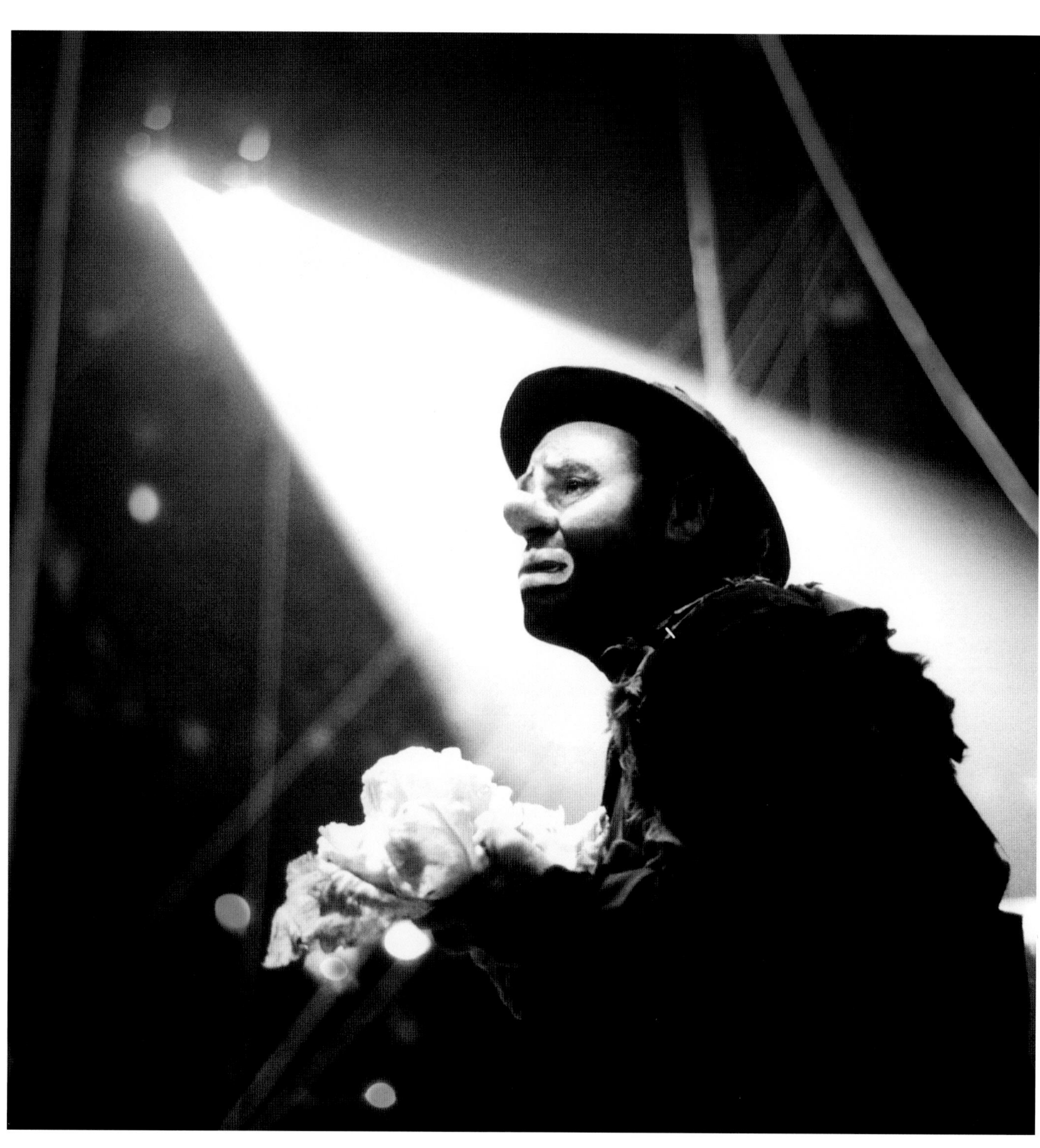

Emmett Kelly, Ringling Bros. and Barnum & Bailey, NYC, 1953

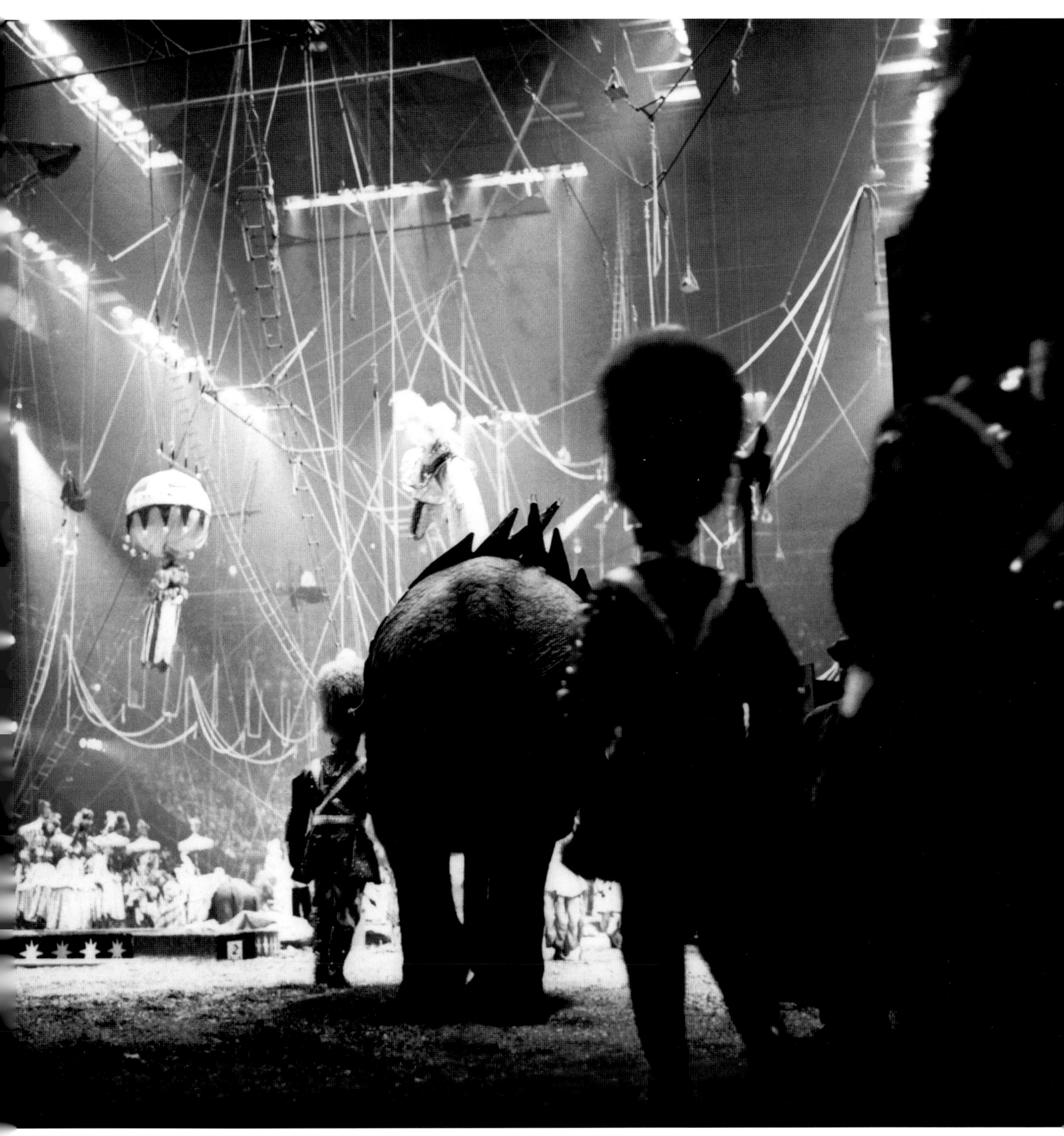

Ringling Bros. and Barnum & Bailey, NYC, 1953

Marilyn Monroe, Ringling Bros. and Barnum & Bailey, NYC, 1953

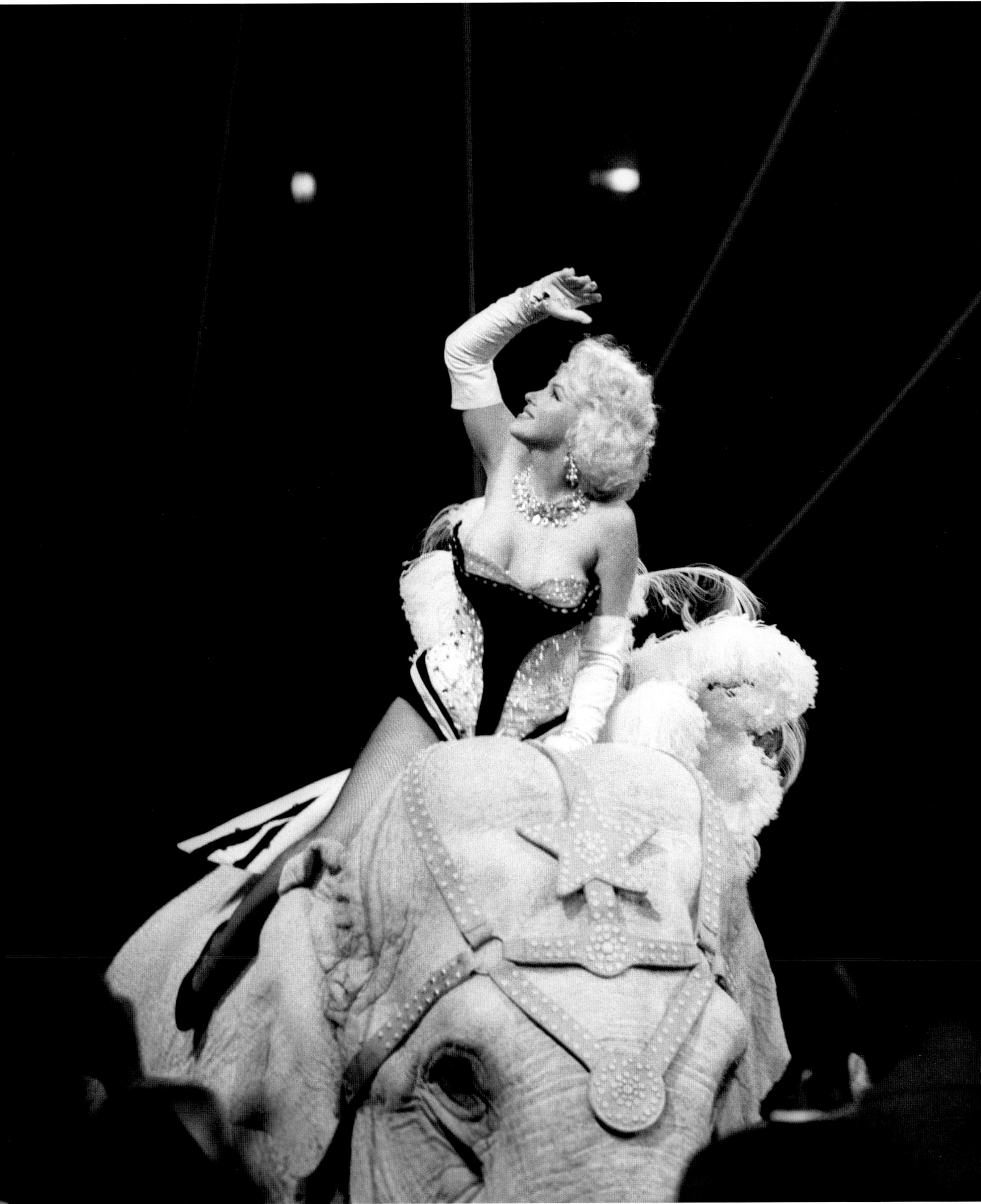

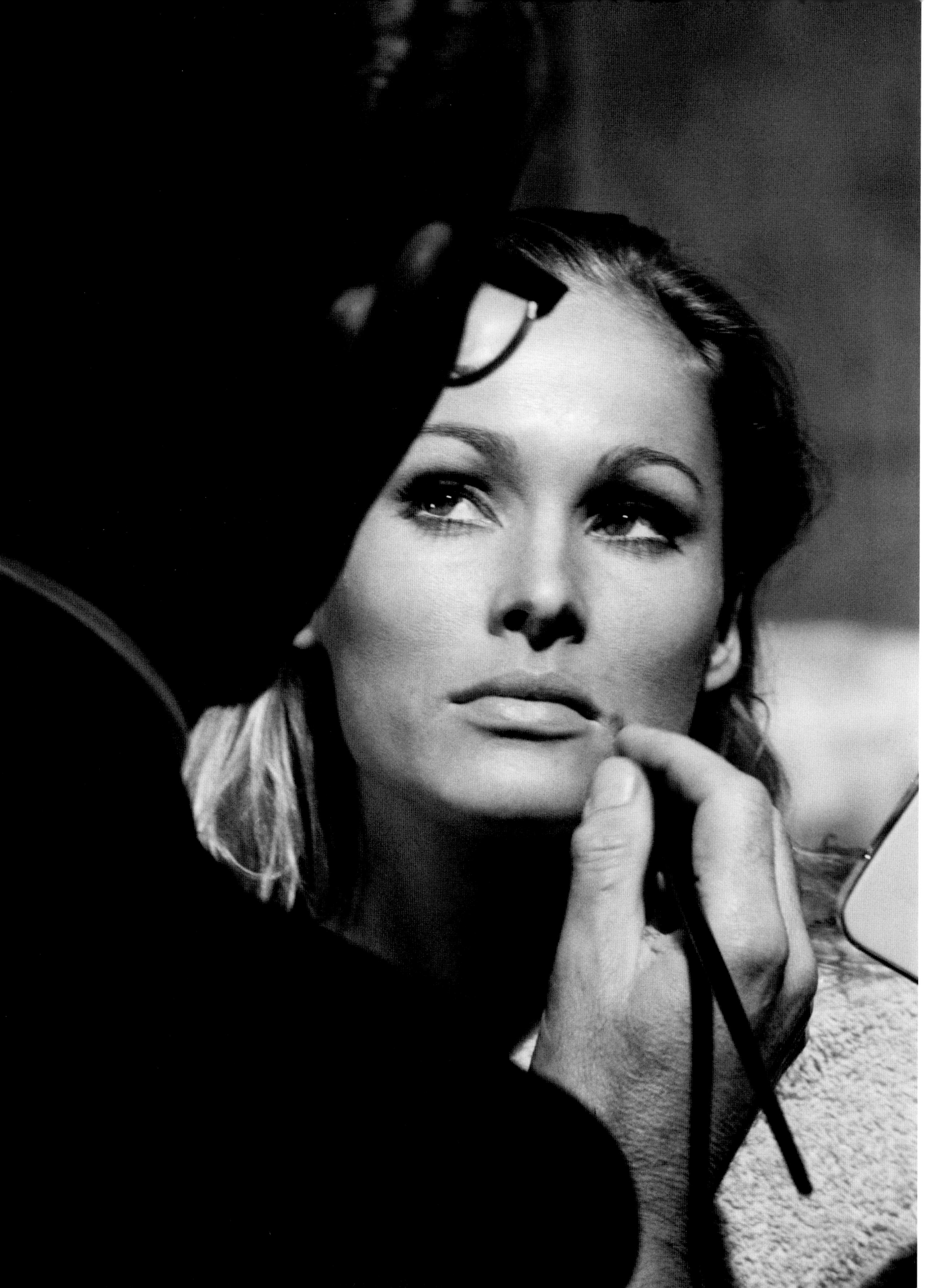

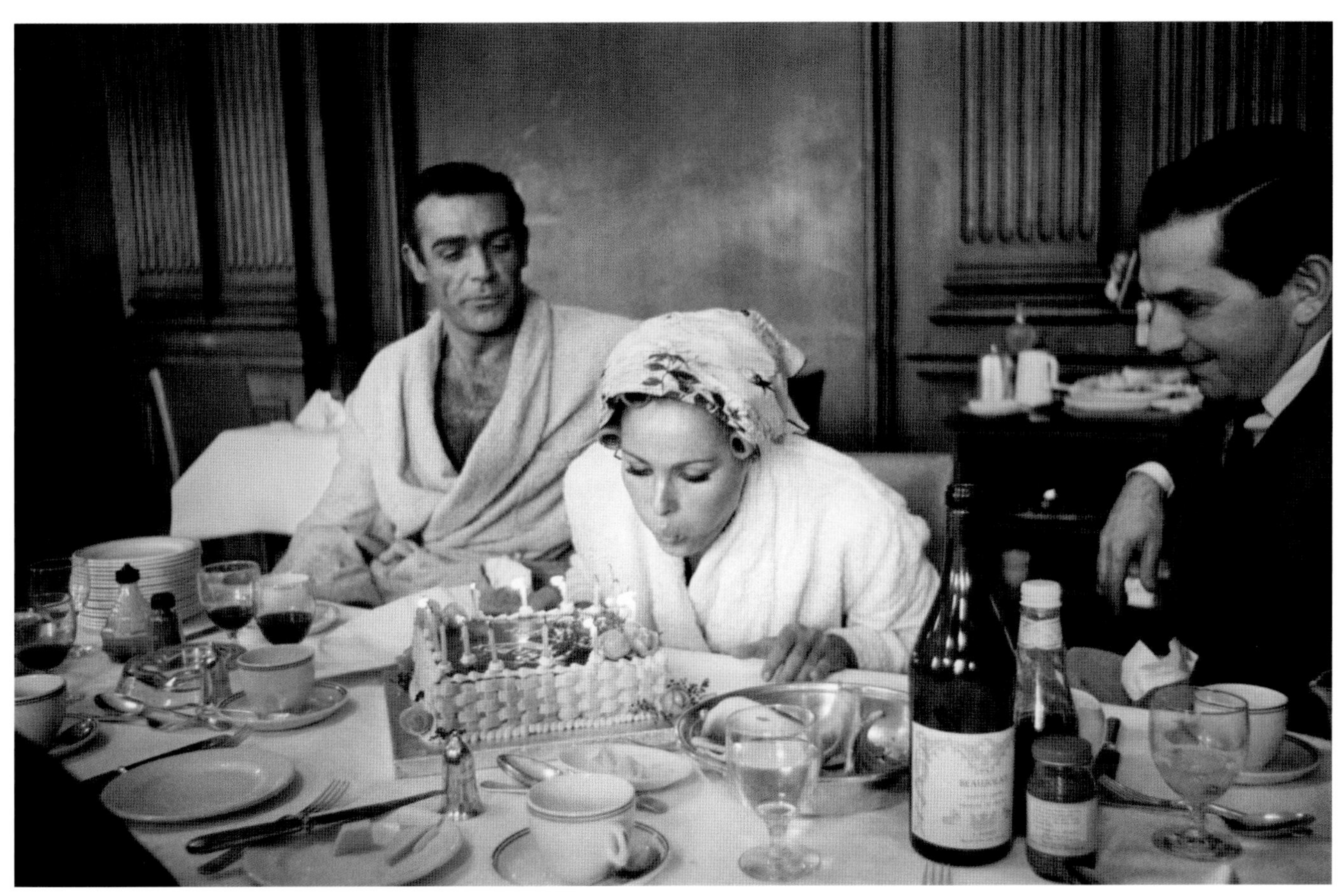

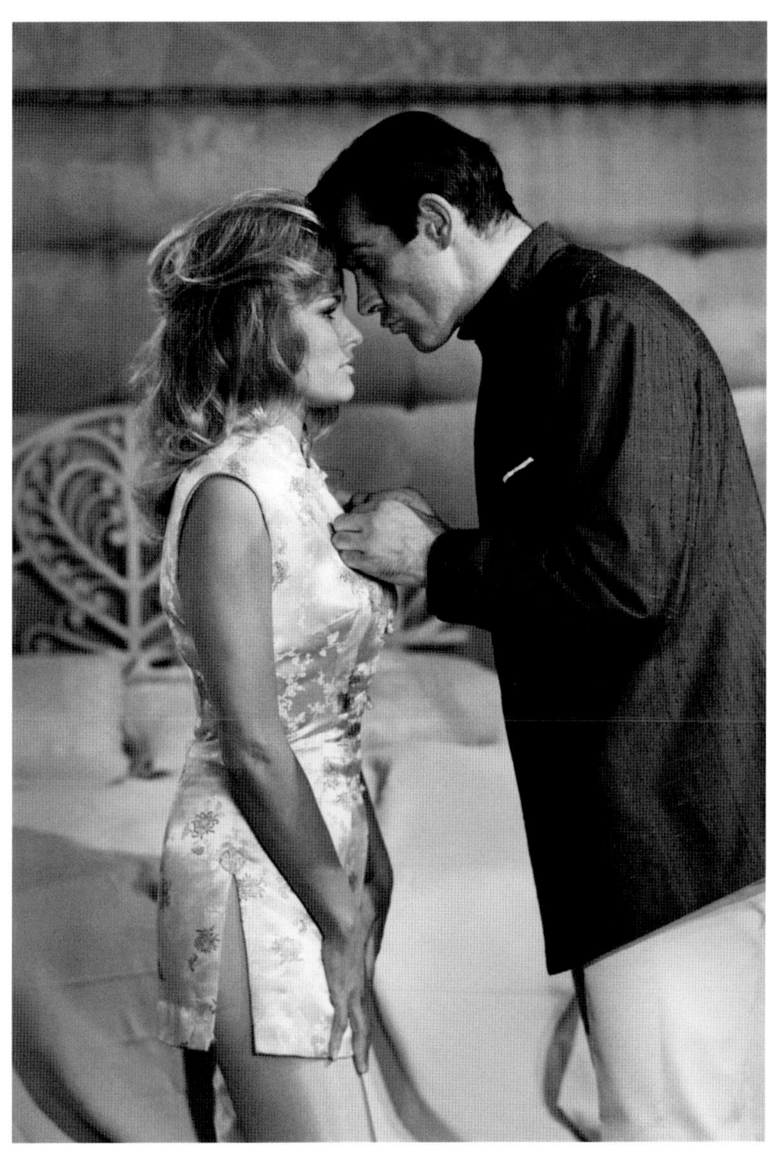

Ursula Andress on the set of *Dr. No*, London, 1960

Ursula Andress' birthday, with Sean Connery on the set of *Dr. No*, London, 1960

Ursula Andress and Sean Connery on the set of *Dr. No*, London, 1960

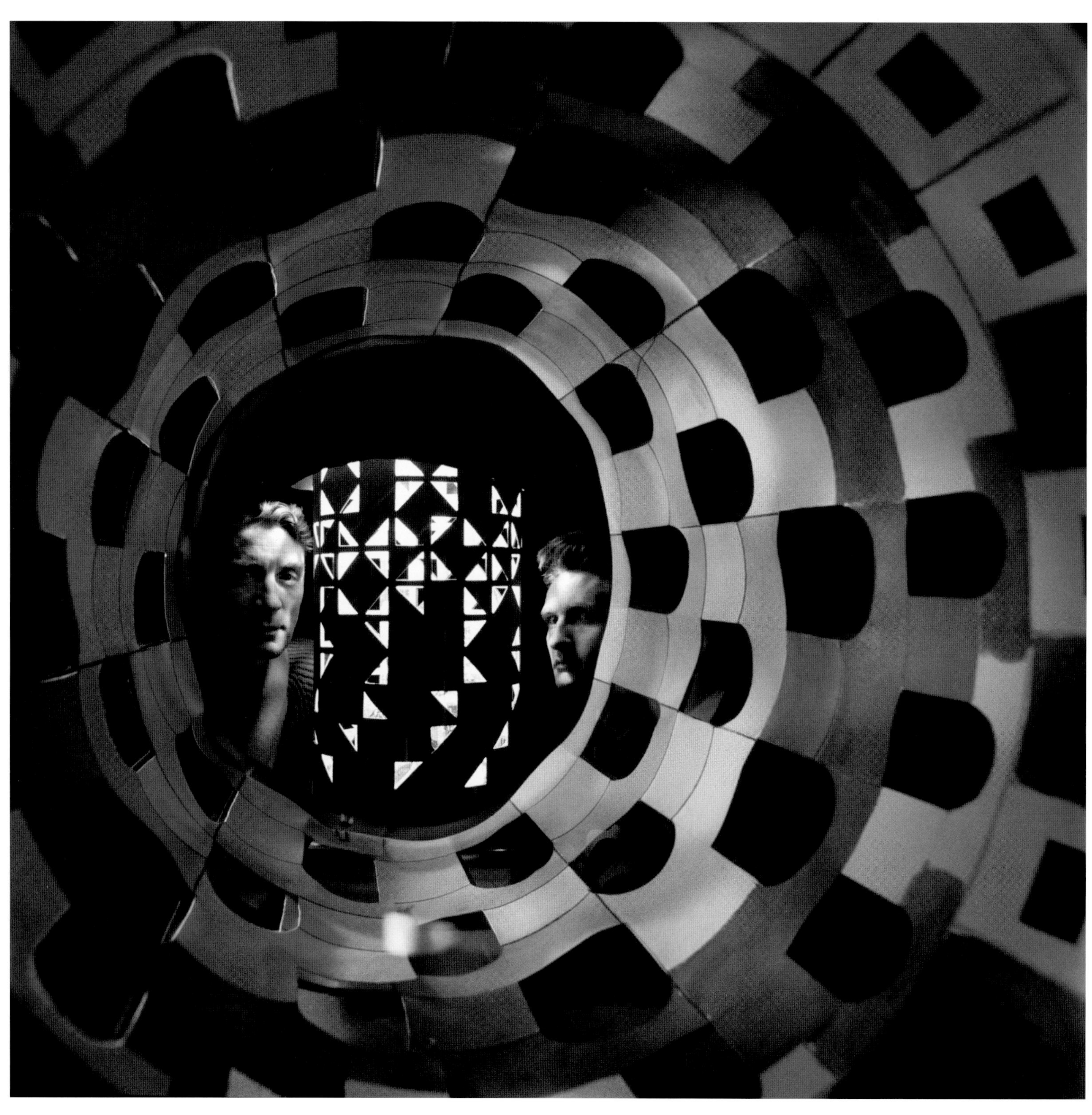

Brion Gysin and Ian Sommerville with The Dream Machine, Paris, 1963

Frank Zappa, Los Angeles, 1989

Metropole Café, NYC, 1948 (overleaf)

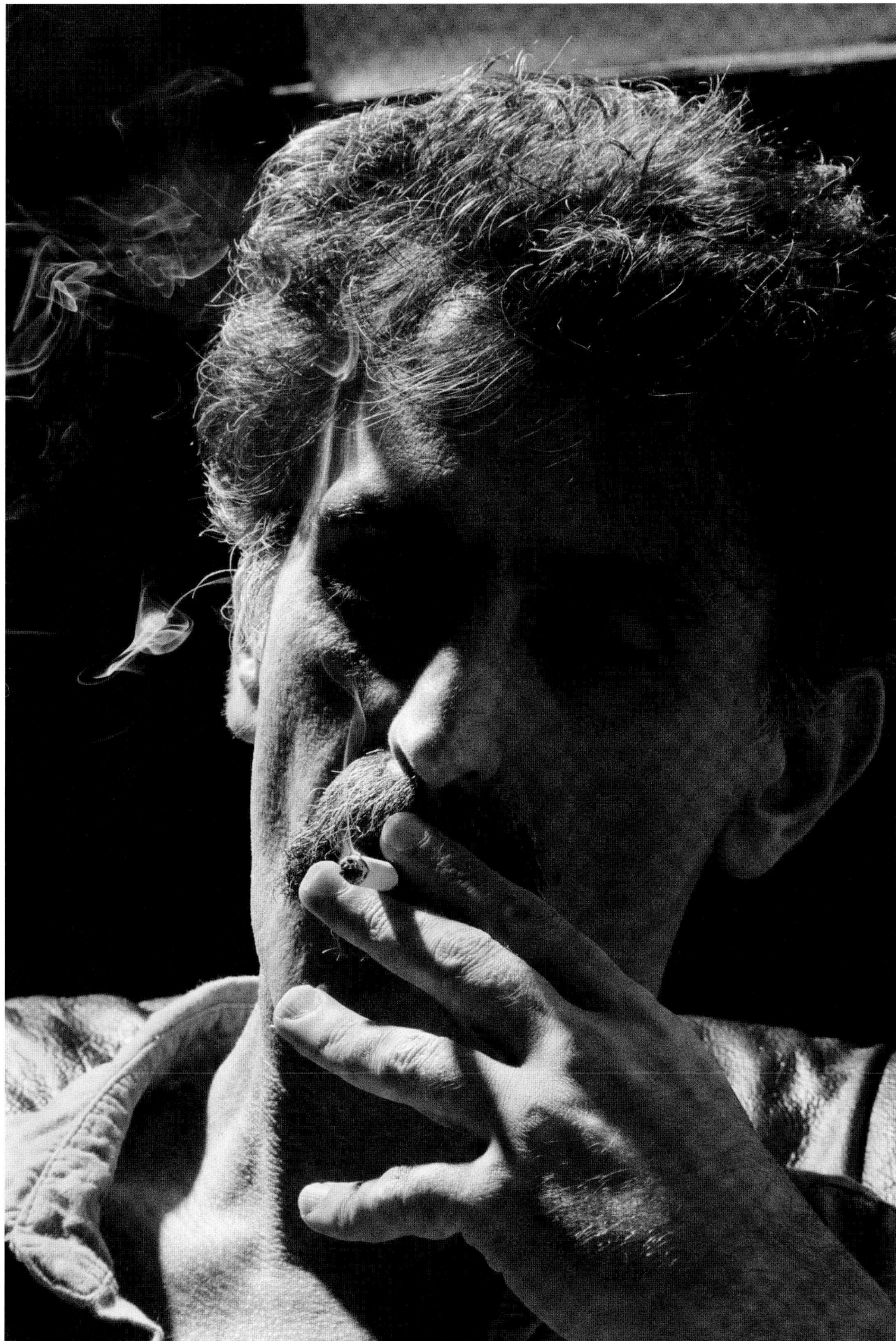

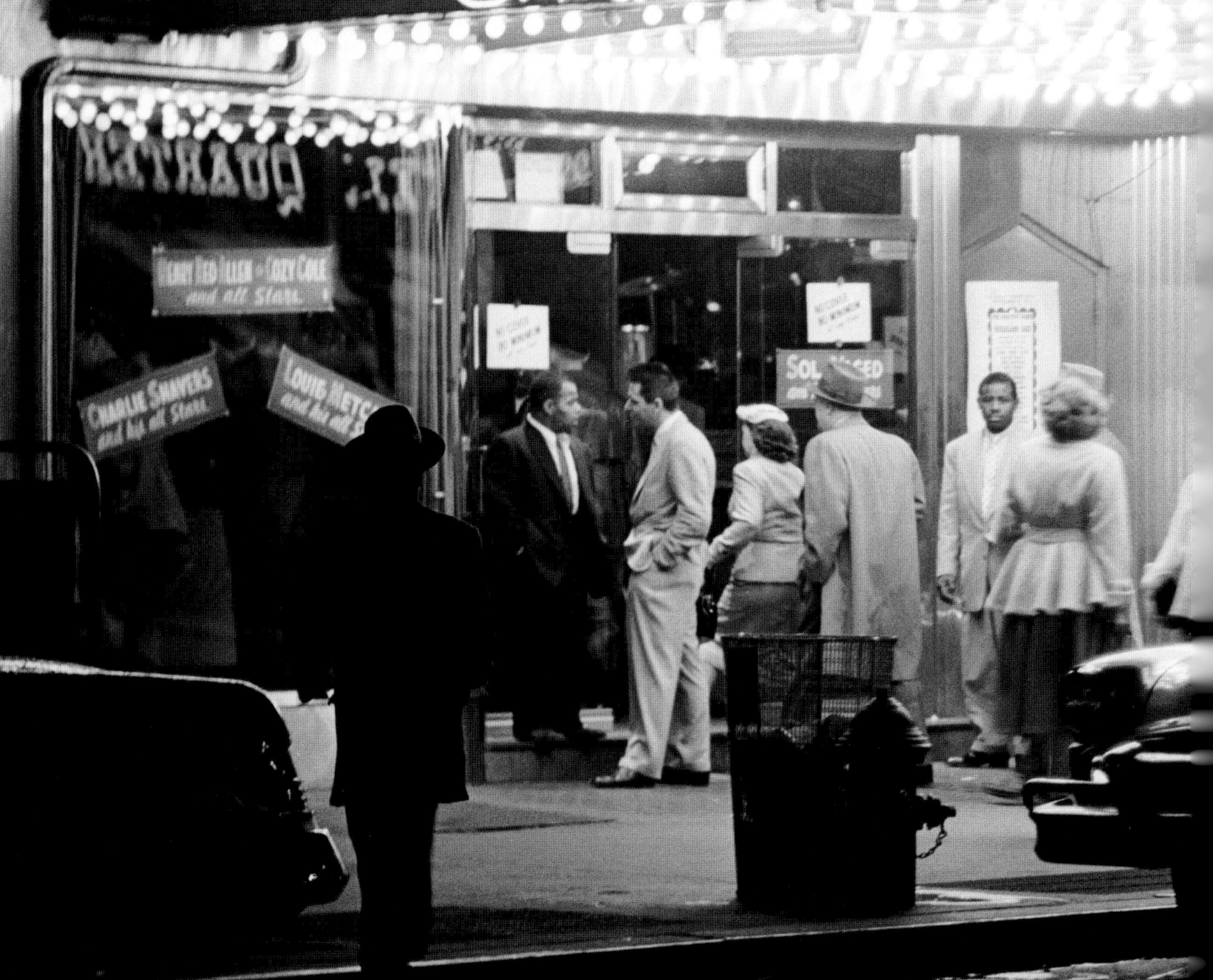
METROPOLE
CAFE
CHARLIE SHAVERS and his all Stars

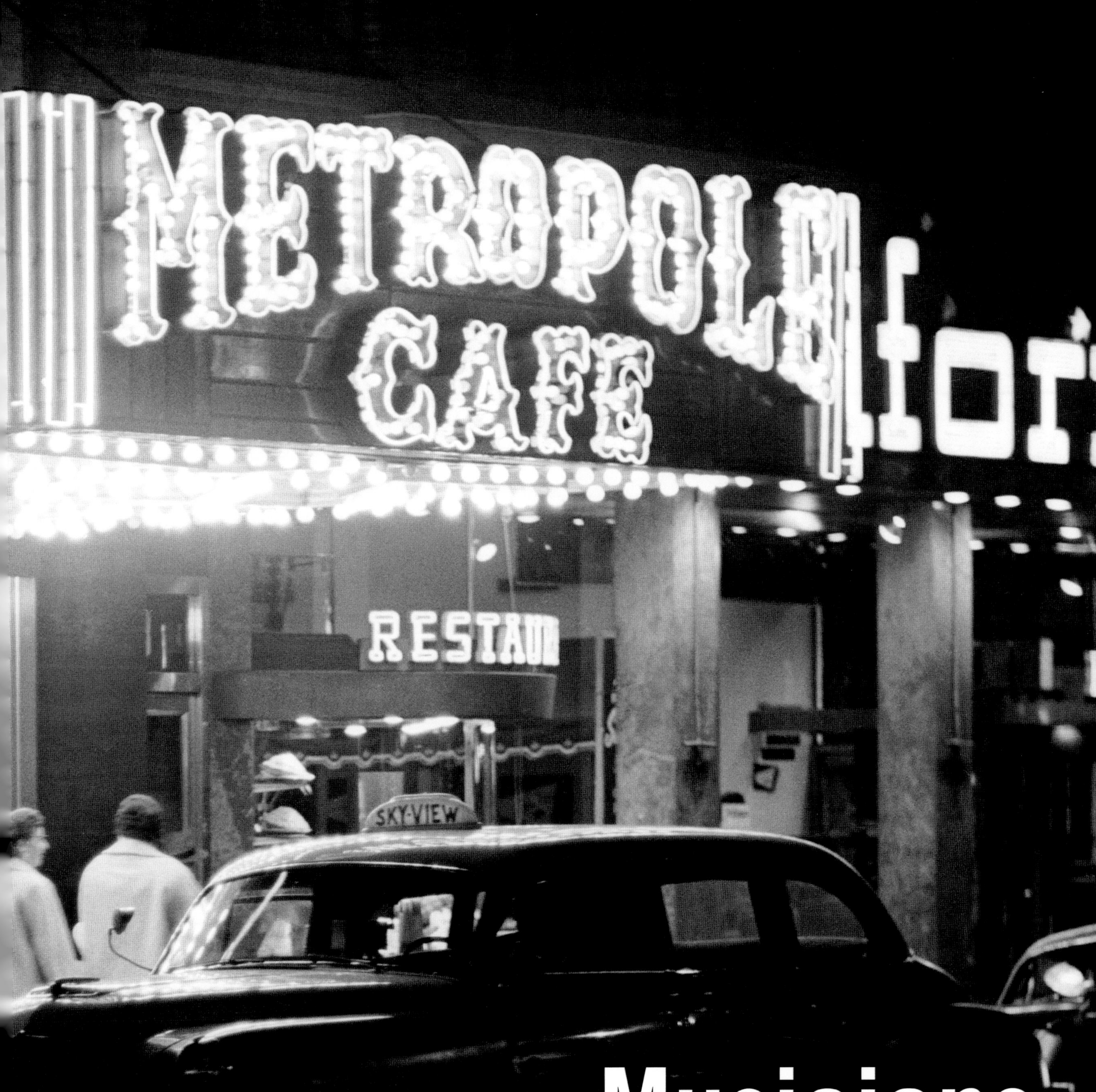

Musicians

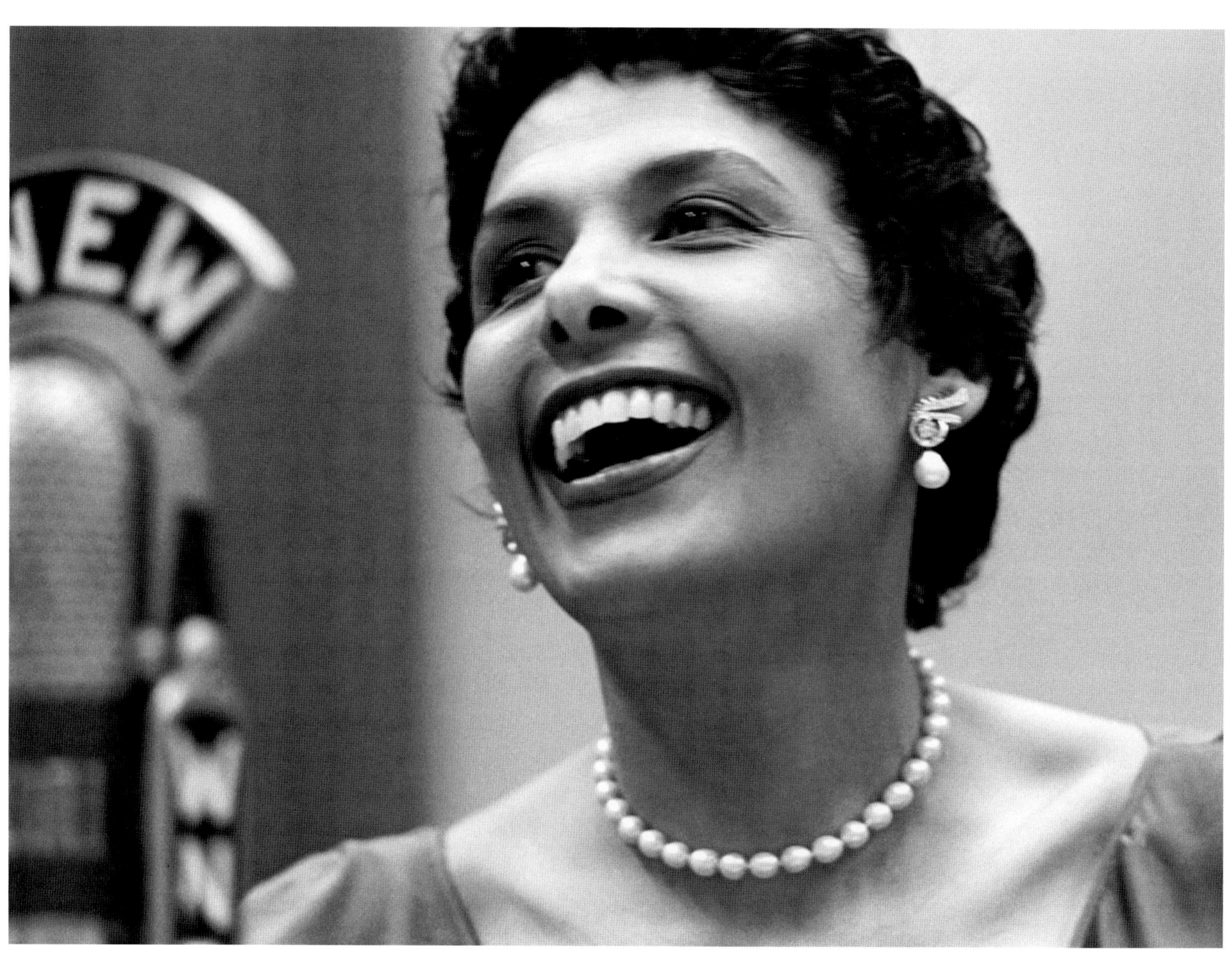

Lena Horne, NYC, 1950

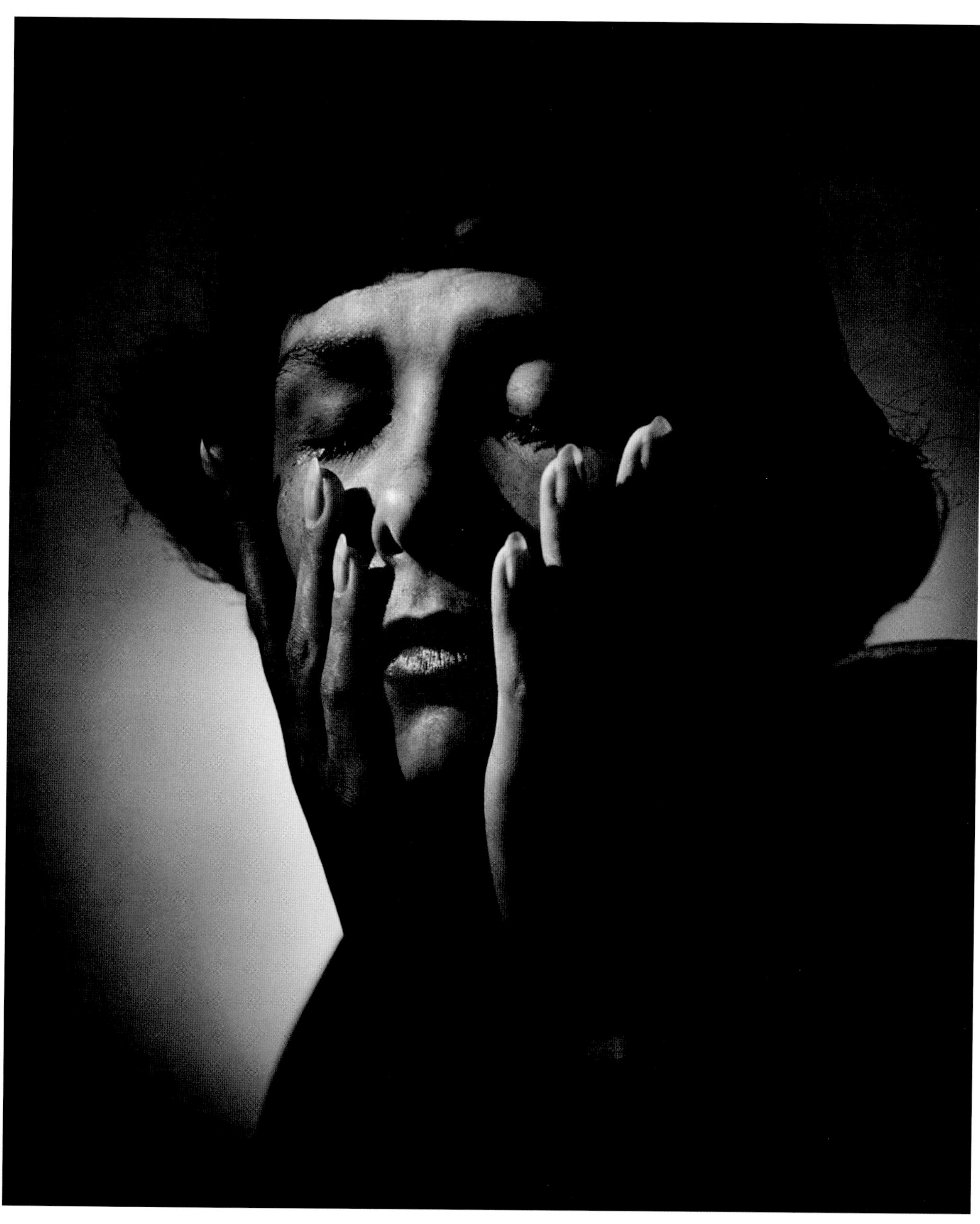

Lena Horne, Sullivan Street studio, NYC, 1948

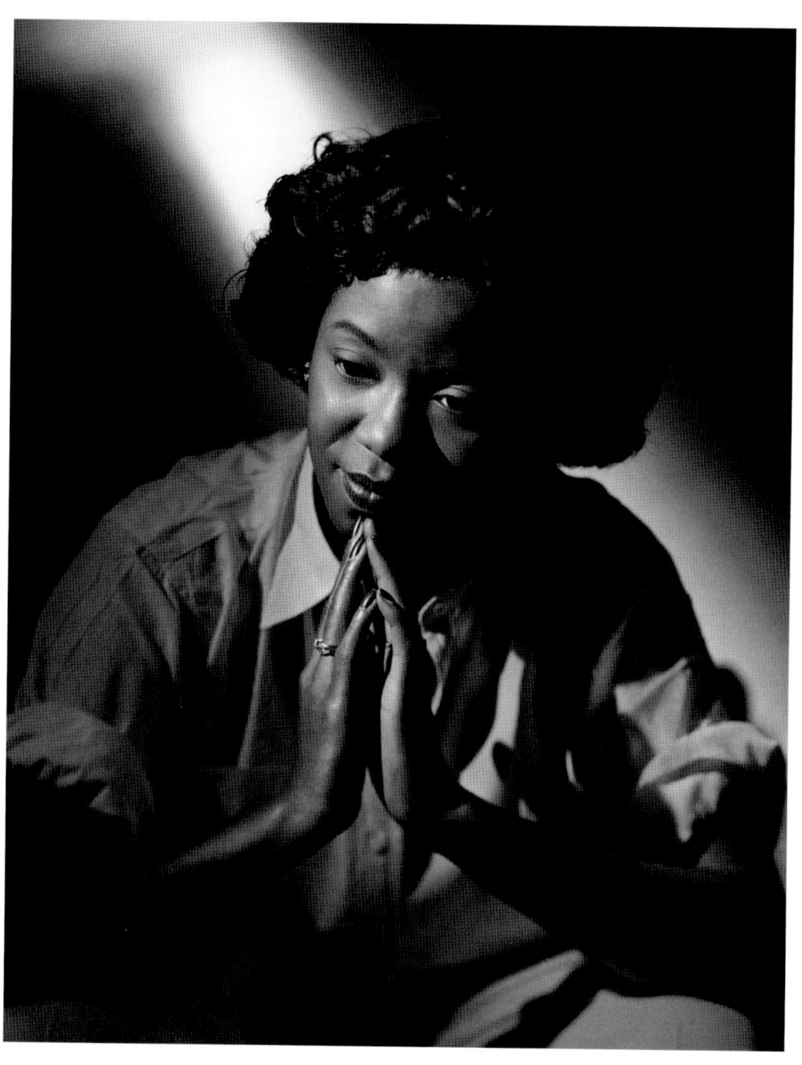

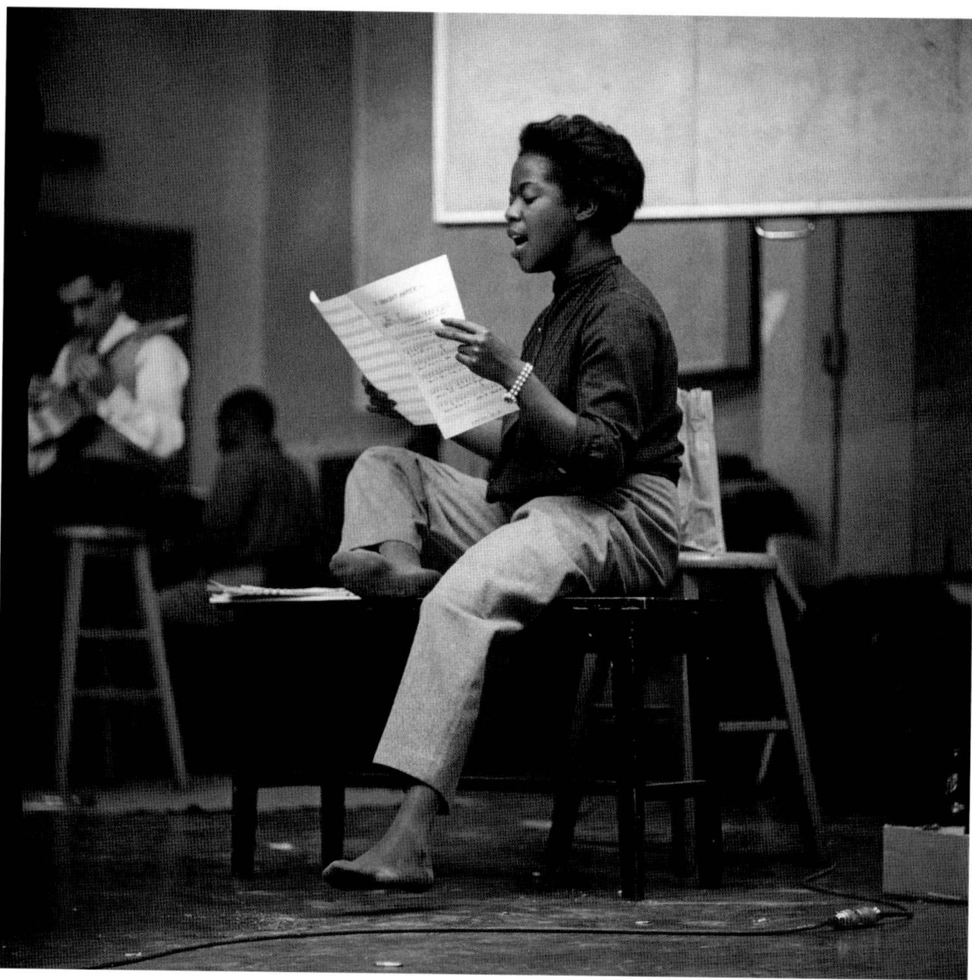

Sarah Vaughan, Sullivan Street studio, NYC, 1948

Sarah Vaughan, NYC, 1950

Sarah Vaughan, Birdland, NYC, 1949

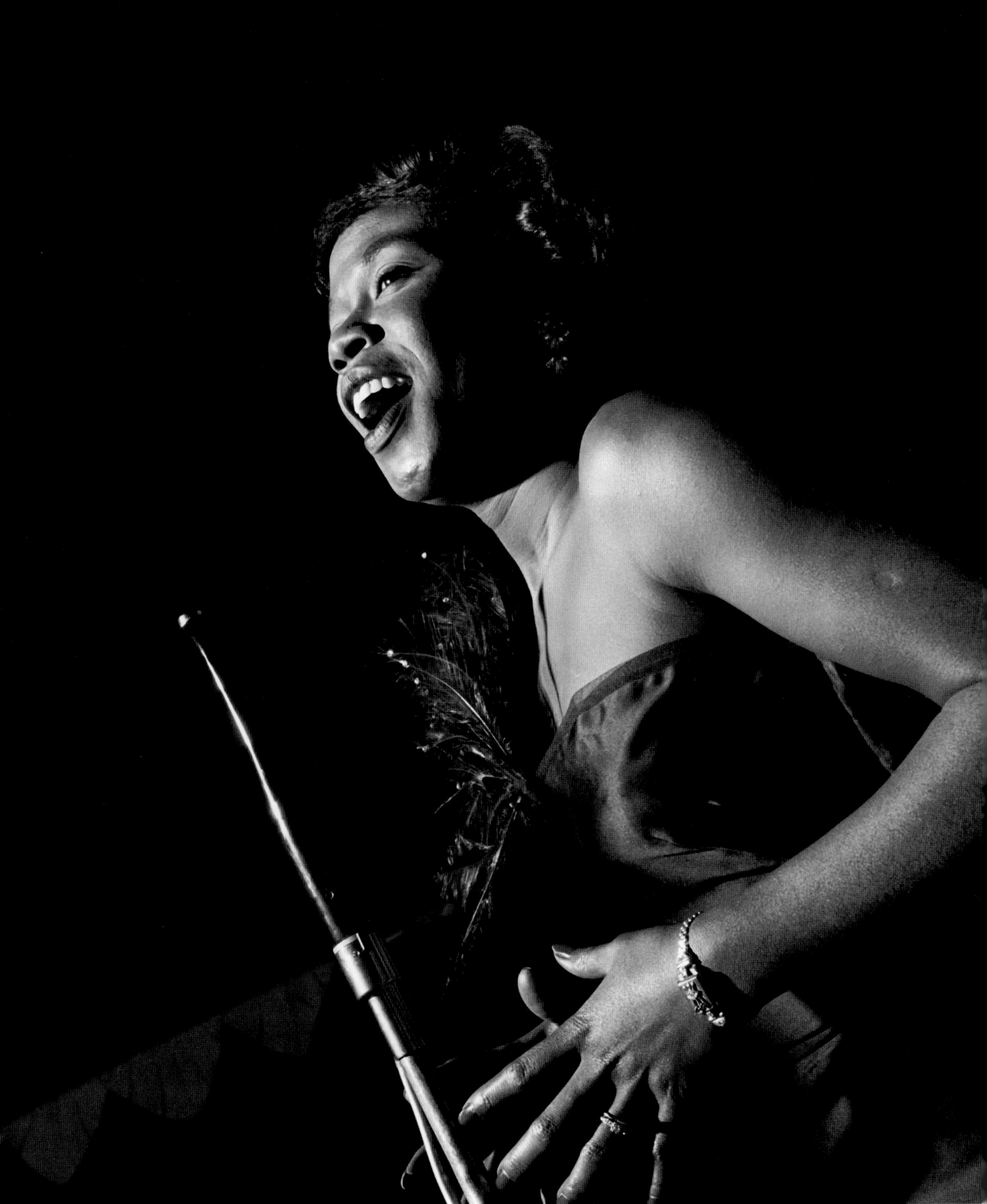

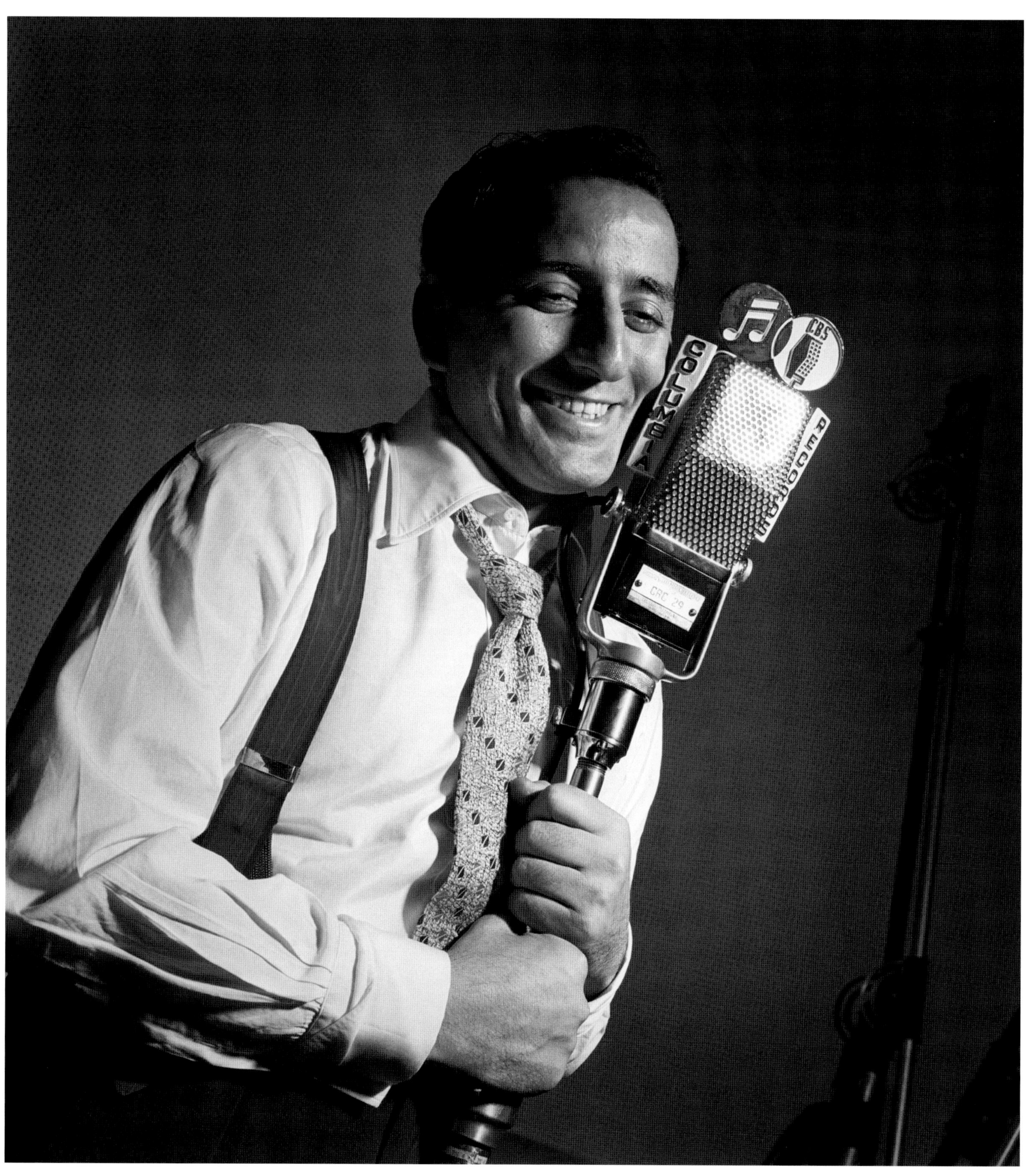

Tony Bennett, NYC, 1950

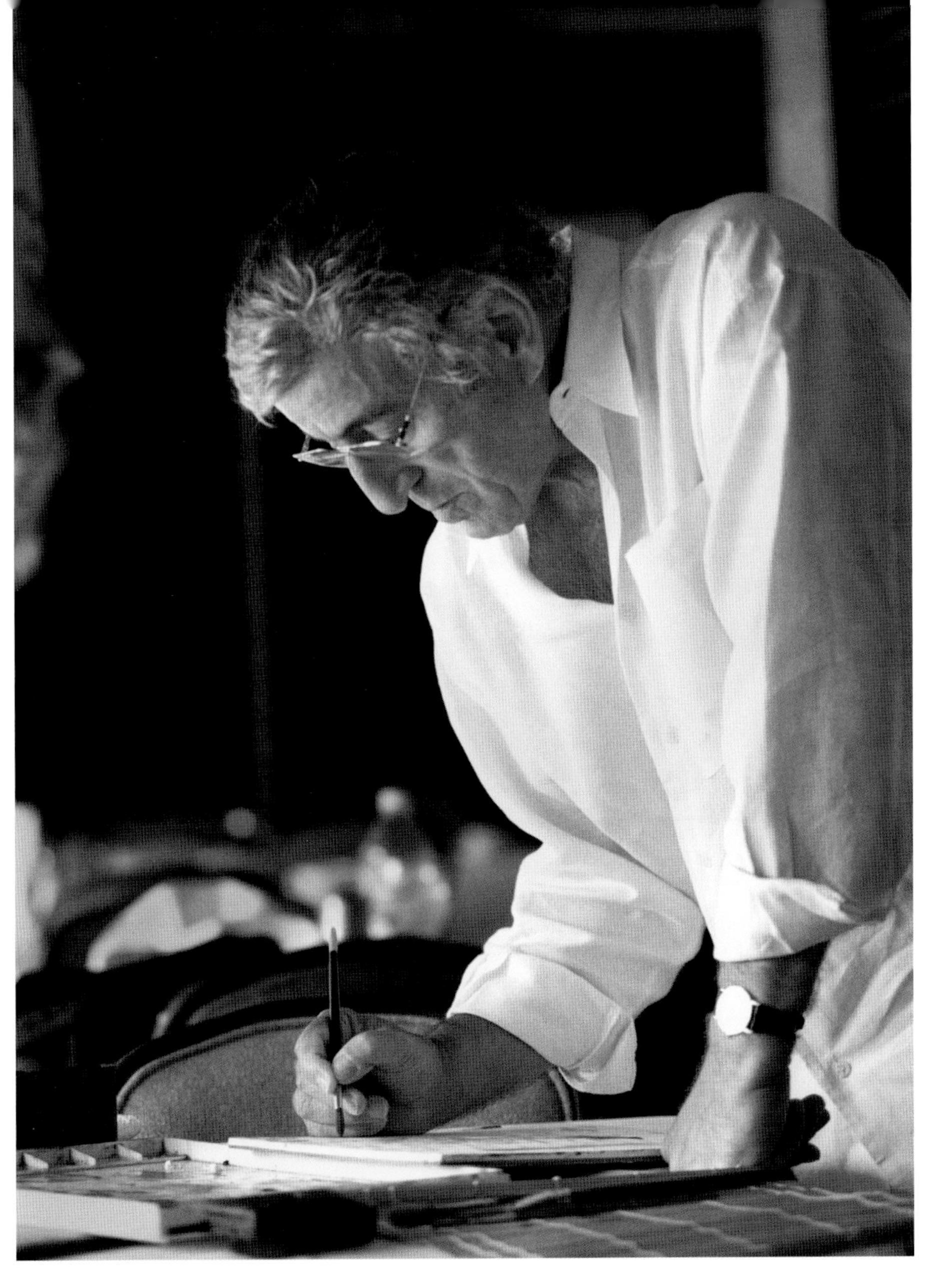

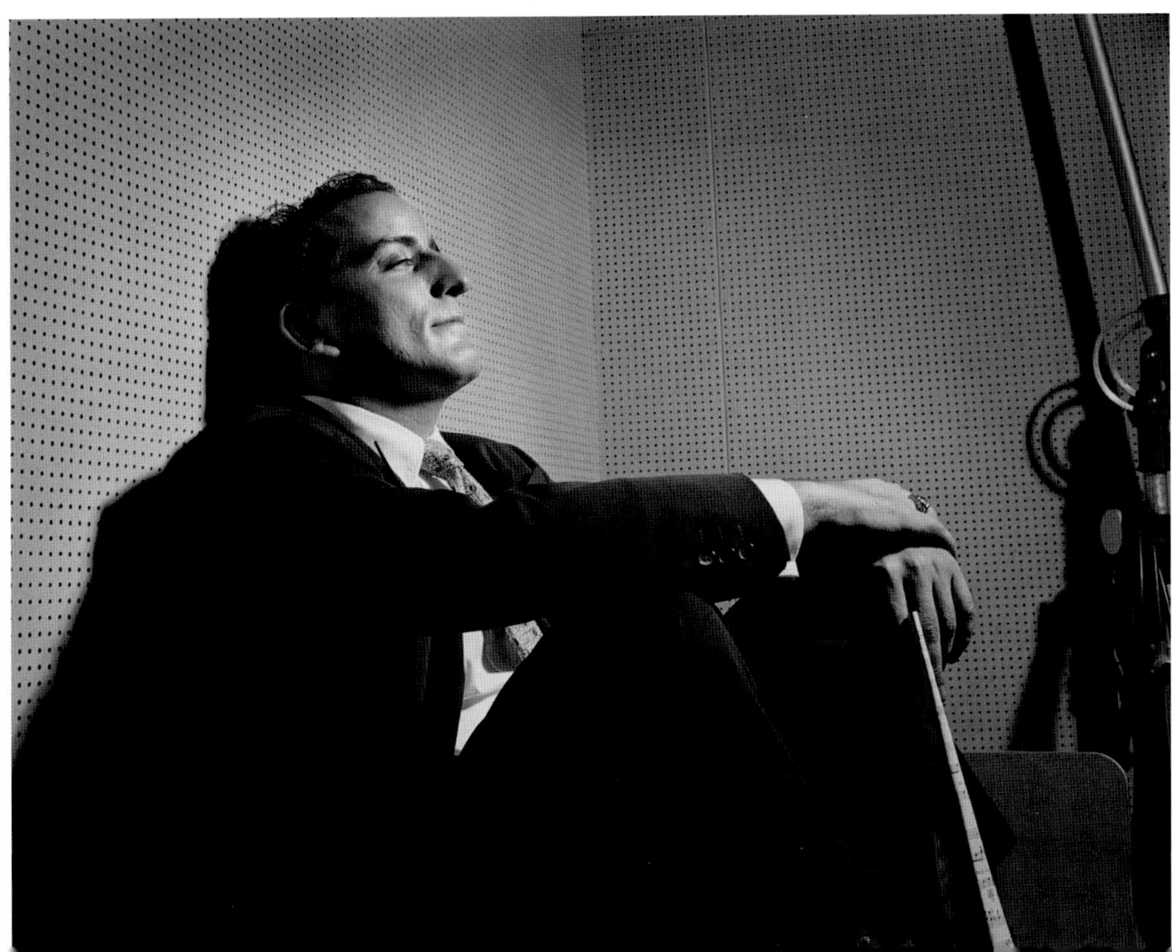

Tony Bennett, New Orleans, 1998

Tony Bennett, NYC, 1950

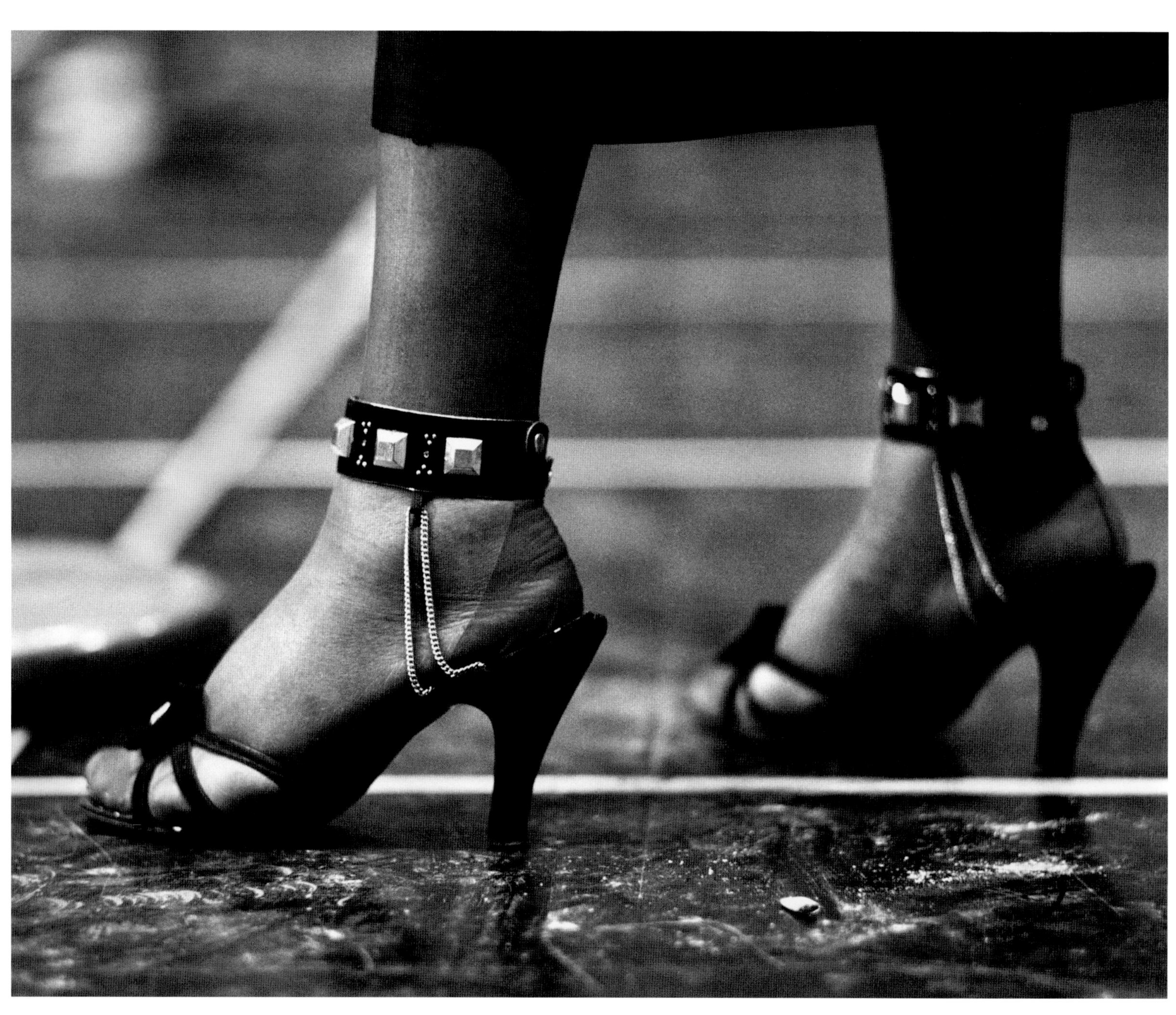

Billie Holiday's Shoes, NYC 1955

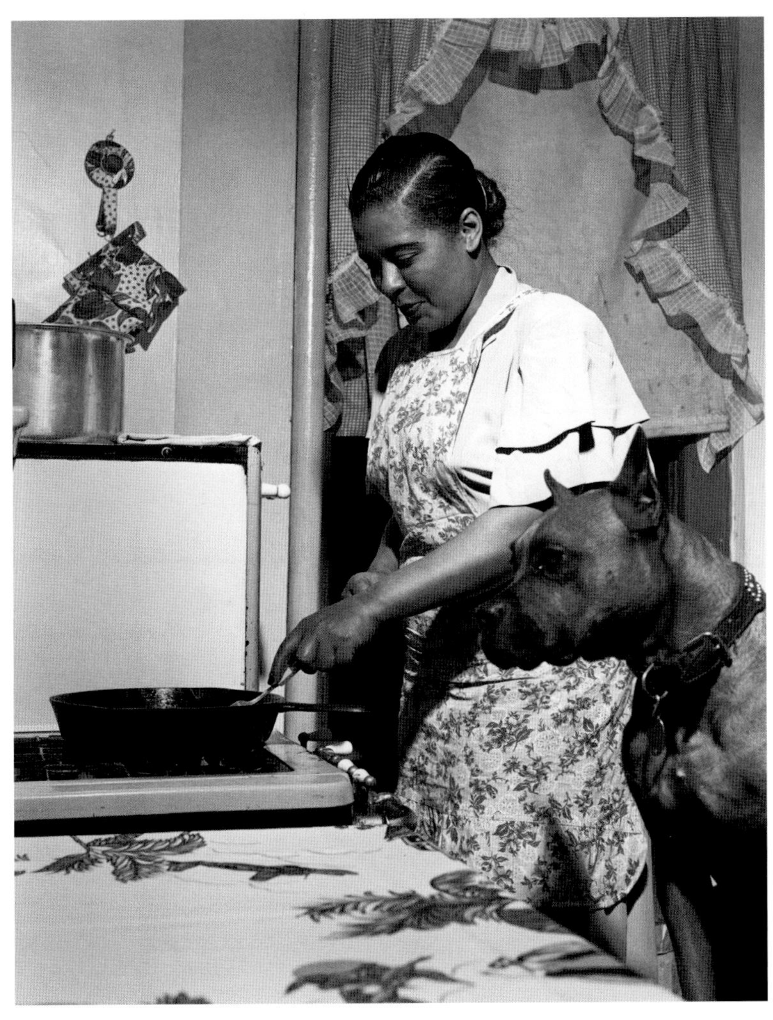

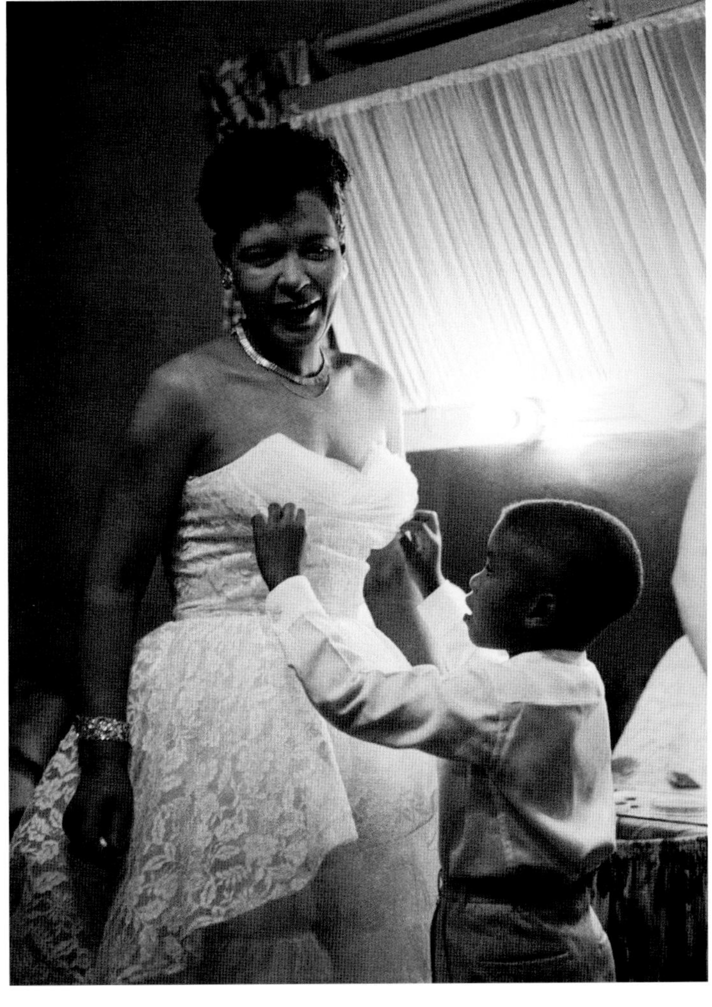

Billie Holiday and her dog Mister, NYC, 1949

Billie Holiday, Hollywood Bowl, Los Angeles, 1953

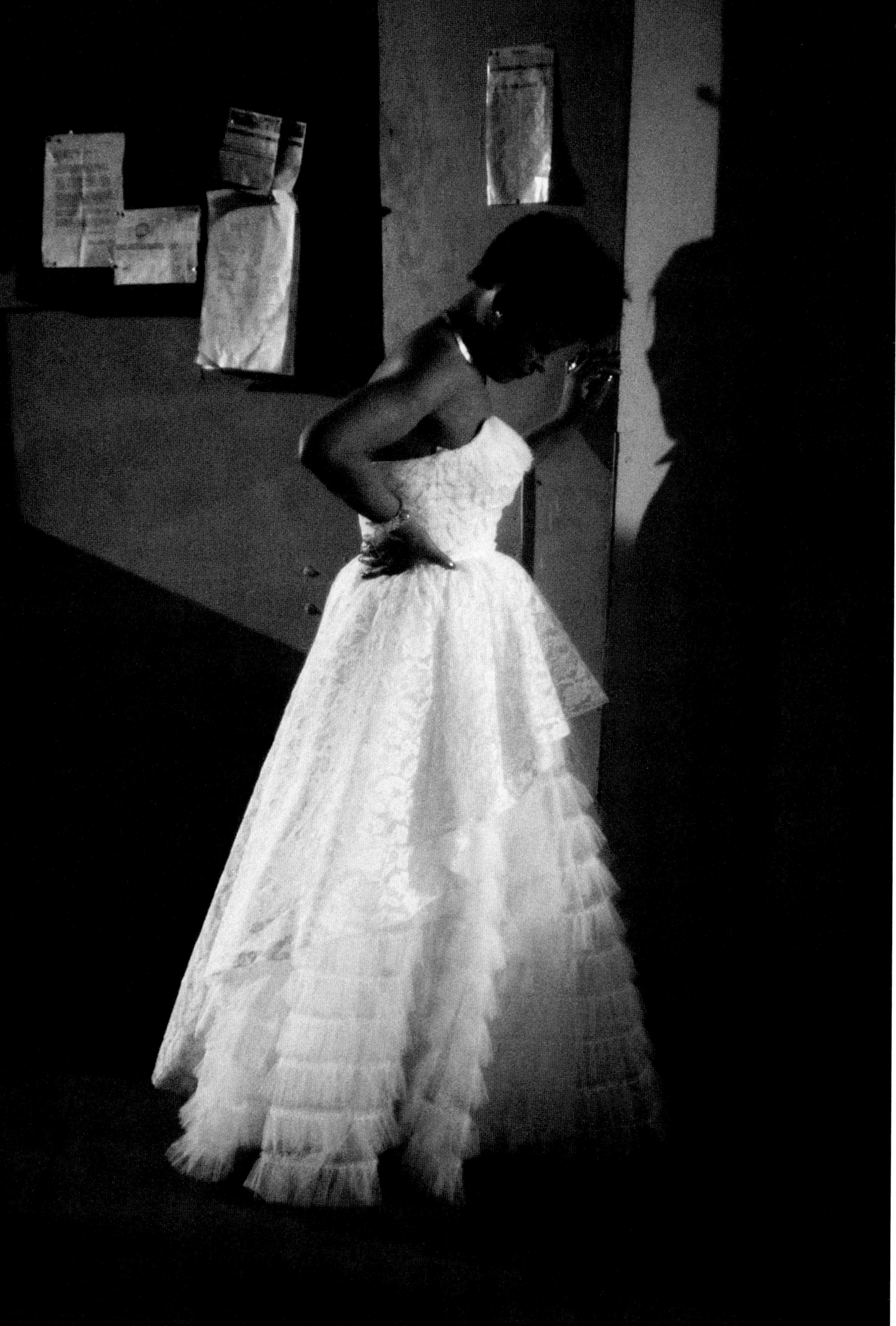

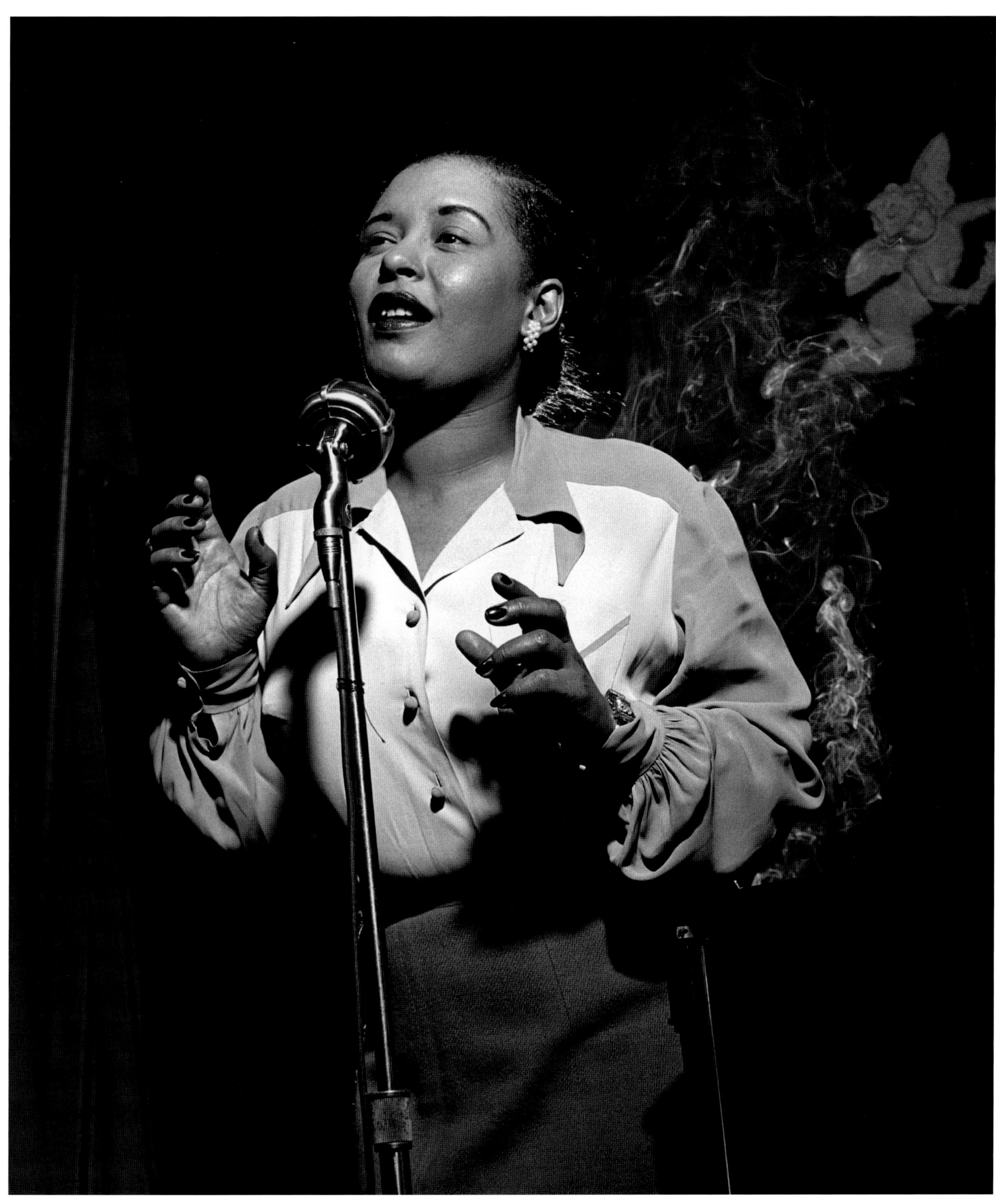

Billie Holiday, Hollywood Bowl, Los Angeles, 1953

Billie Holiday, NYC, 1949

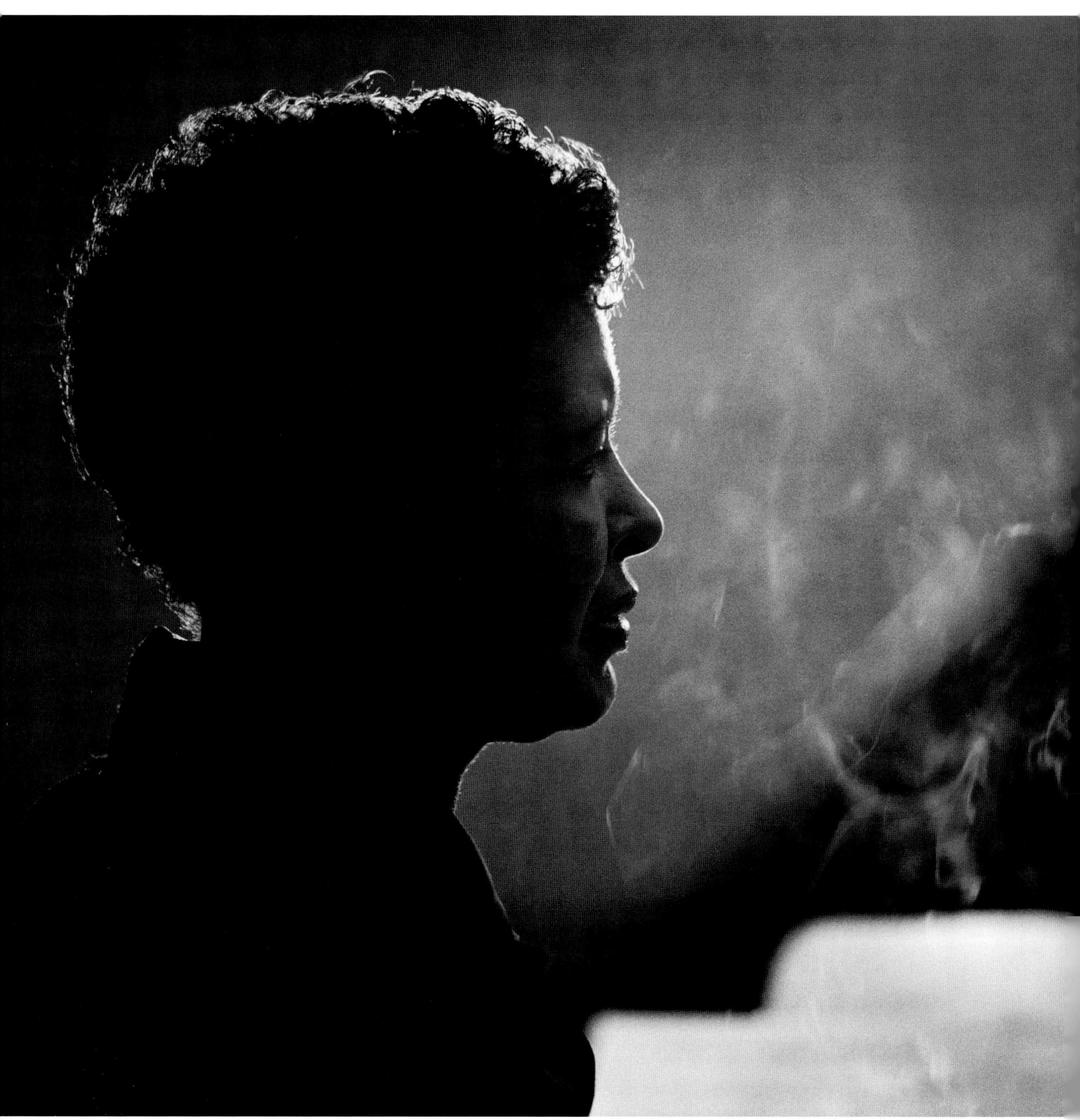

Billie Holiday, NYC, 1955

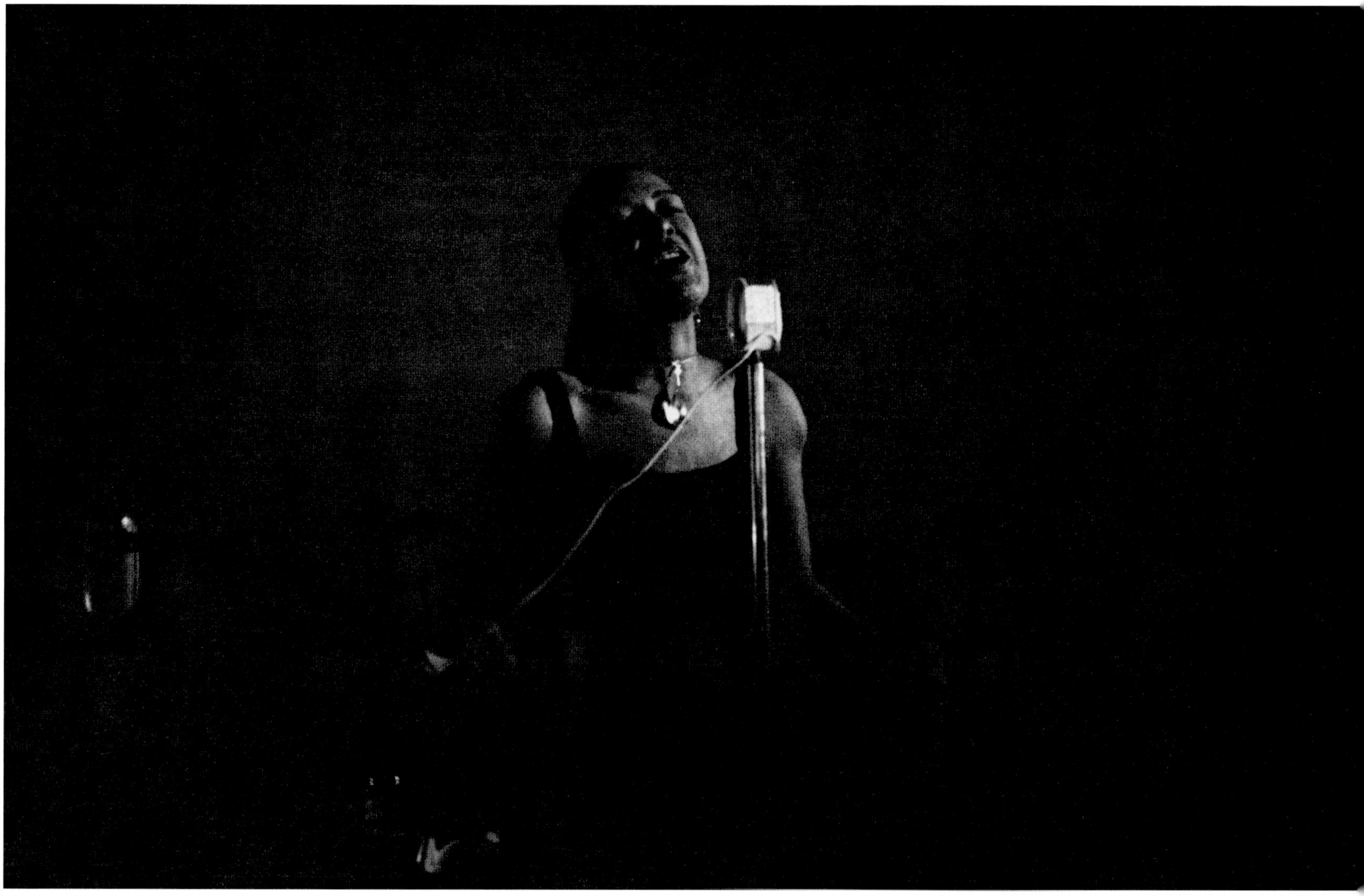

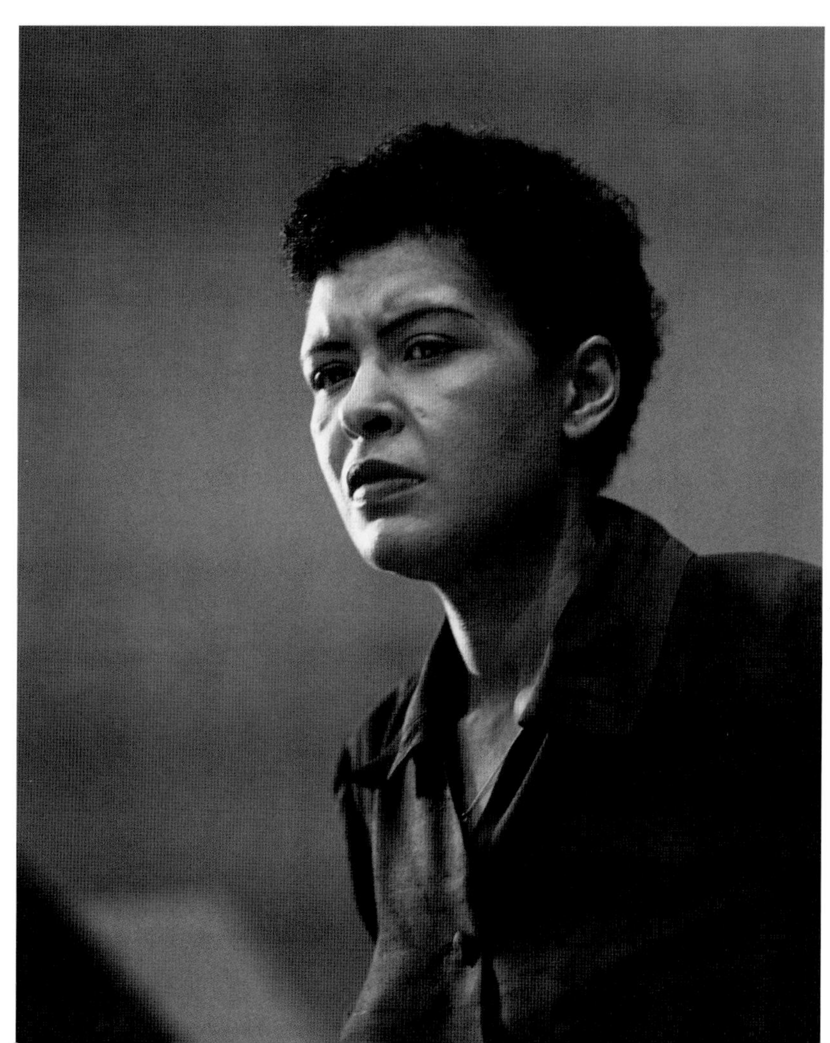

Billie Holiday, NYC, 1953

Billie Holiday, NYC, 1955

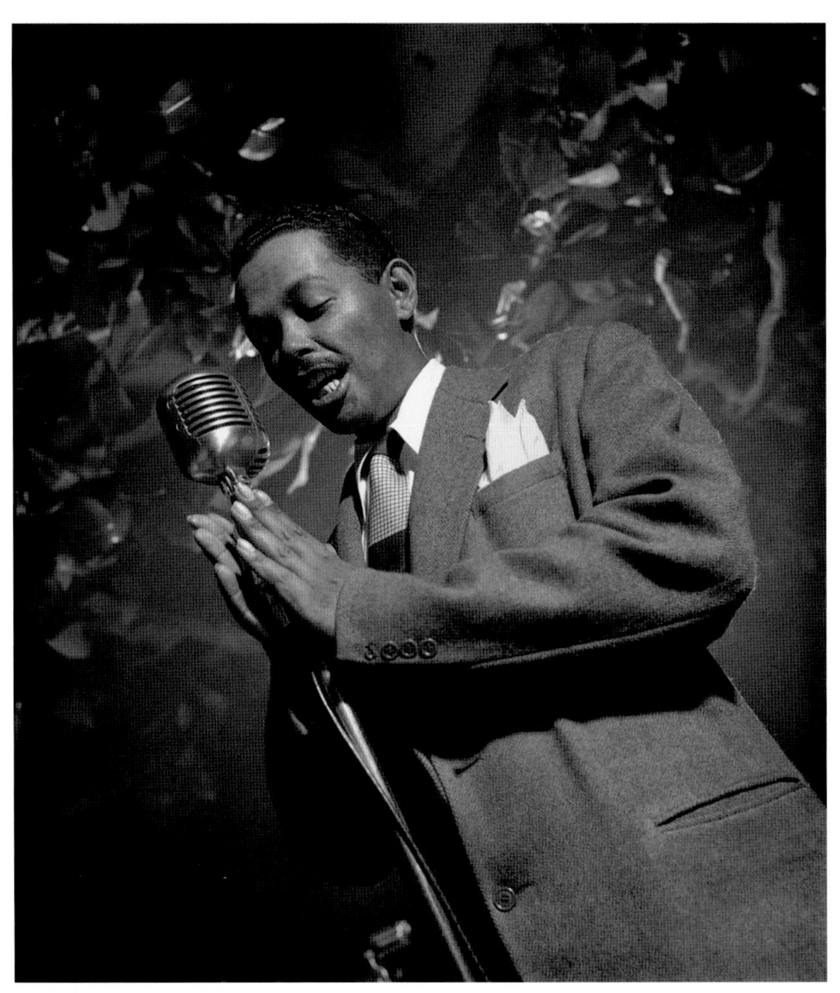

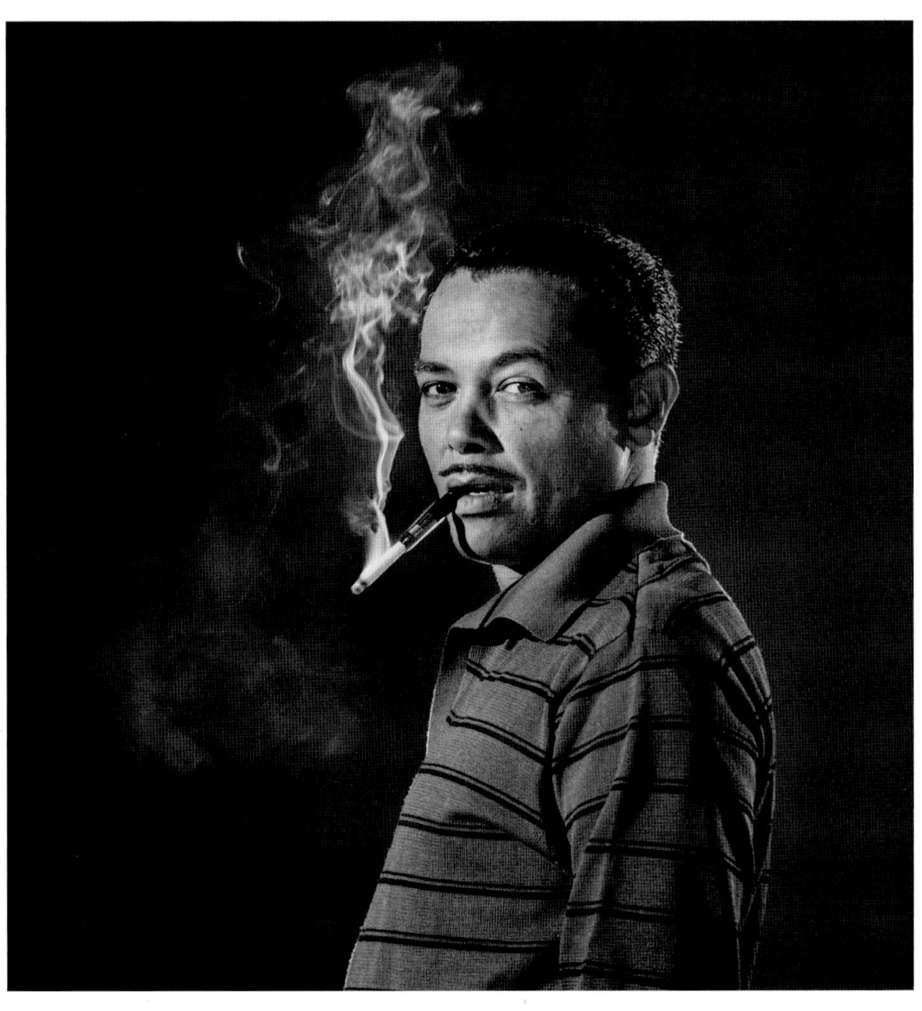

Billy Eckstine, Royal Roost, NYC, 1948

Billy Eckstine, Royal Roost, NYC, 1963

Billy Eckstine and Cliff Smalls, Royal Roost, NYC, 1948

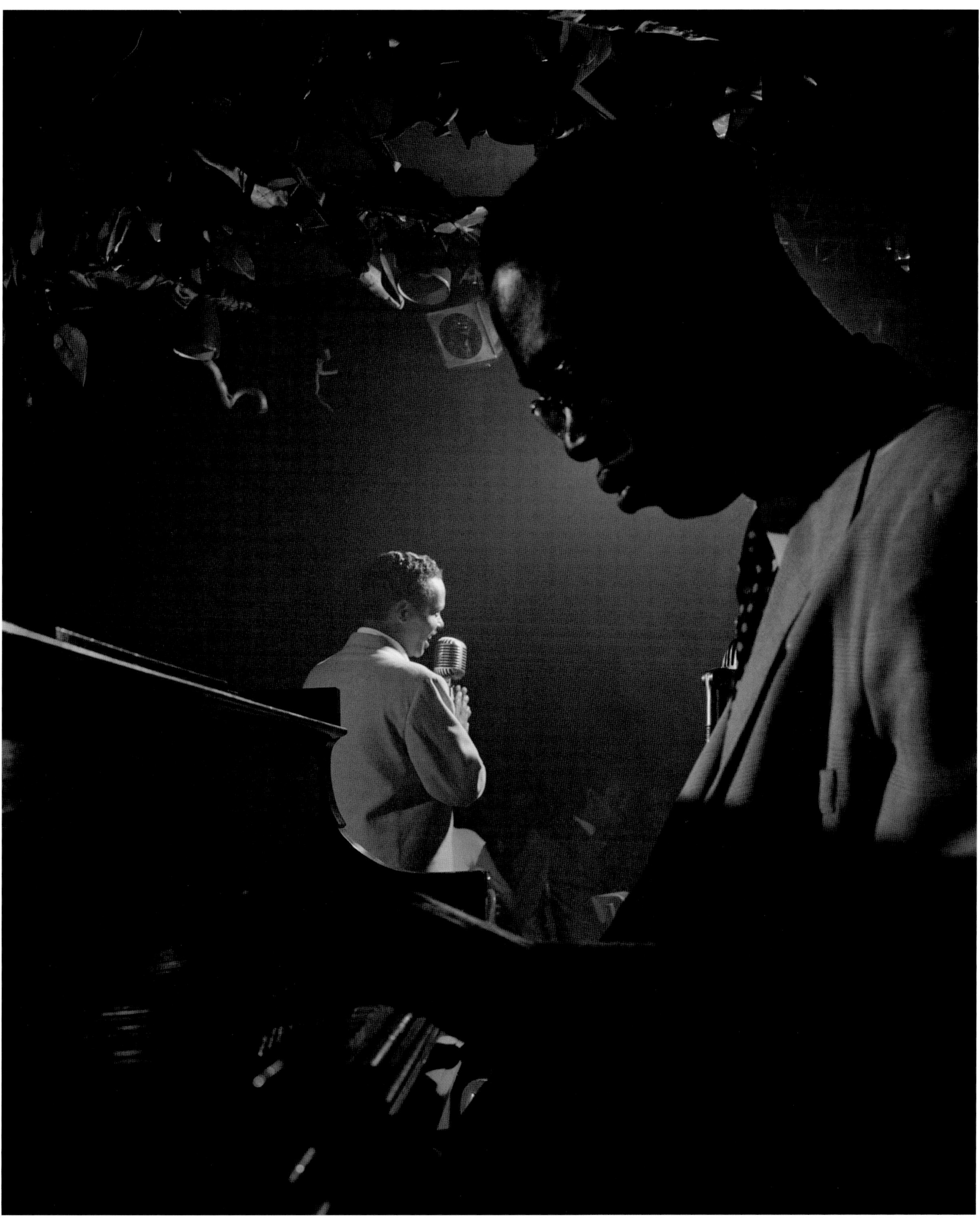

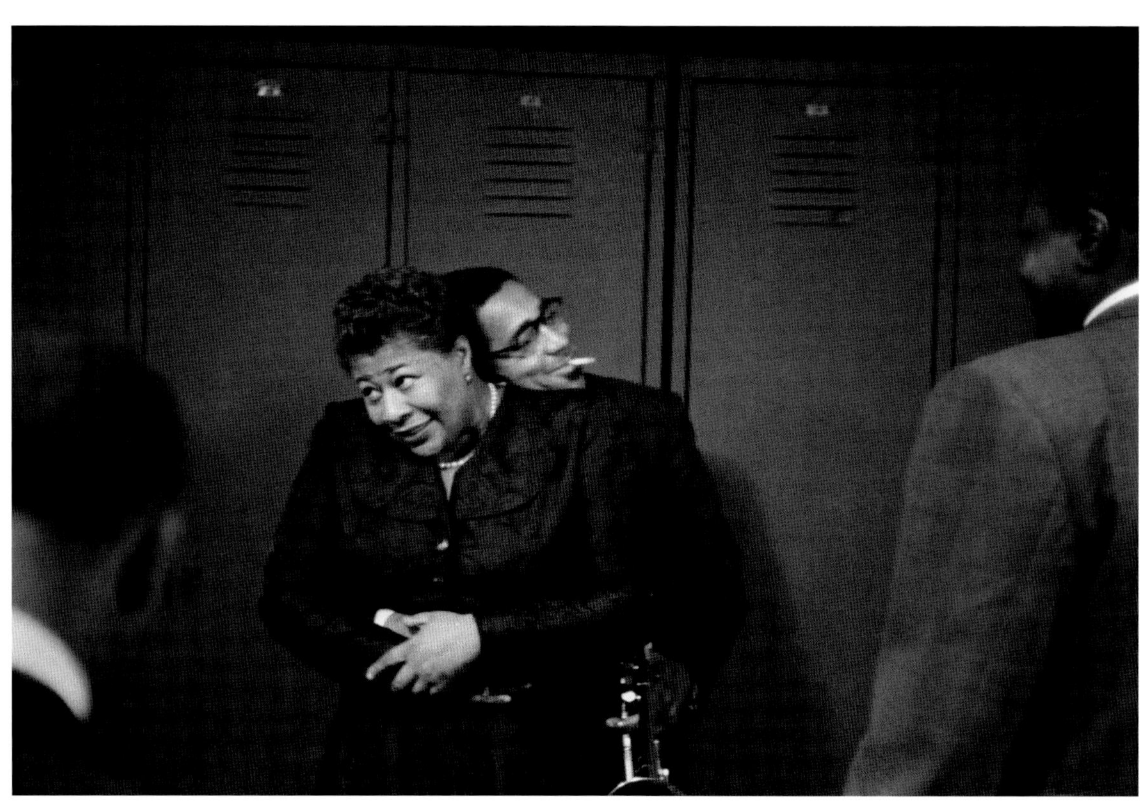

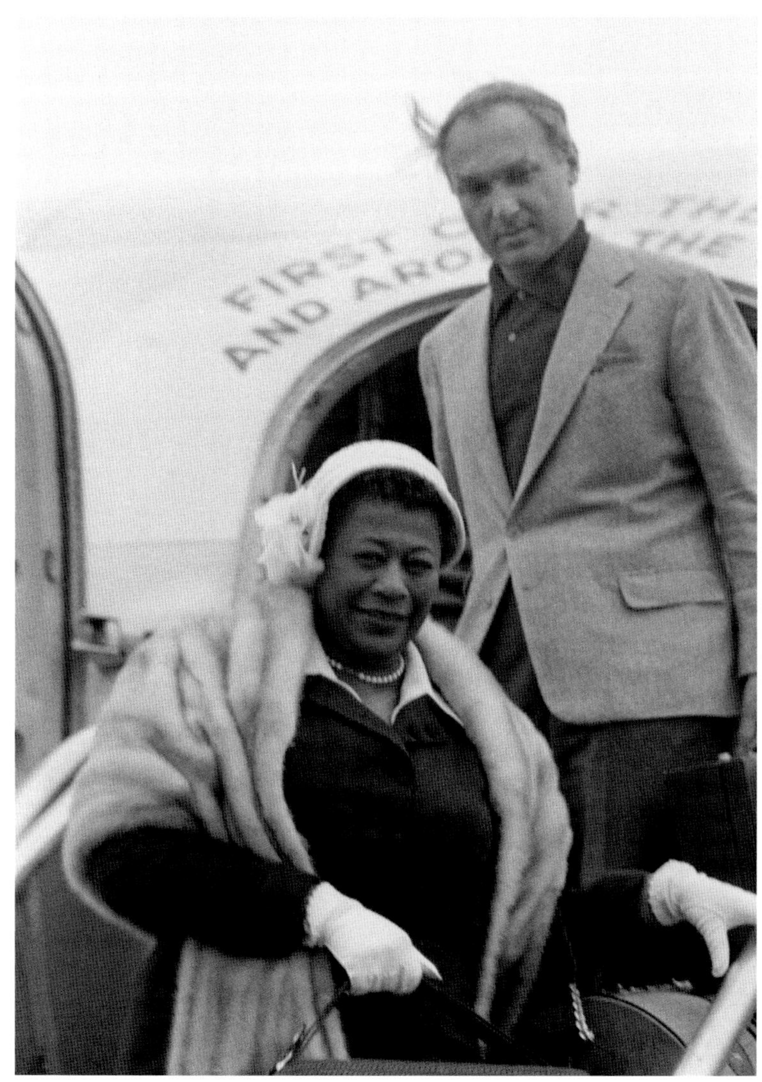

Ella Fitzgerald and Dizzy Gillespie, Carnegie Hall, NYC, 1950

Ella Fitzgerald and Norman Granz, Nice, France, 1958

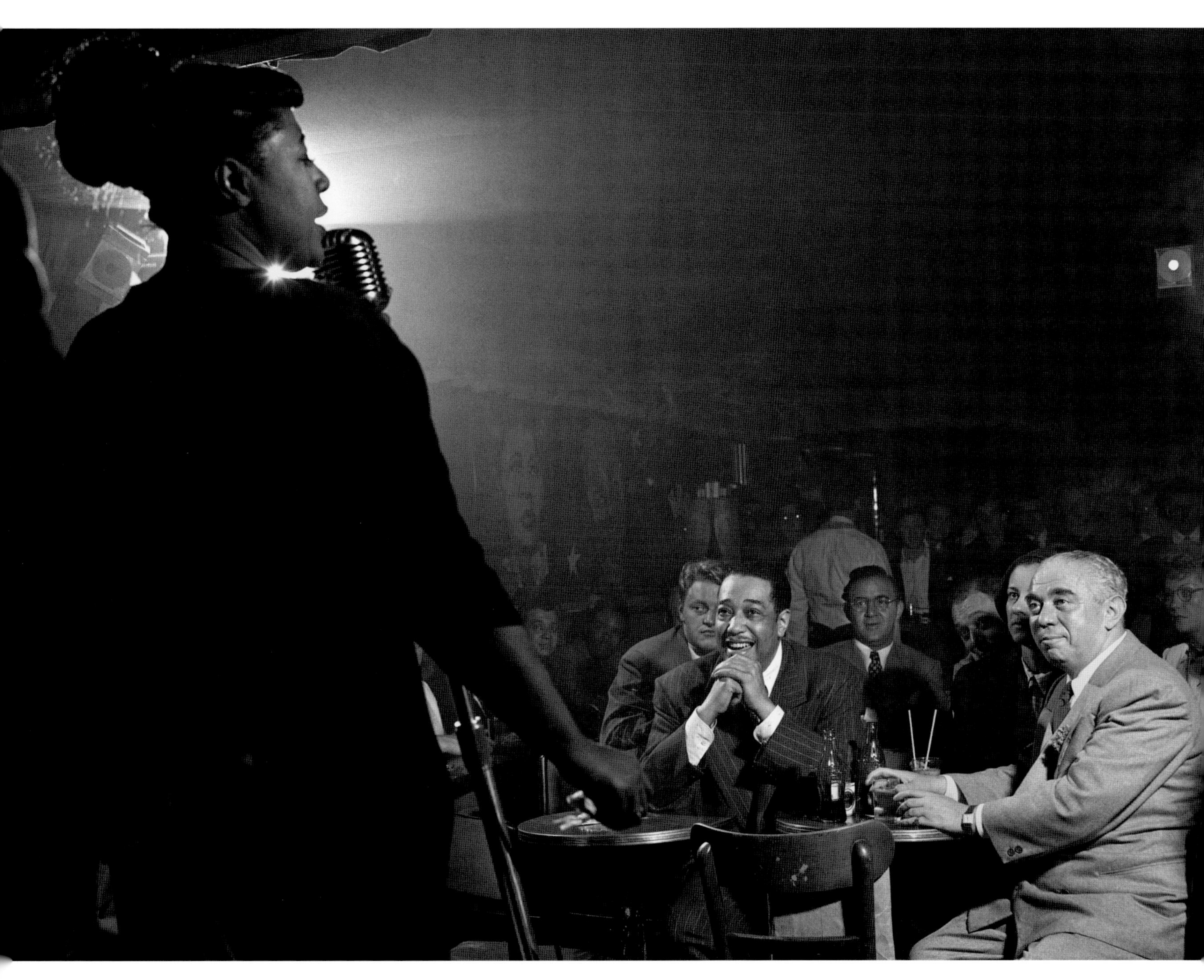

Ella Fitzgerald, Stan Hasselgard, Duke Ellington, Benny Goodman and Jack Robbins, Downbeat Club, NYC, 1949

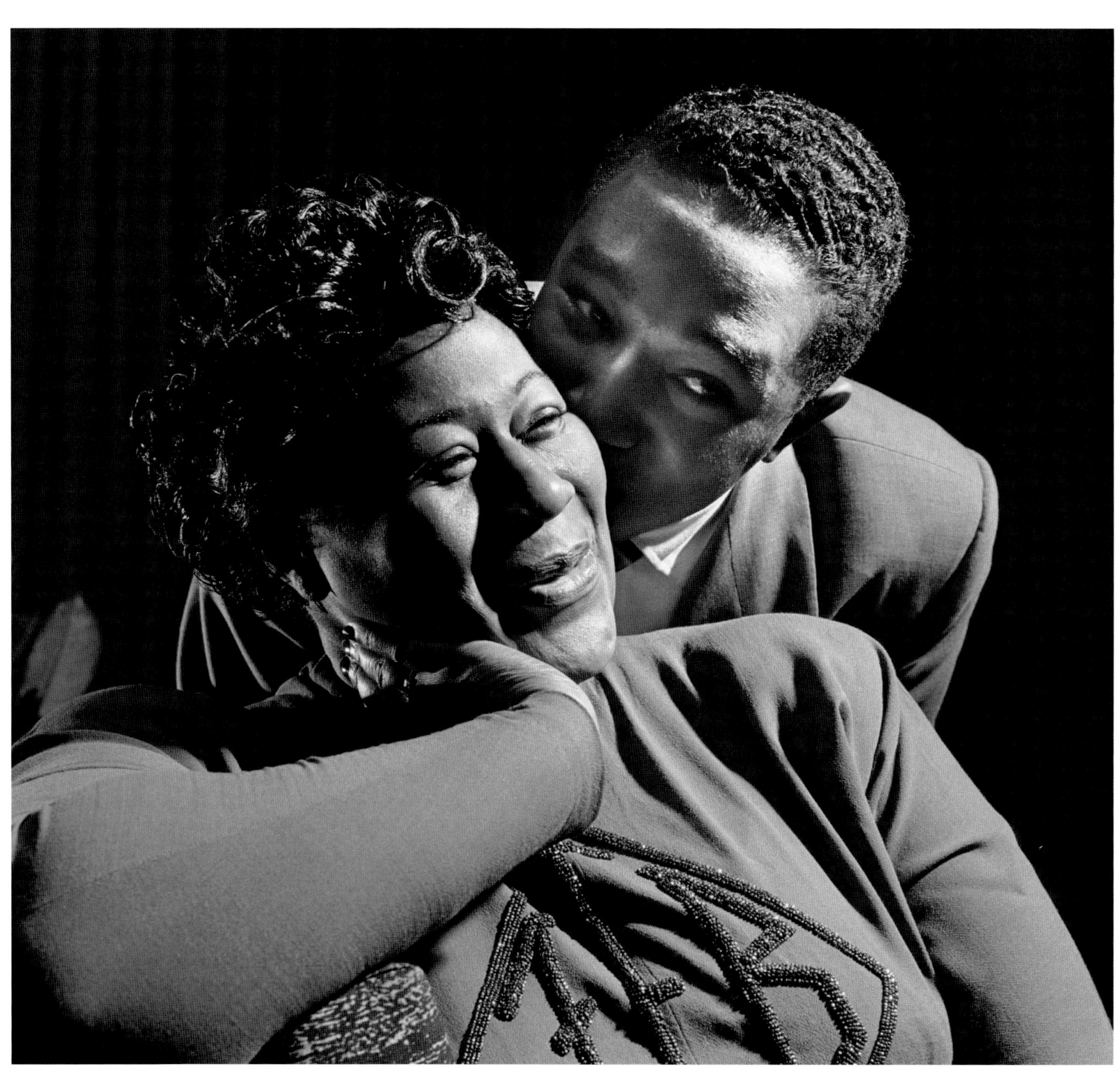

Ella Fitzgerald and Ray Brown, Sullivan Street studio, NYC, 1949

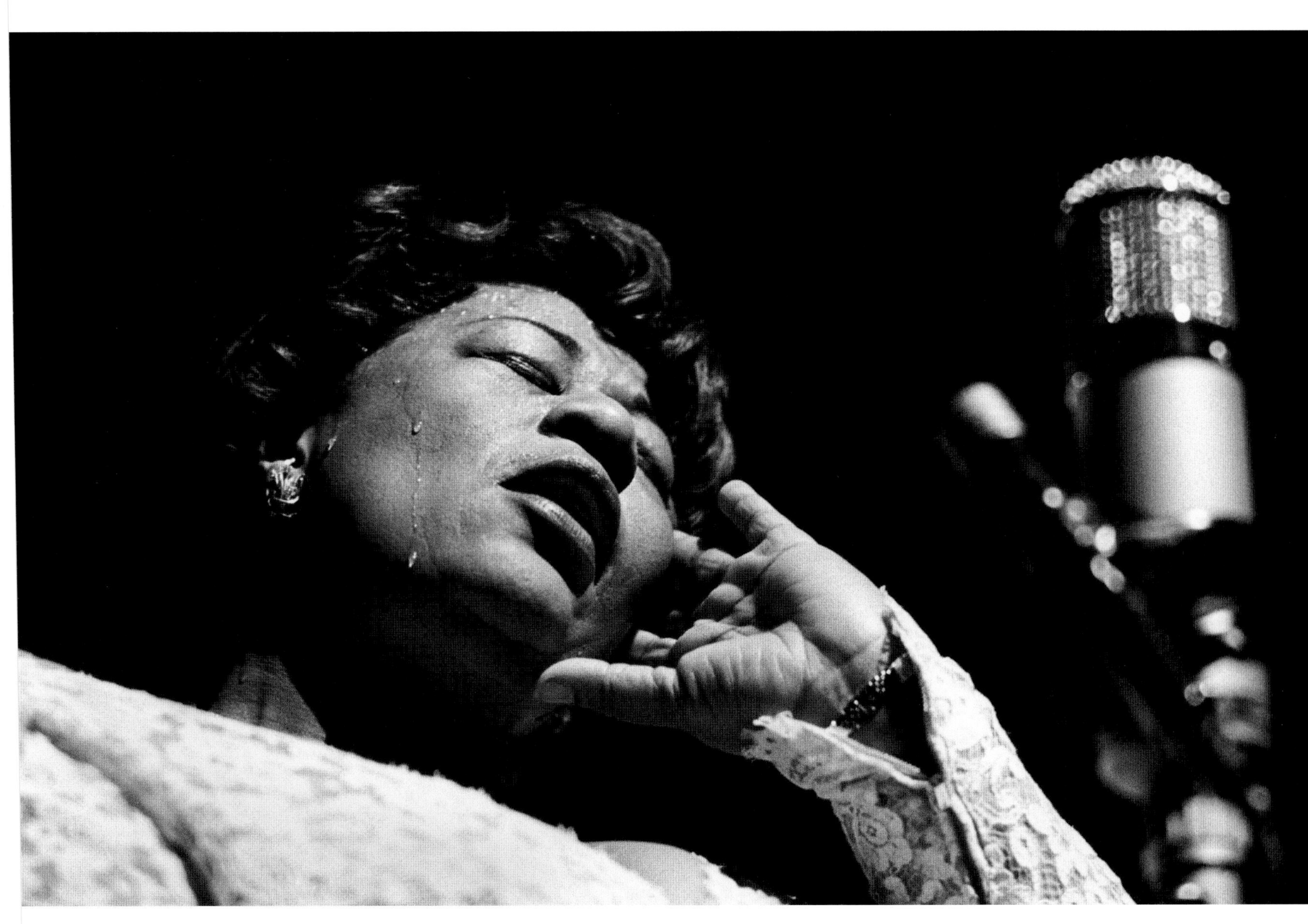

Ella Fitzgerald, Olympia Theatre, Paris, 1960

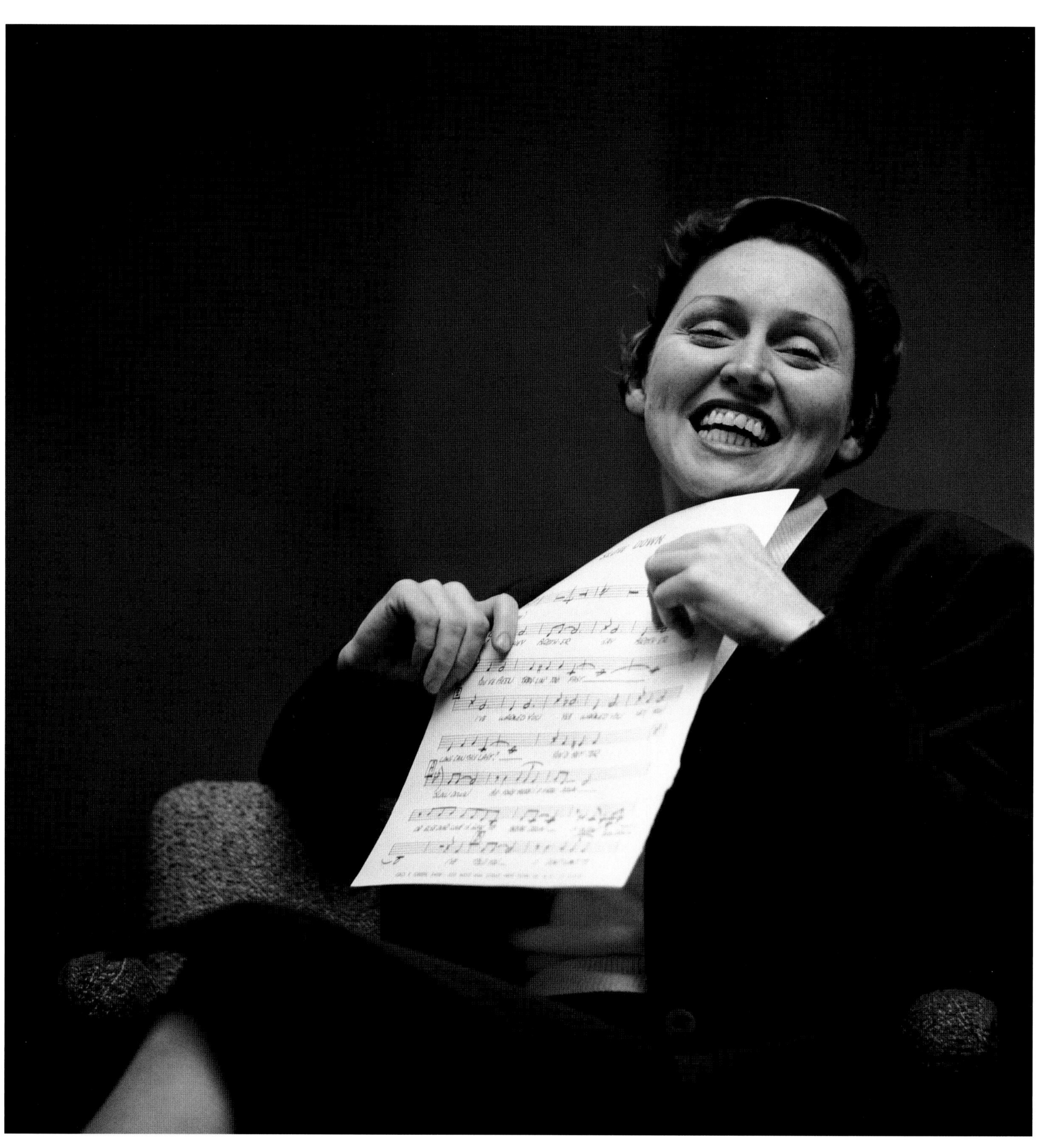

Anita O'Day, NYC, 1955

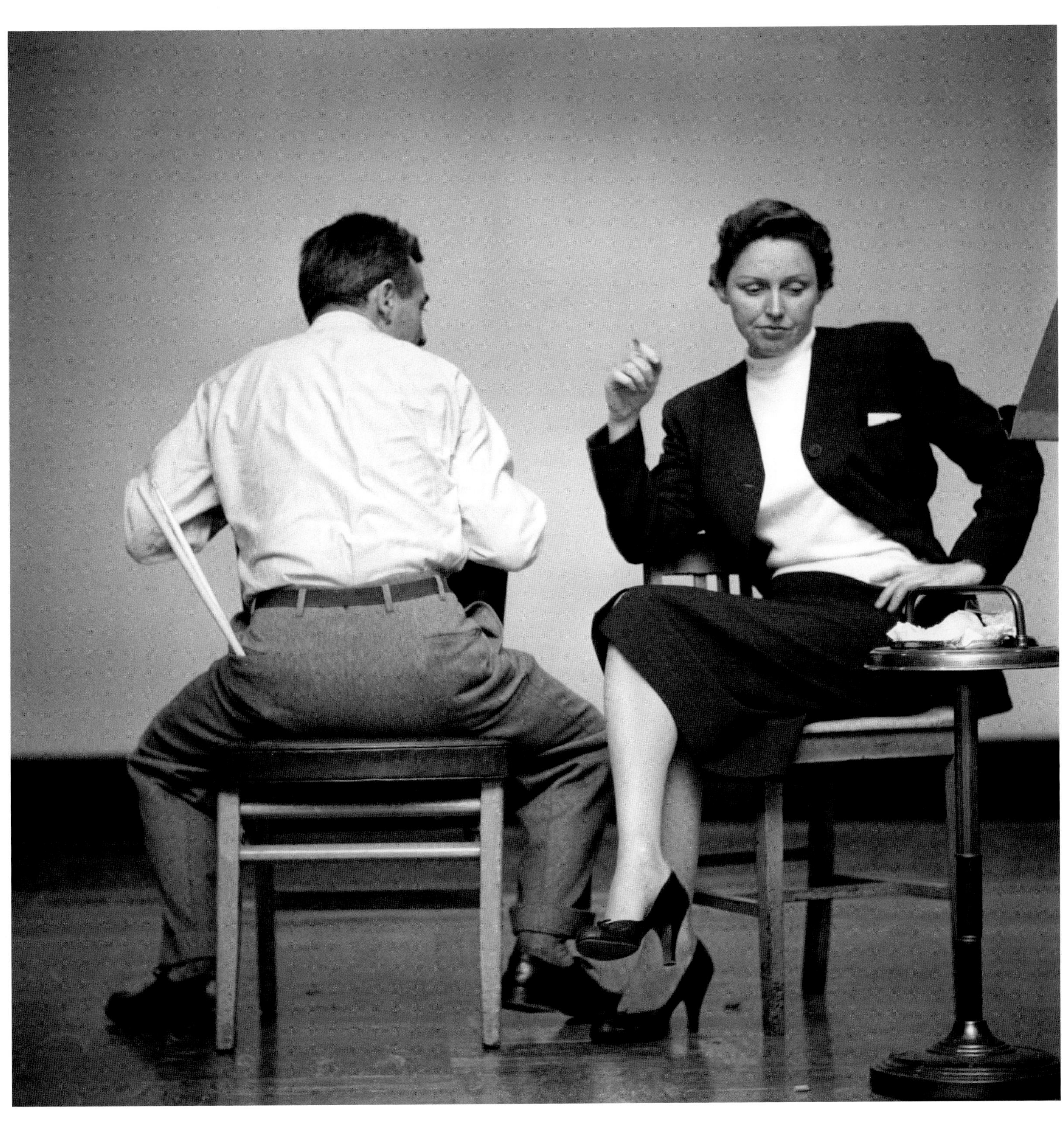

Gene Krupa and Anita O'Day, NYC, 1955

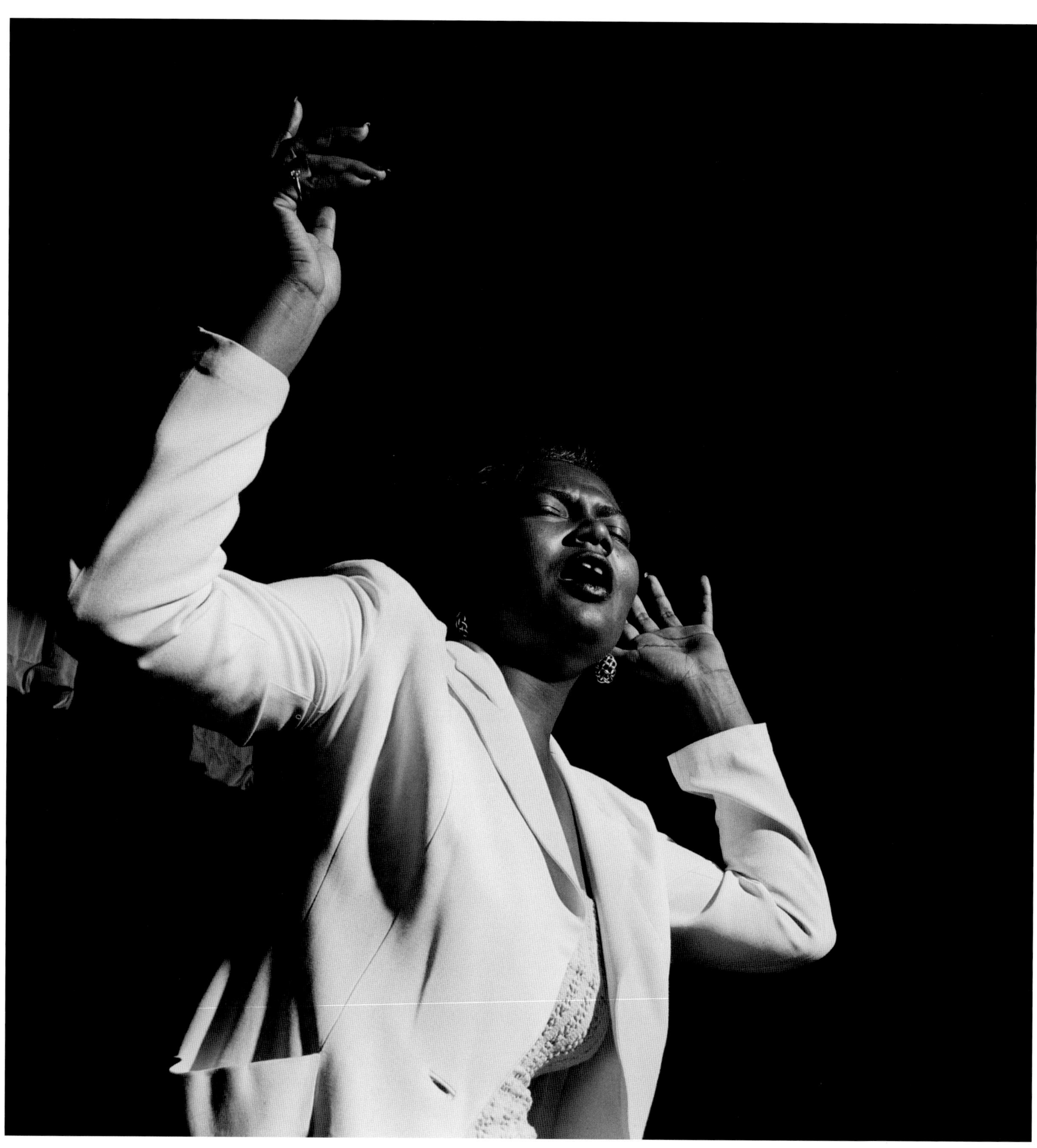

Pearl Bailey, Birdland, NYC, 1950

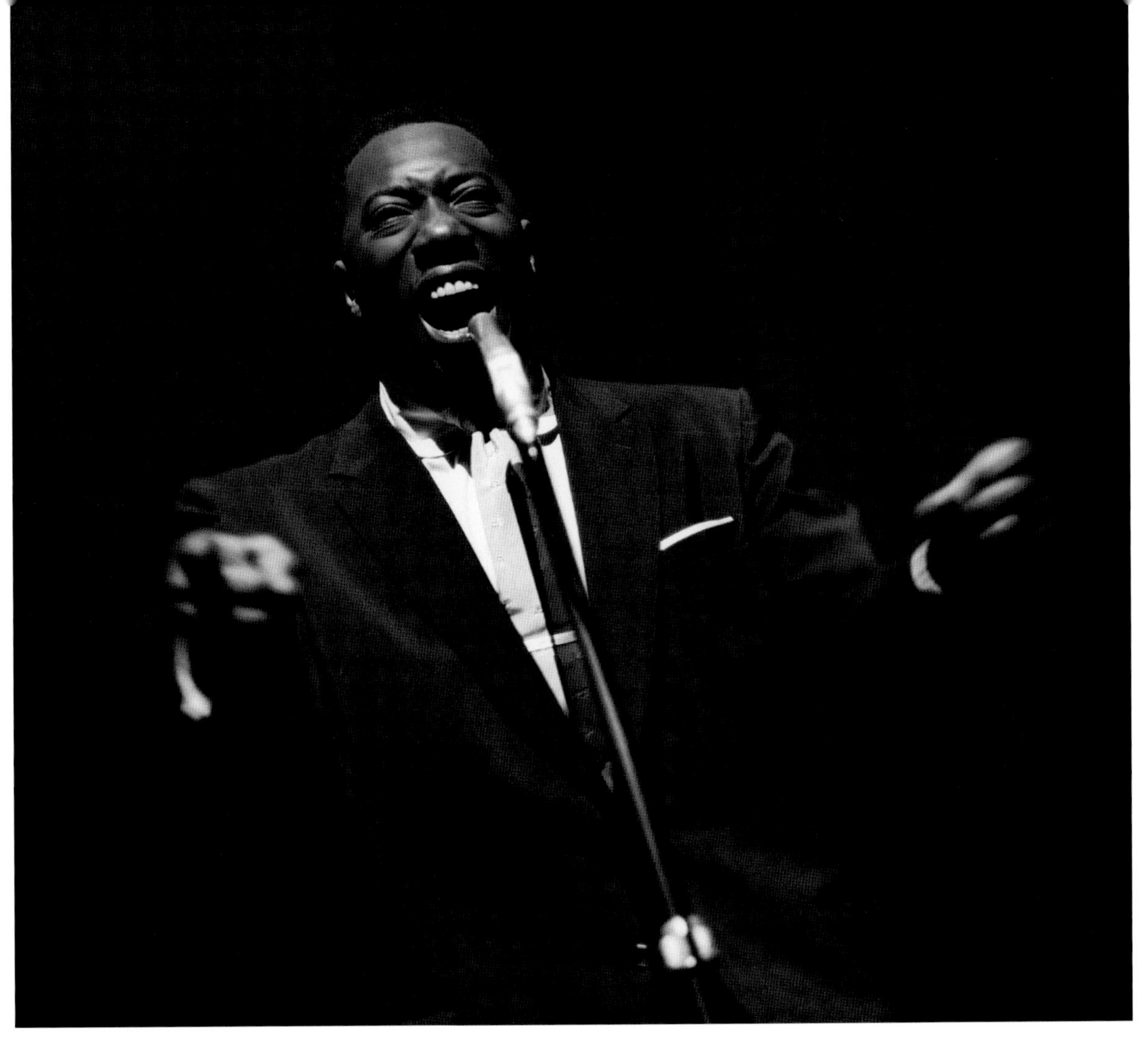

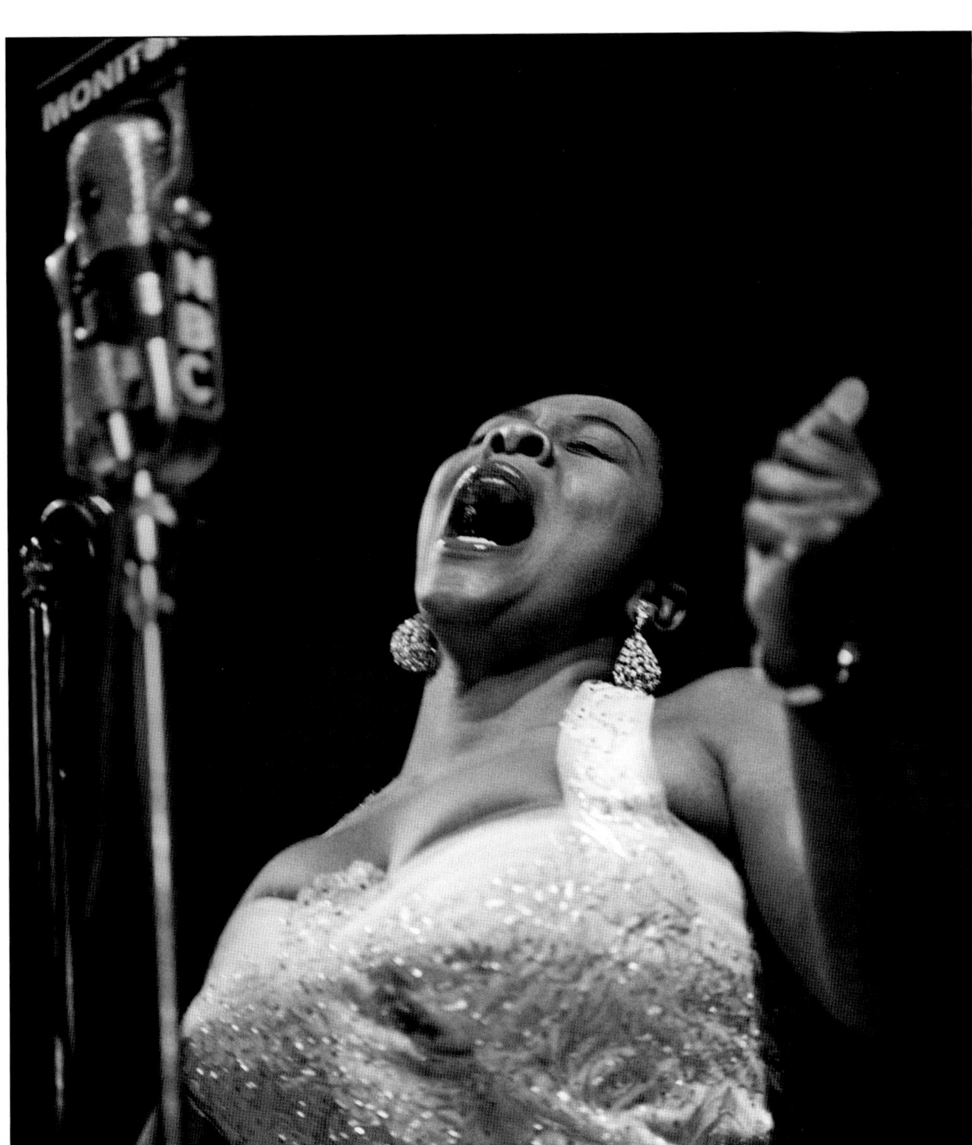

Joe Williams, NYC, 1954

Dinah Washington, Newport, 1955

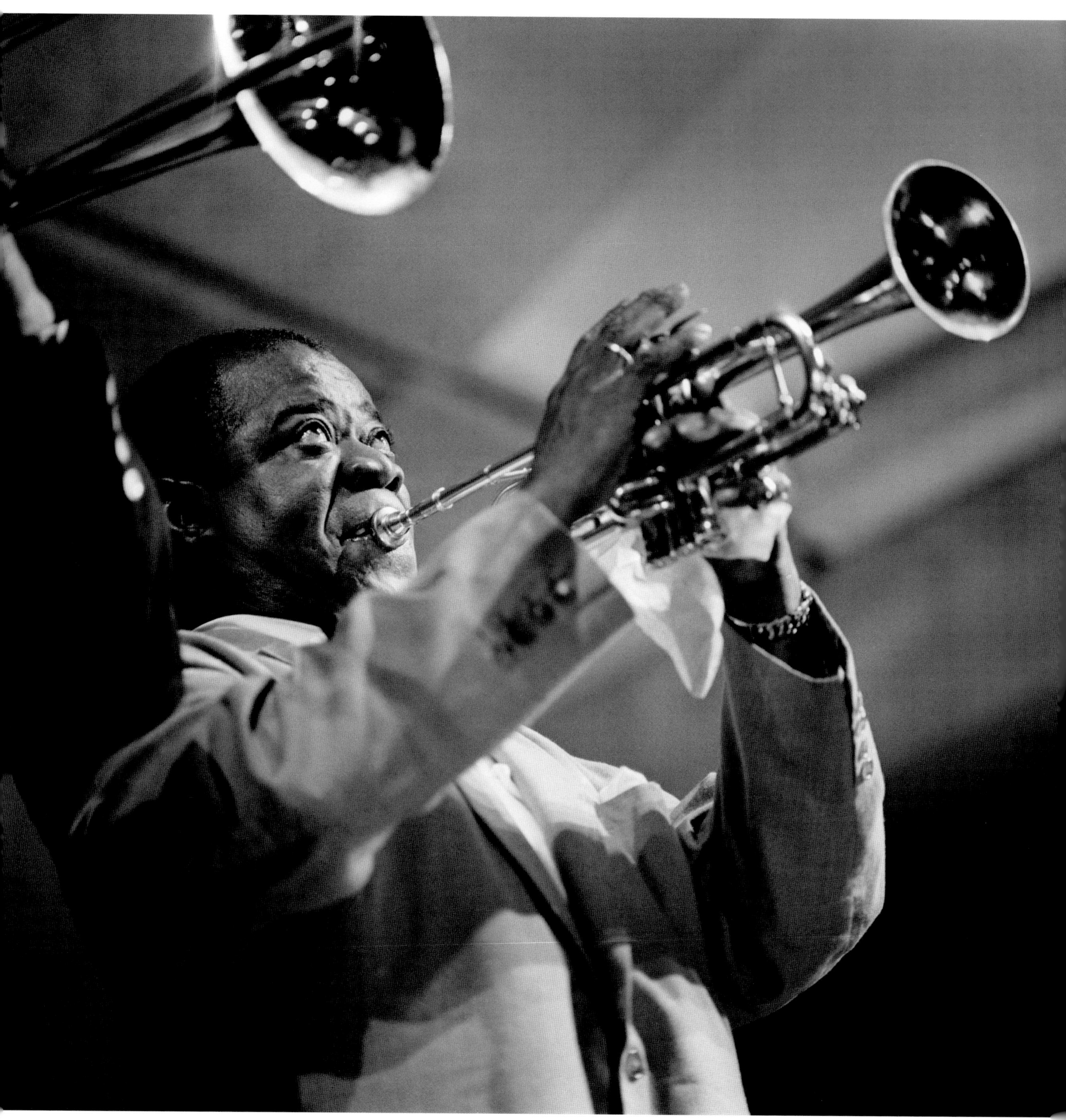

Louis Armstrong, Newport, 1955

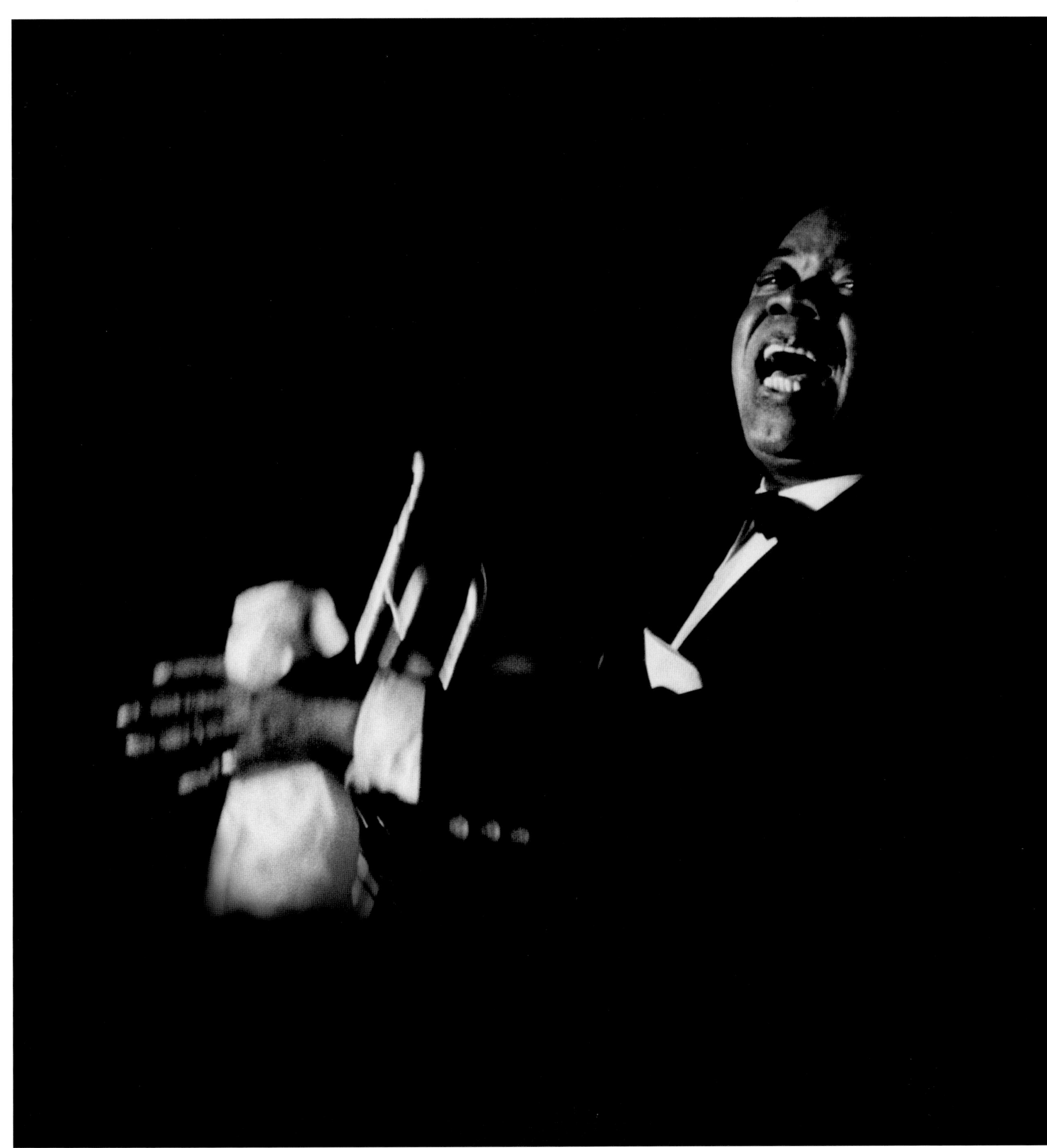

Louis Armstrong, Paris, 1960

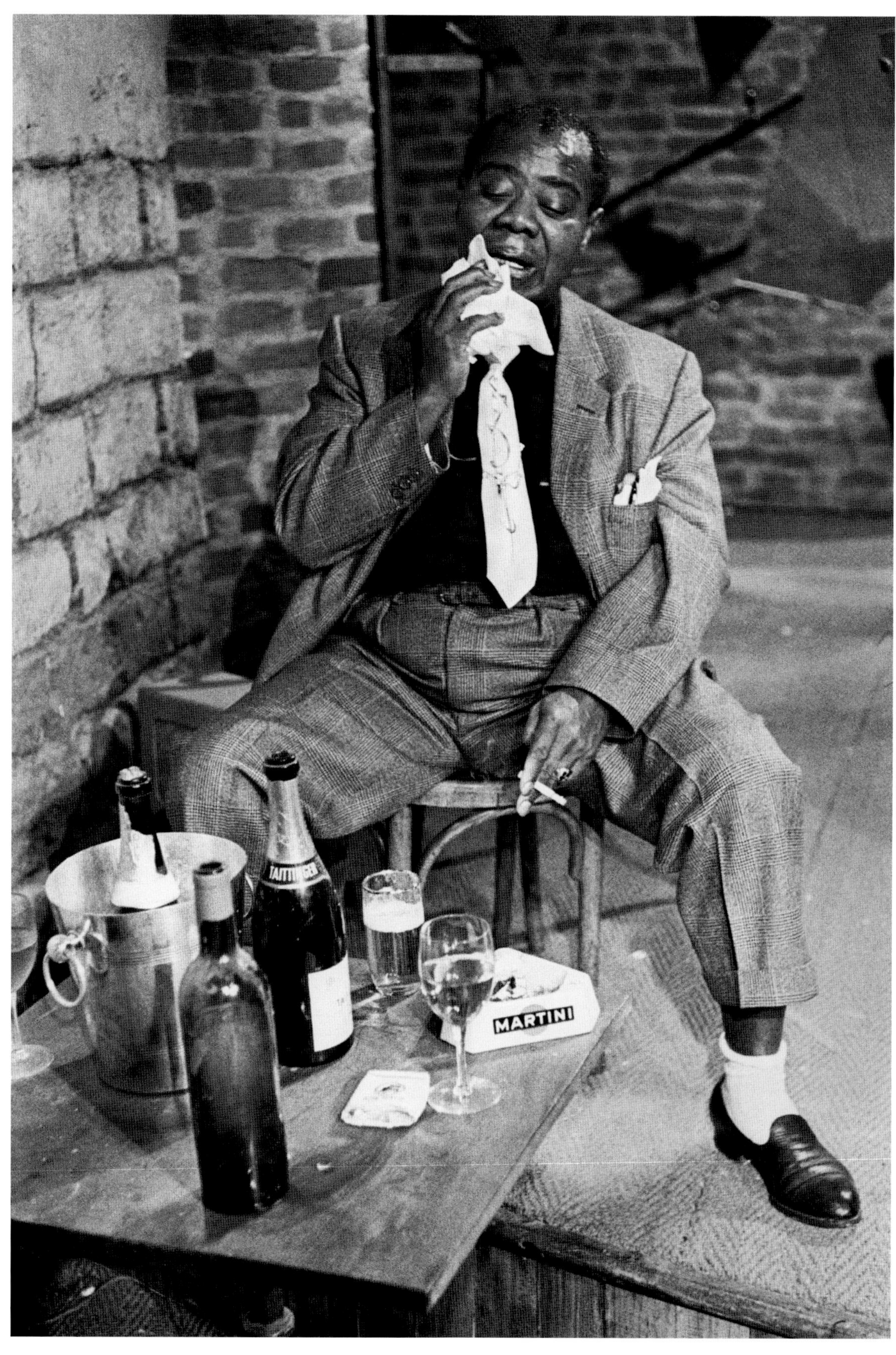

Louis Armstrong on the set of *Paris Blues*, Paris, 1960

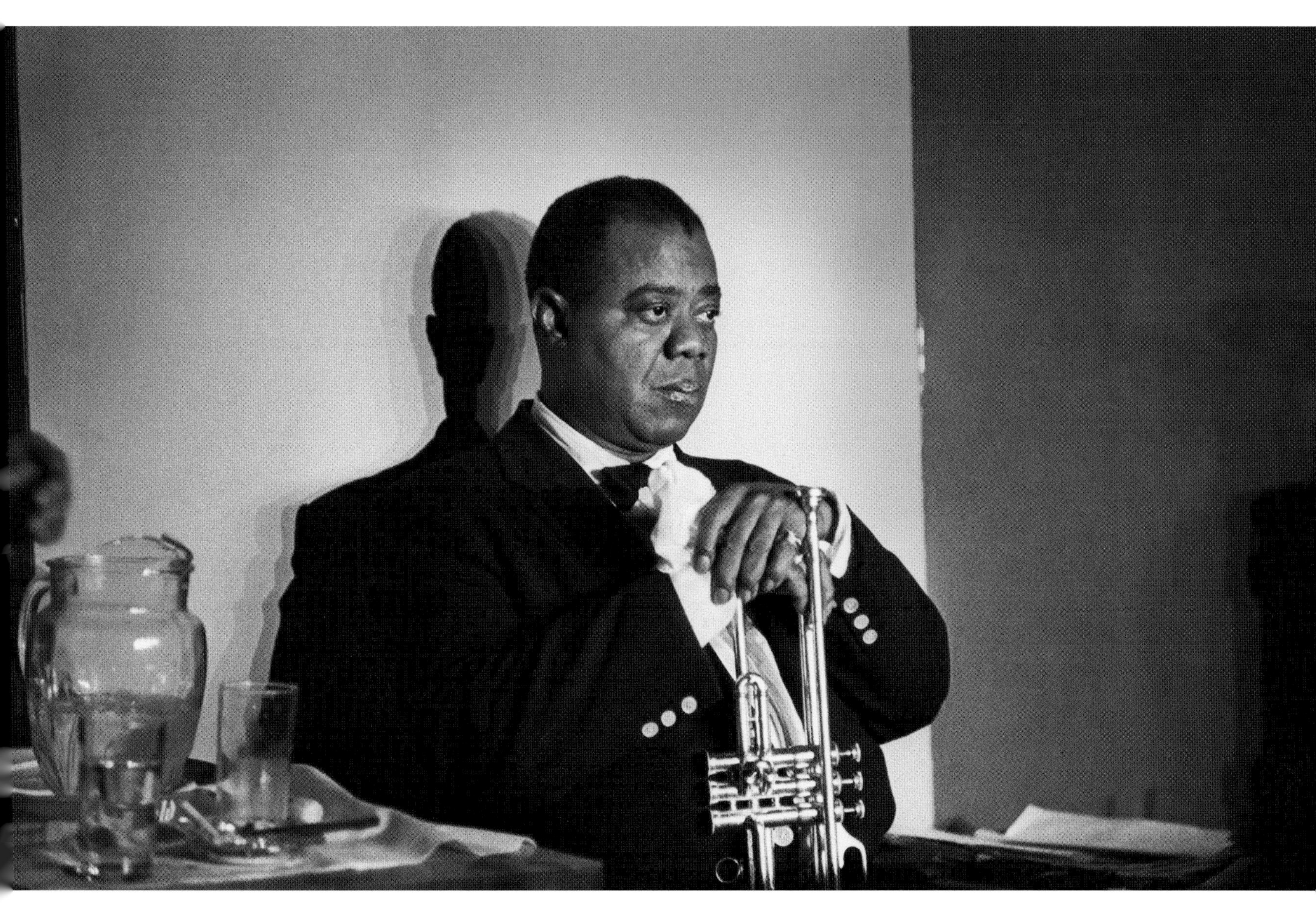

Louis Armstrong, Olympia Theatre, Paris, 1960

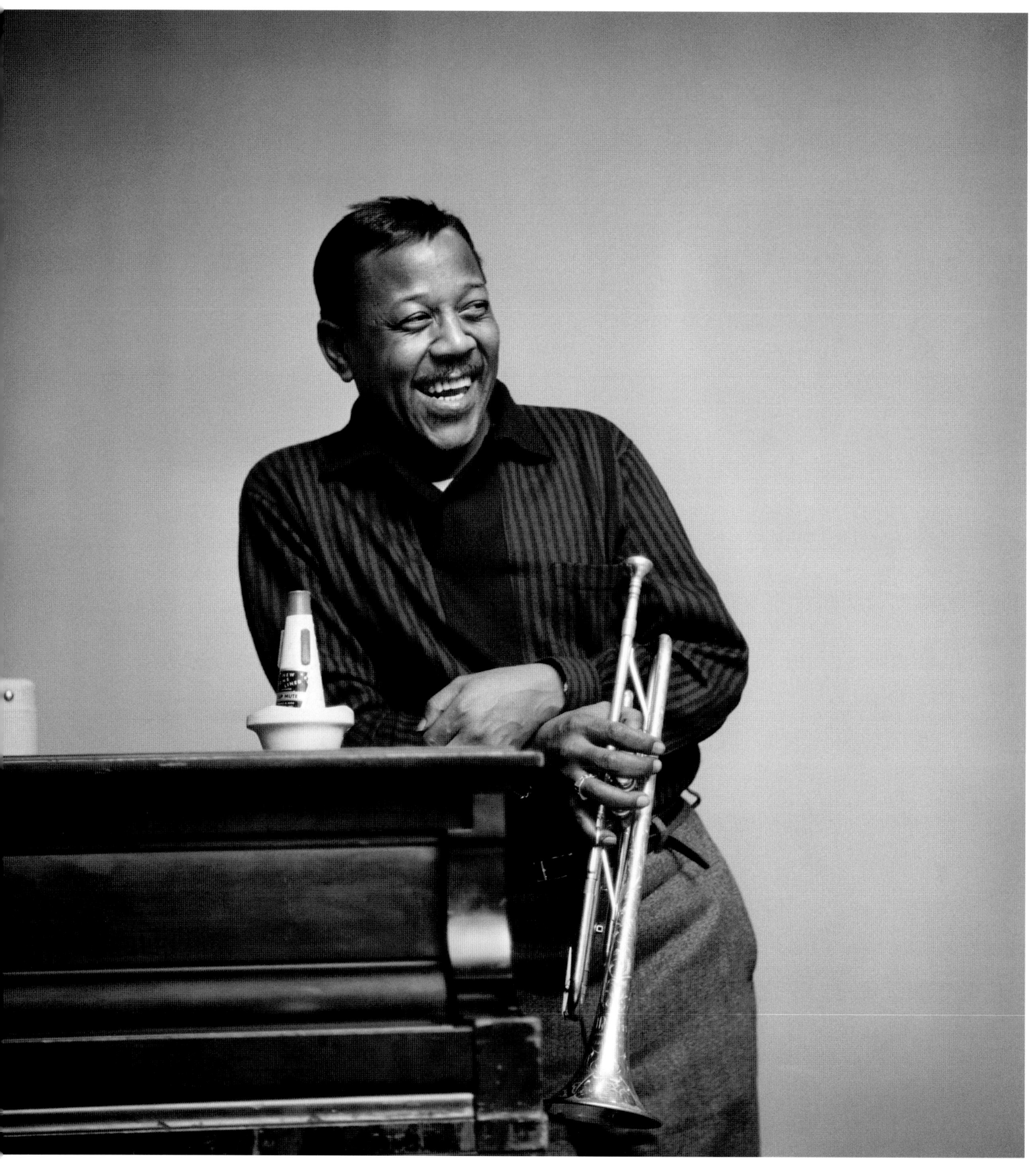

Roy Eldridge, NYC, 1952

Roy Eldridge, NYC, 1954

Fats Navarro, Royal Roost, NYC, 1948

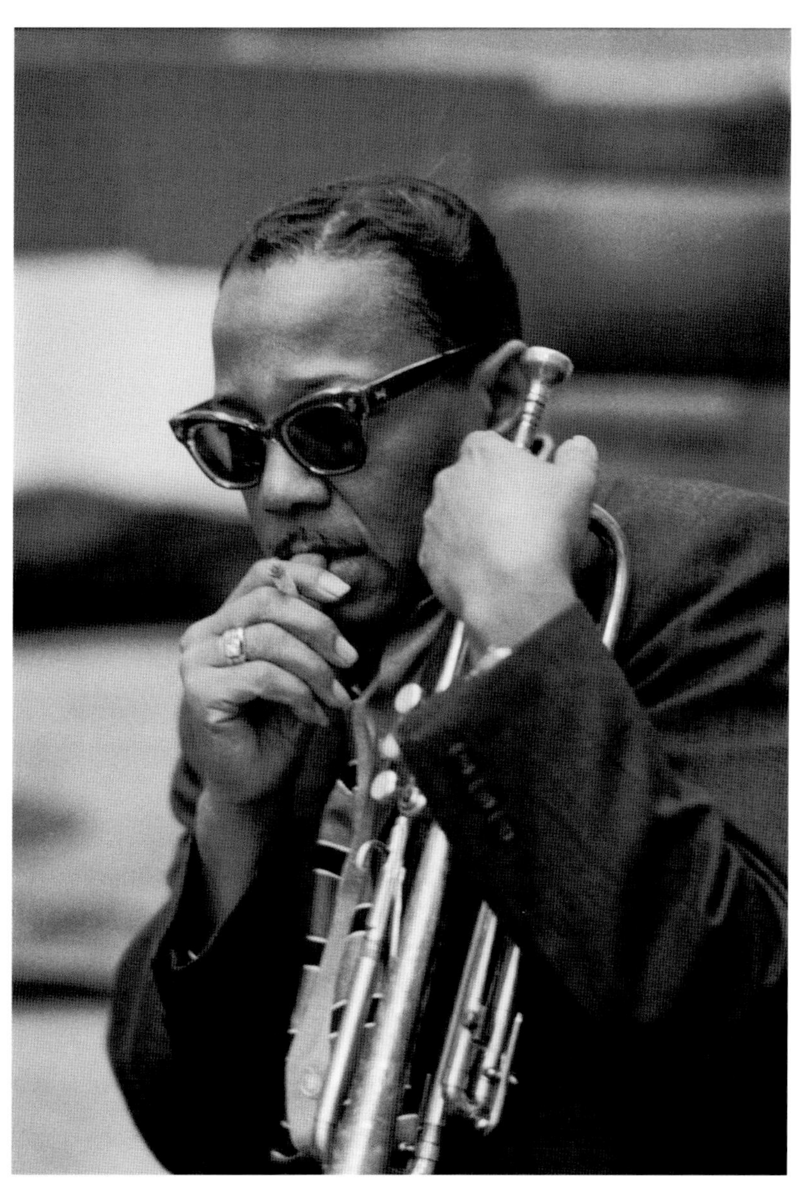

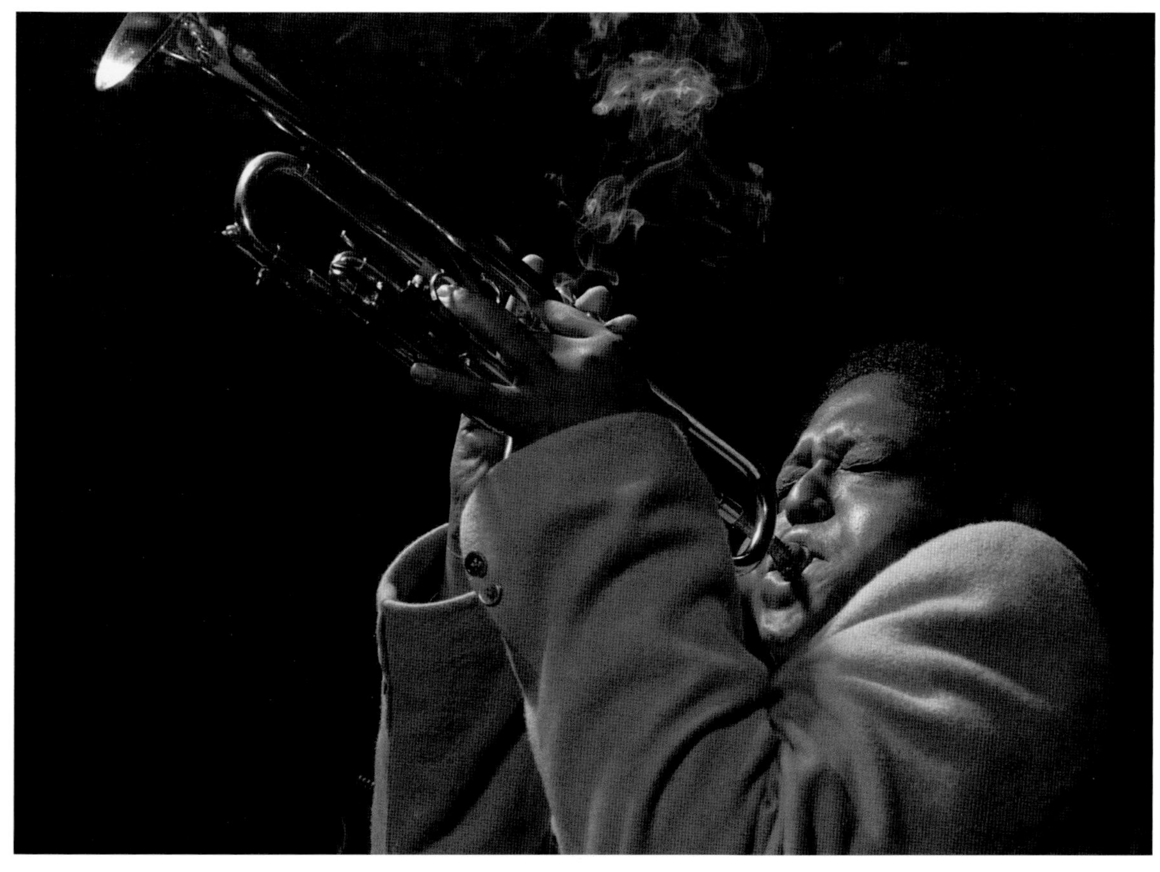

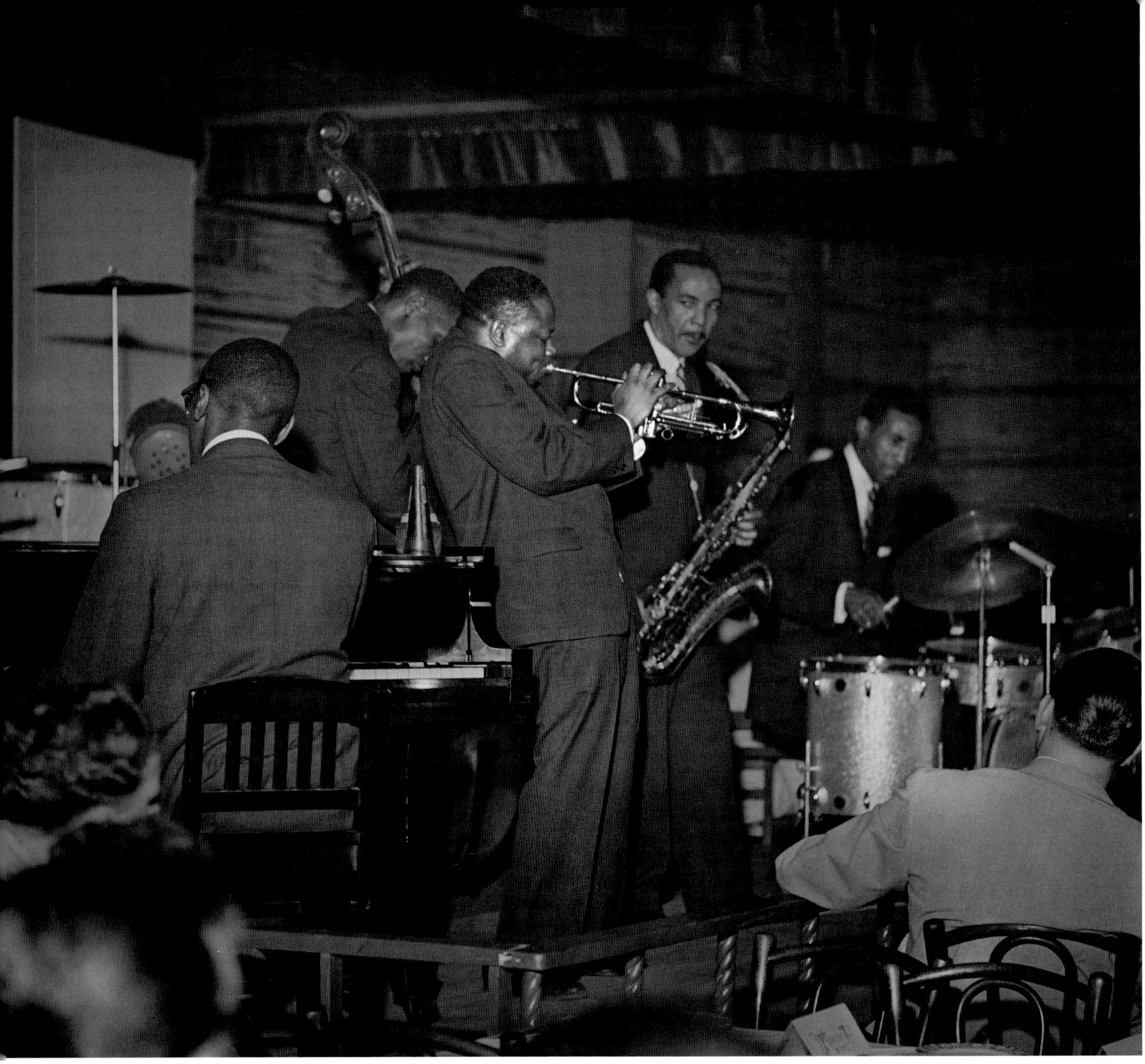

Richie Powell, George Morrow, Clifford Brown, Harold Land and Max Roach, NYC, 1954

Clifford Brown and Max Roach, Birdland, NYC, 1954

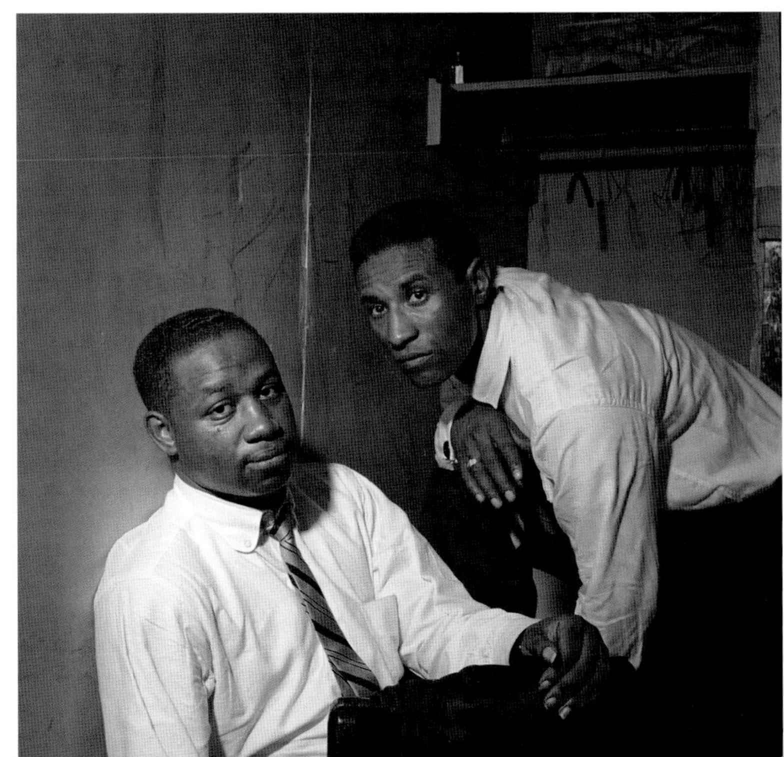

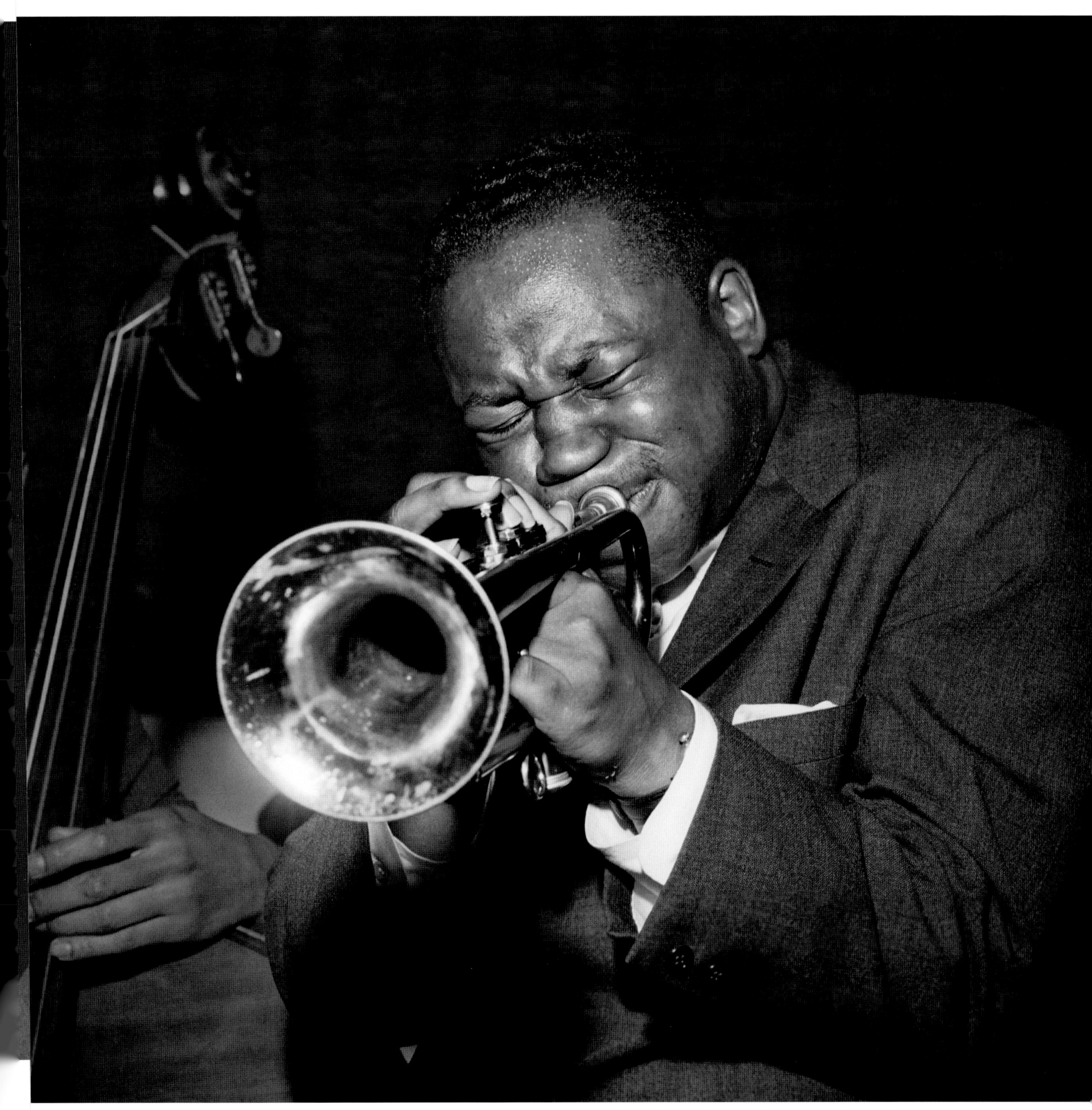

Clifford Brown, Birdland, NYC, 1954

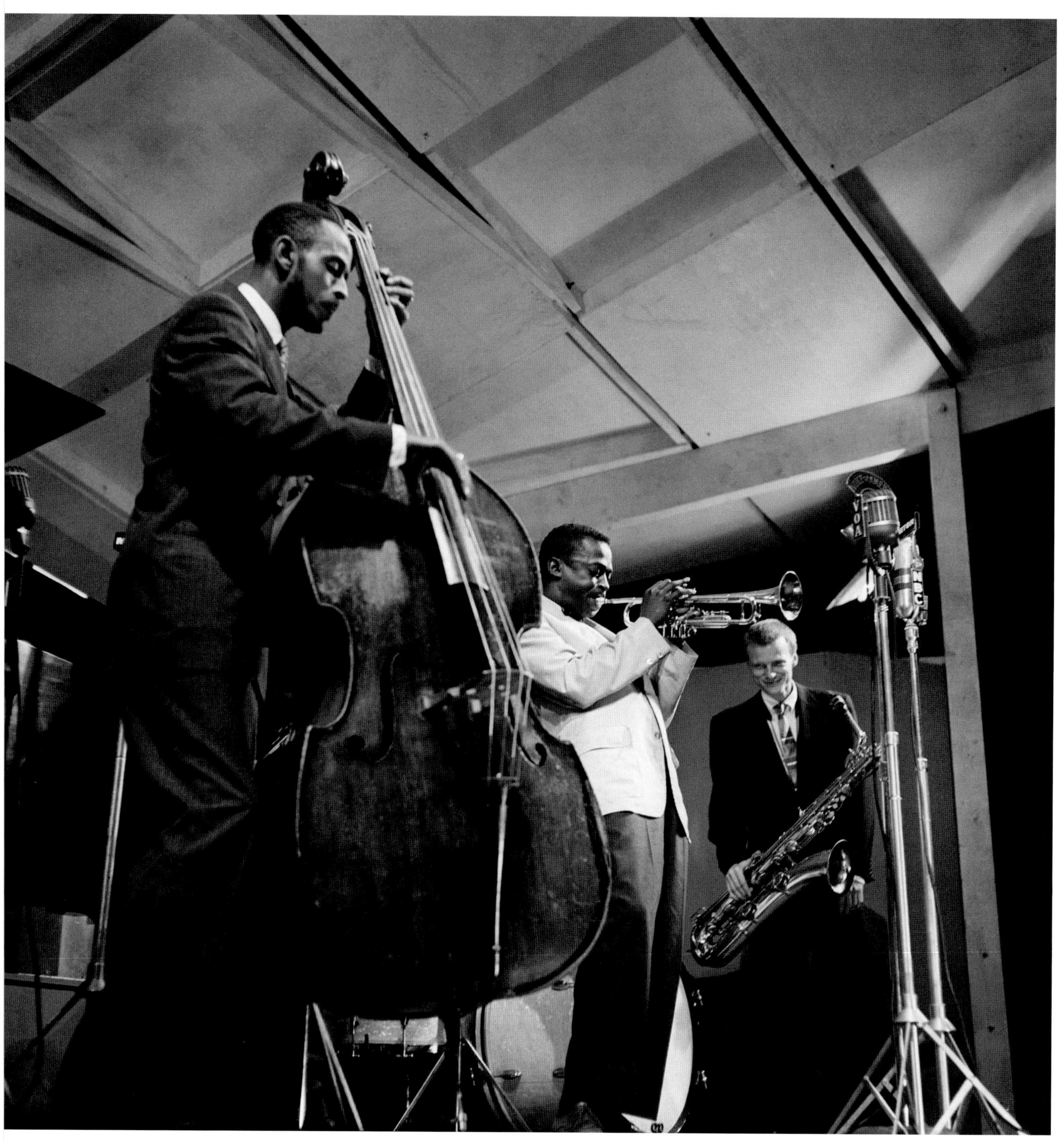

Percy Heath, Miles Davis and Gerry Mulligan, Newport, 1955

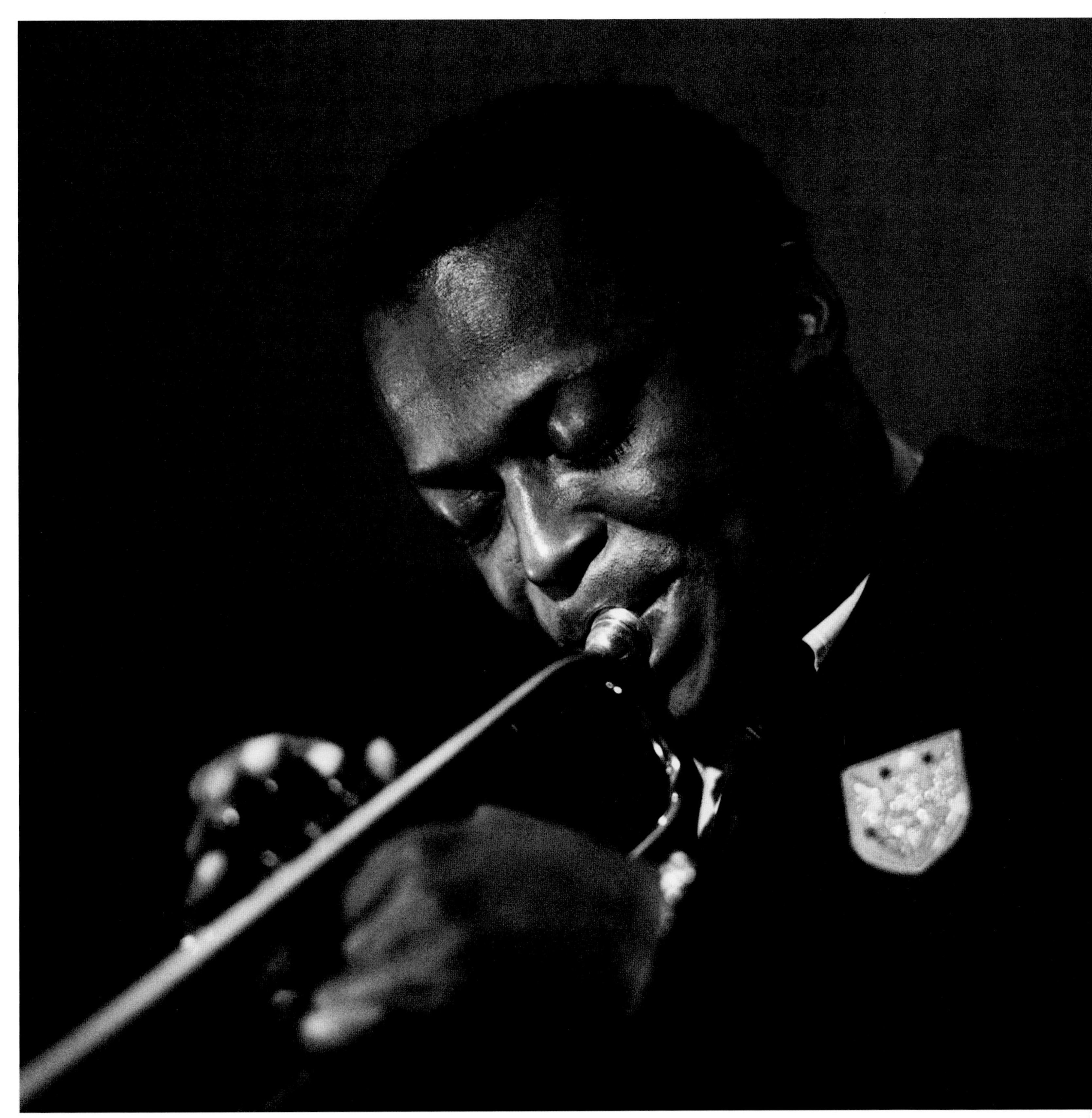

Miles Davis, Birdland, NYC, 1949

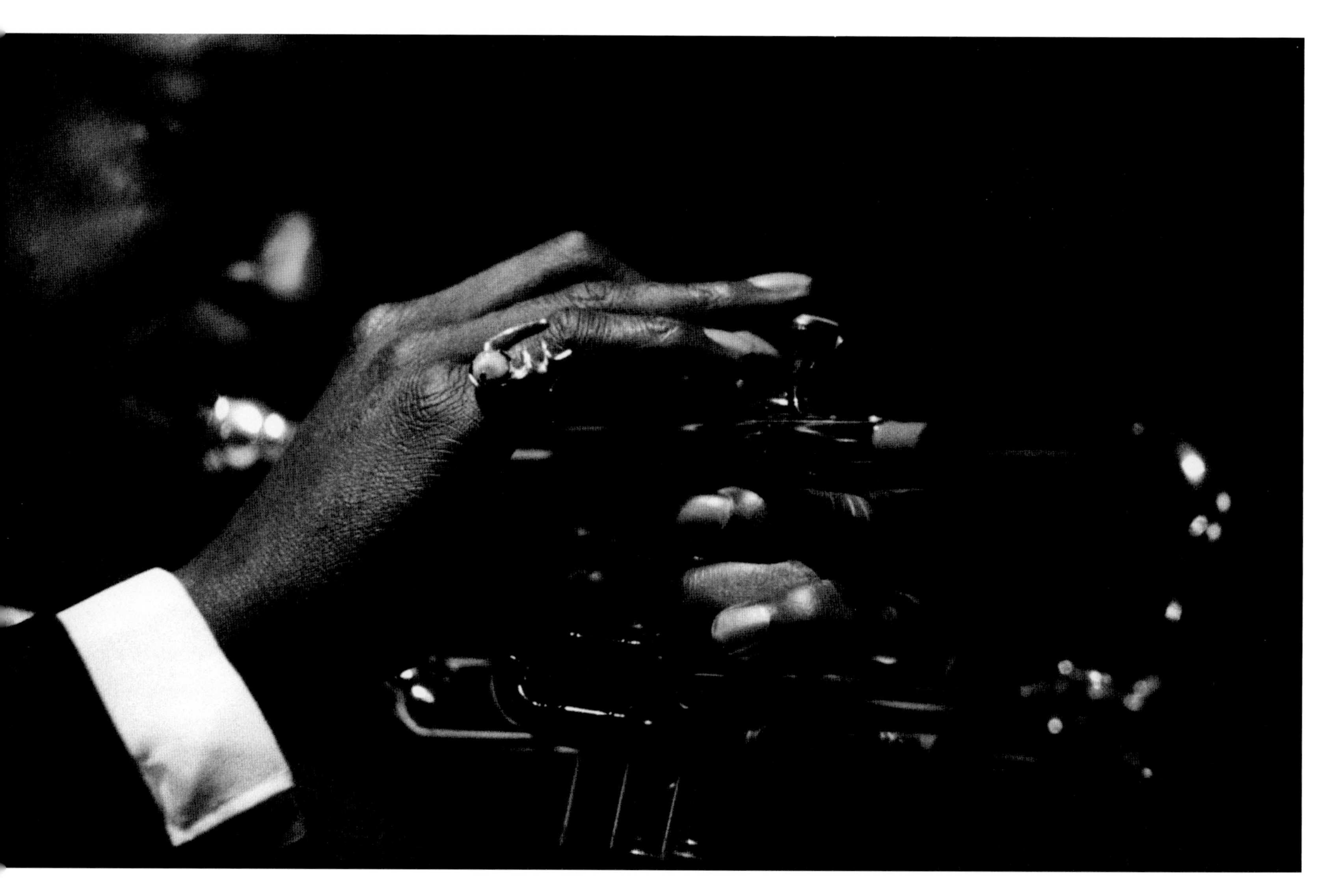

Miles Davis, NYC, 1953

Miles Davis, Royal Festival Hall, London, 1989

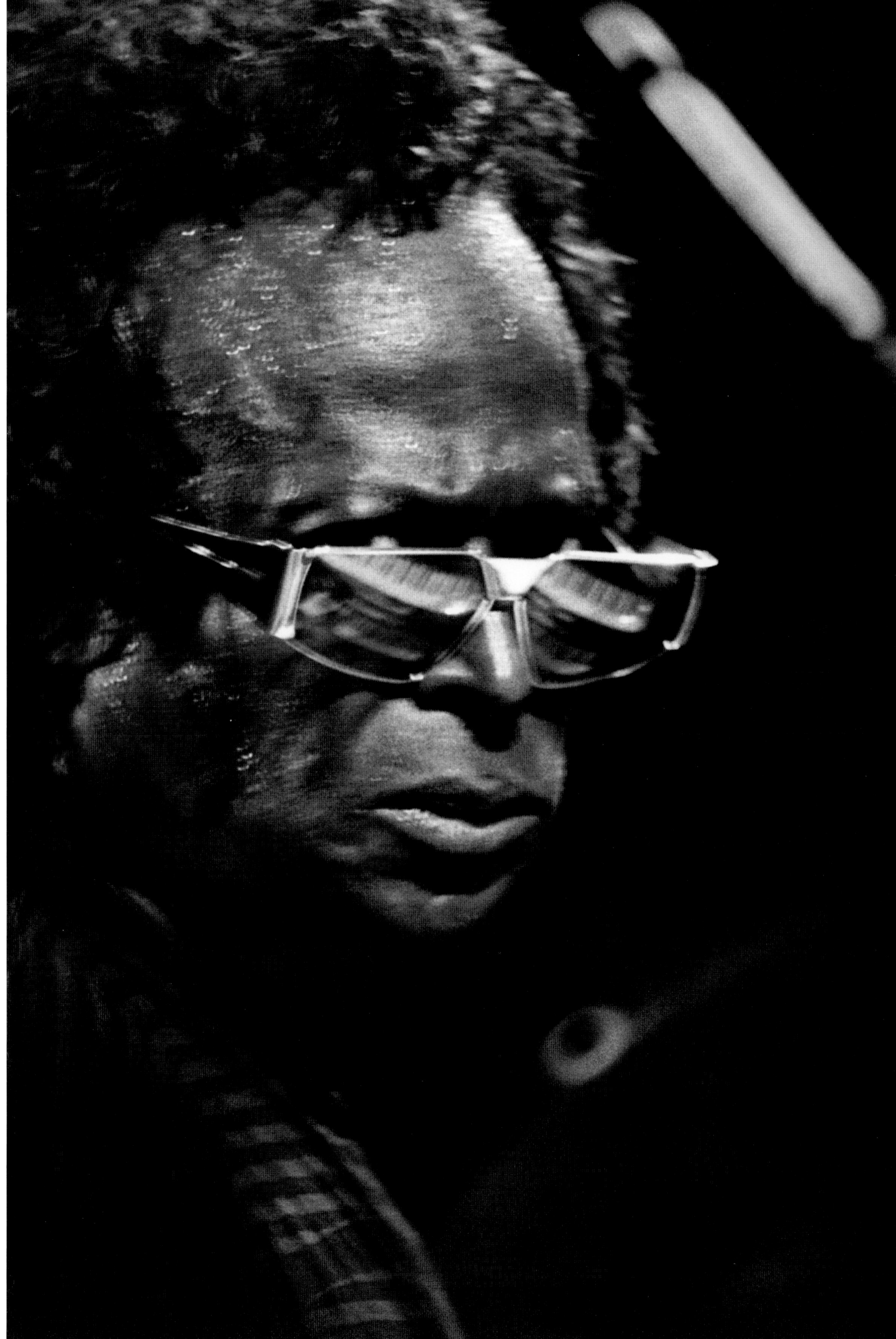

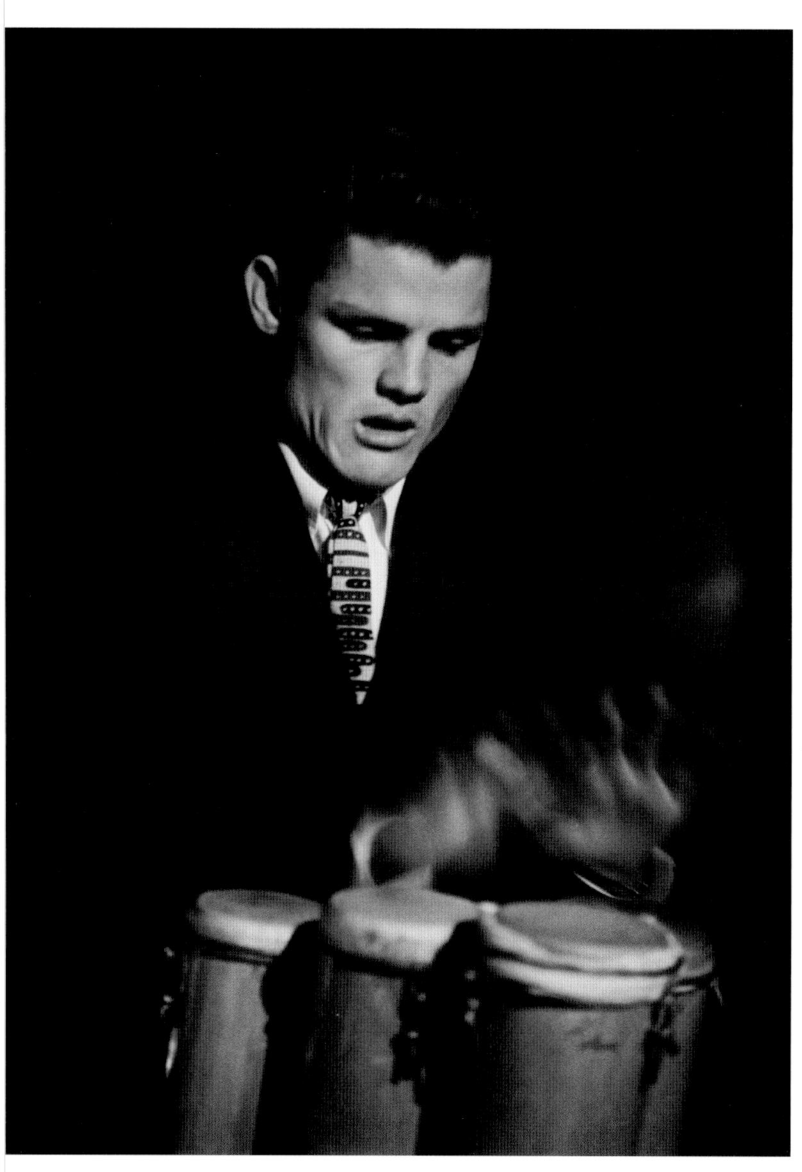

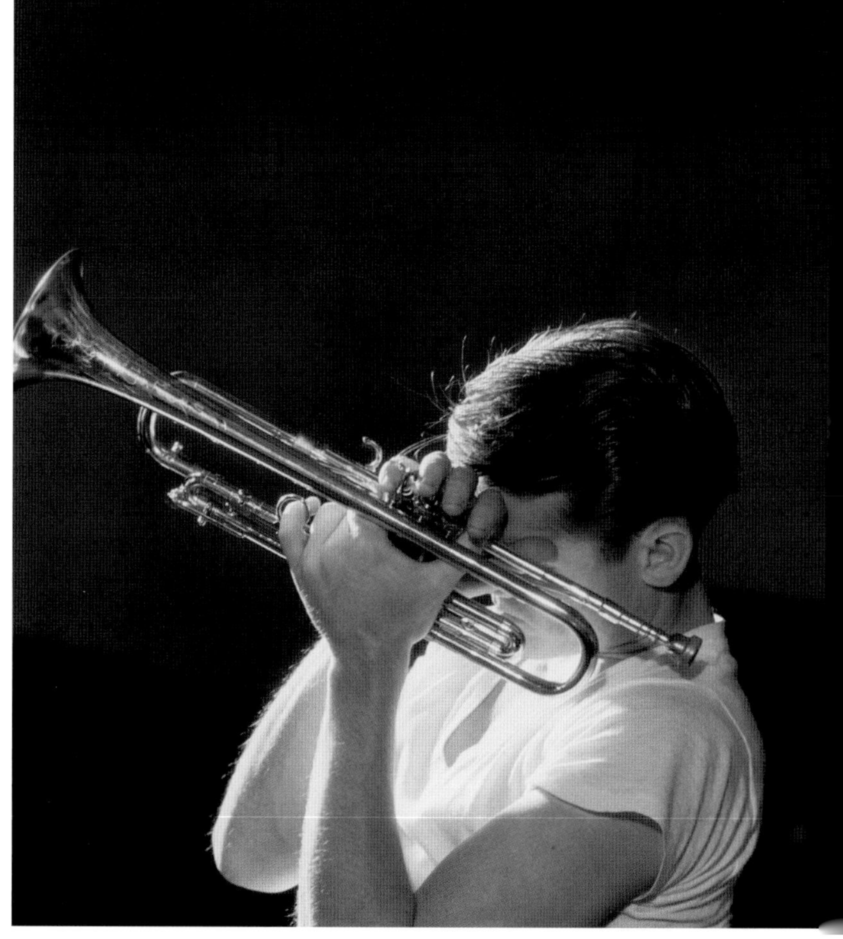

Chet Baker, NYC, 1955

Chet Baker, NYC, 1956

Chet Baker in dressing room mirror, NYC, 1955

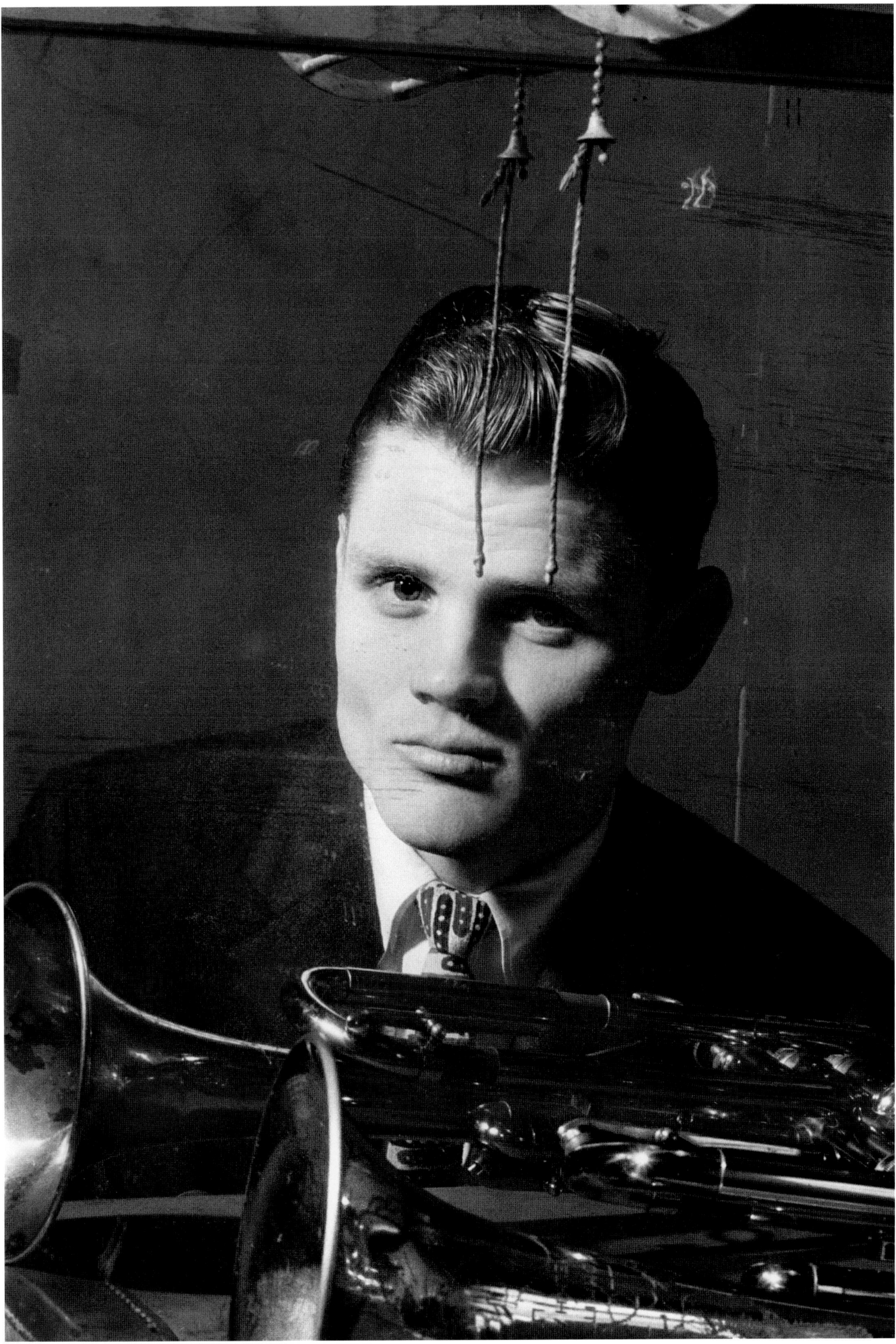

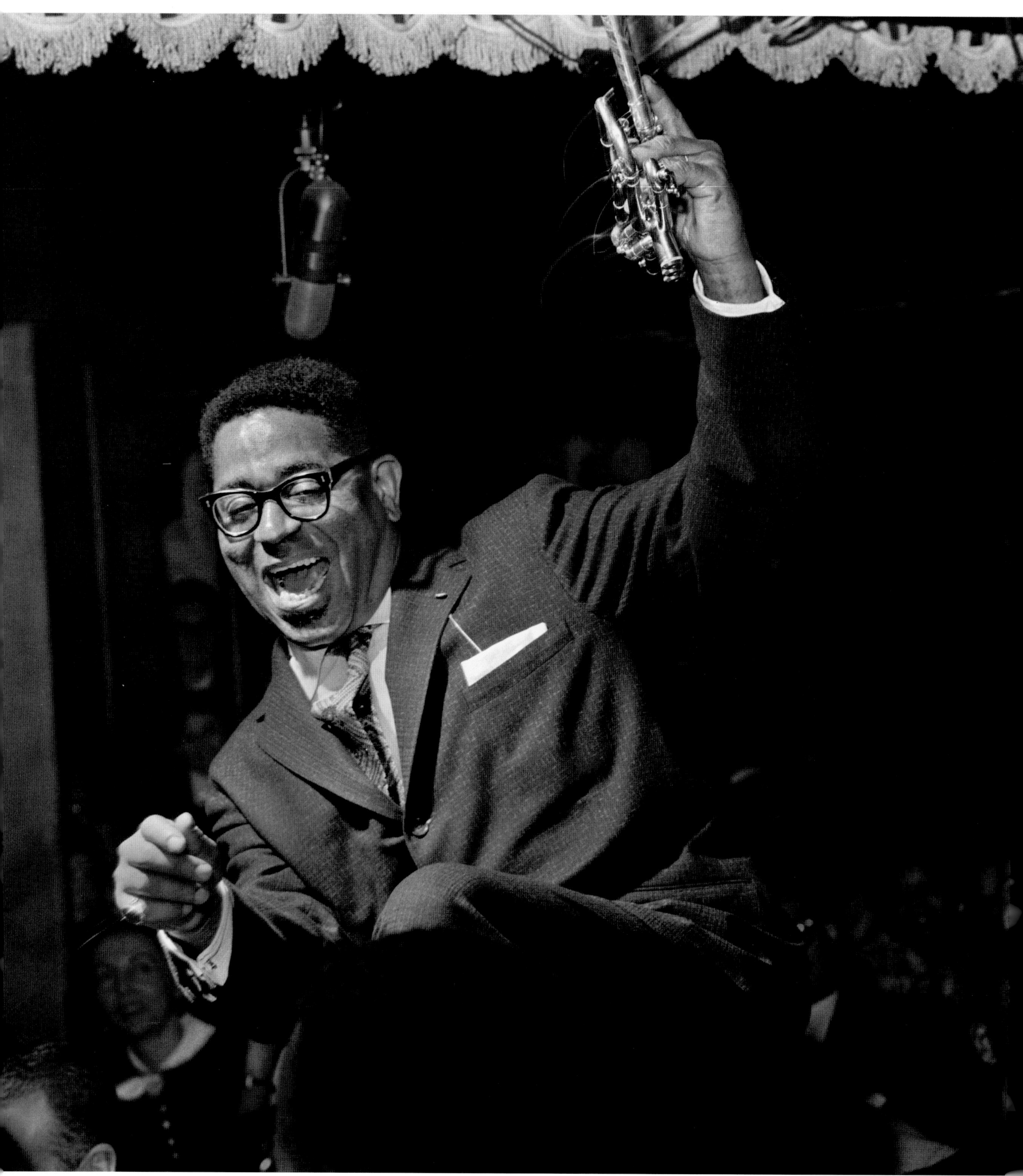

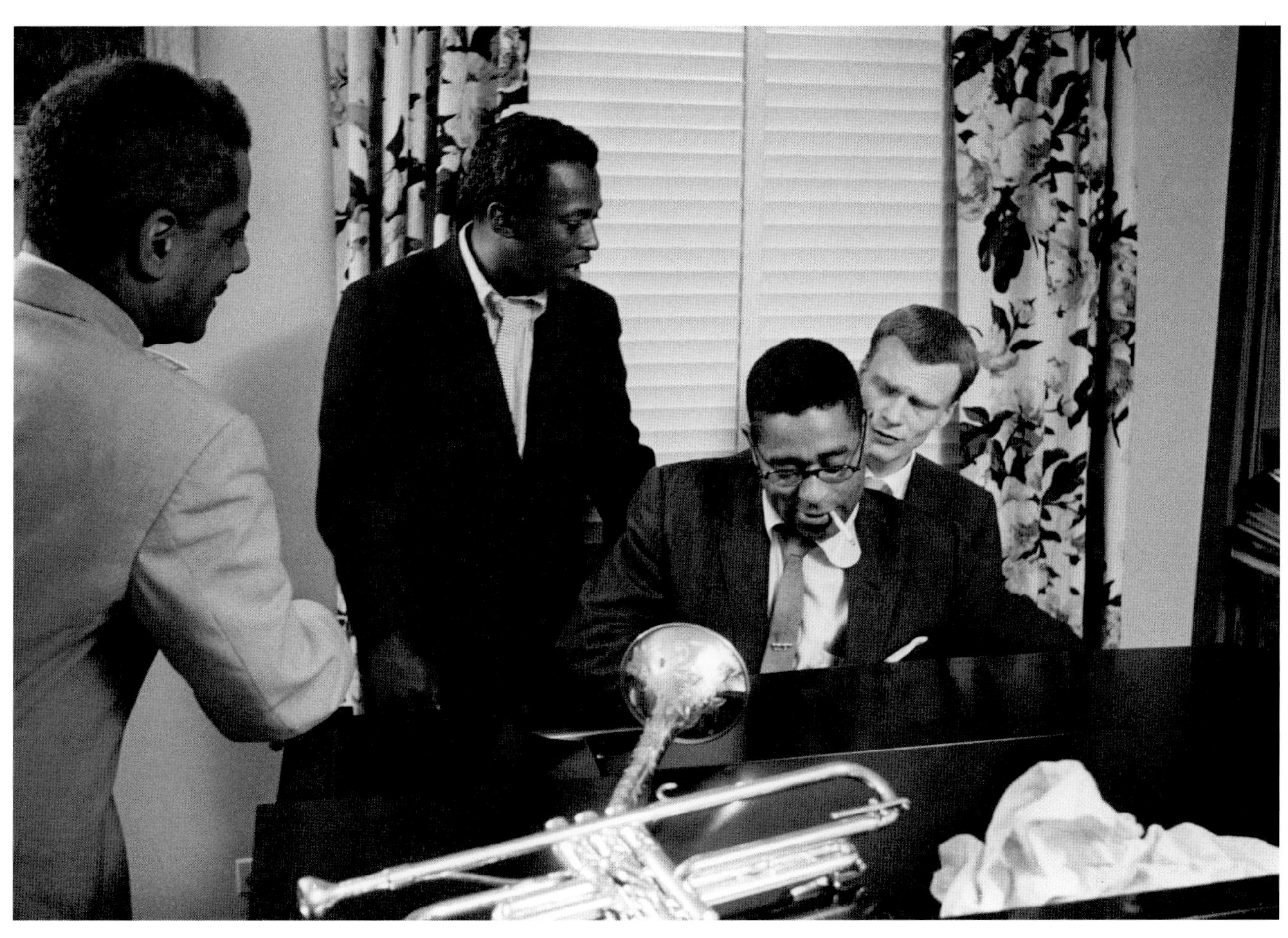

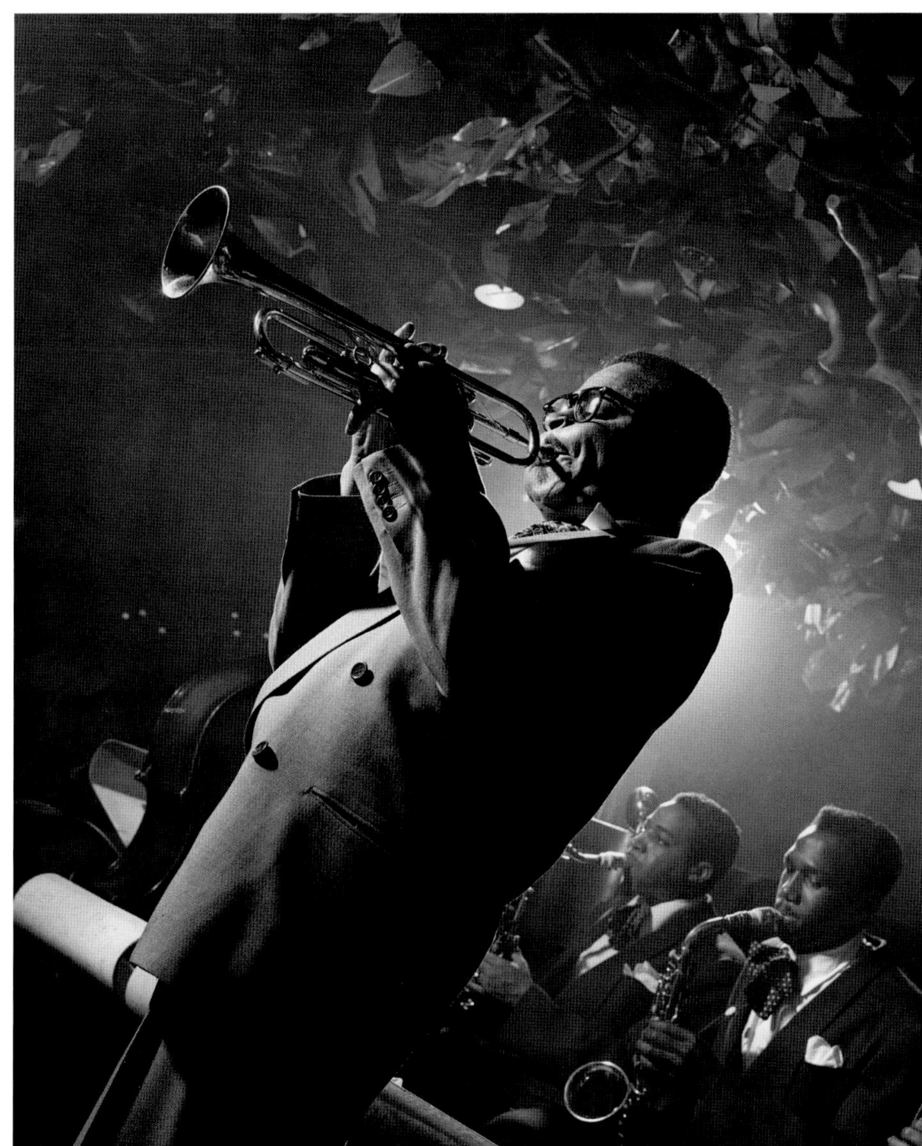

Dizzy Gillespie, Birdland, NYC, 1955 (opposite)

Teddy Wilson, Miles Davis, Dizzy Gillespie and Gerry Mulligan, Hazel Scott's house, Paris, 1948

Dizzy Gillespie, Royal Roost, NYC, 1948

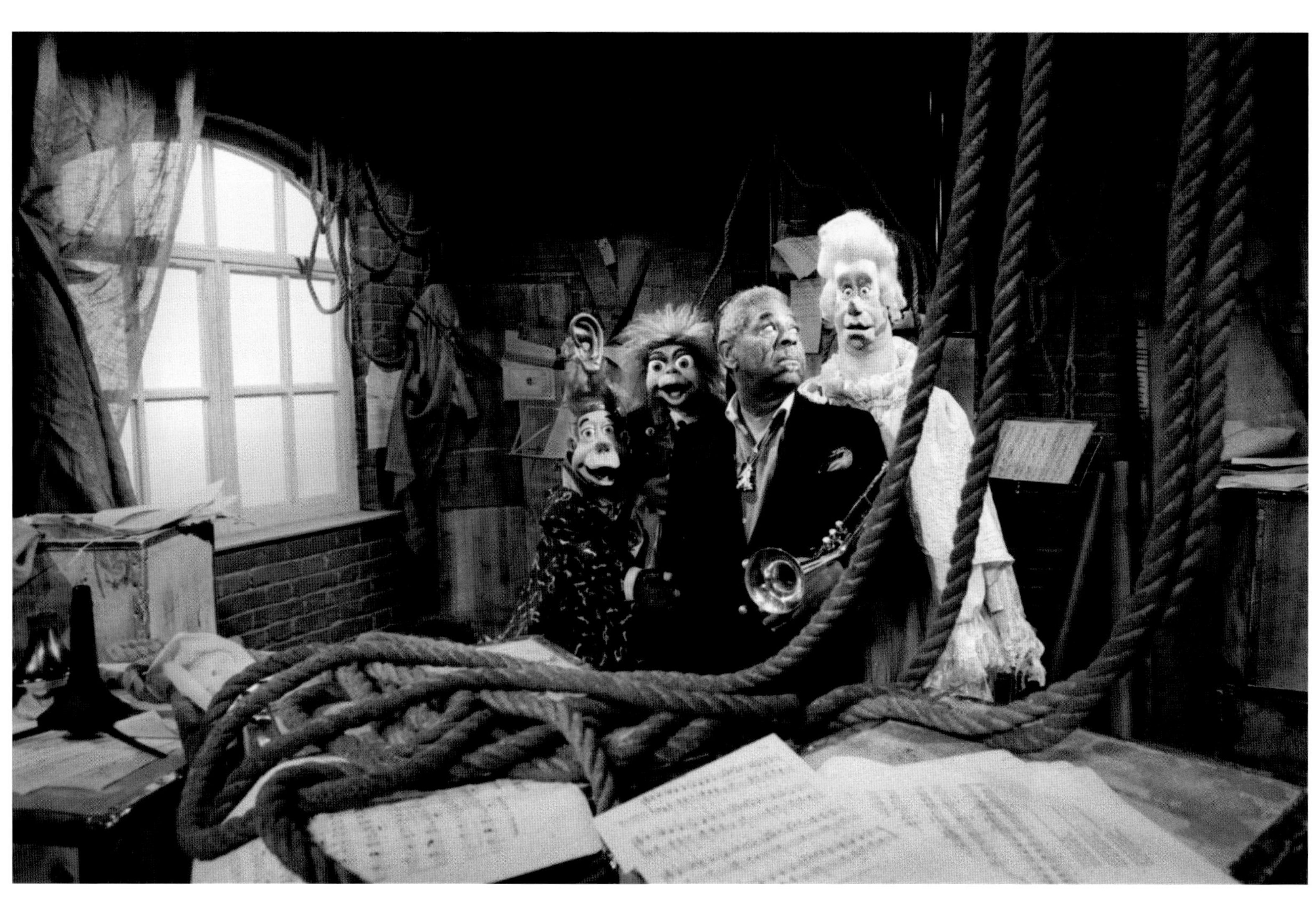

Dizzy Gillespie with muppets, London, 1988

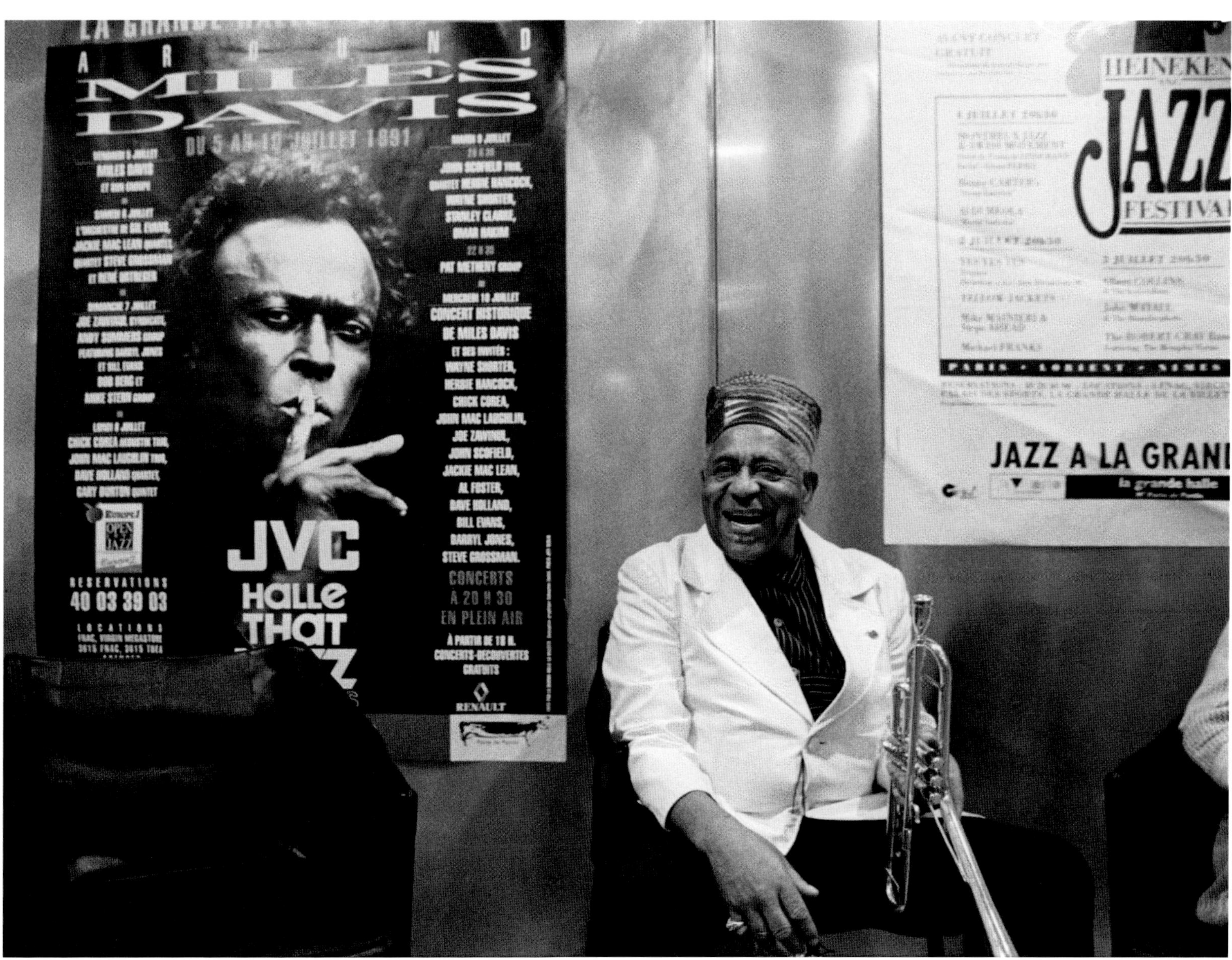

Dizzy Gillespie, Paris, 1991

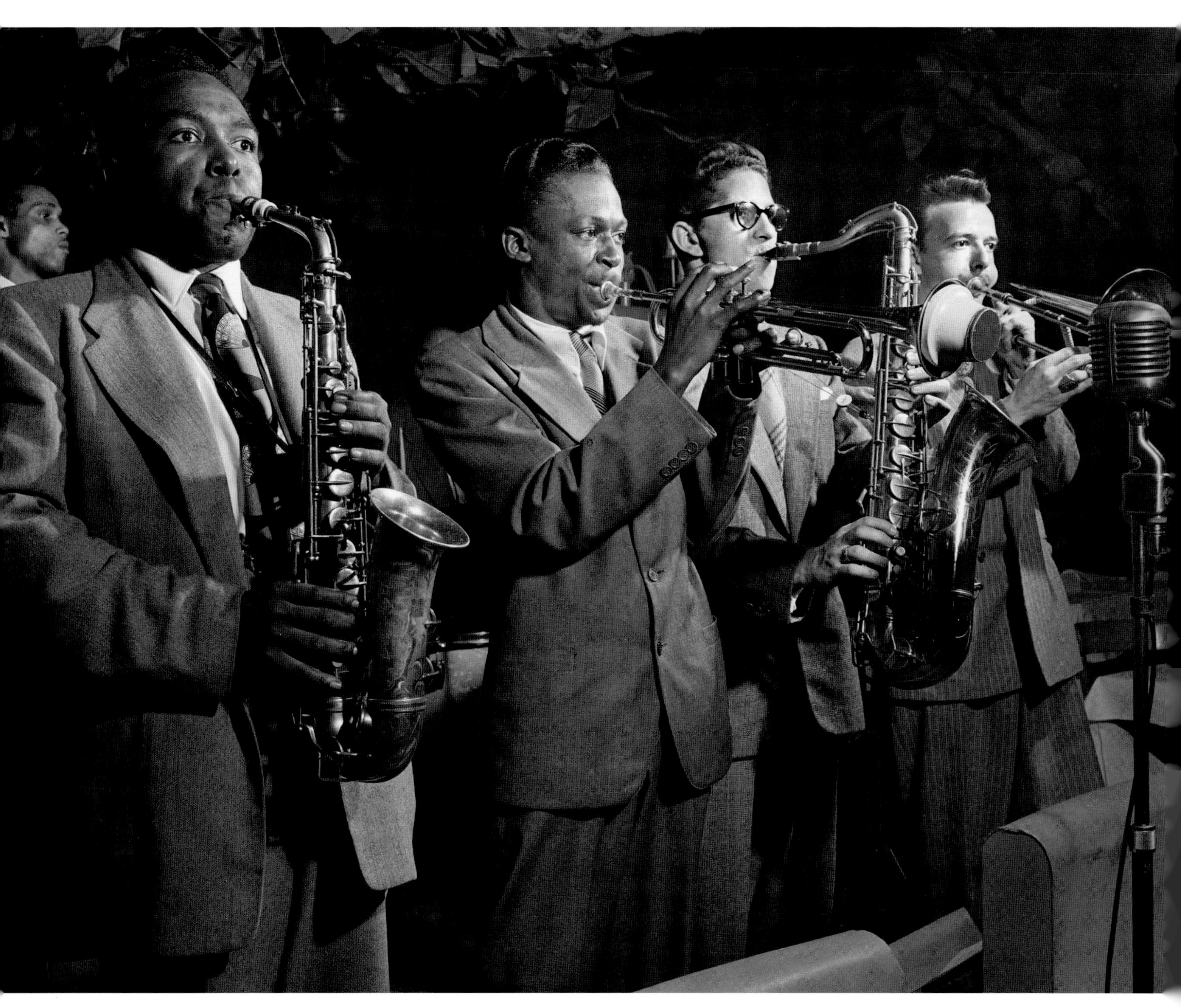

Charlie 'Bird' Parker, Miles Davis, Kai Winding and Allan Eager, Royal Roost, NYC, 1948

Charlie 'Bird' Parker and Dizzy Gillespie, Royal Roost, NYC, 1949

Joe Gordon, Ermet Perry, Dizzy Gillepsie, Carl 'Bama' Warwick and Quincy Jones, Birdland, NYC, 1955

Sonny Stitt and Dizzy Gillespie, NYC, 1953

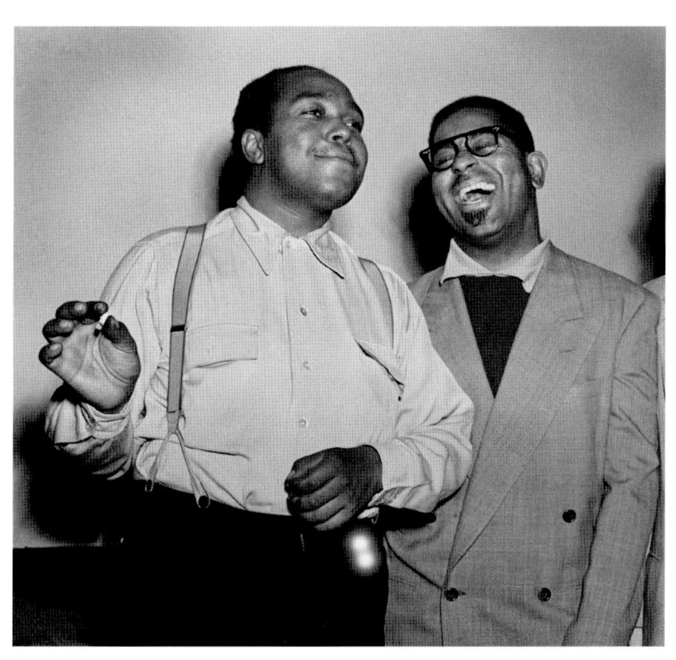

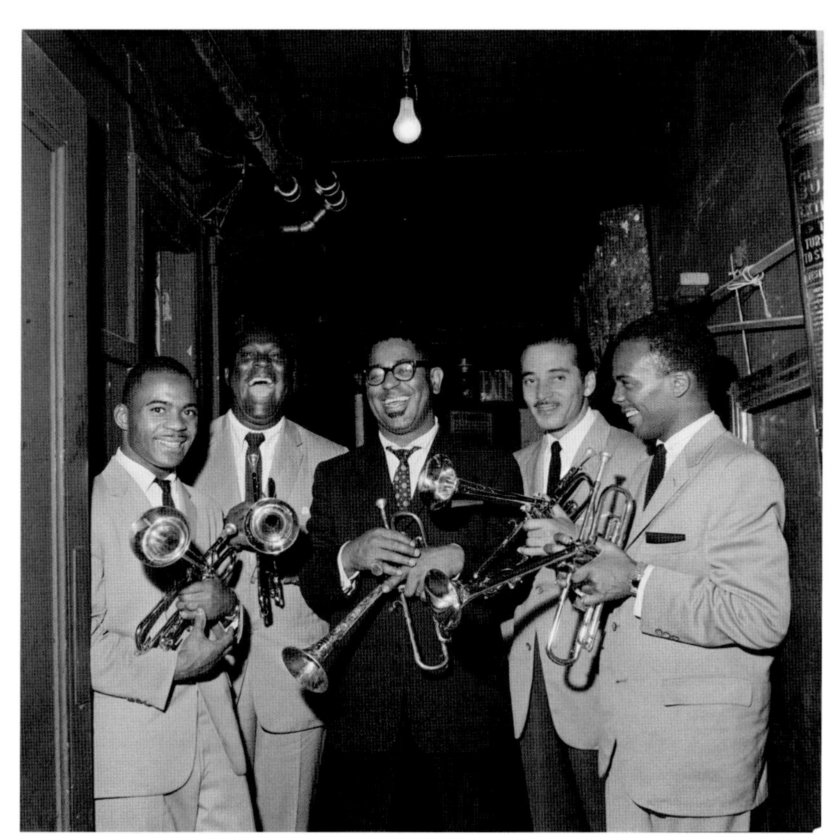

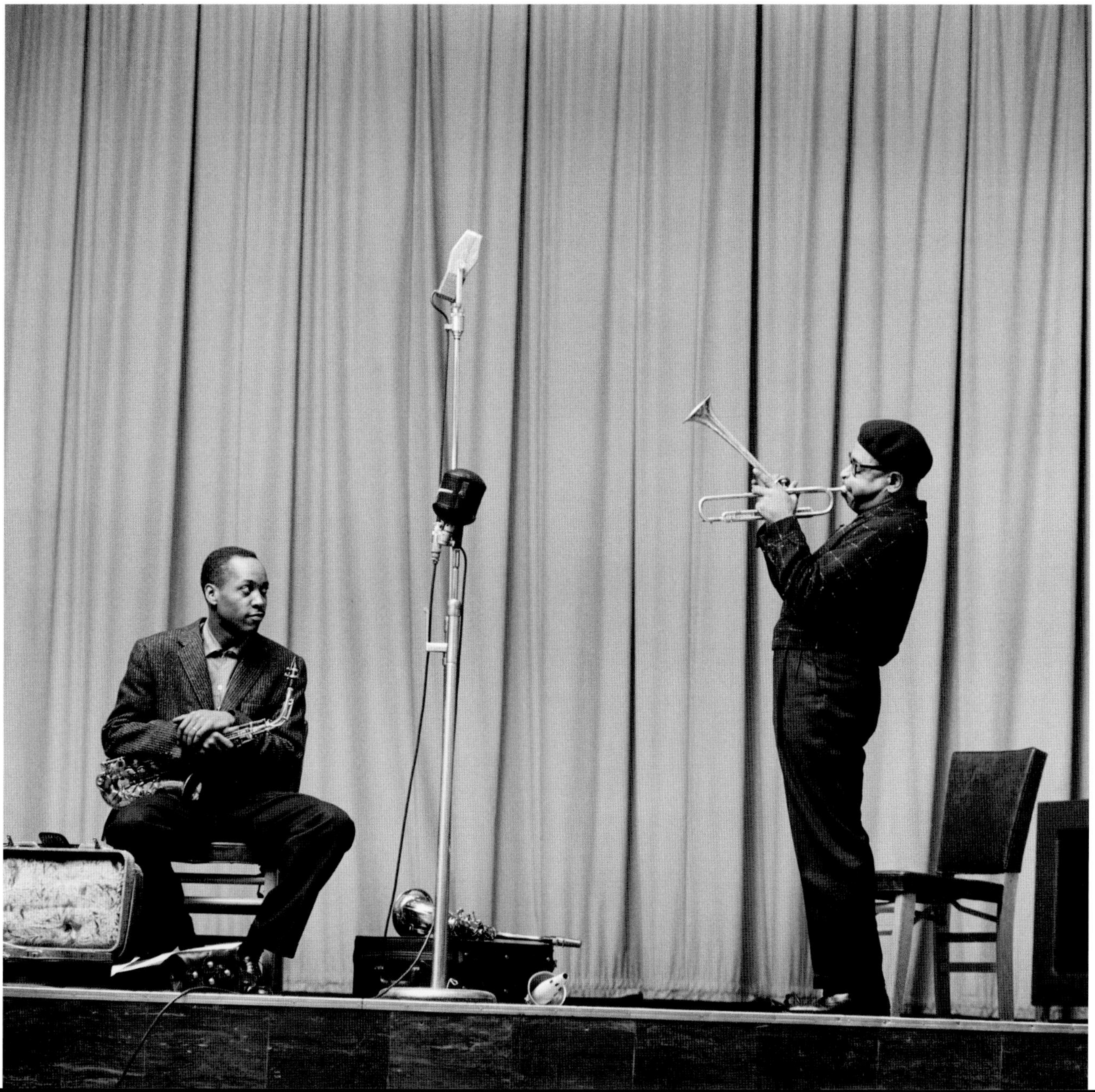

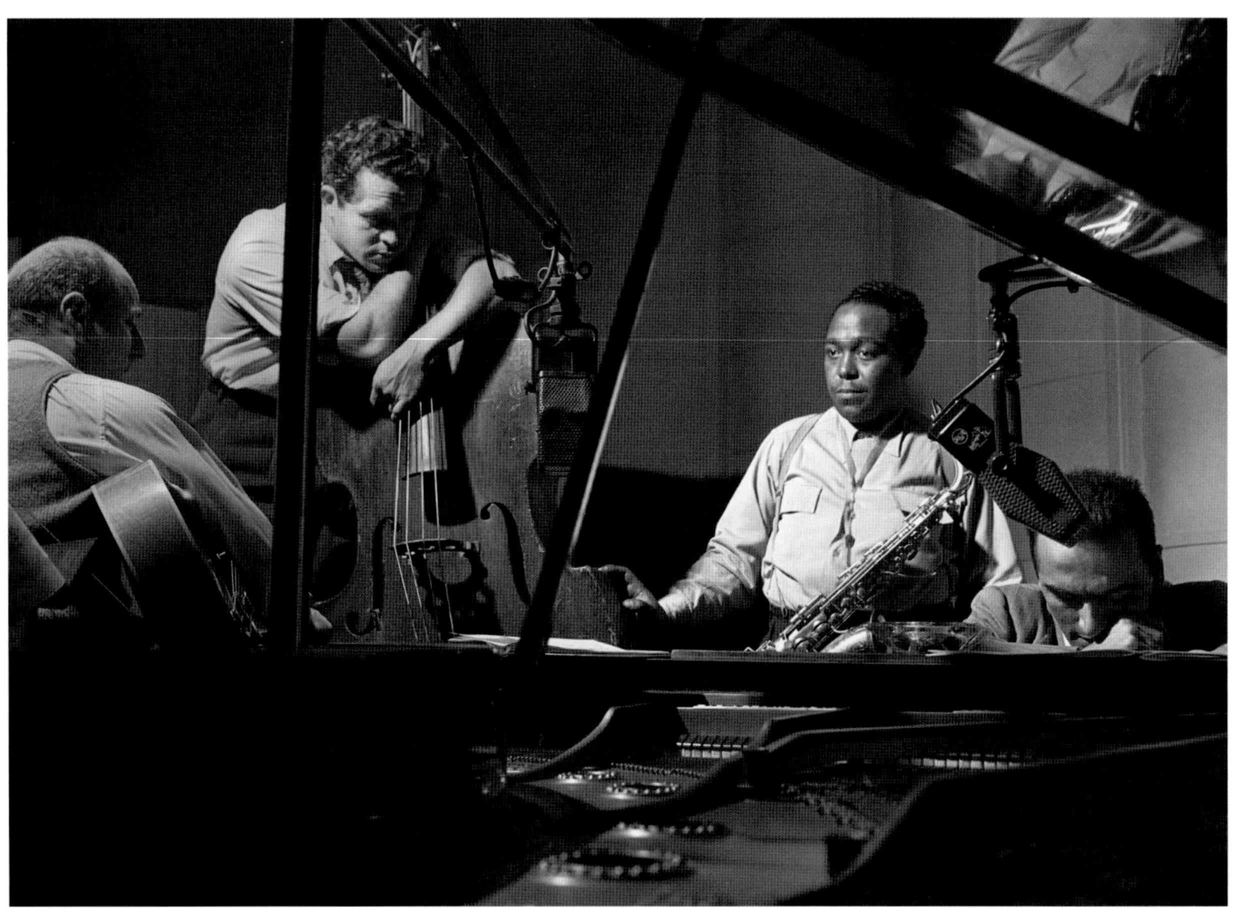

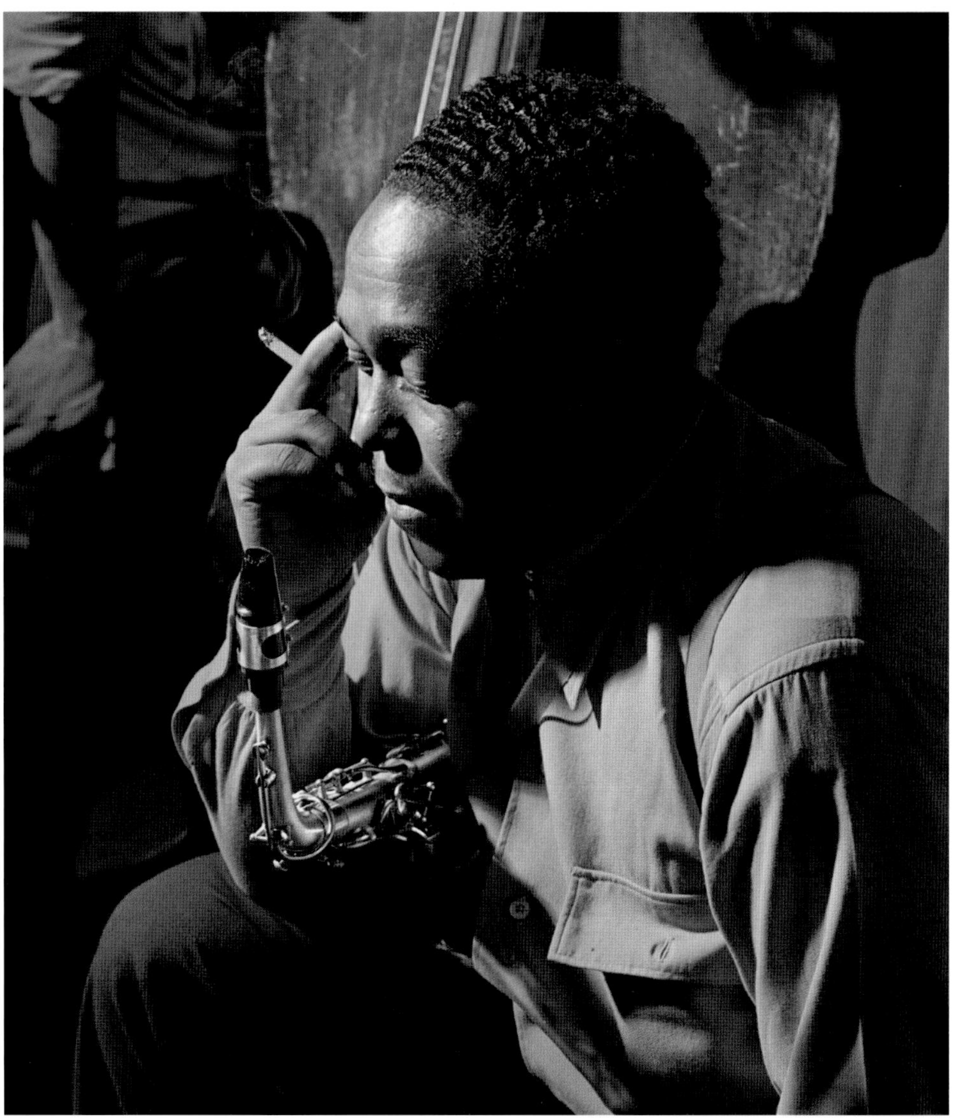

The Metronome All Stars (Eddie Safranski, Billy Bauer, Charlie 'Bird' Parker, Lennie Tristano), NYC, 1949

Charlie 'Bird' Parker, NYC, 1949

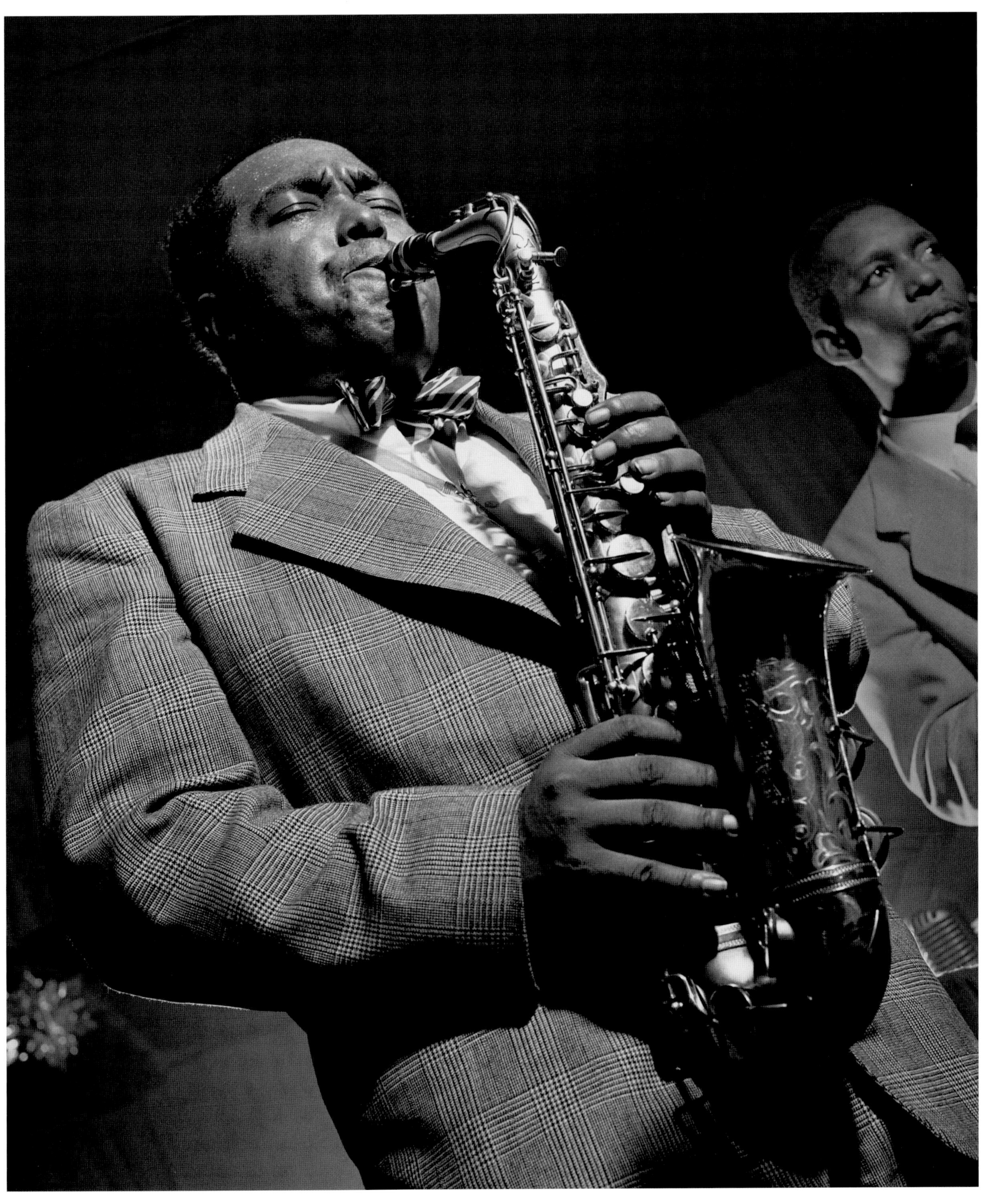

Charlie 'Bird' Parker, Birdland, NYC, 1949

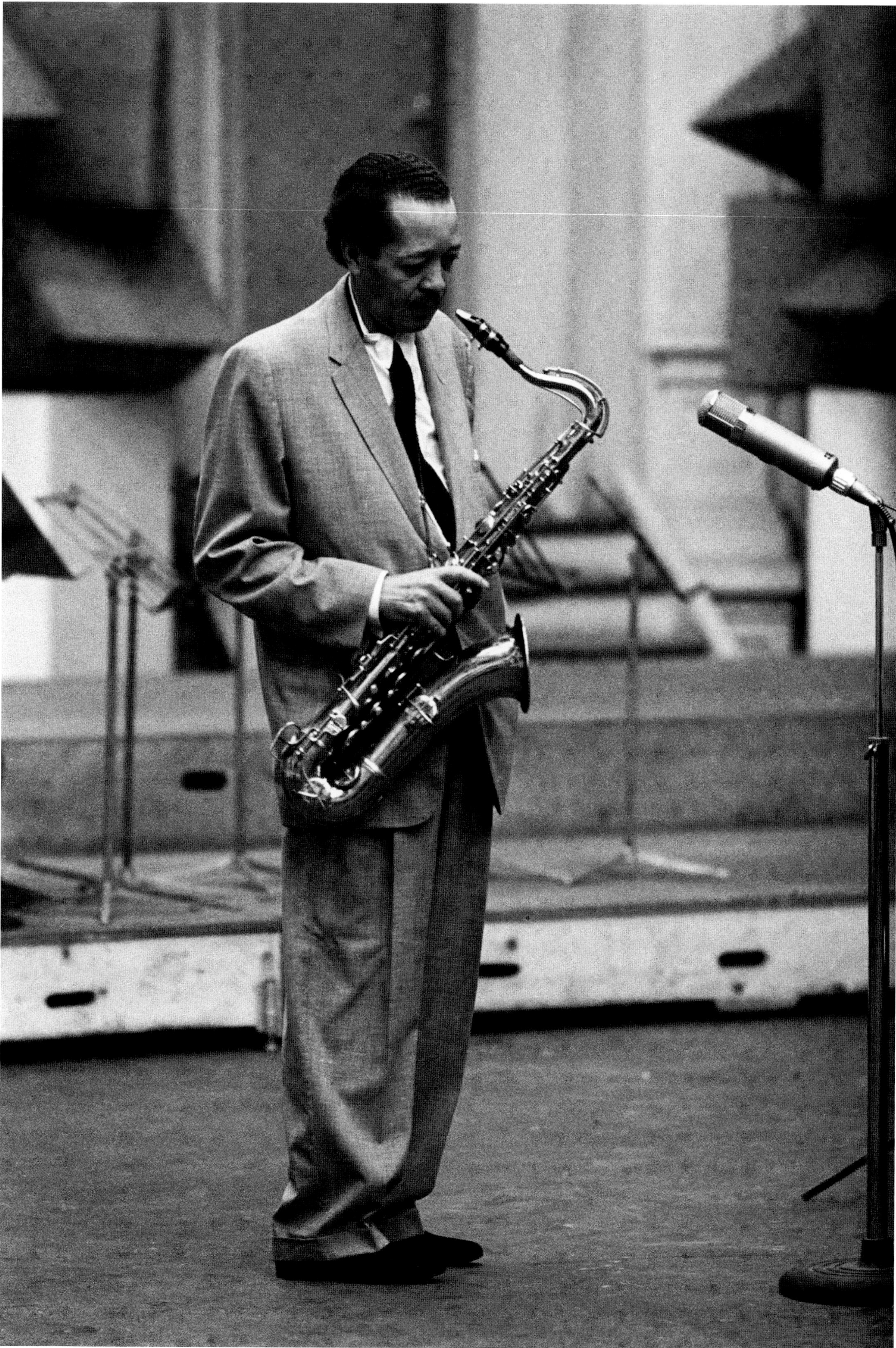

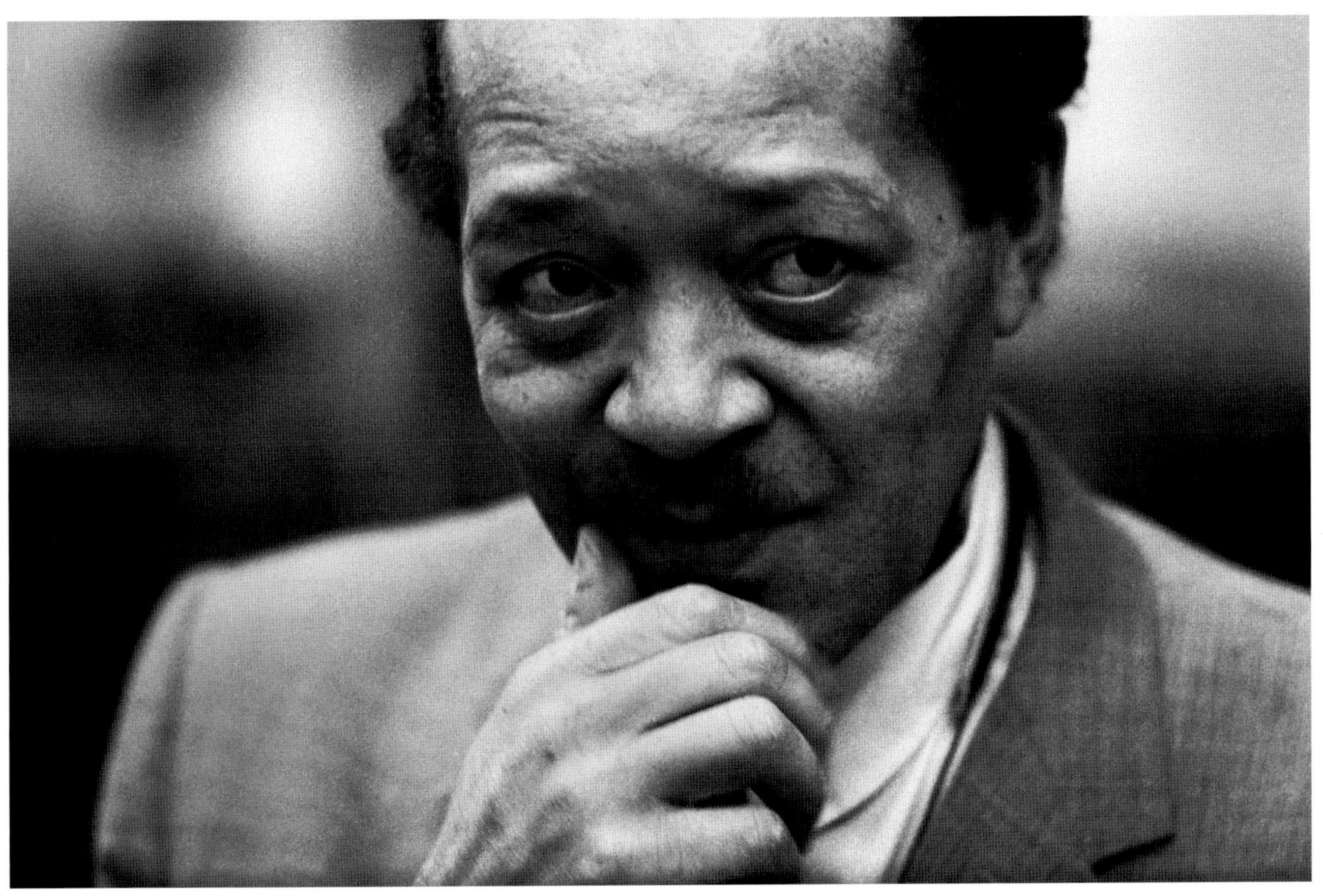

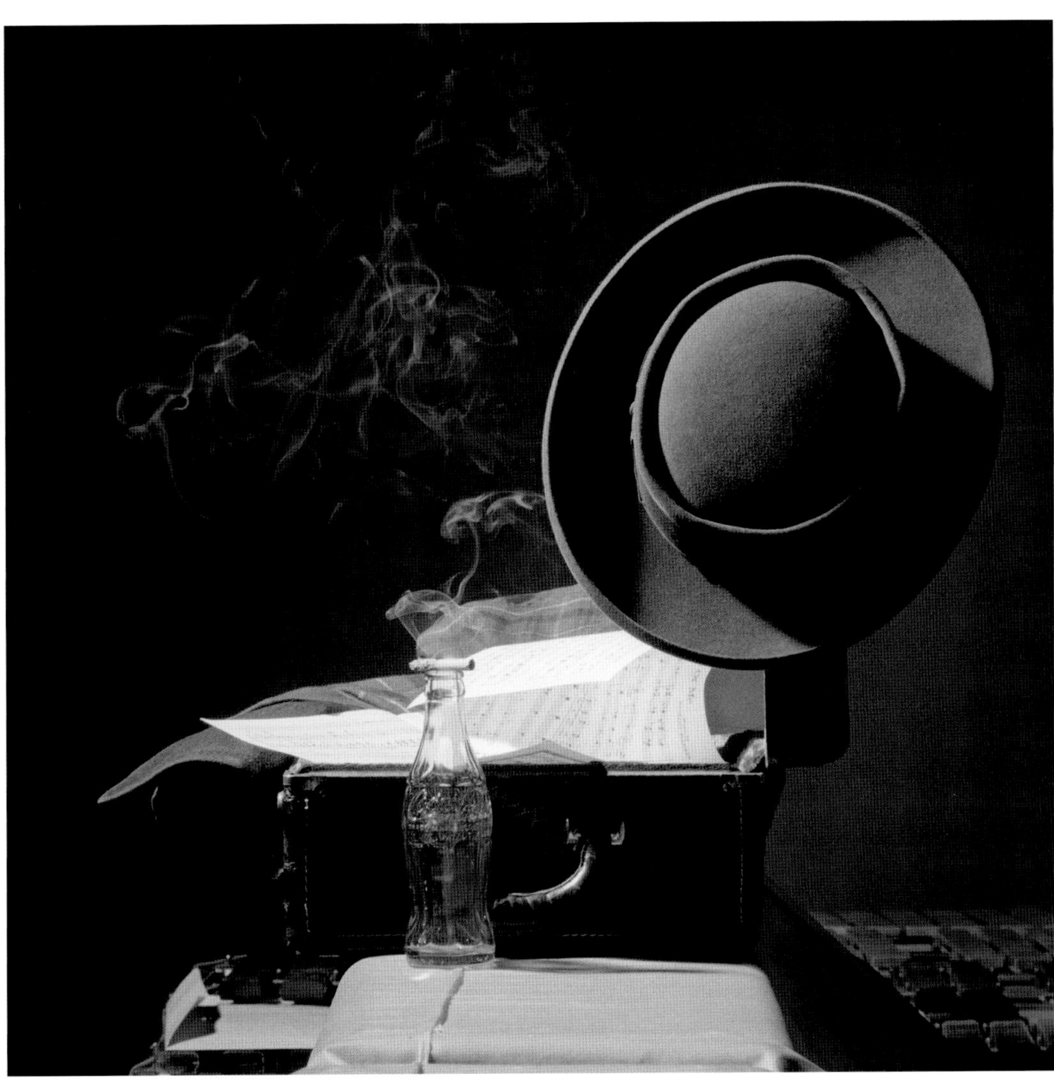

Lester 'Prez' Young, Paris, 1958

Lester 'Prez' Young, Paris, 1958

Lester Young still life, NYC, 1948

Dexter Gordon, Royal Roost, NYC, 1948

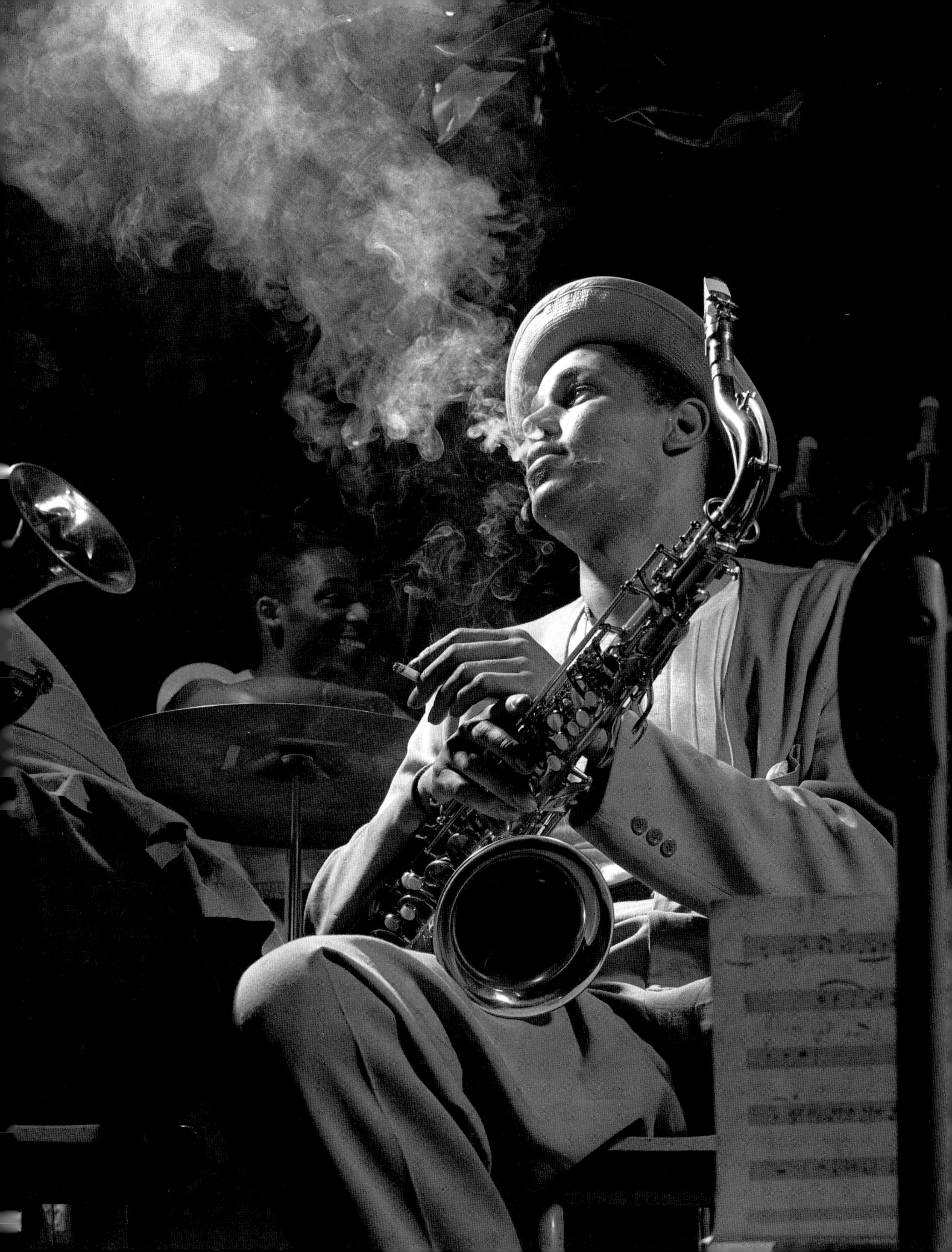

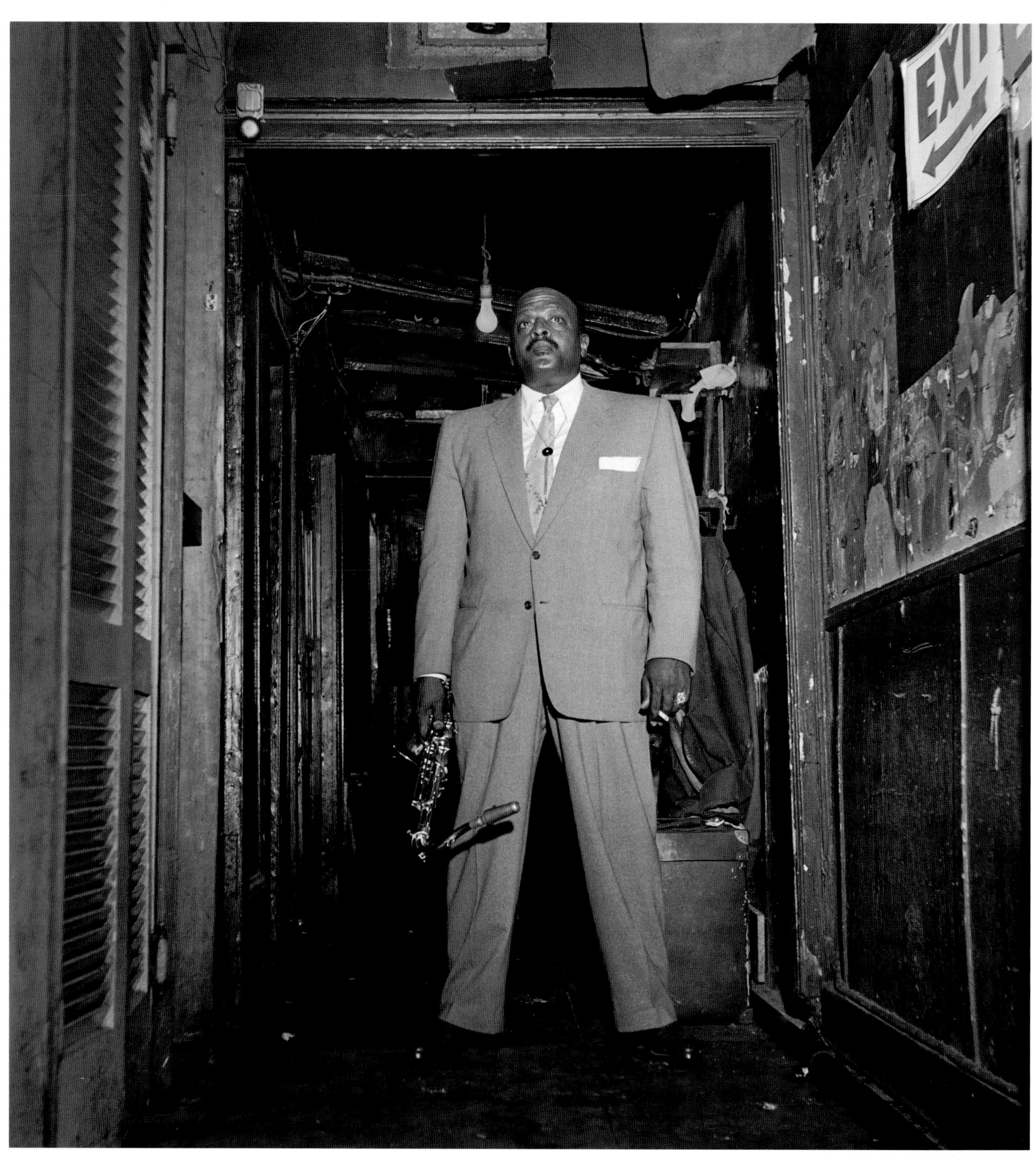

Ben Webster, Birdland, NYC, 1950

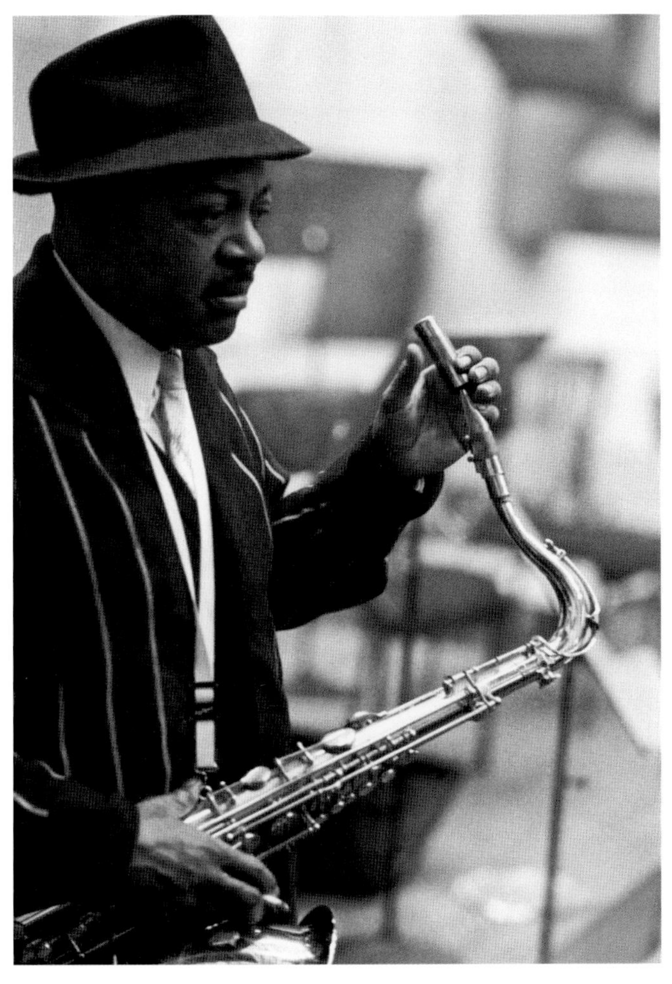

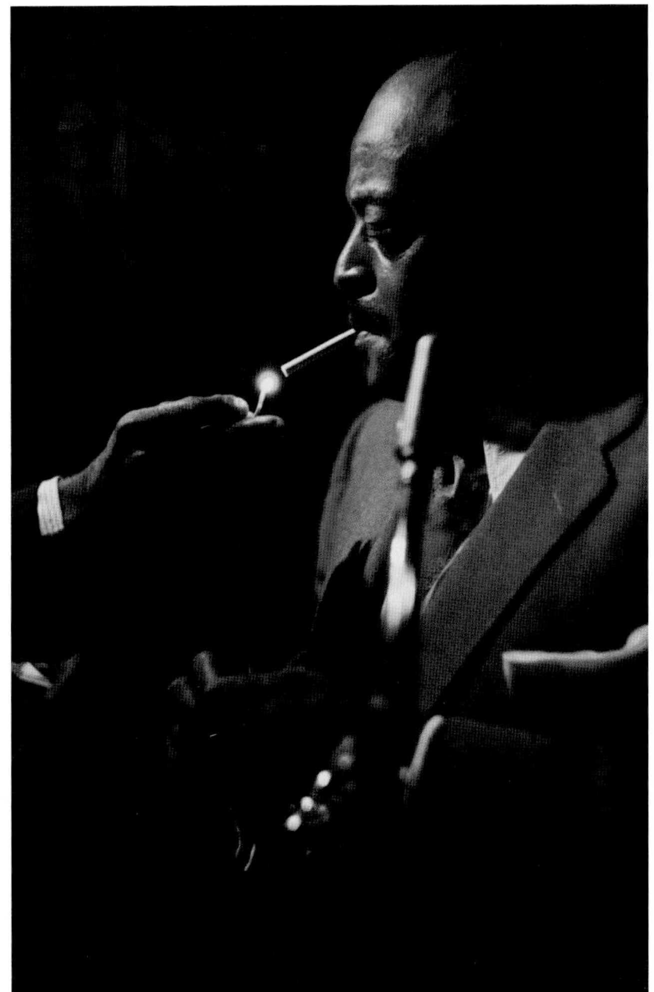

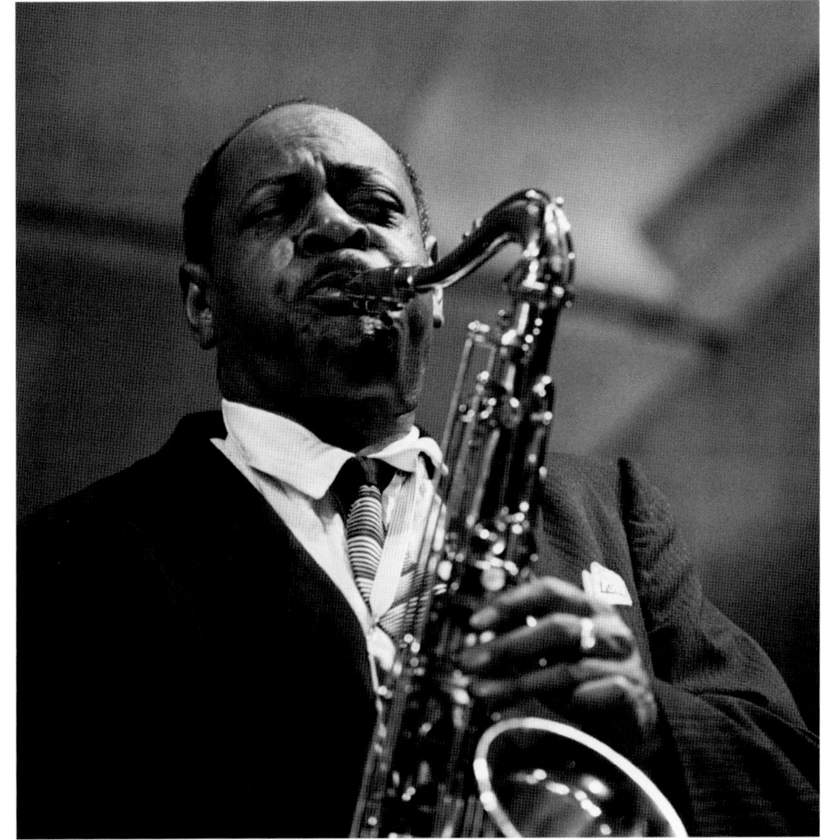

Coleman Hawkins, Paris, 1958

Ben Webster, Birdland, NYC, 1950

Coleman Hawkins, Newport, 1955

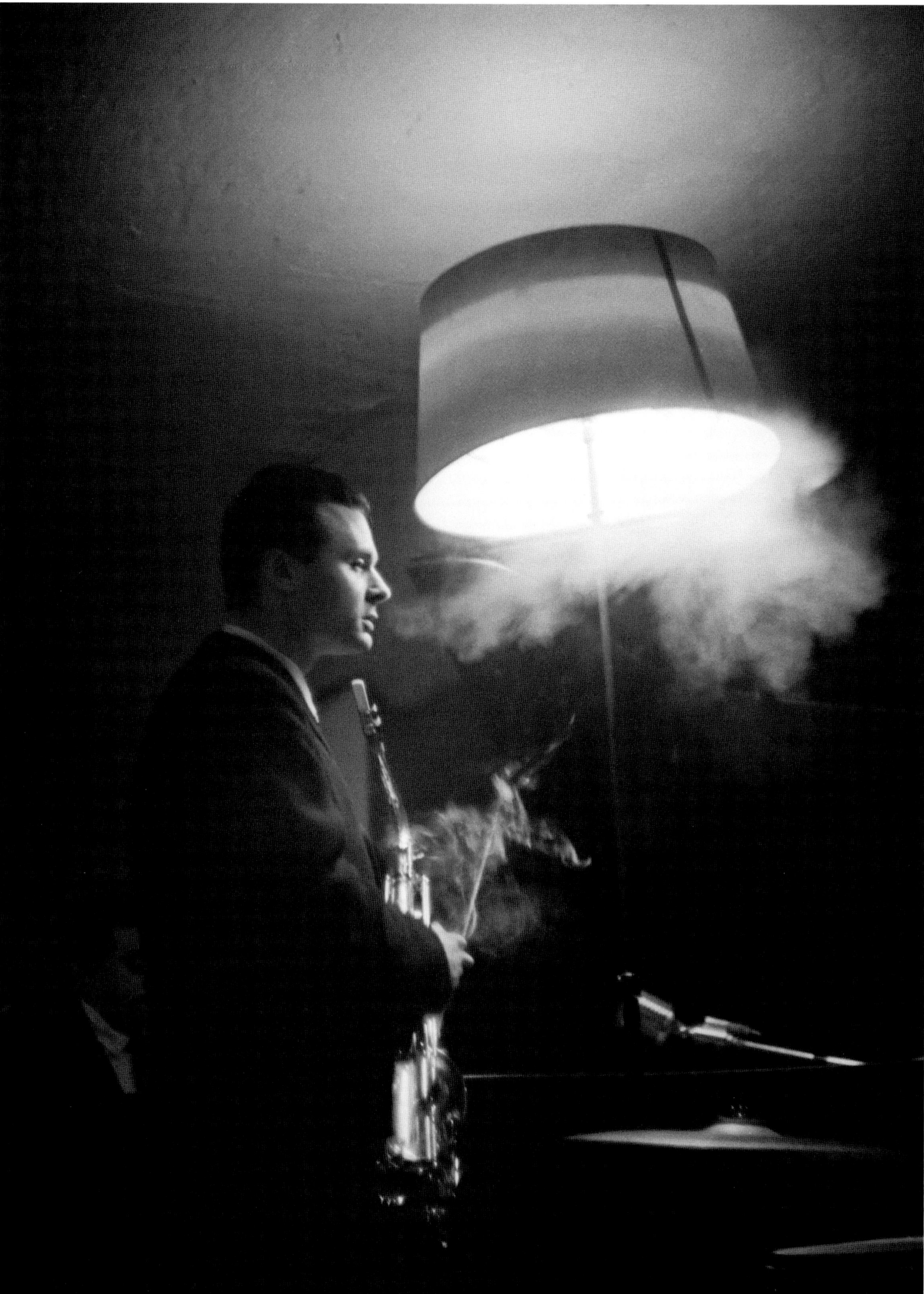

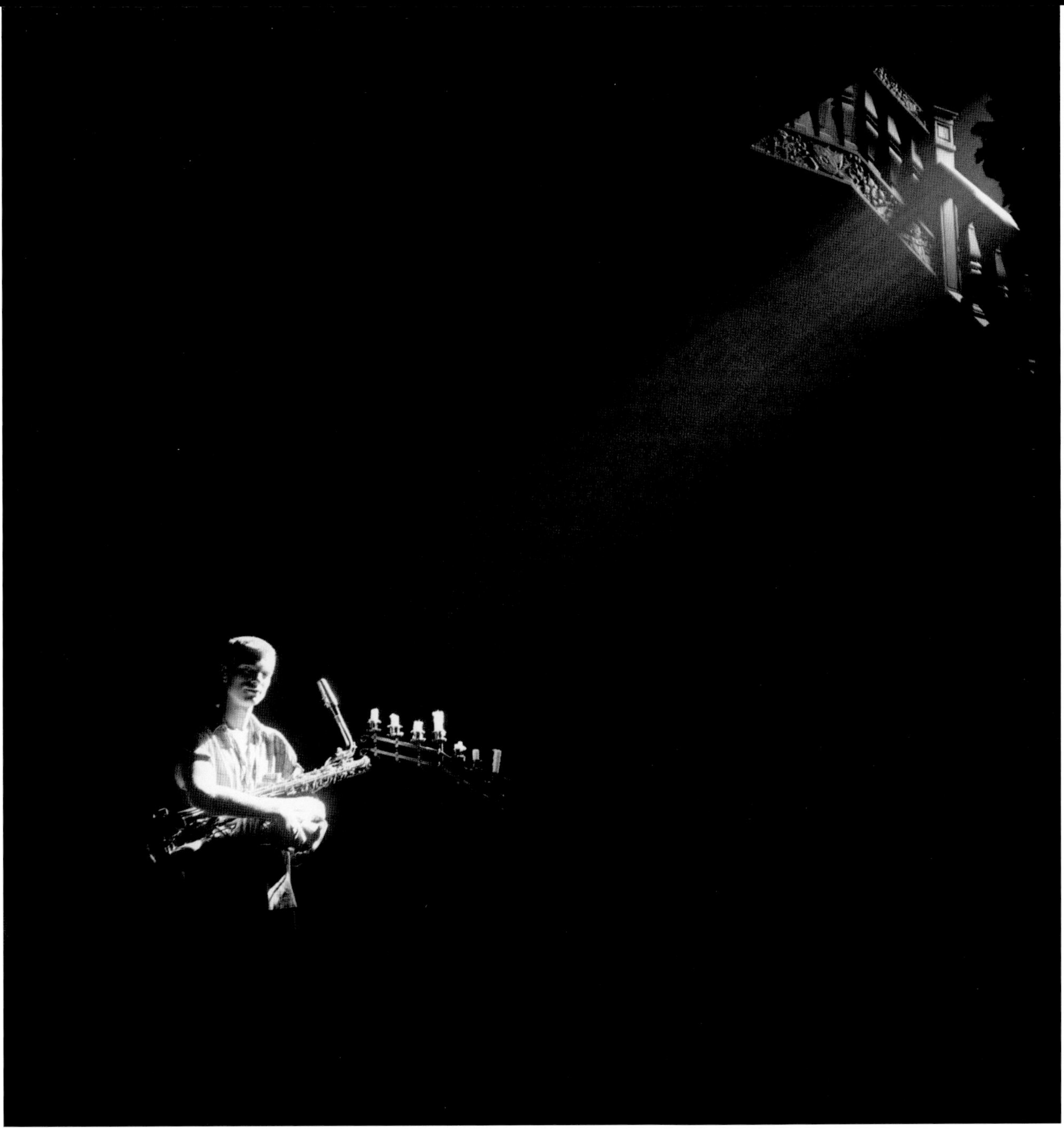

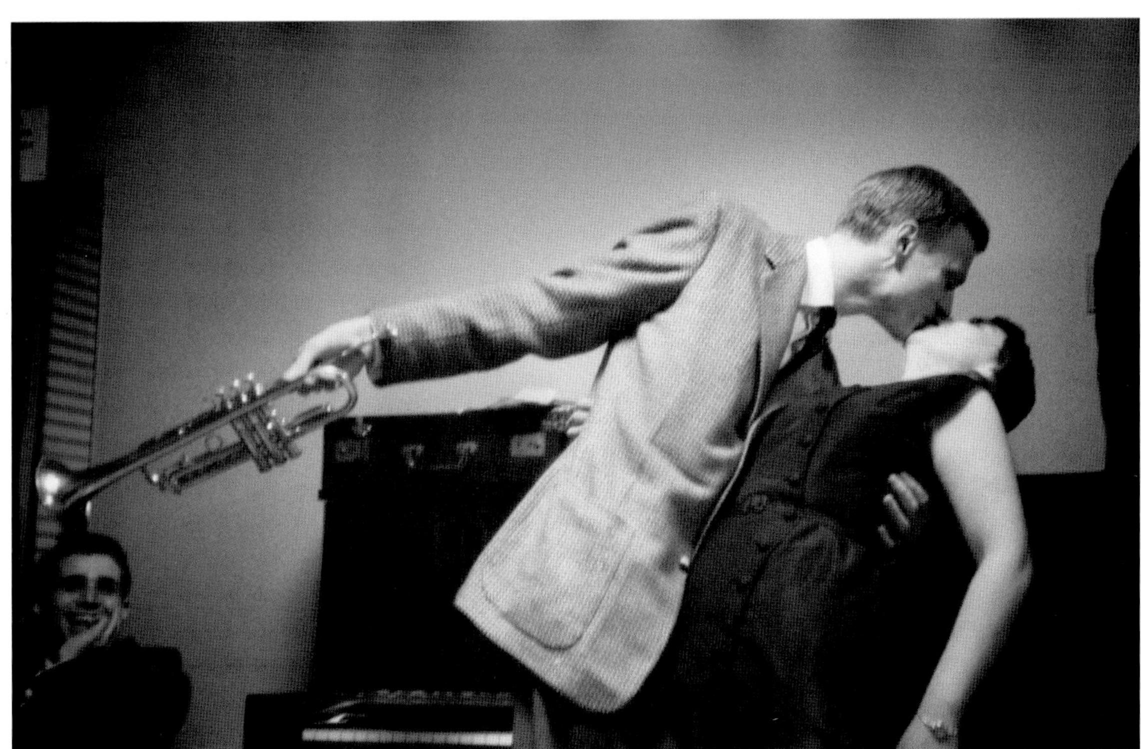

Stan Getz, Club St Germain, Paris, 1960

Gerry Mulligan, Newport, 1955

Gerry Mulligan, Carnegie Hall, NYC, 1953

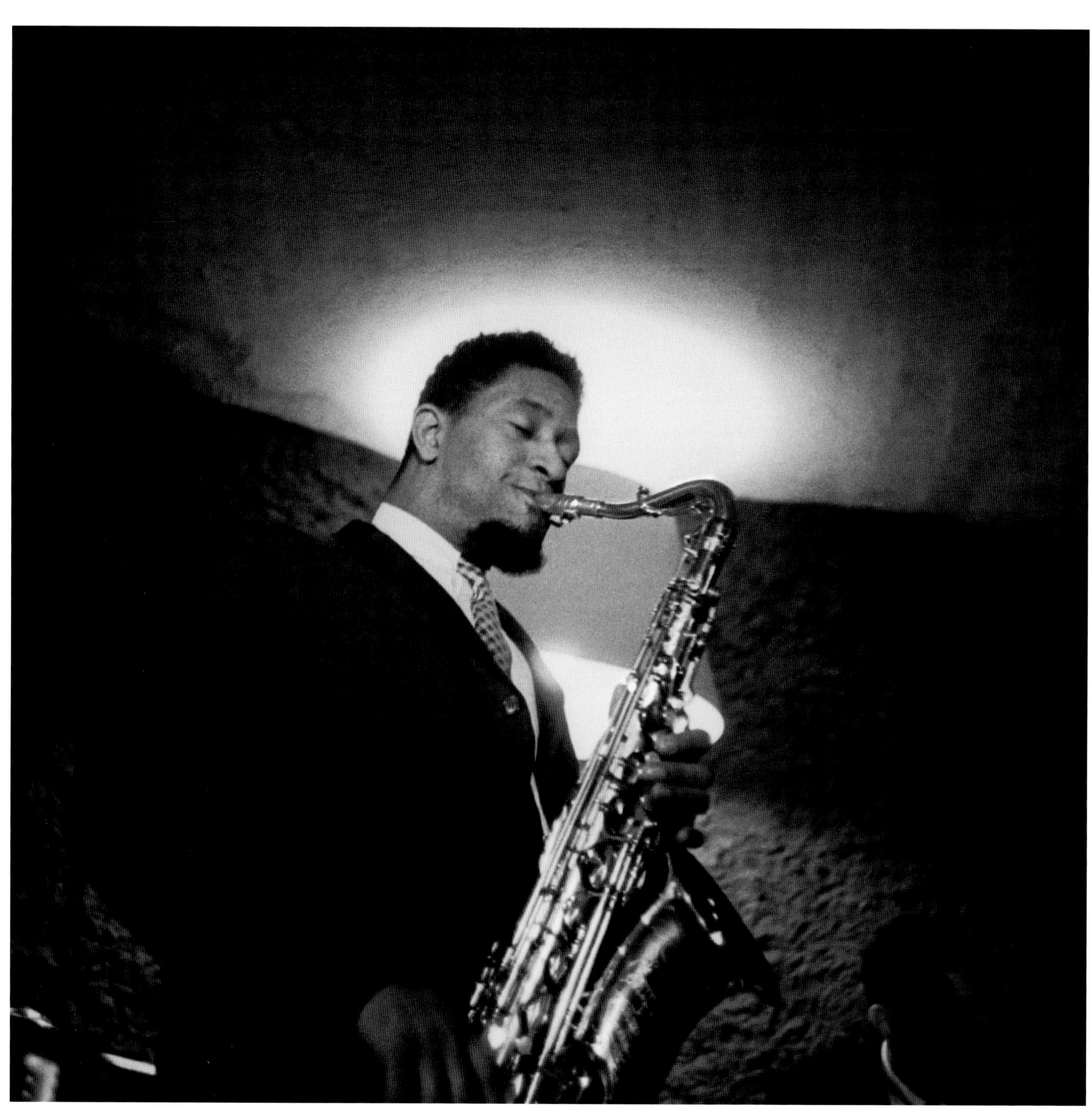

Sonny Rollins, Club St Germain, Paris, 1960

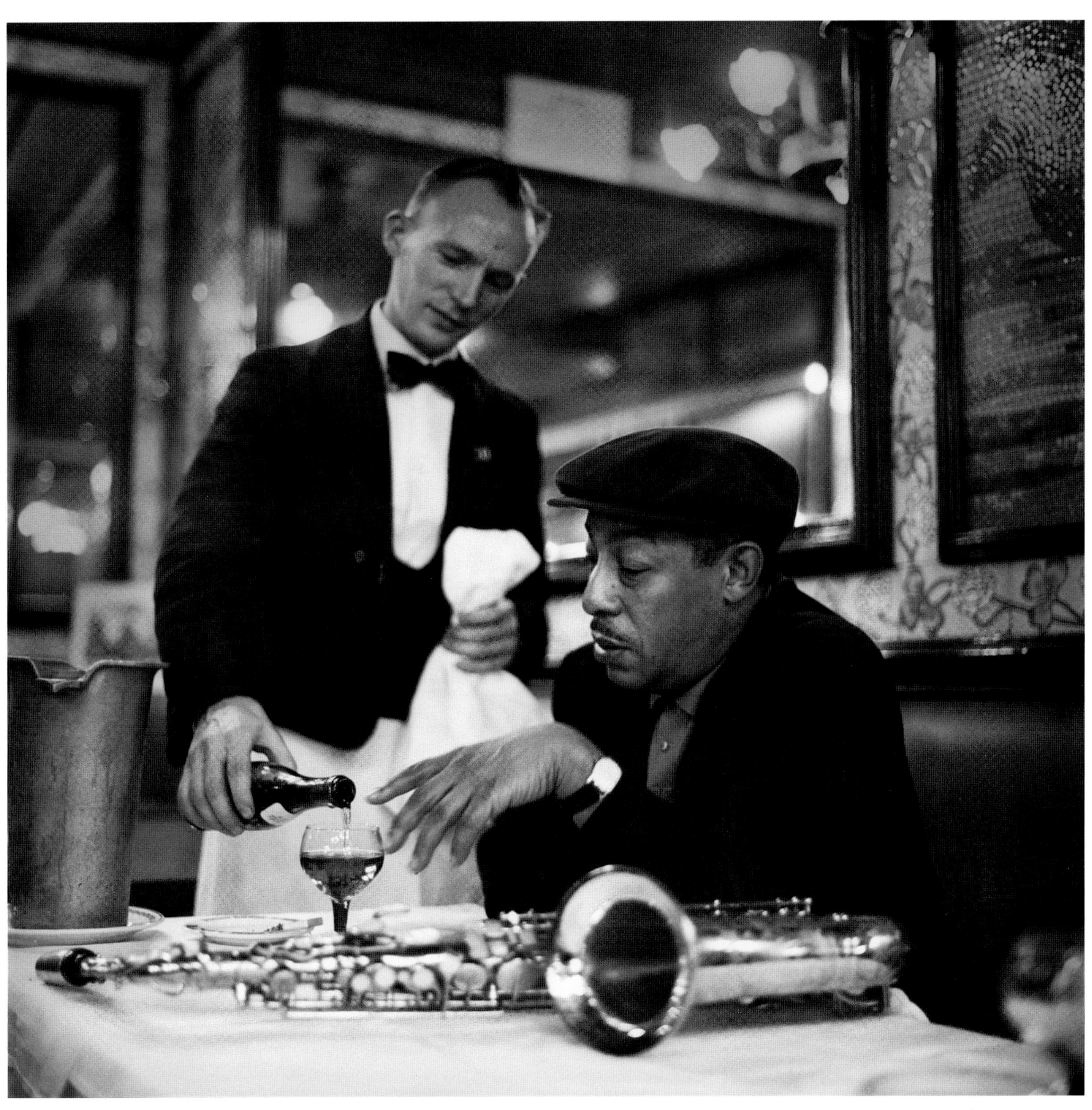

Johnny Hodges, Brasserie Lipp, Paris, 1958

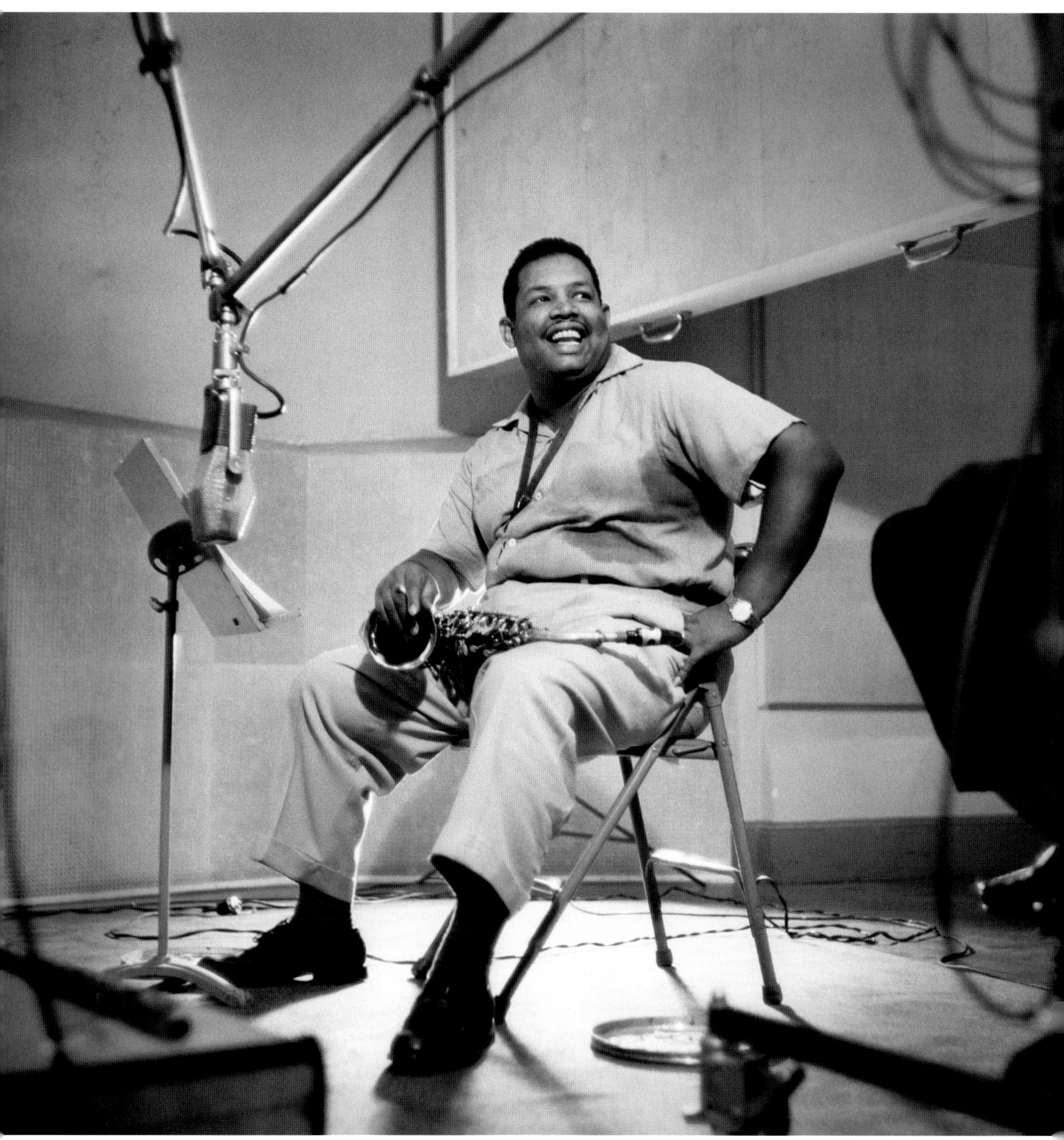

'Cannonball' Adderley, NYC, 1956

Jimmy Cleveland, Nat Adderley, 'Cannonball' Adderley, Bobby Shad, Quincy Jones, Jerome Richardson and Cecil Payne, NYC, 1956

Nat Adderley and 'Cannonball' Adderley, Amsterdam, 1960

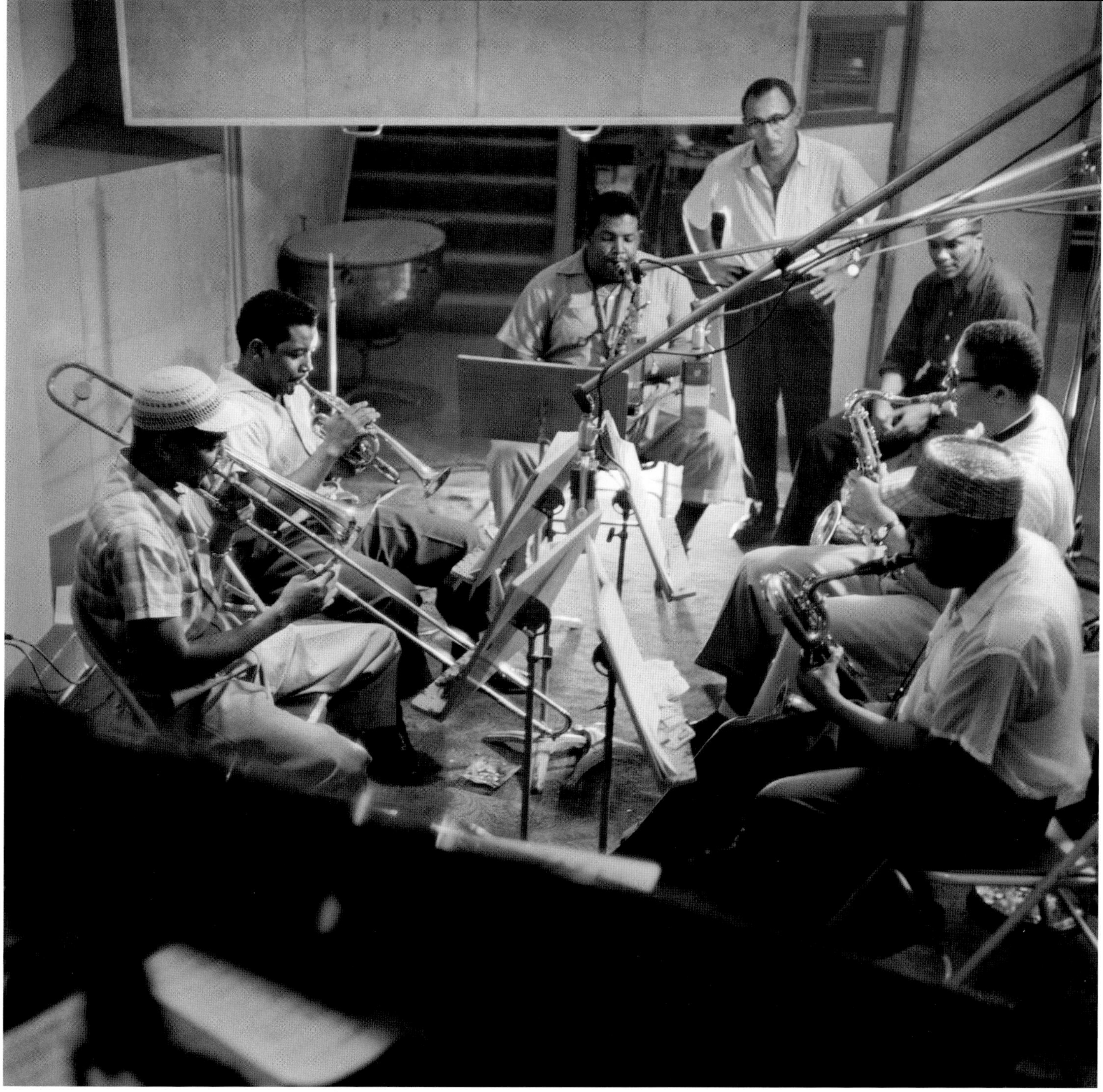

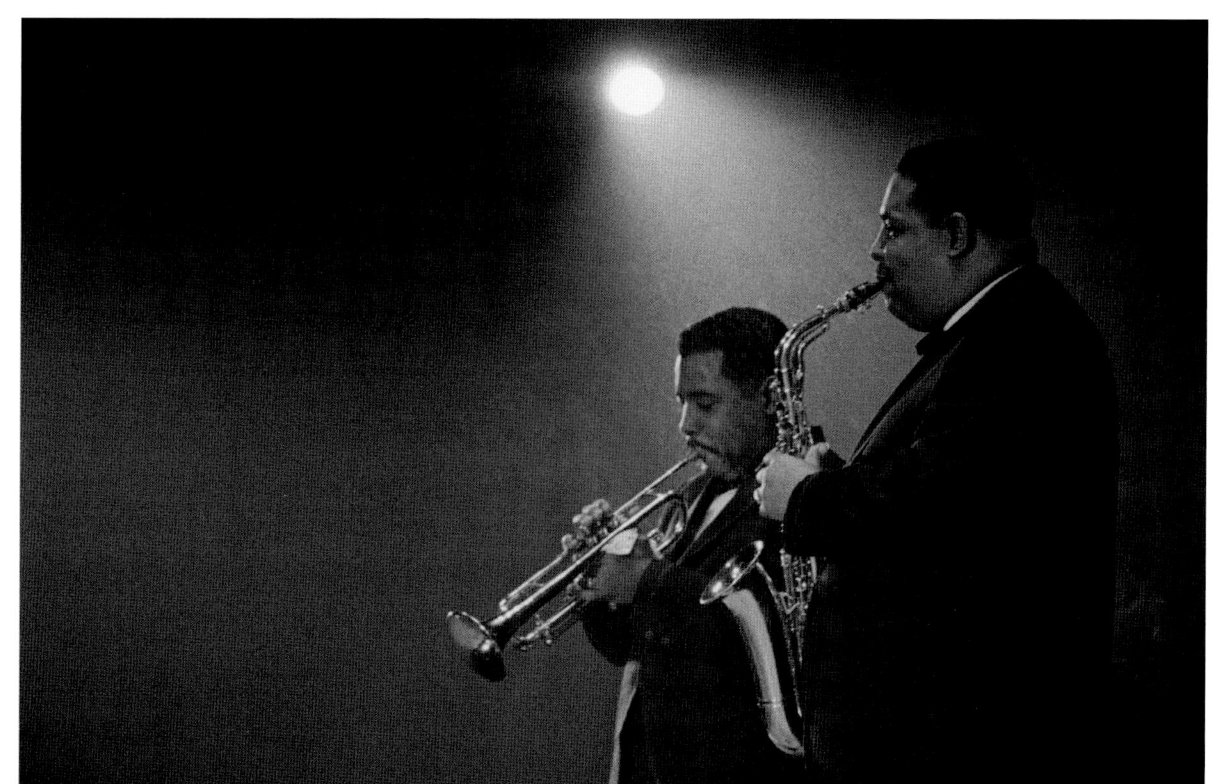

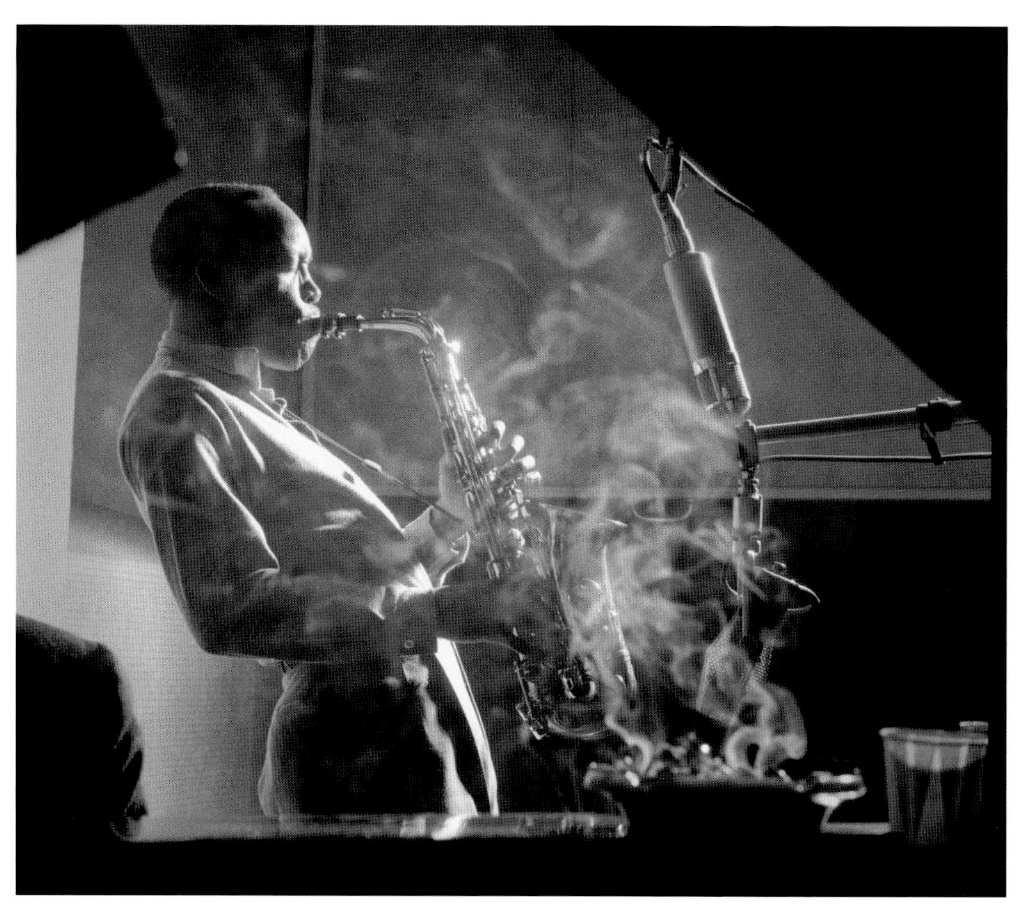

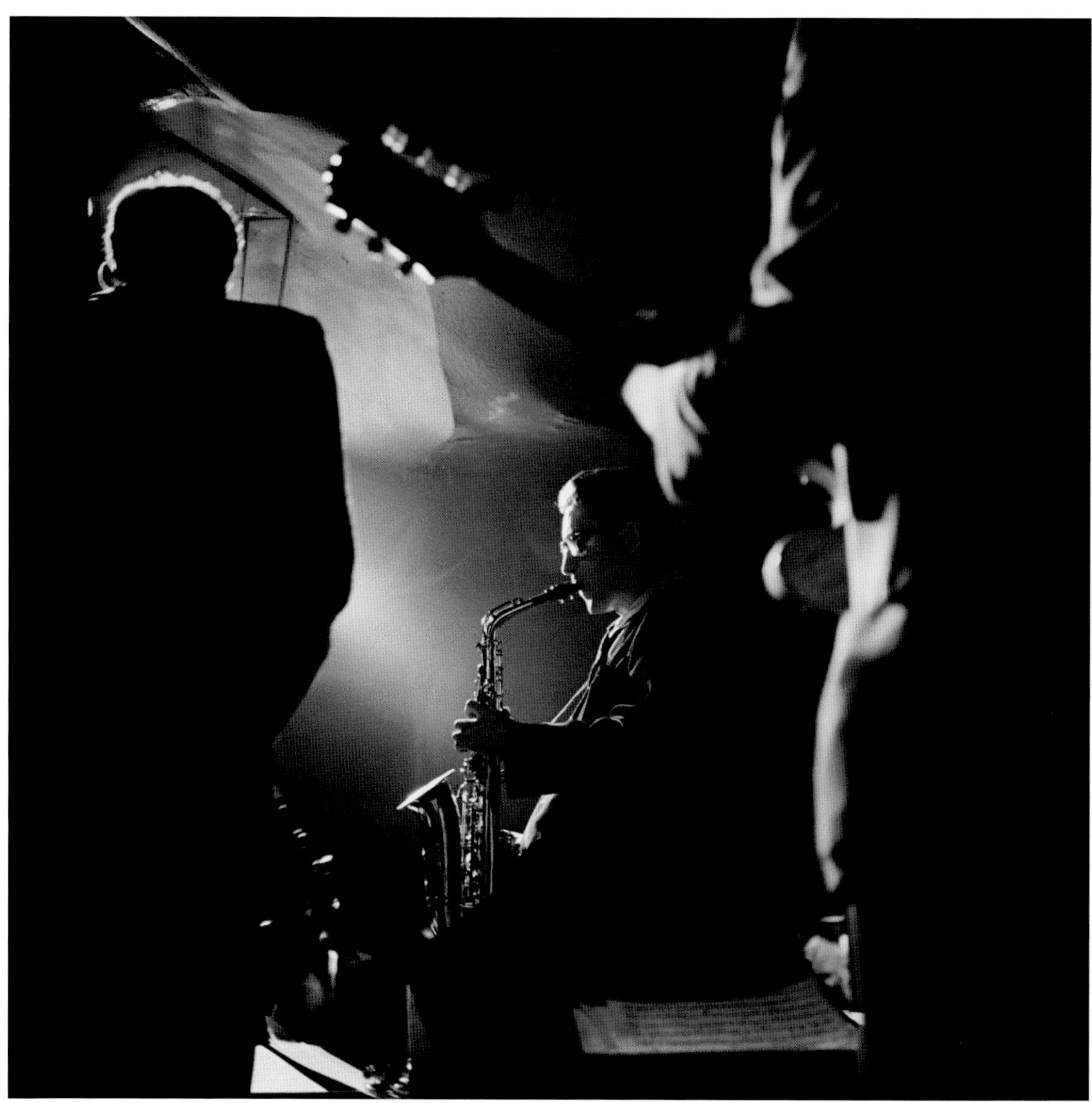

Sonny Stitt, NYC, 1953

Lee Konitz, Birdland, NYC, 1949

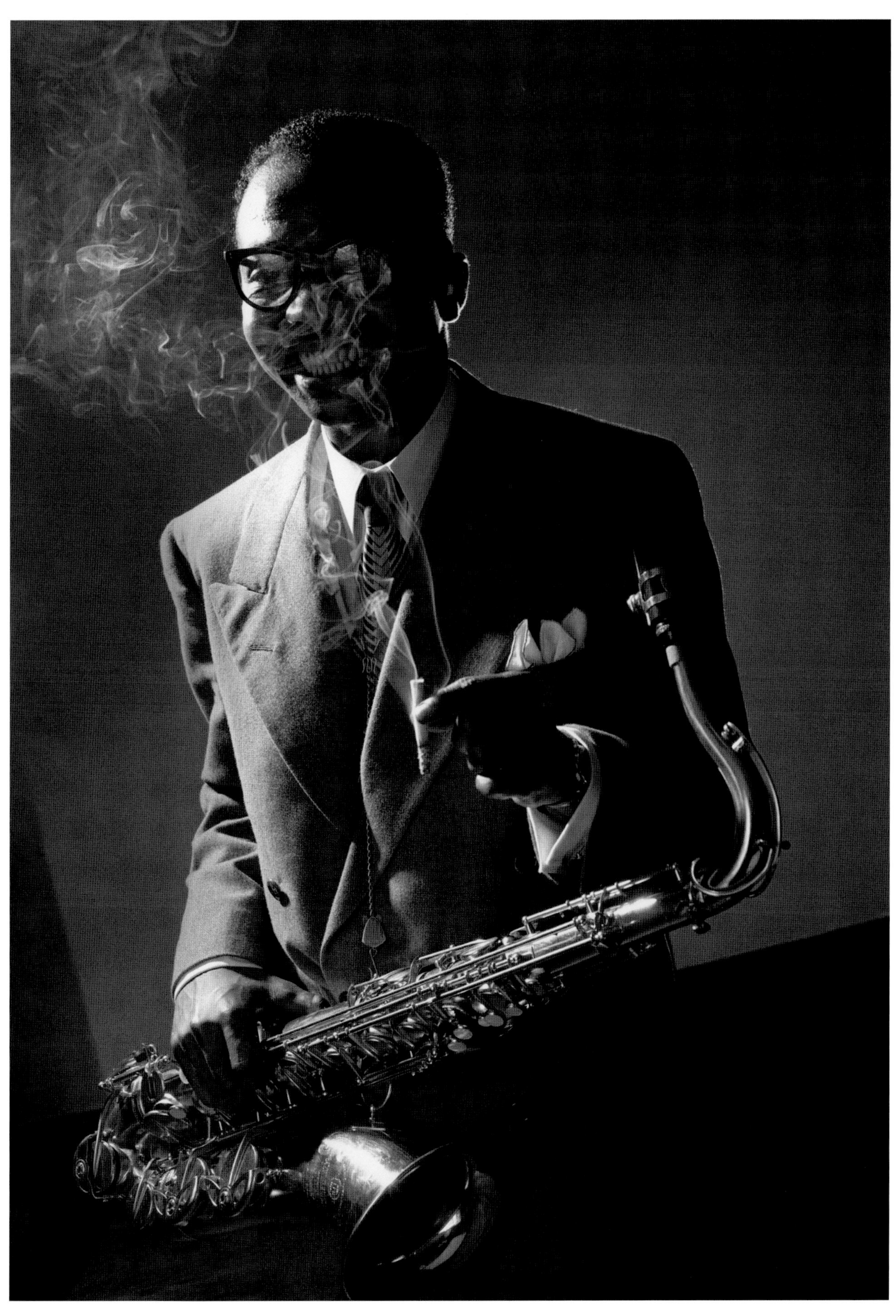

James Moody, Sullivan Street studio, NYC, 1951

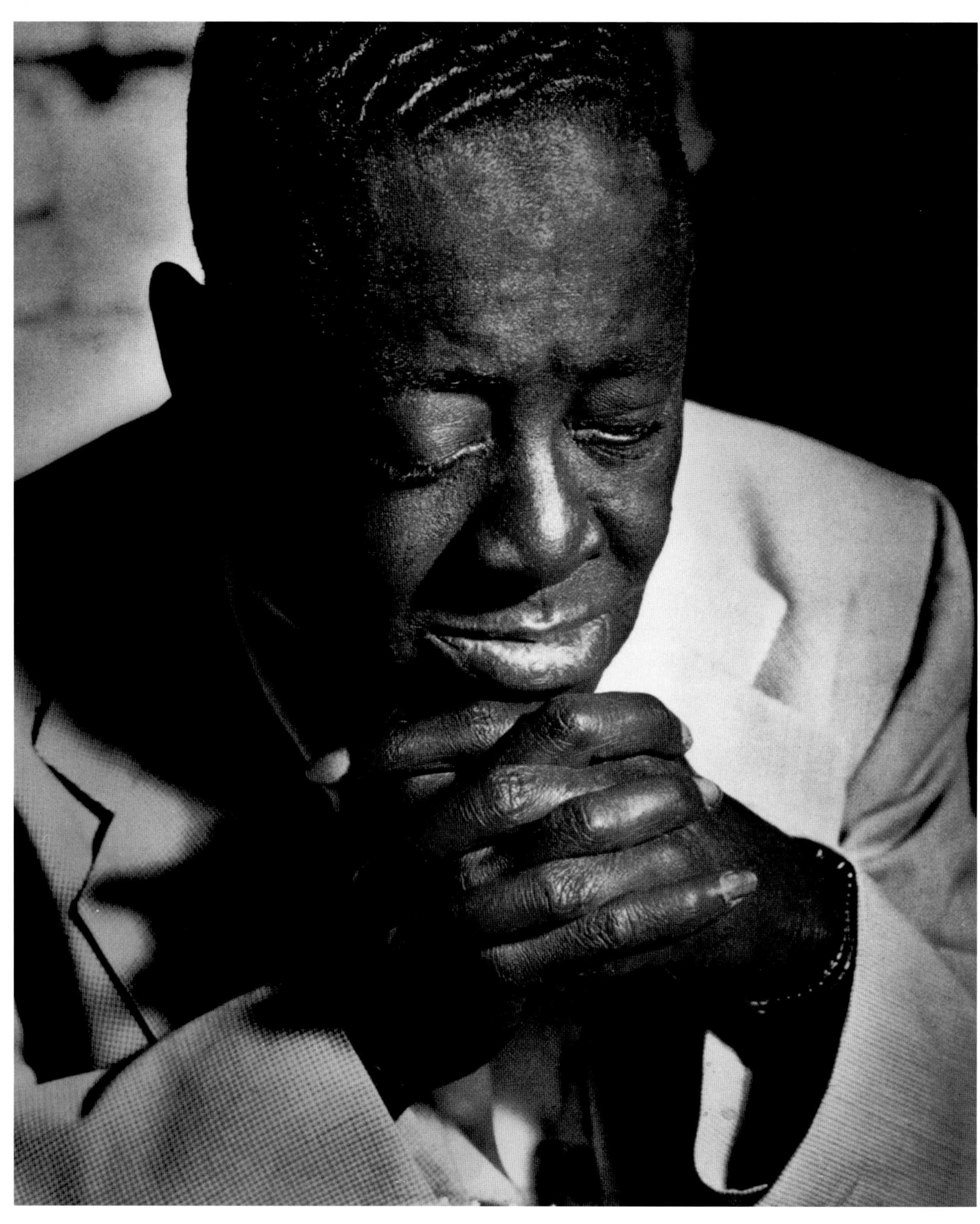

Art Tatum, Los Angeles, 1955

Bud Powell, Birdland, NYC, 1949

Earl 'Fatha' Hines, Carnegie Hall, NYC, 1953

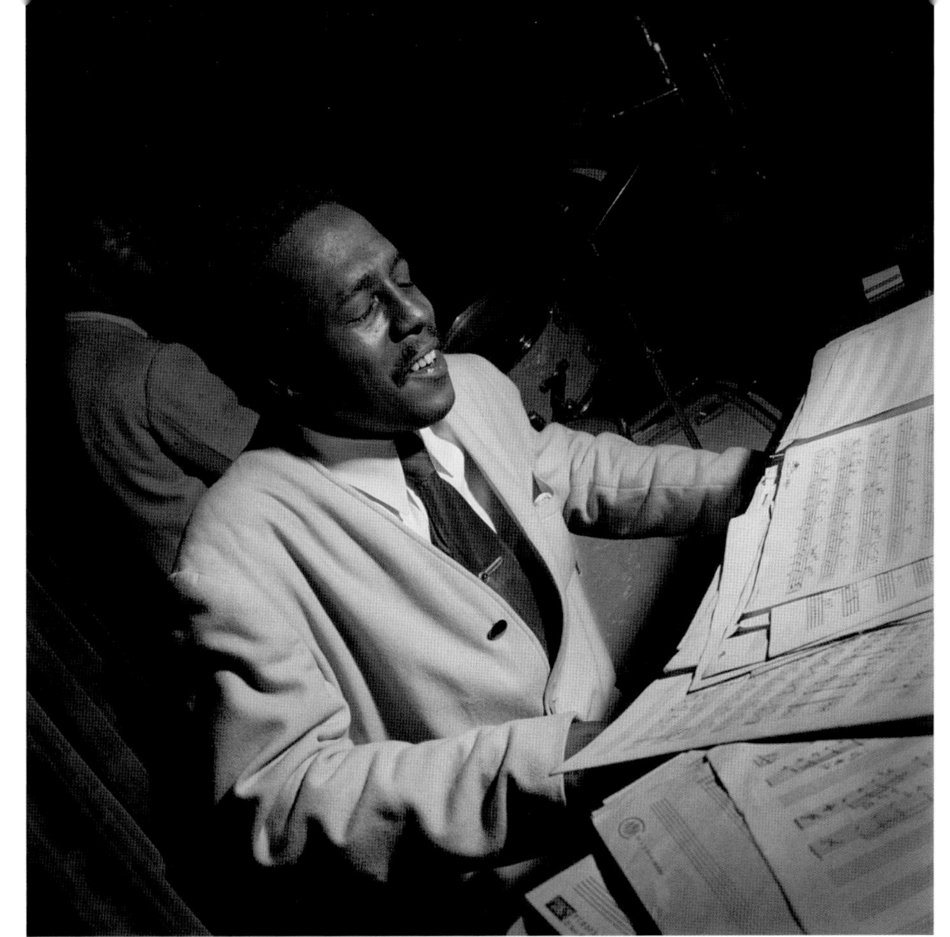

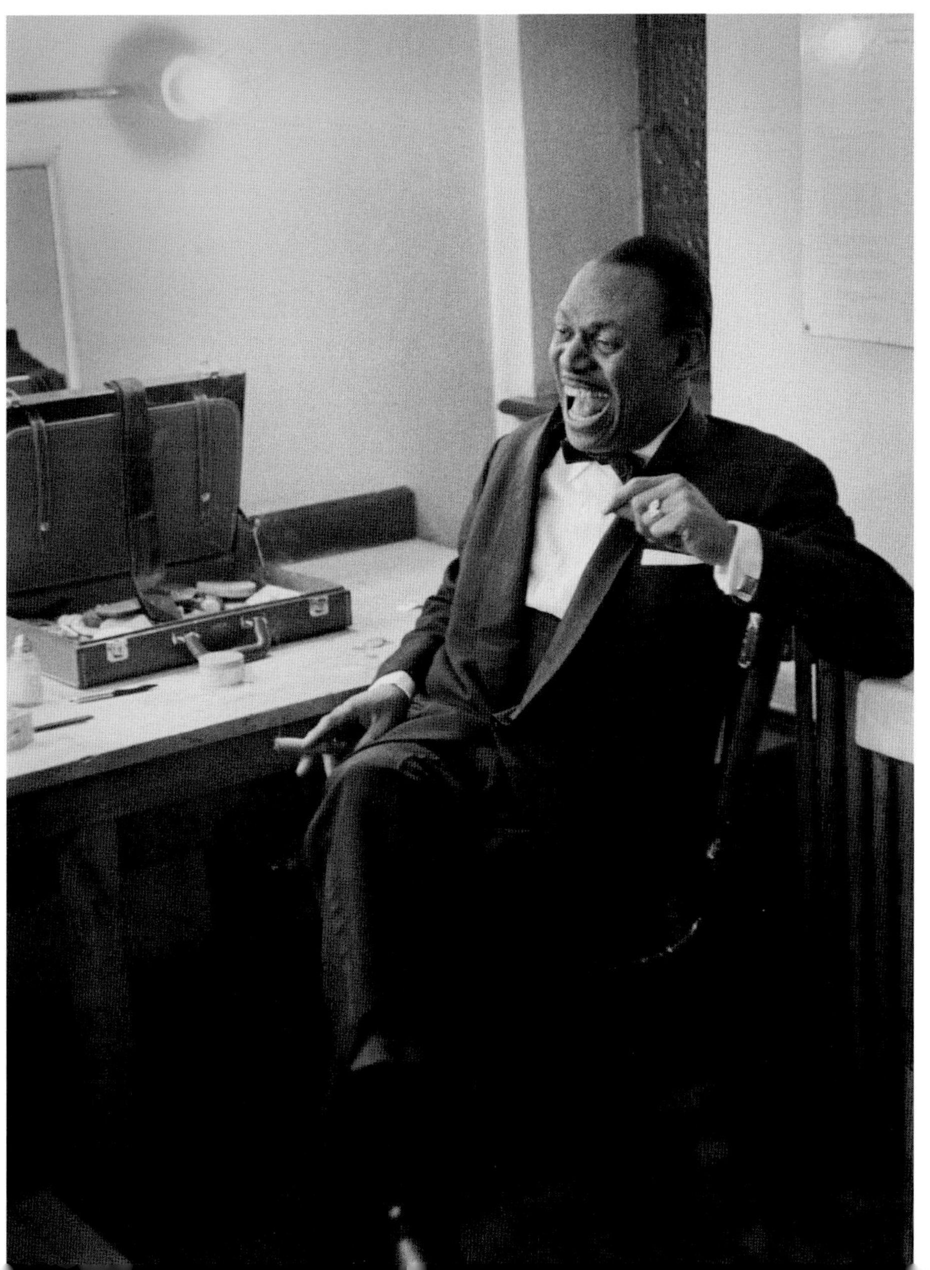

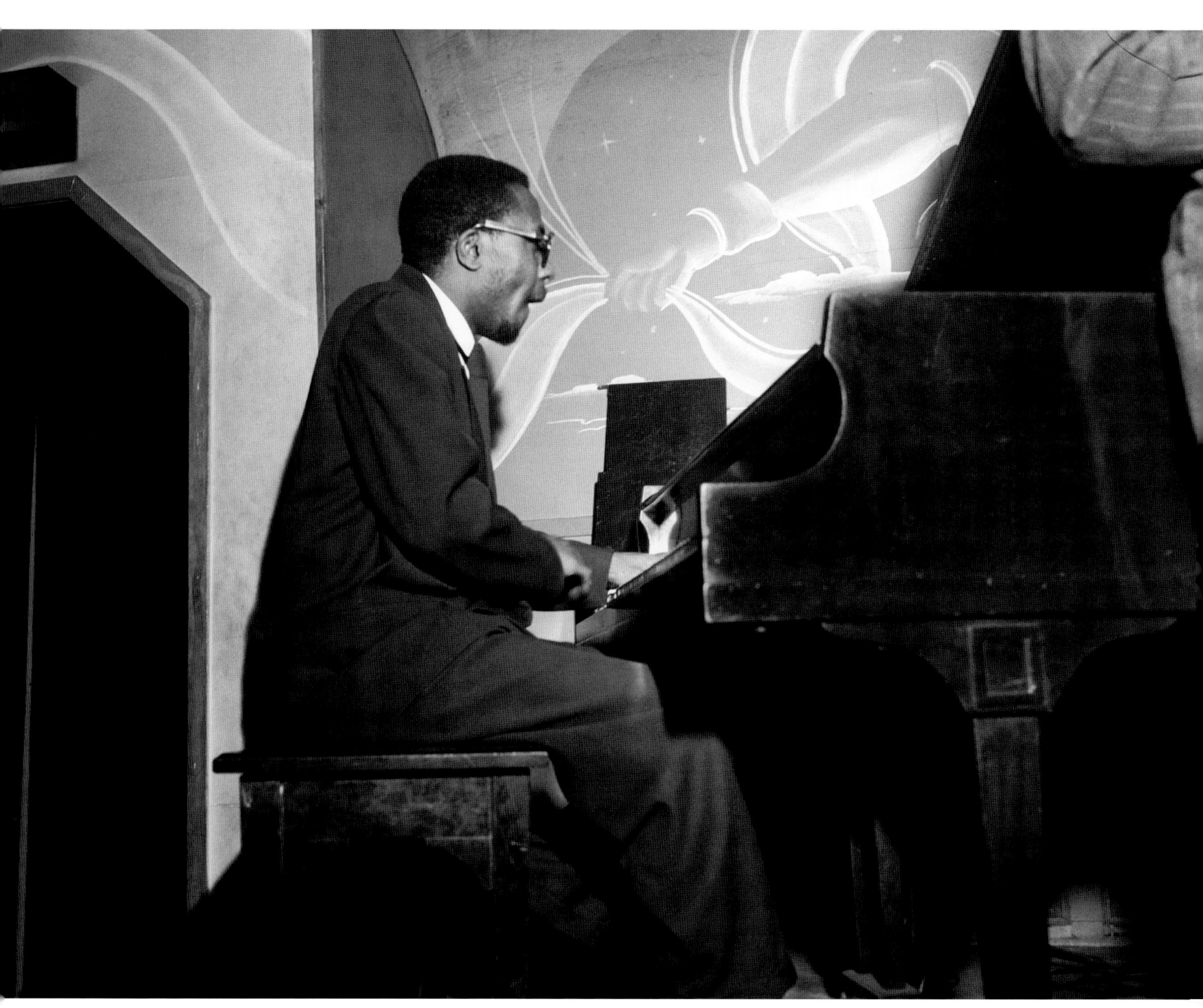

Thelonious Monk, Minton's Playhouse, NYC, 1949

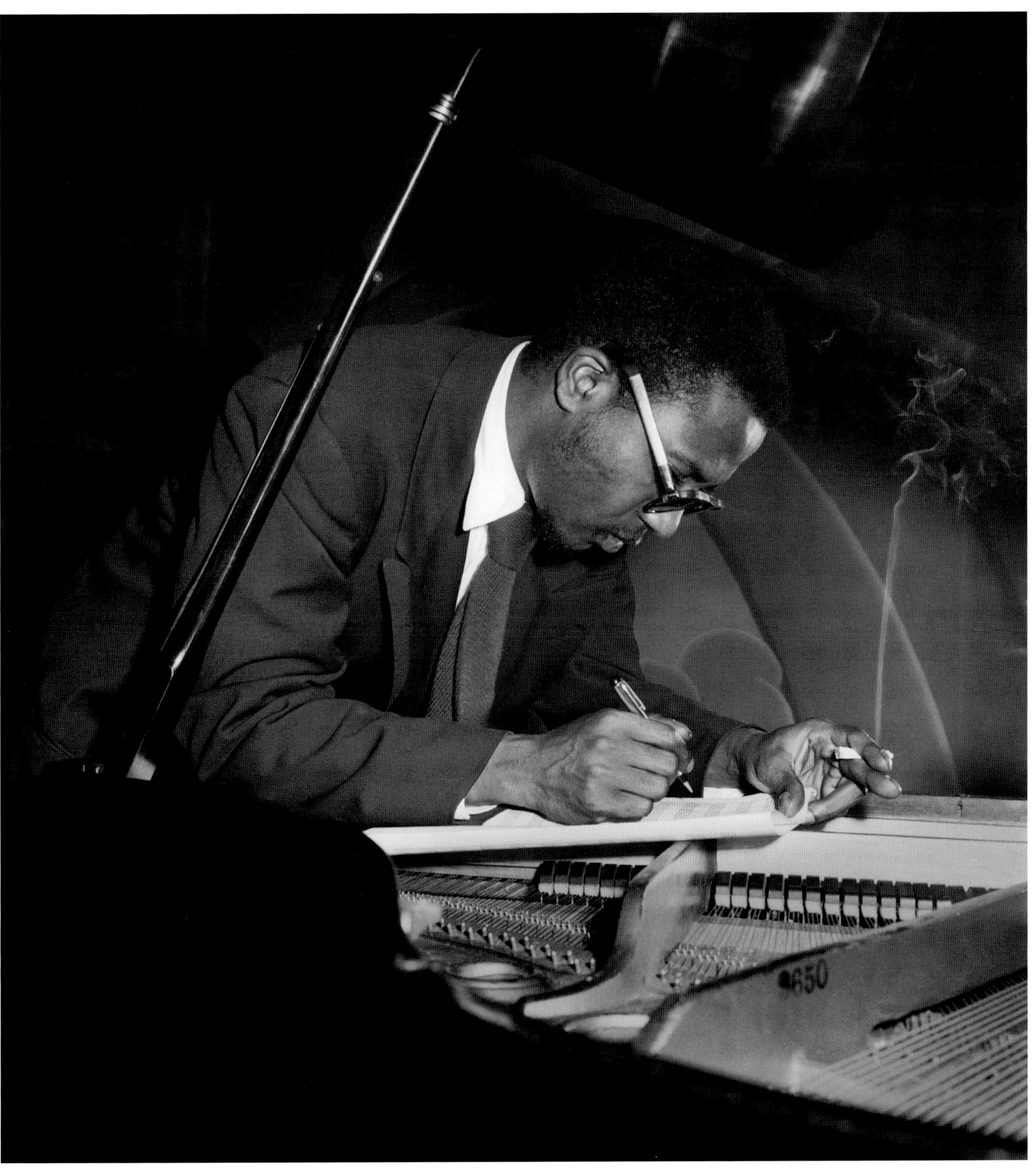

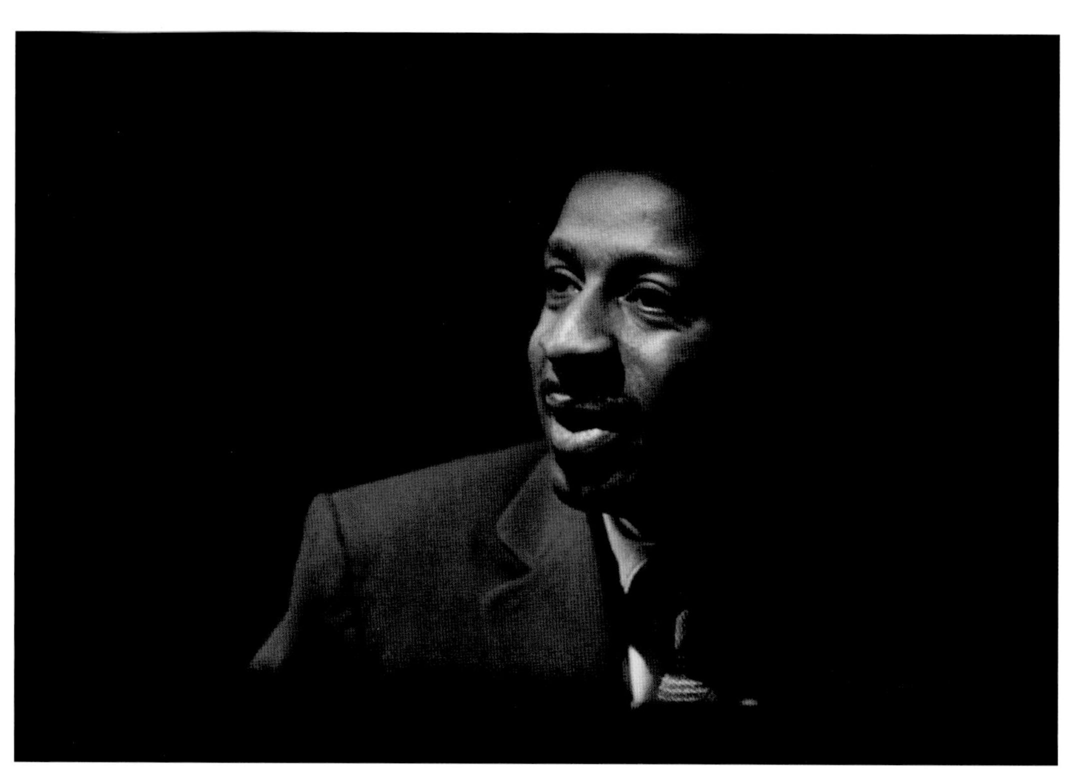

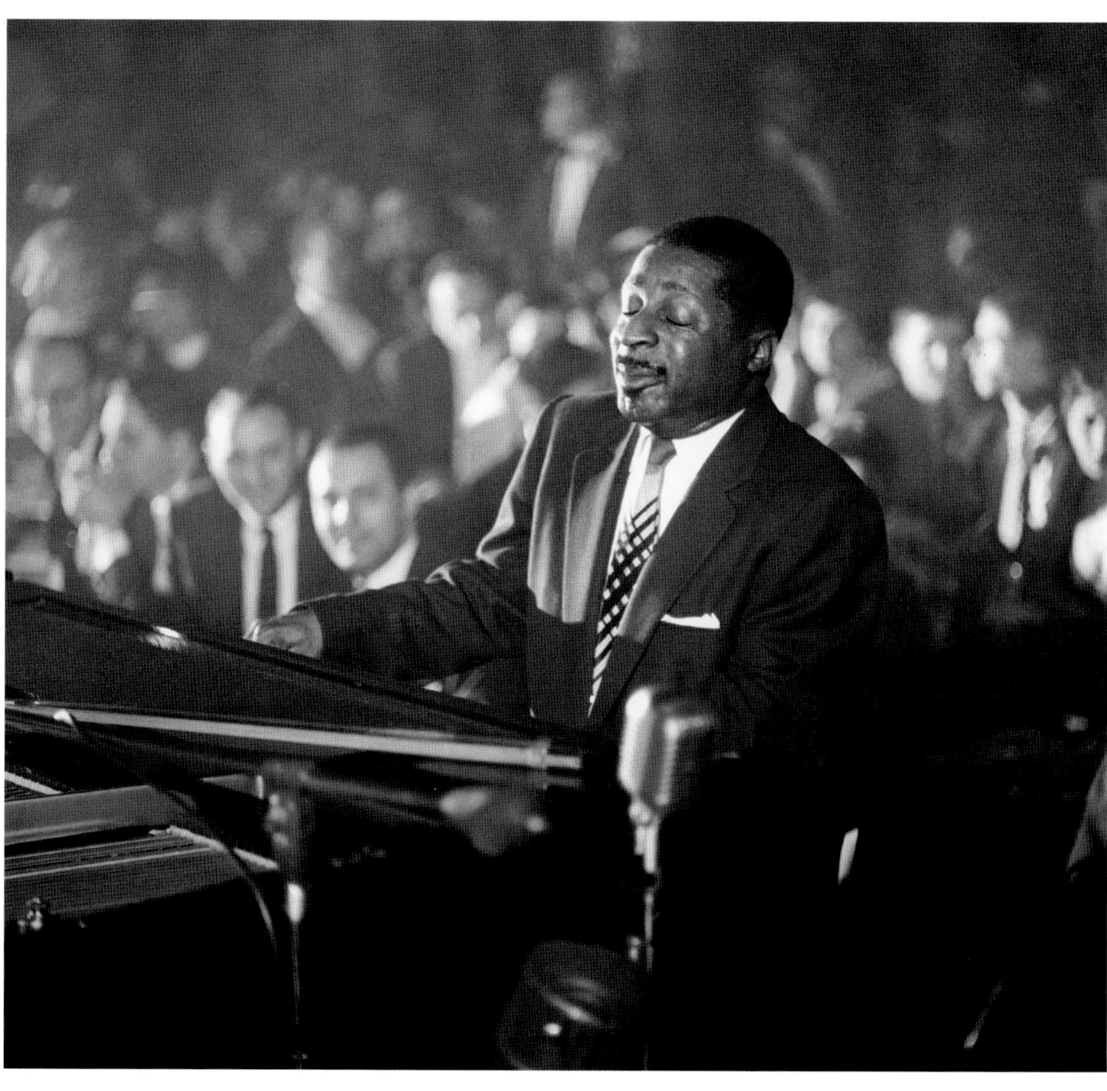

Errol Garner, NYC, 1953

Errol Garner, Bop City, NYC, 1953

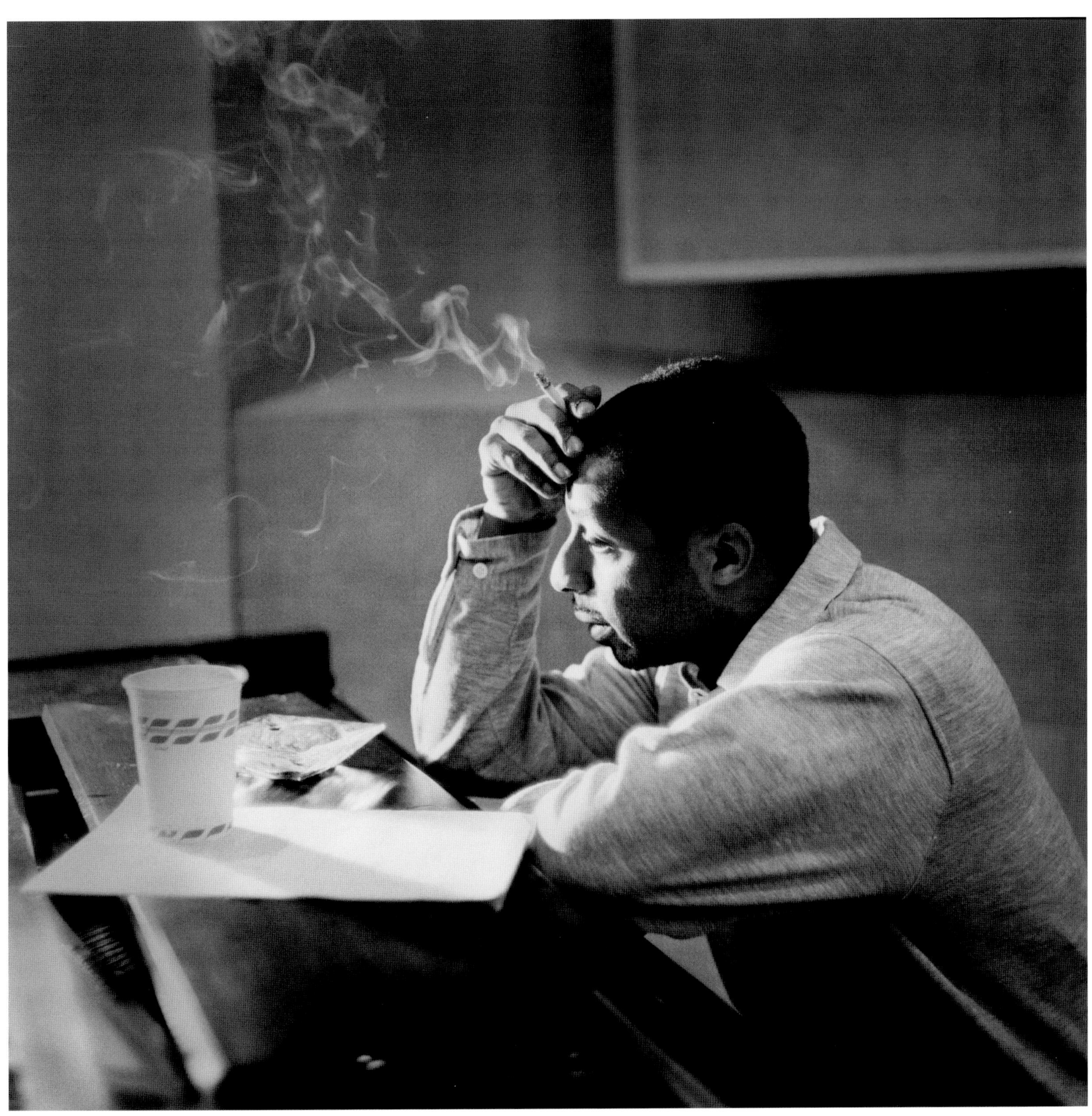

Errol Garner, NYC, 1953

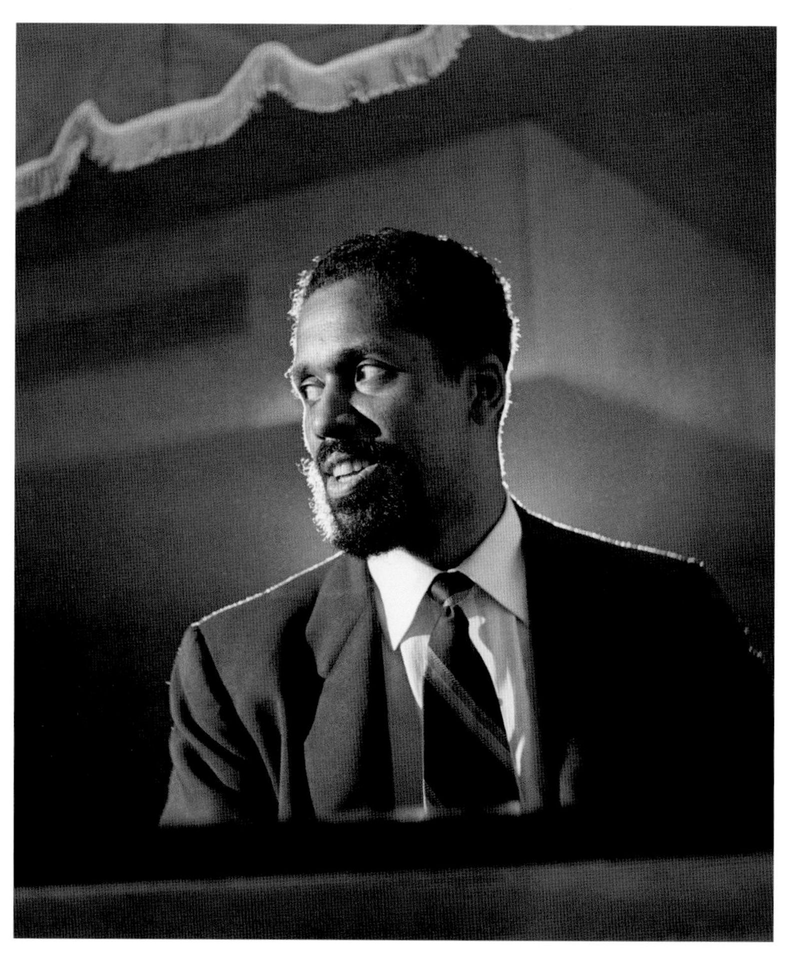

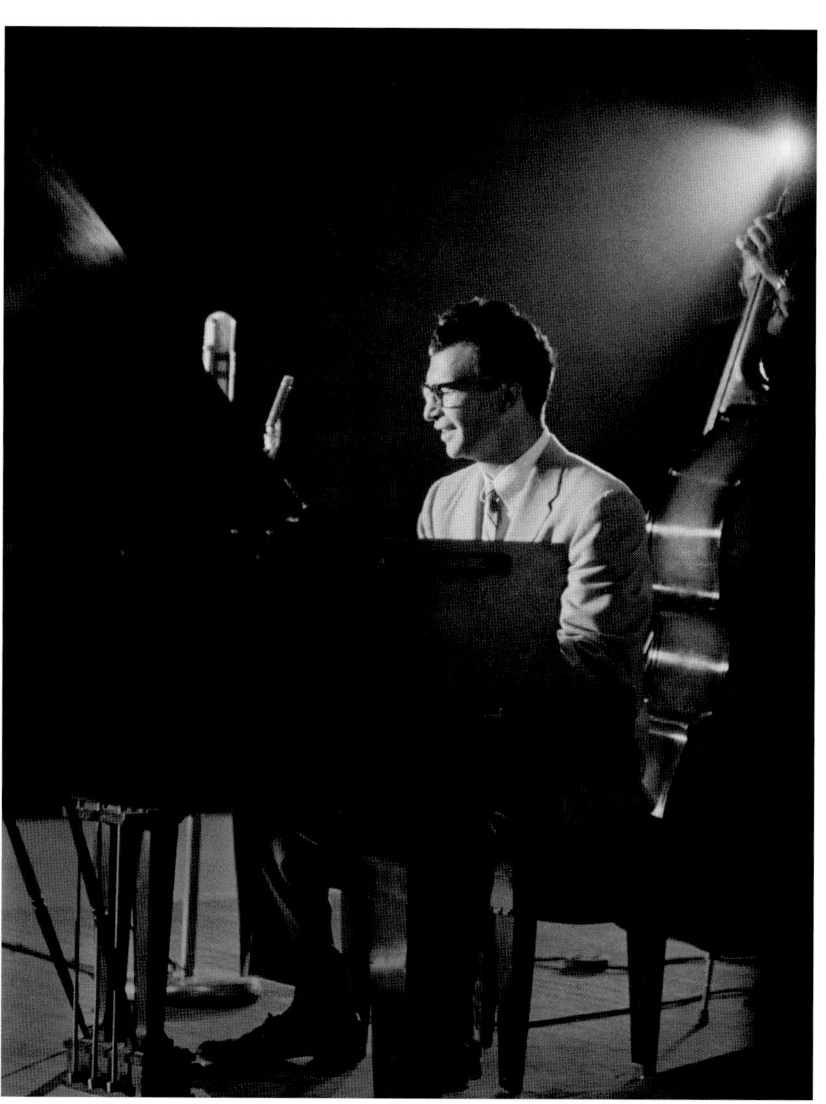

John Lewis, Birdland, NYC, 1957

Dave Brubeck, Hollywood Bowl, Los Angeles, 1953

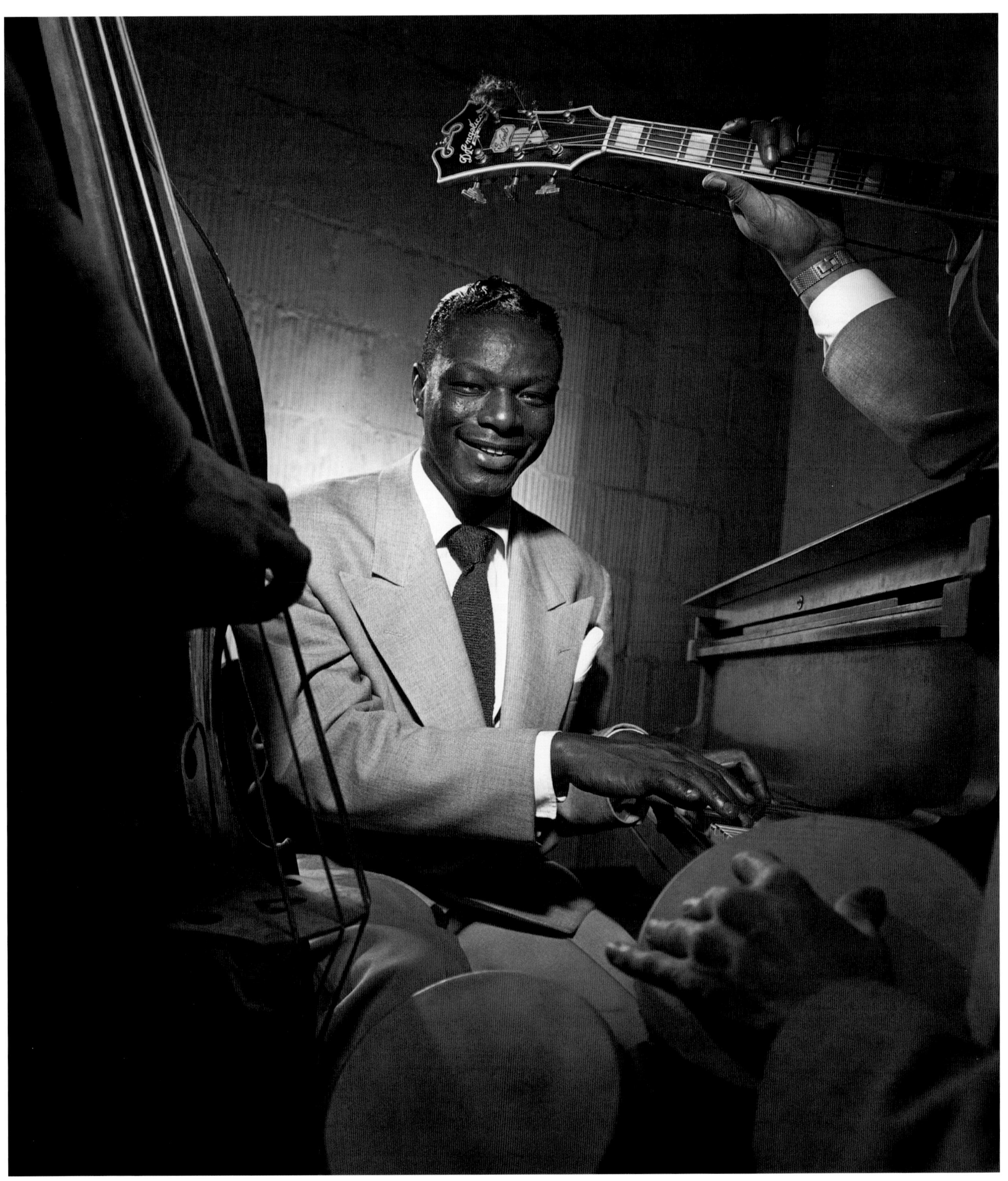

Nat King Cole, Sullivan Street studio, NYC, 1949

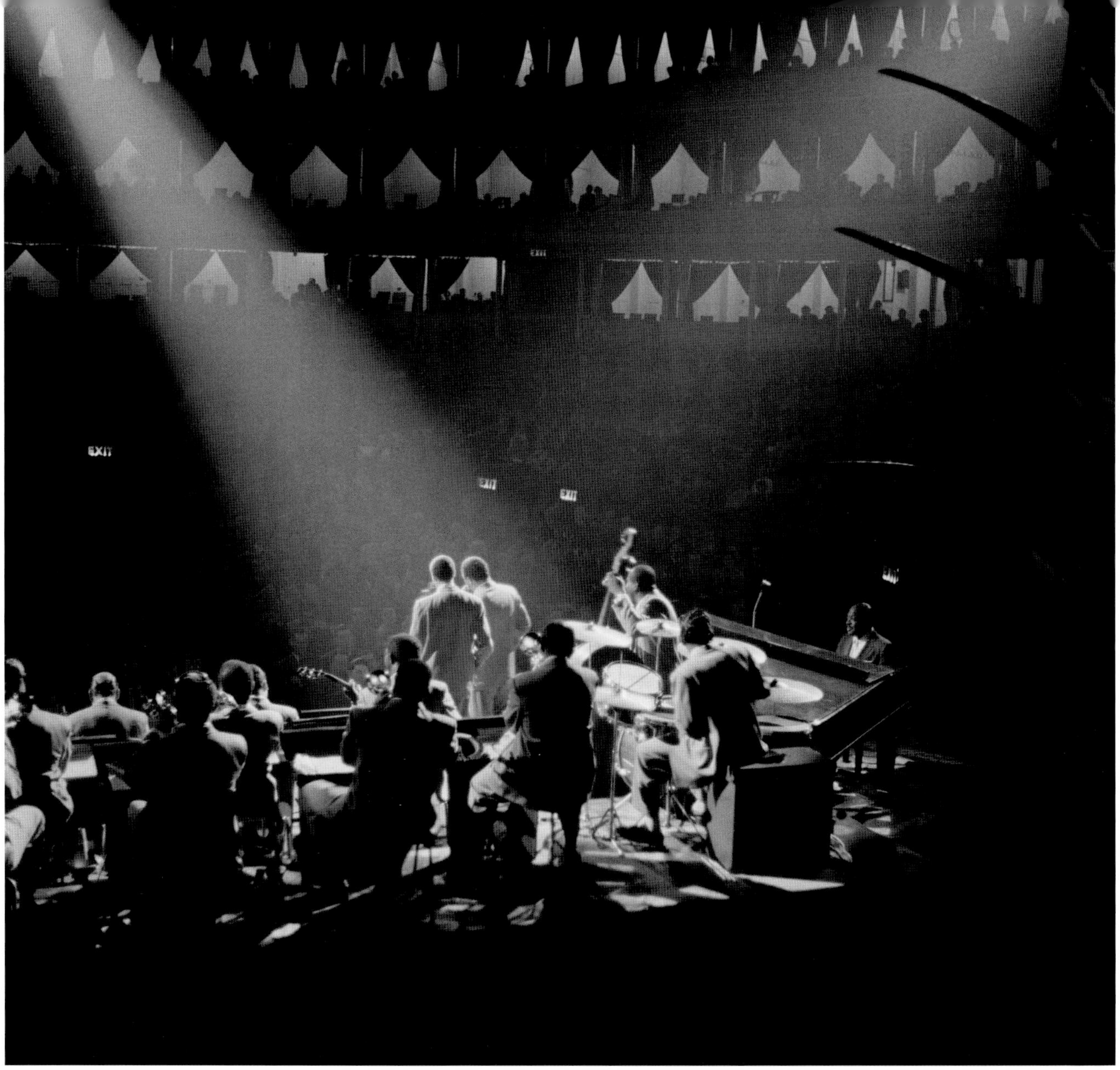

Count Basie, Royal Albert Hall, London, 1958

Count Basie, Paris, 1960

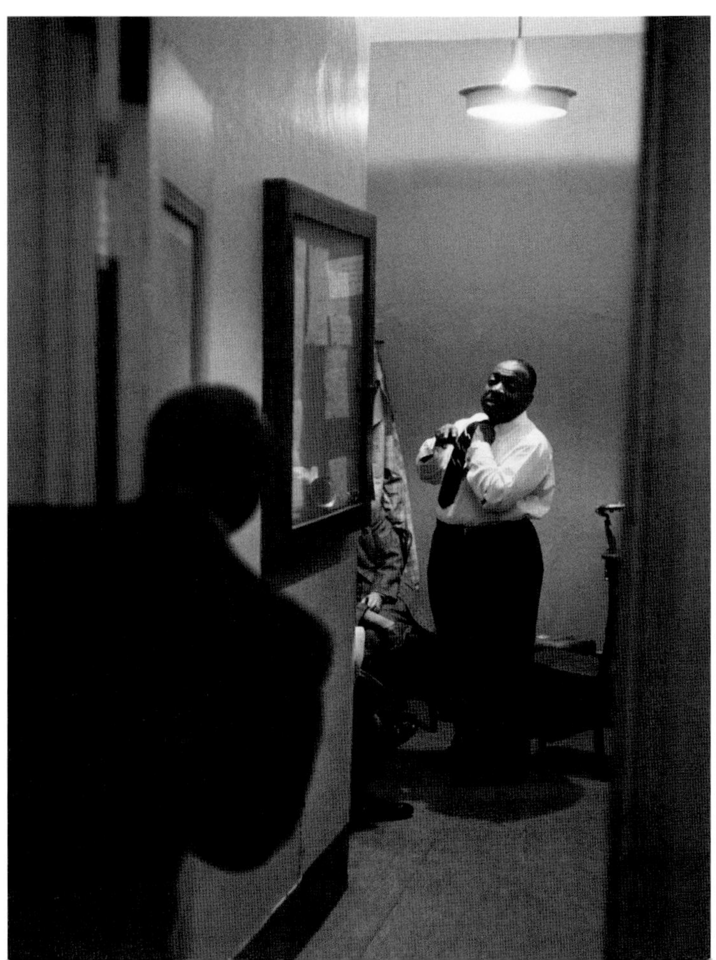

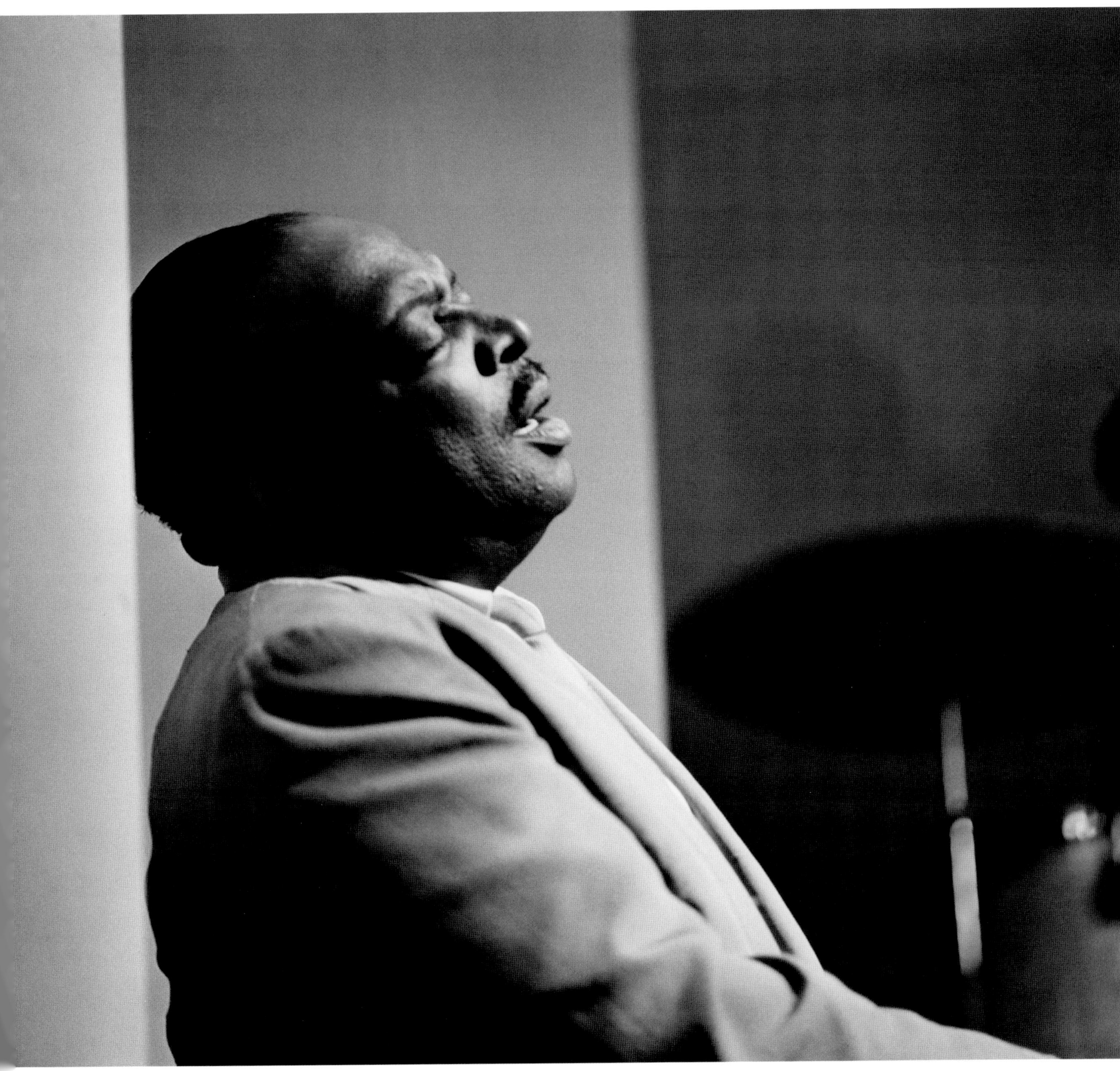

Count Basie, Newport, 1955

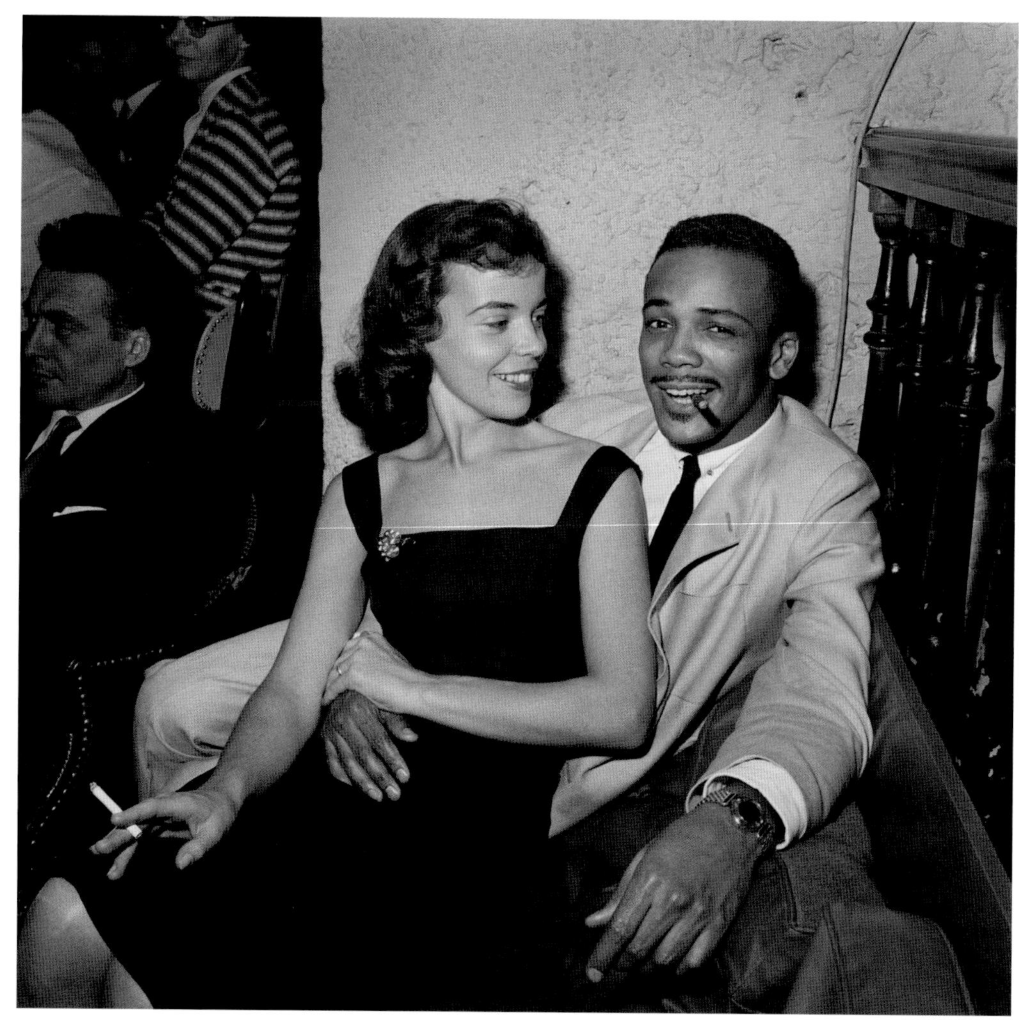

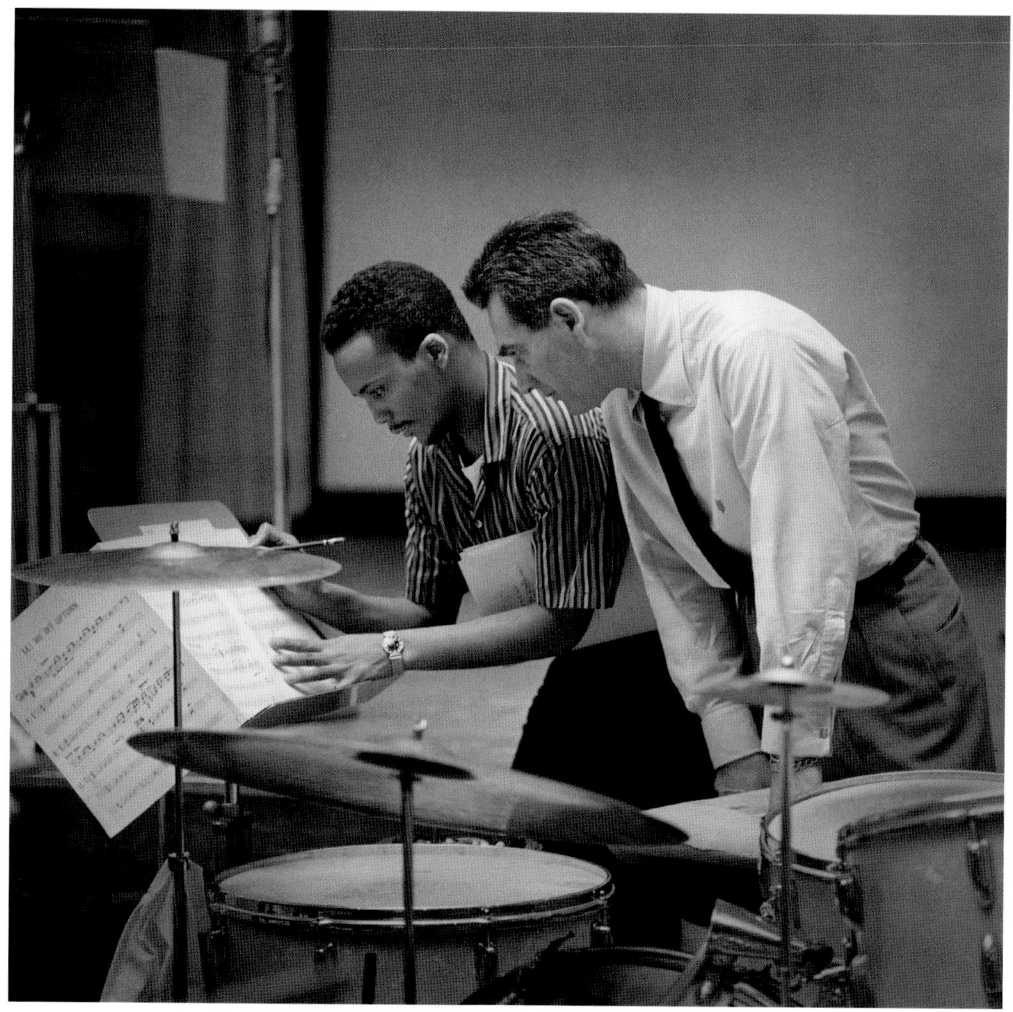

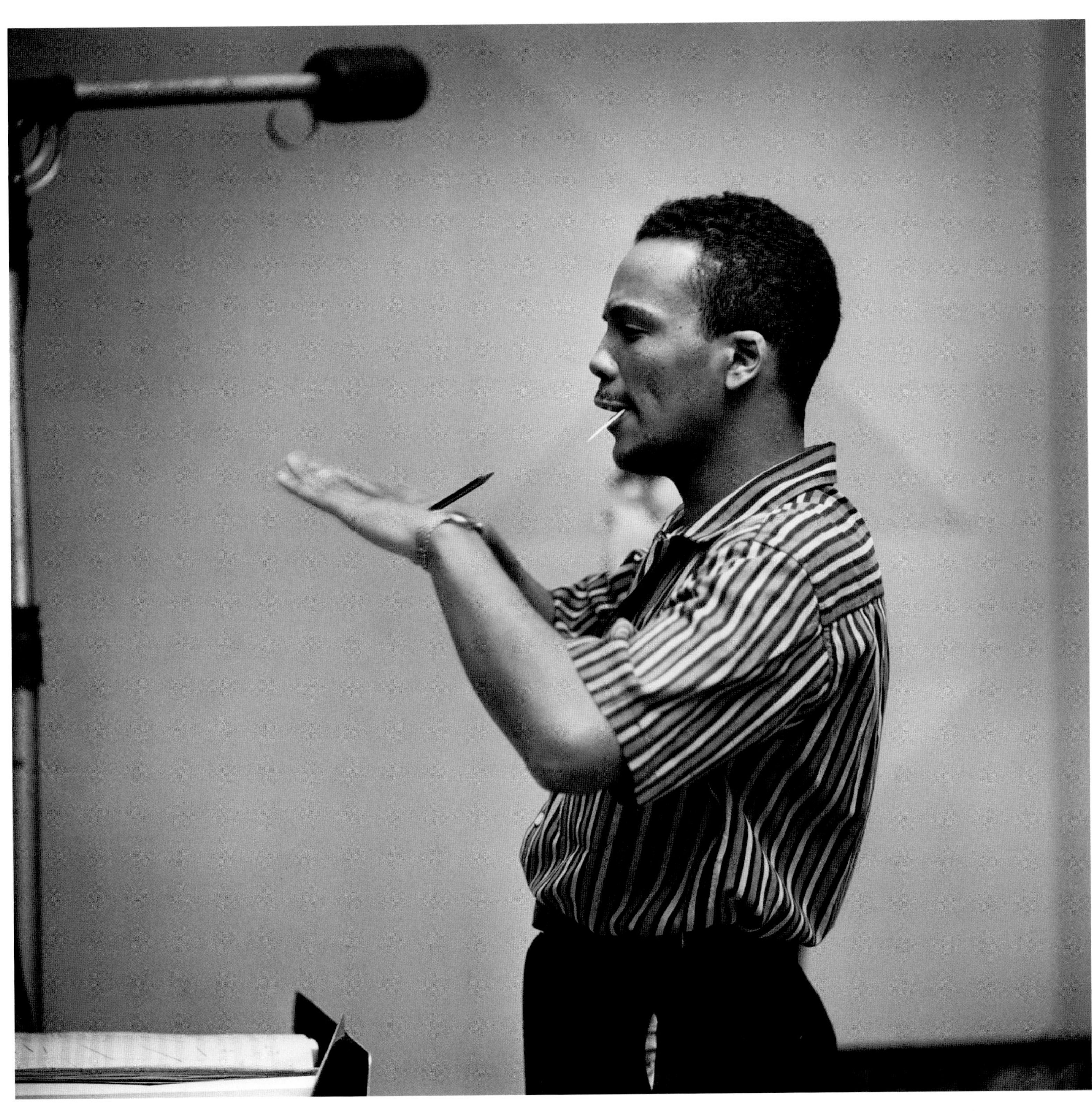

Quincy Jones, Club St Germain, Paris, 1950

Quincy Jones and Gene Krupa, NYC, 1955

Quincy Jones, NYC, 1955

Quincy Jones and Big Band, NYC, 1955

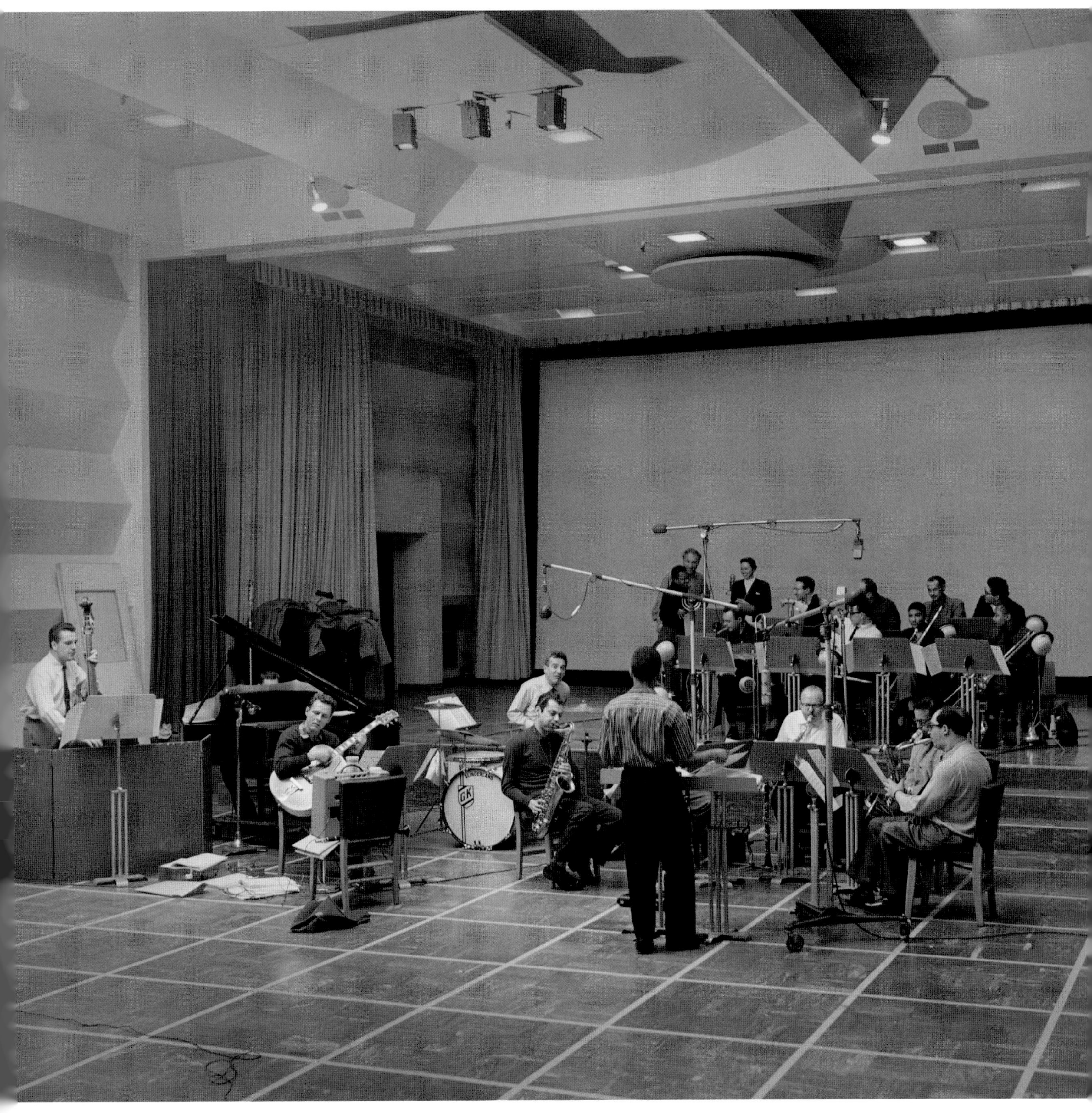
GK

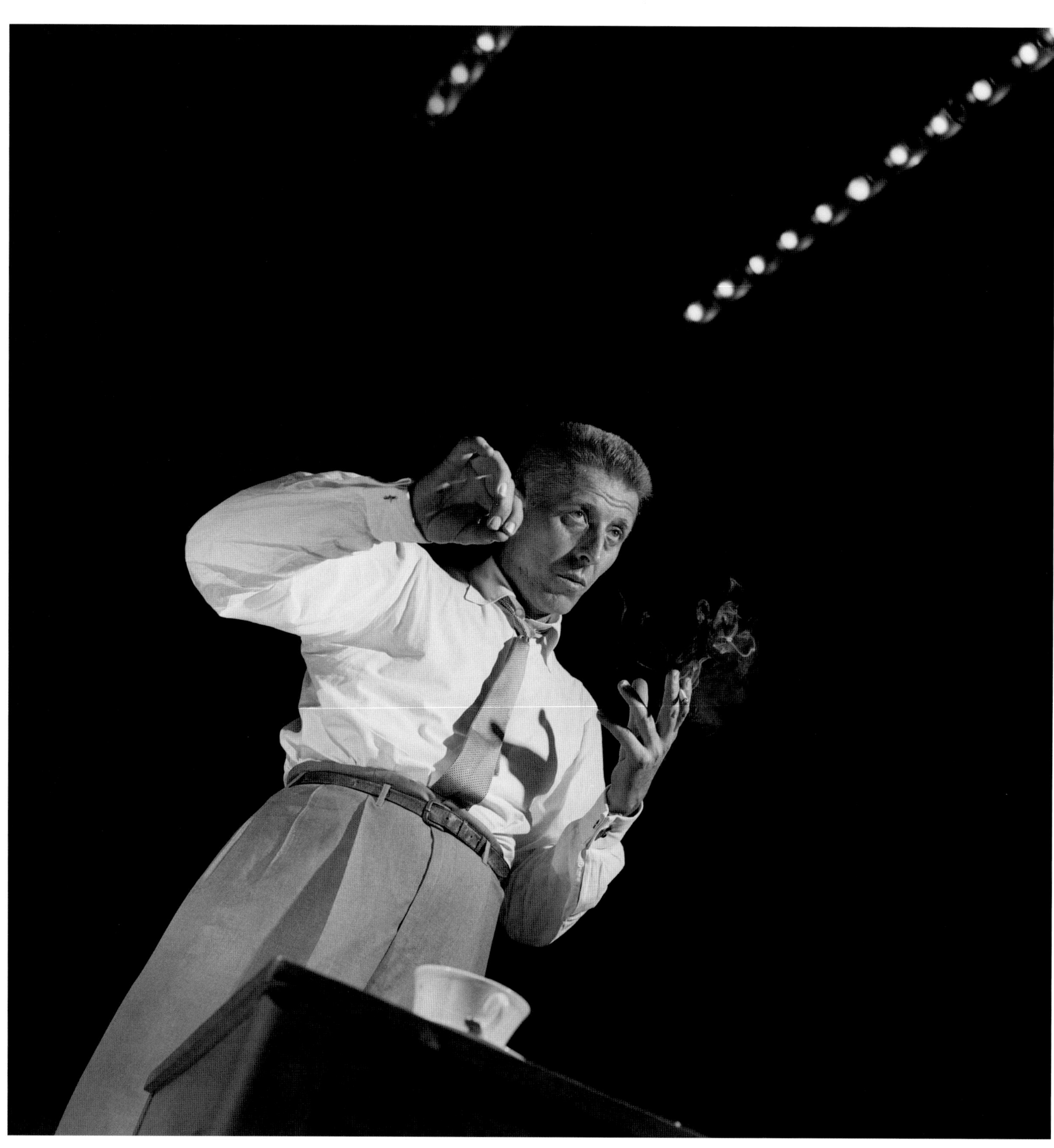

Stan Kenton, Atlanta, 1950

Woody Herman, Royal Roost, NYC, 1948

Stan Kenton, Atlanta, 1950

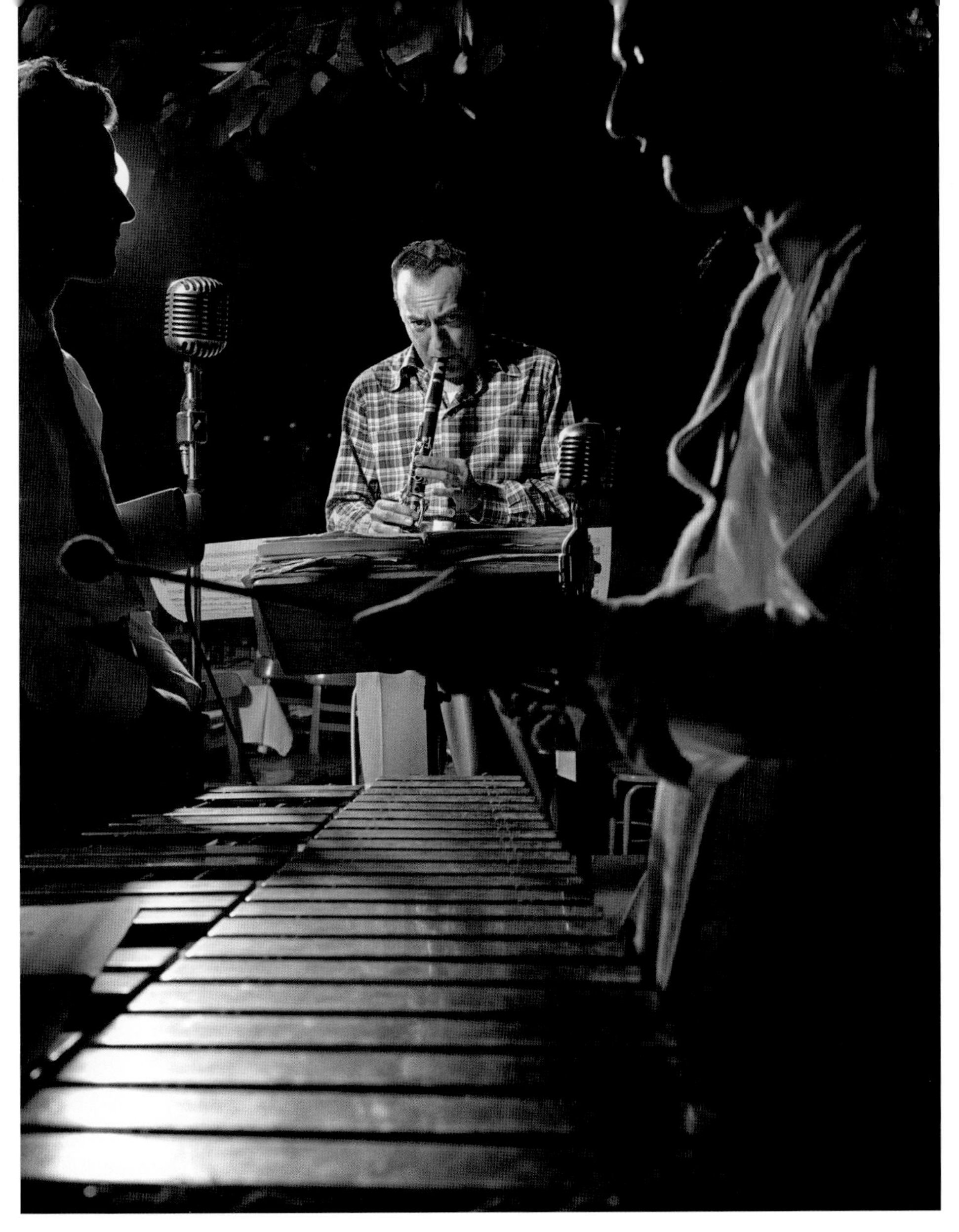

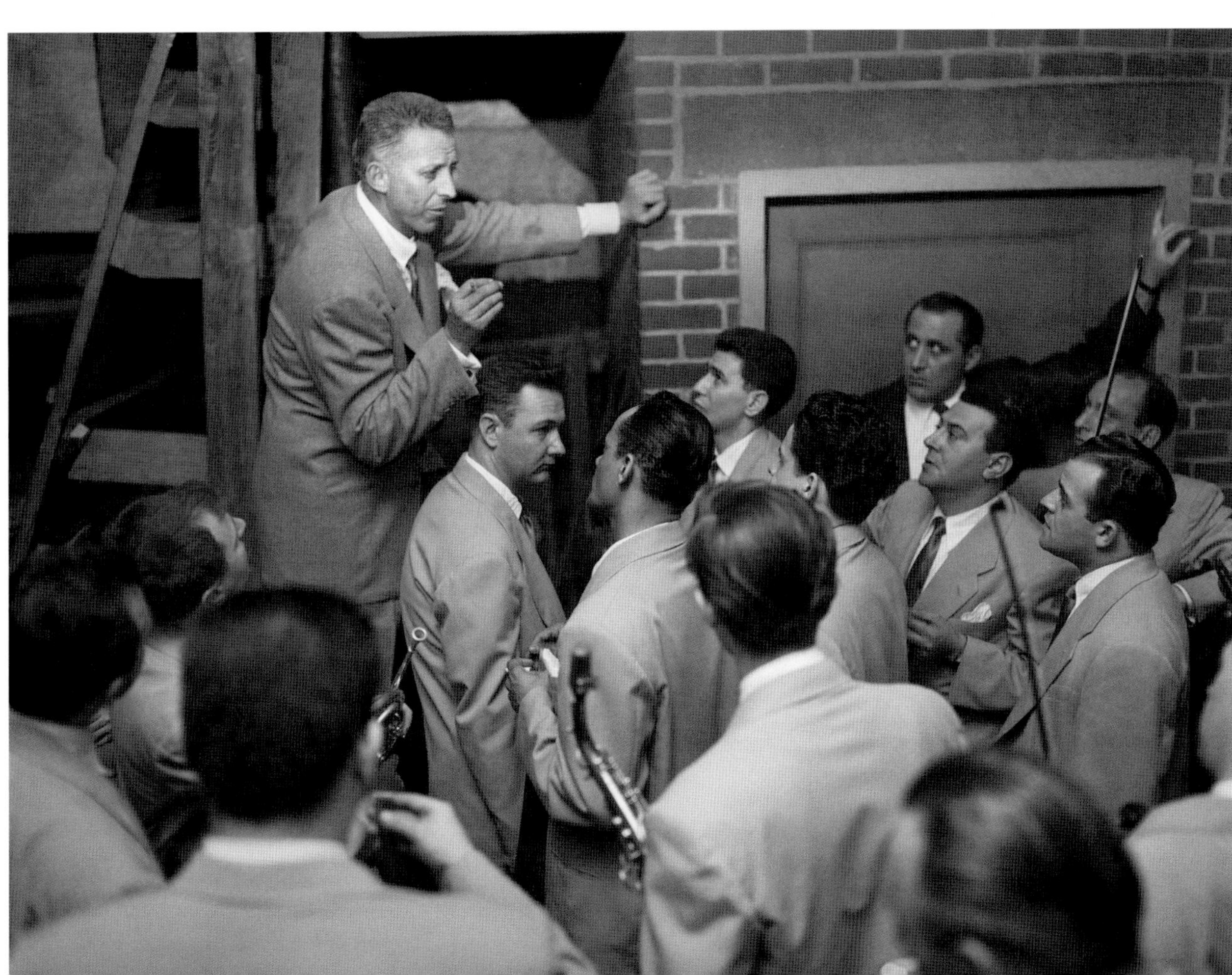

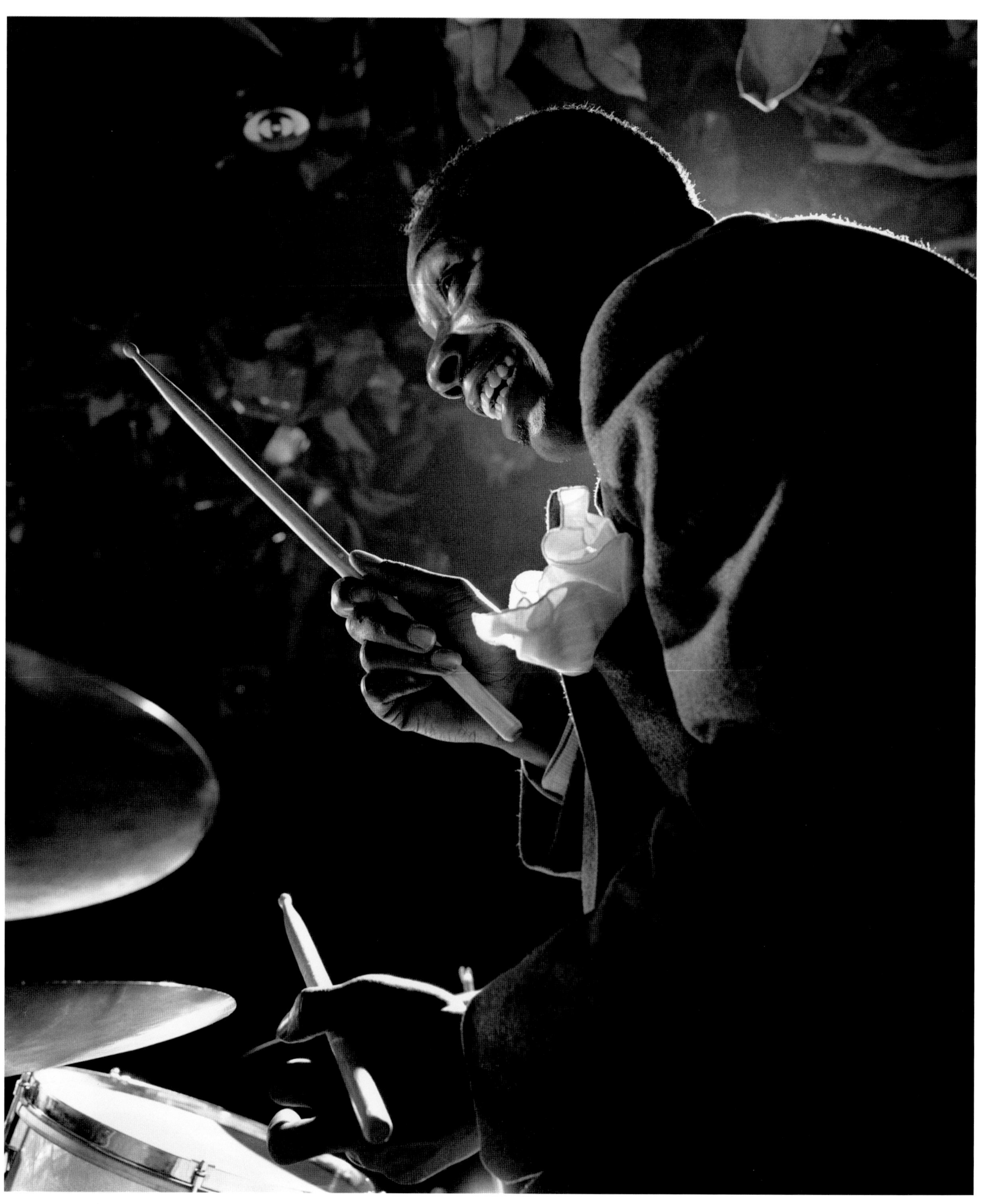

Kenny Clarke, Royal Roost, NYC, 1948

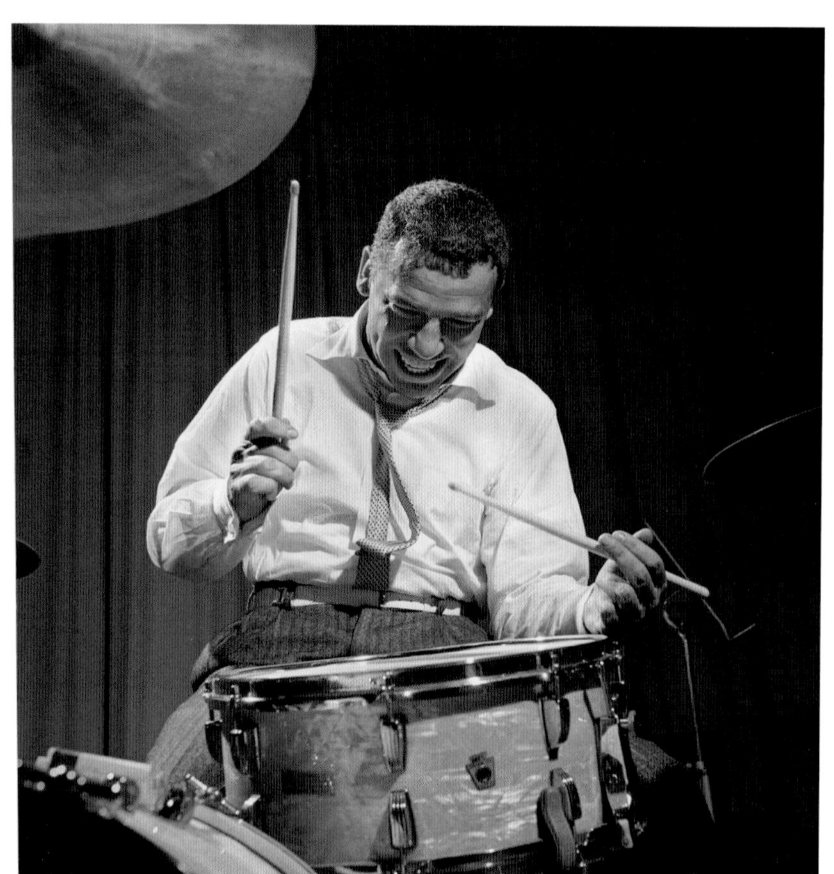

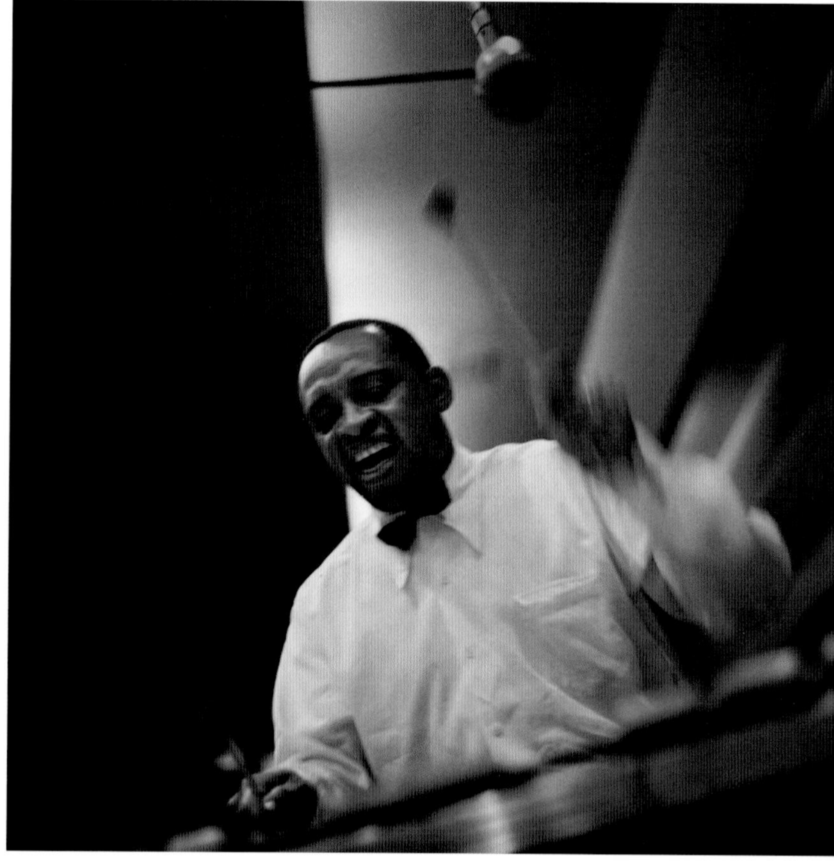

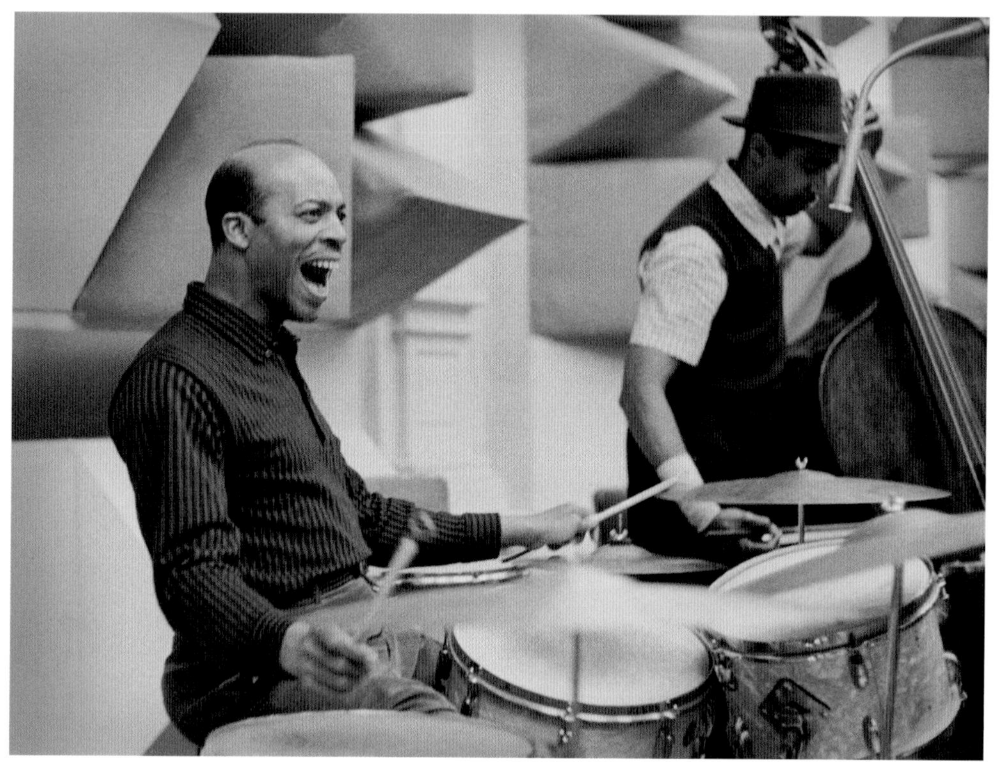

Buddy Rich, NYC, 1954

Lionel Hampton, NYC, 1954

Jo Jones and Ray Brown, NYC, 1958

Cozy C

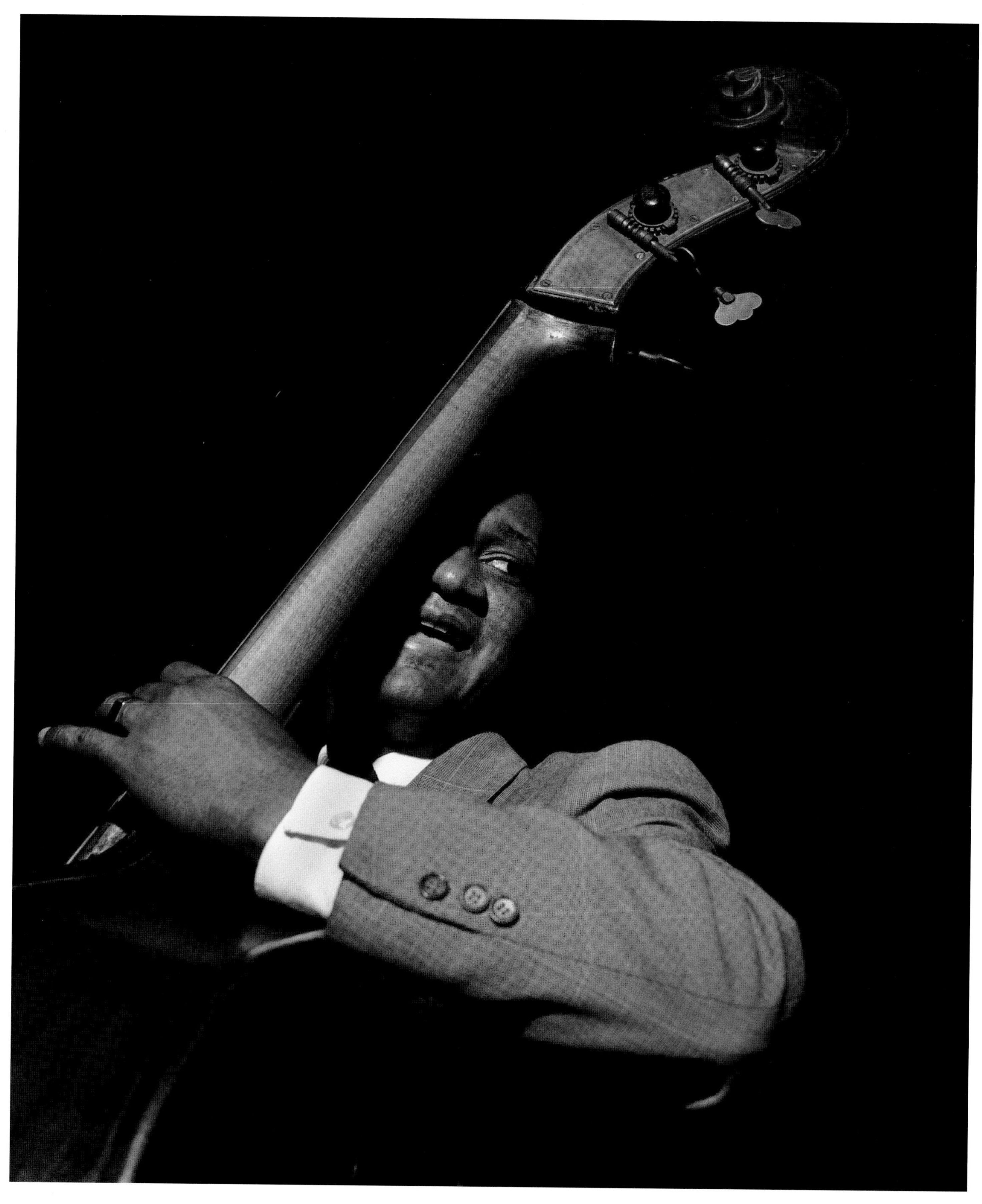

Oscar Pettiford, NYC, 1950

Percy Heath, Birdland, NYC, 1953 (opposite)

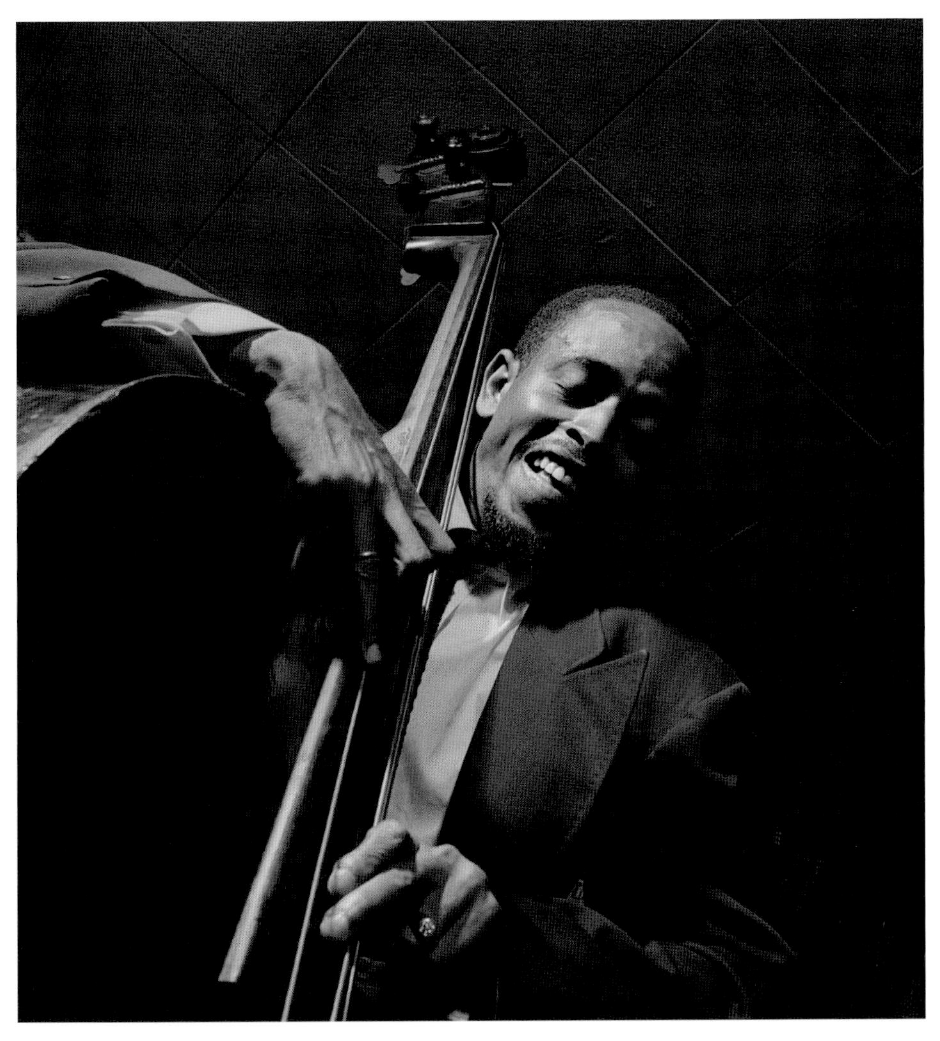

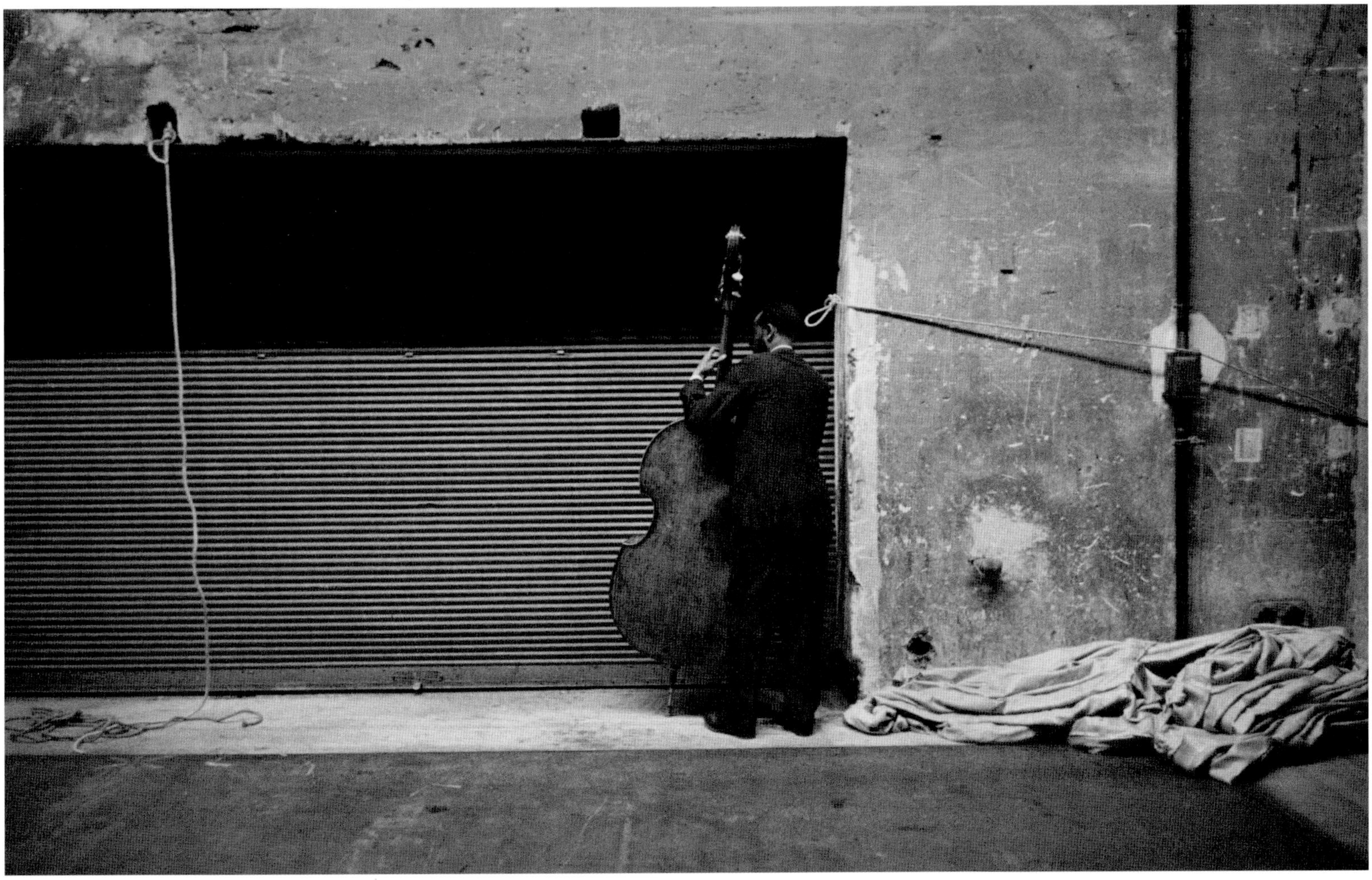

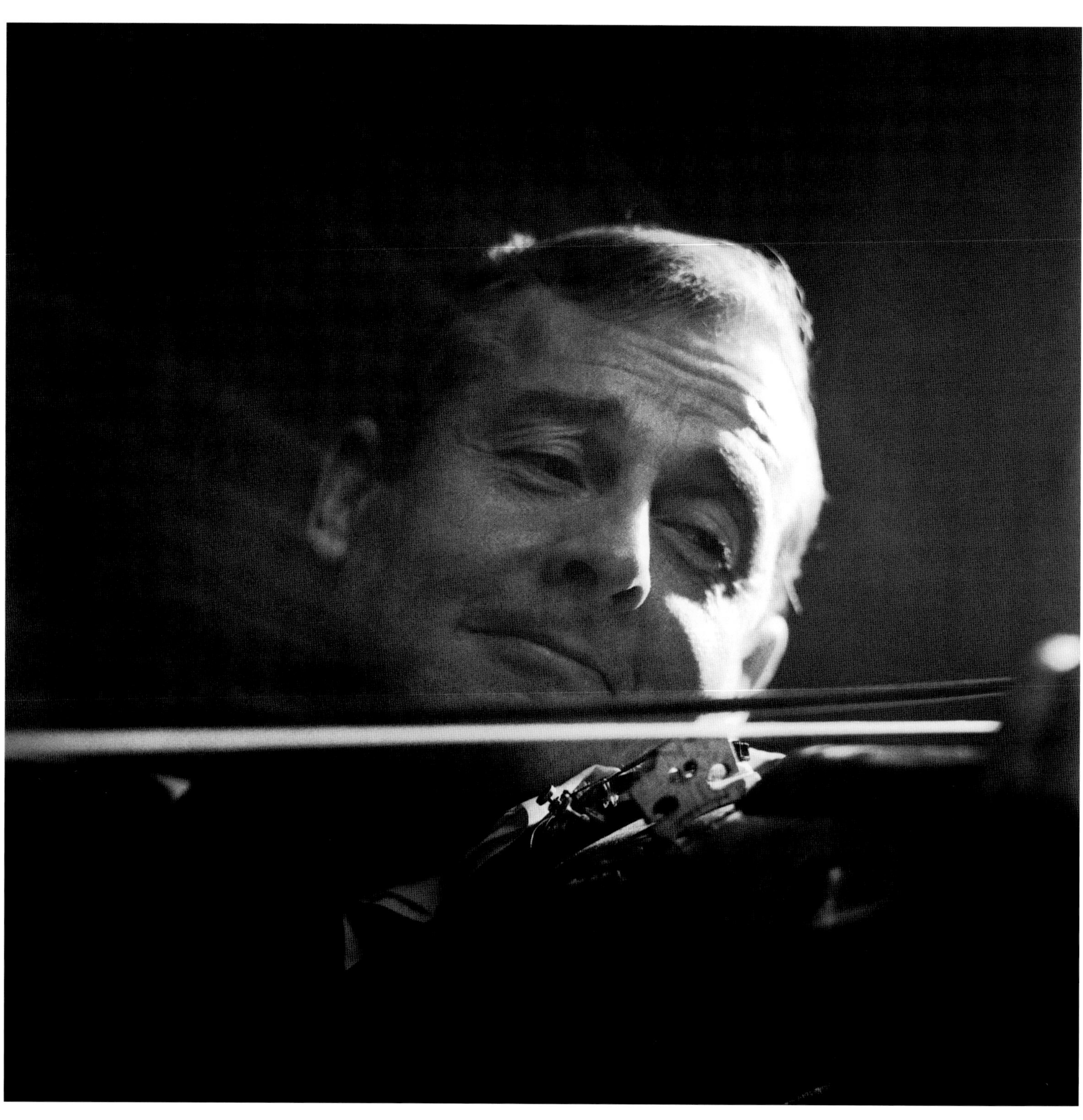

Stephane Grappelli, Paris, 1958

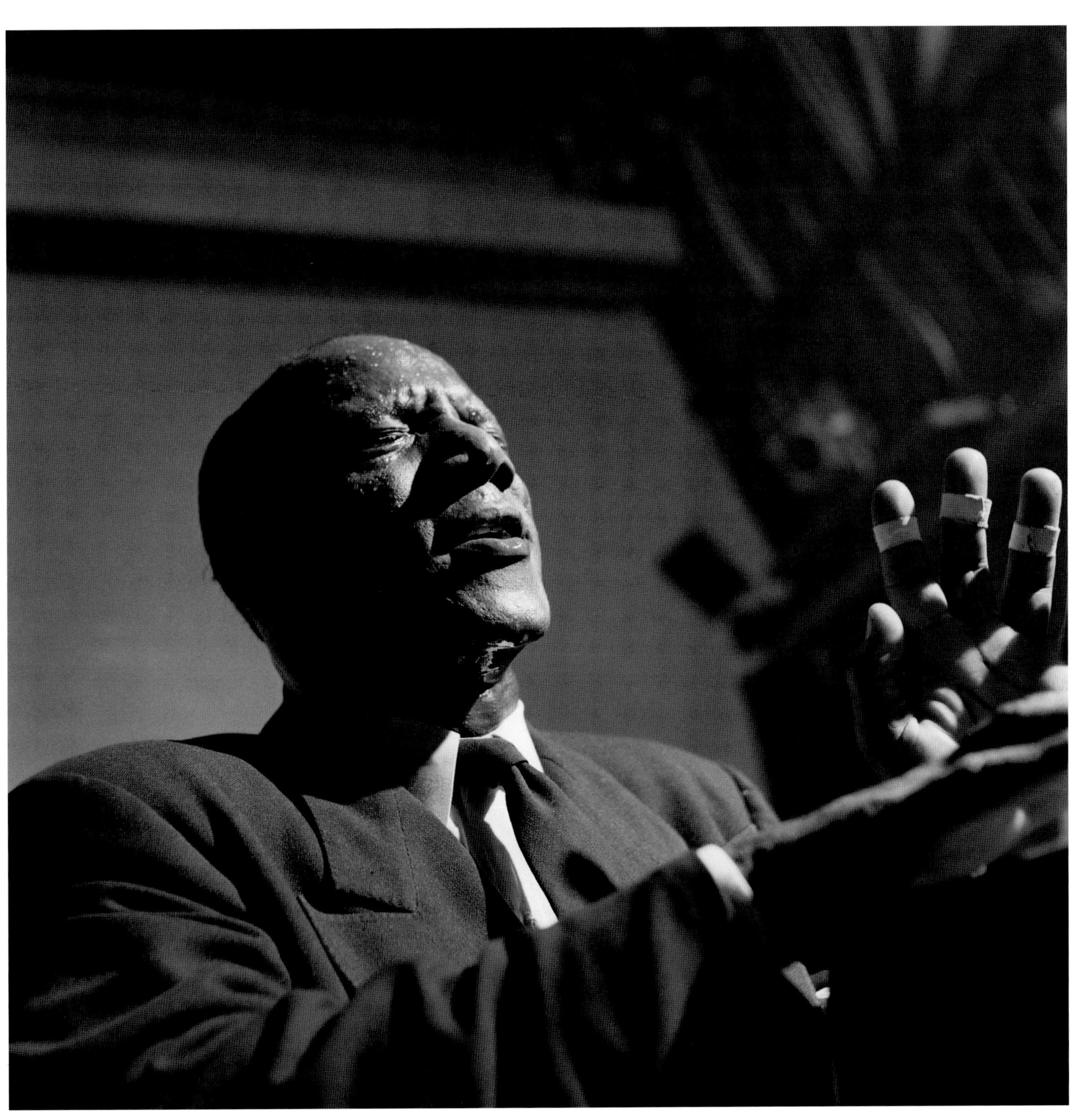

Candido Camero, Birdland, NYC, 1954

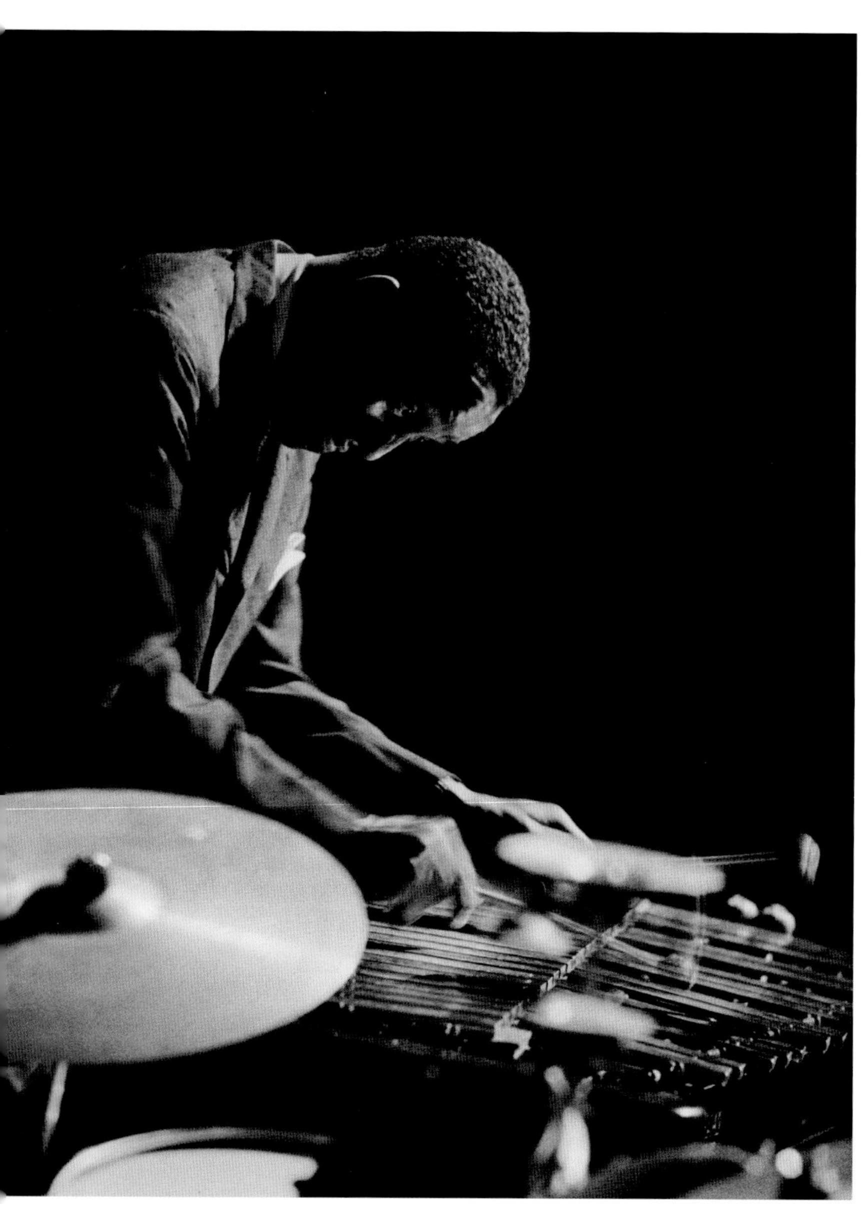

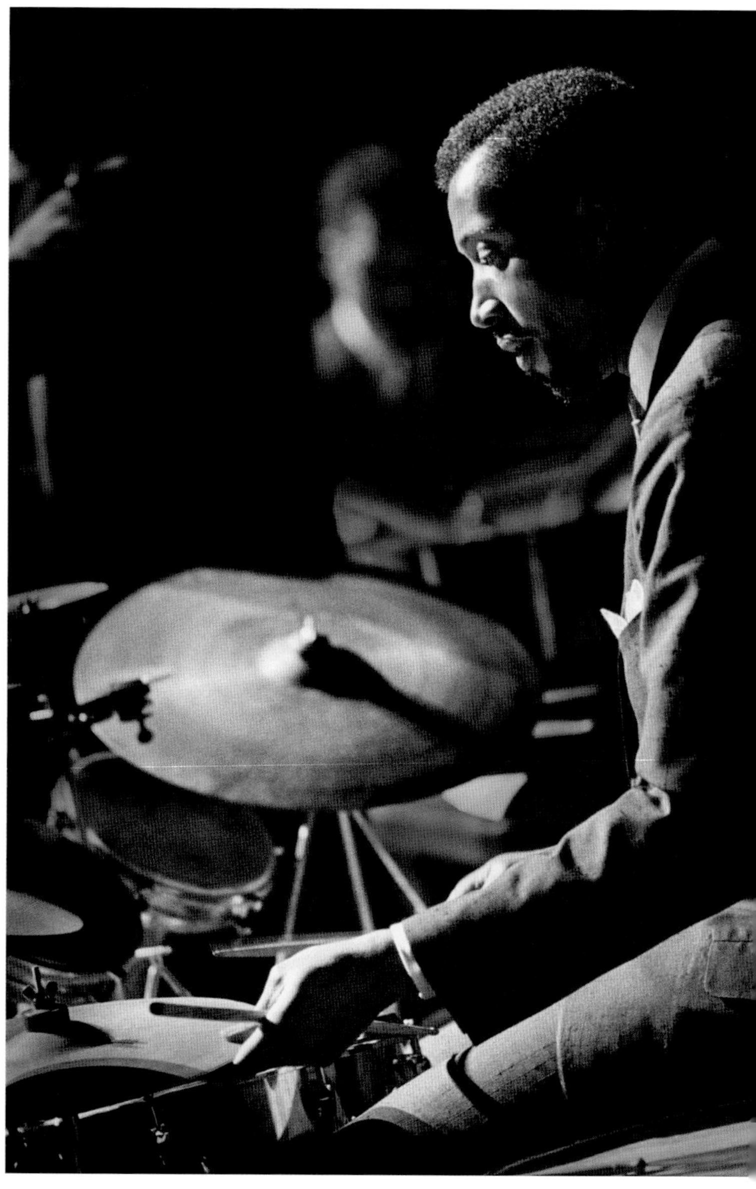

Milt Jackson, Olympia Theatre, Paris, 1960

Connie Kay, Olympia Theatre, Paris, 1960

Modern Jazz Quartet (Connie Kay, Milt Jackson, Percy Heath and John Lewis), Olympia Theatre, Paris, 1957

Paris, 1968 (overleaf)

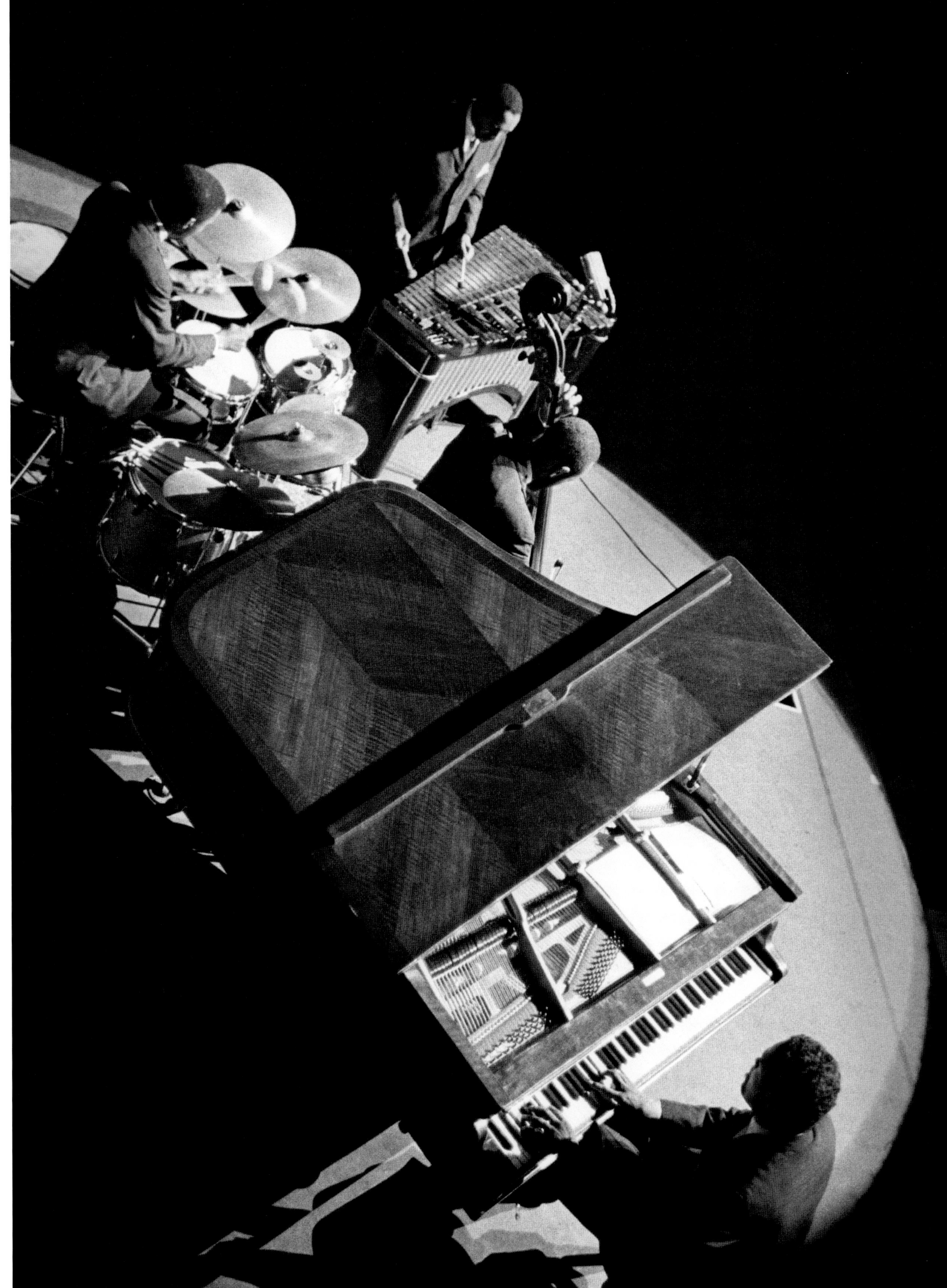

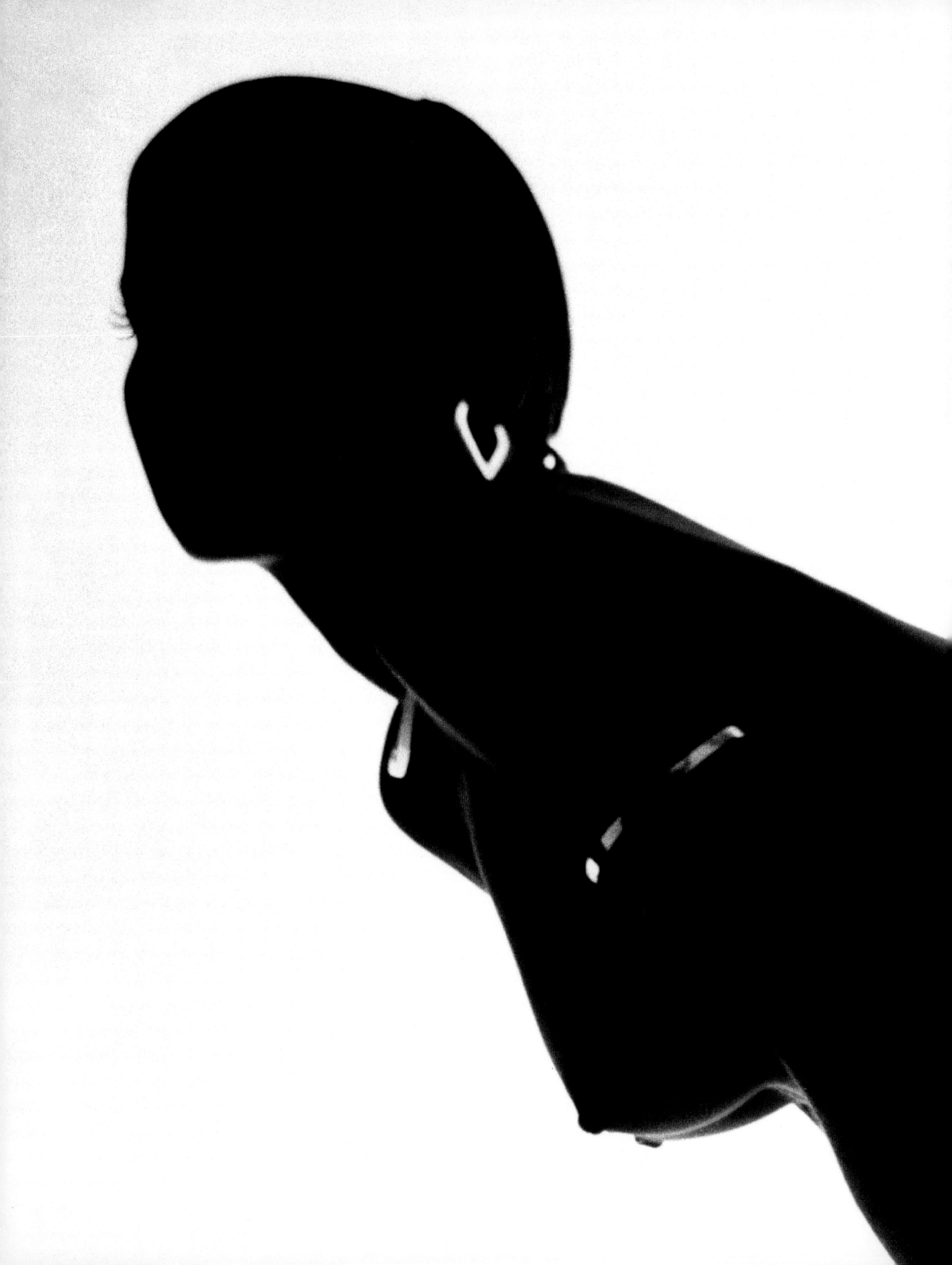

Fashion and Nudes

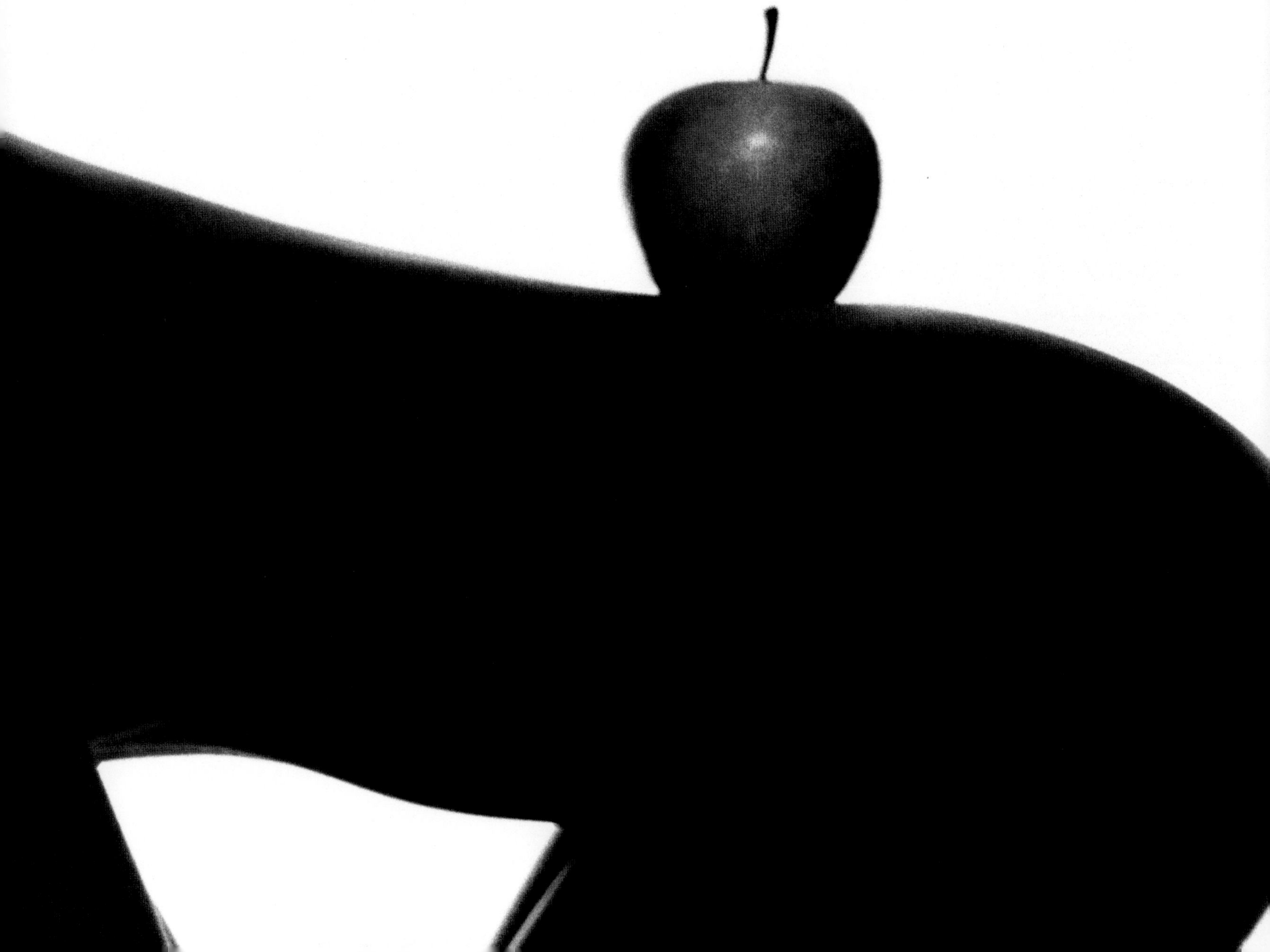

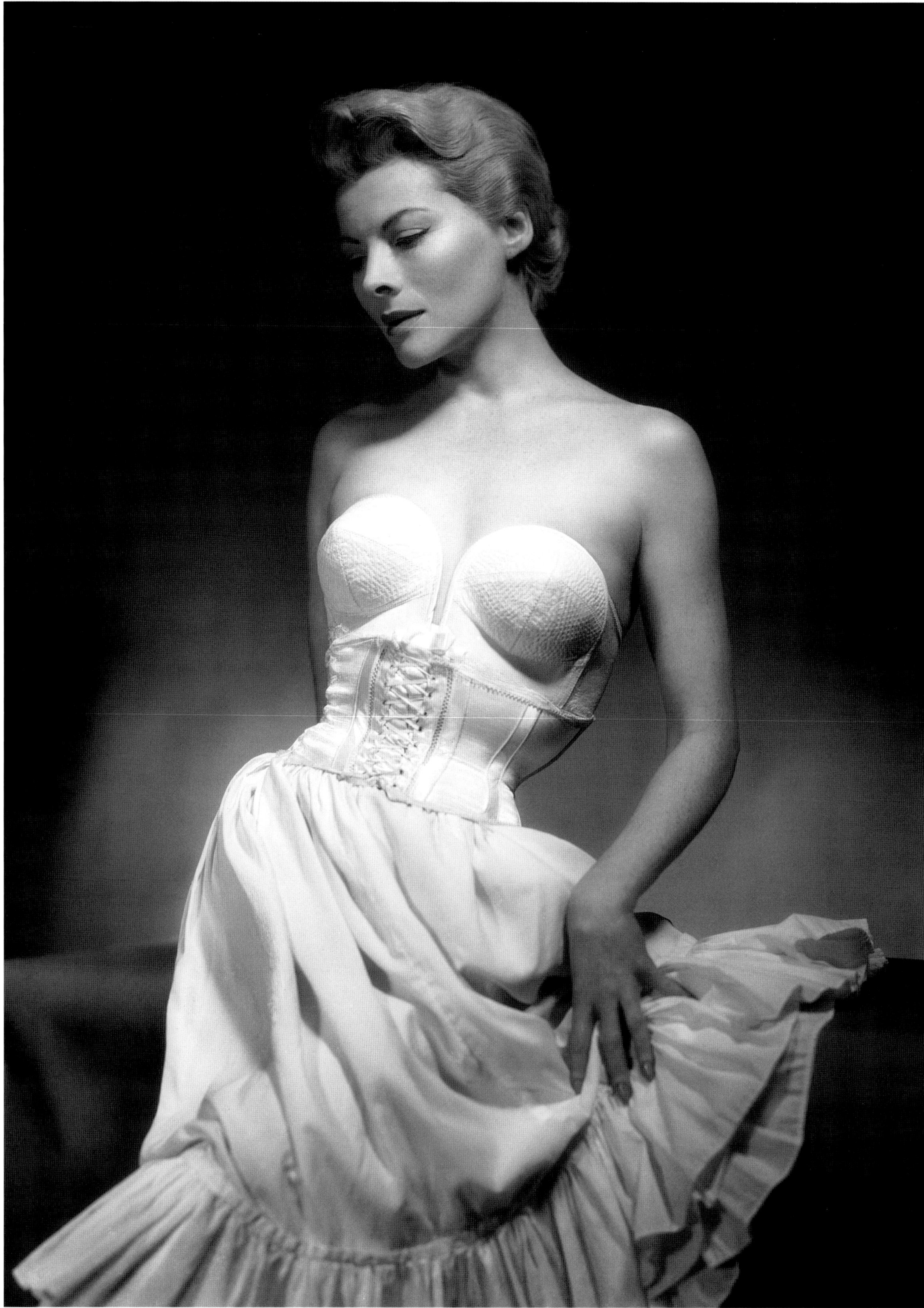

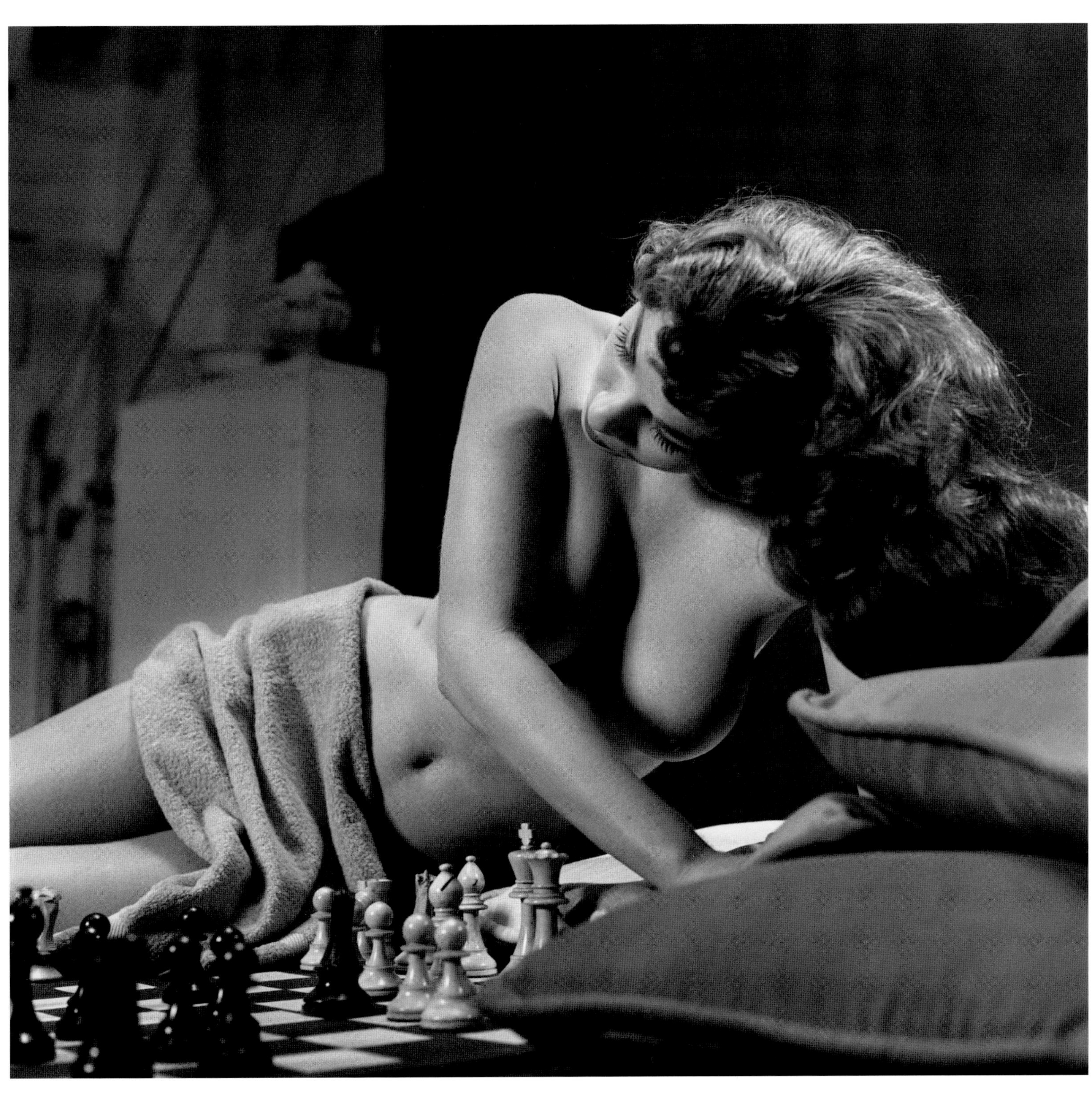

Advertisement for Charis Corporation, NYC, 1953

Gloria, *Playboy* session, NYC, 1956

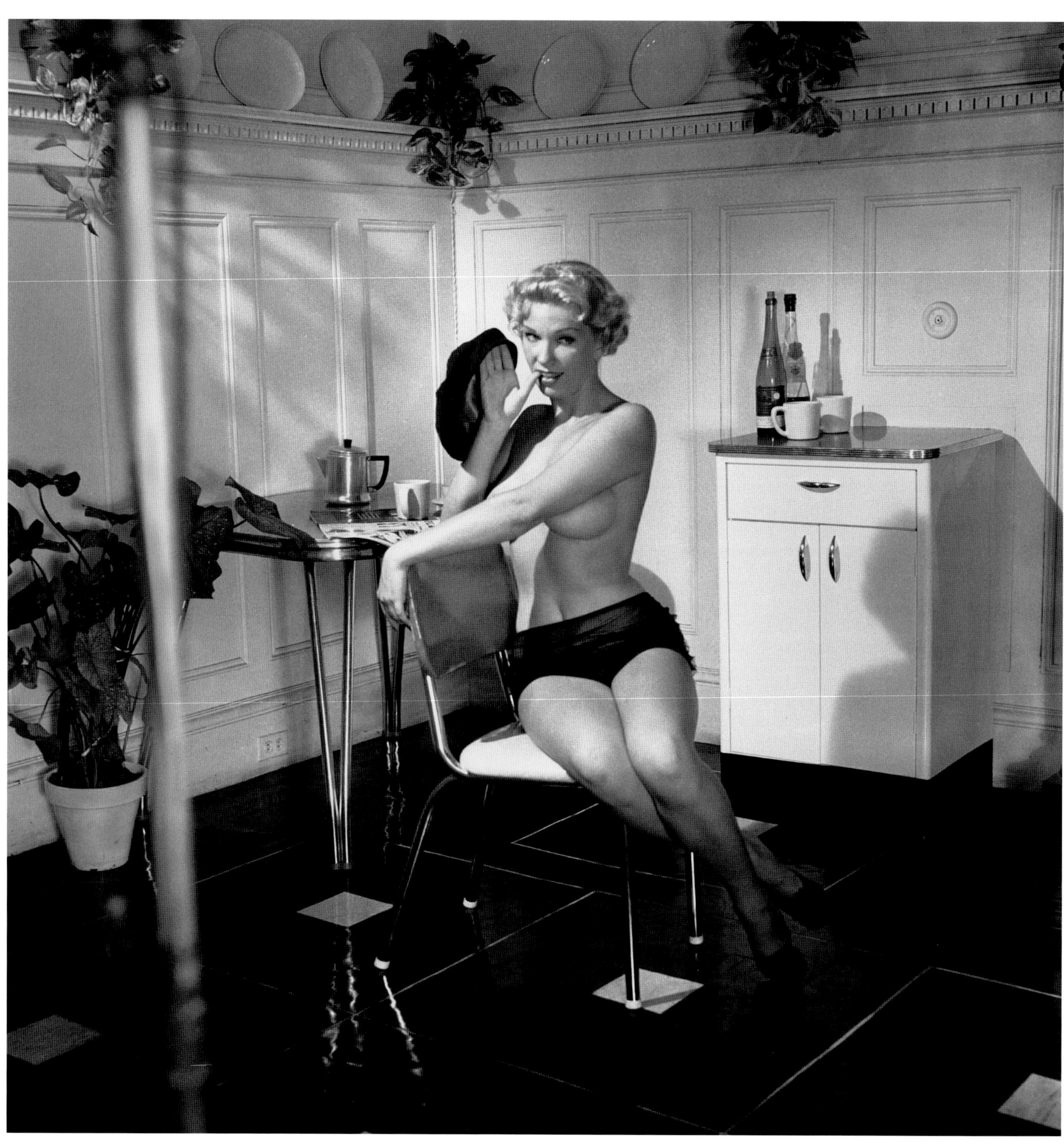

Marion, *Playboy* session, NYC, 1956

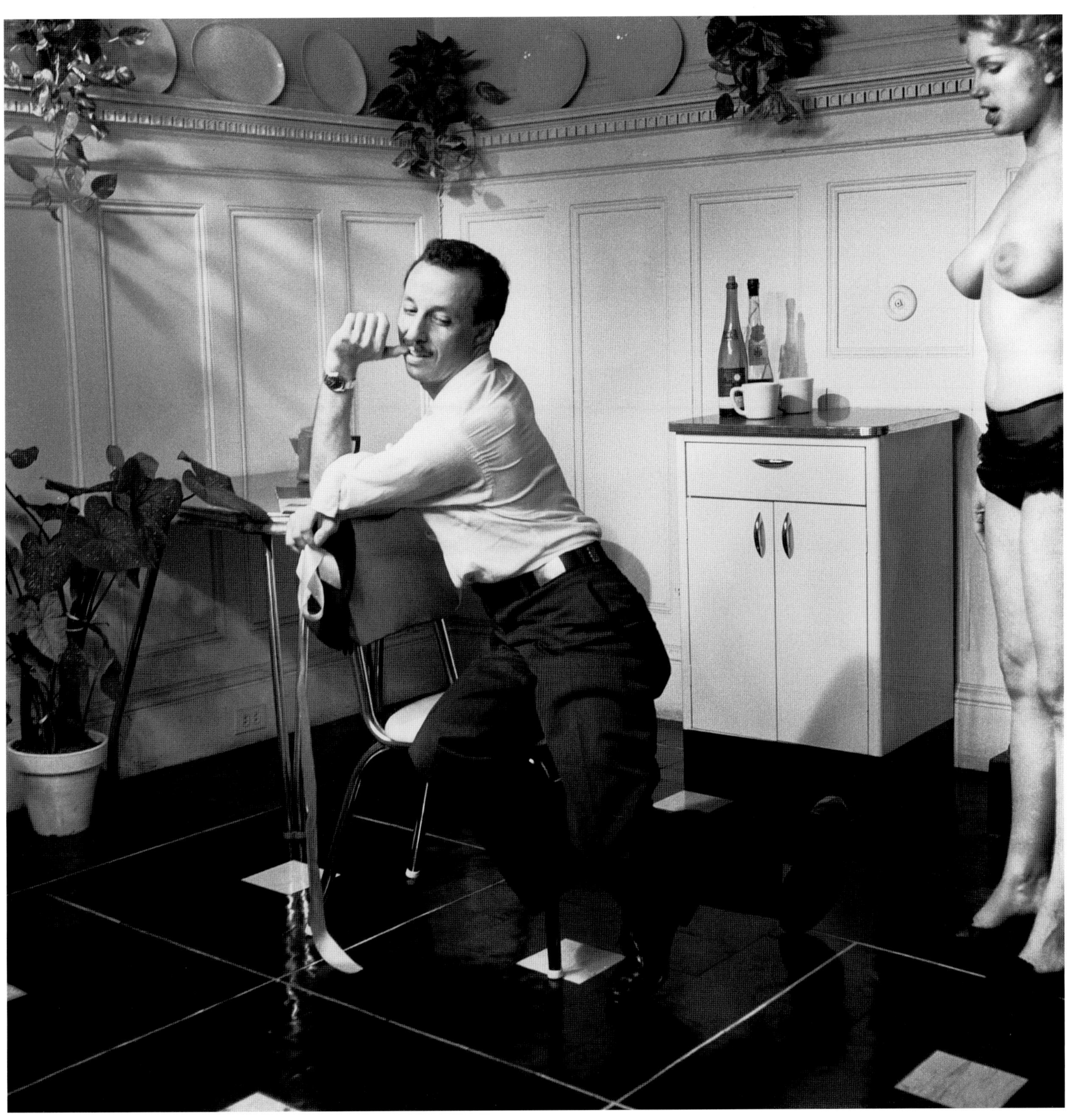

Herman Leonard, *Playboy* session, NYC, 1956

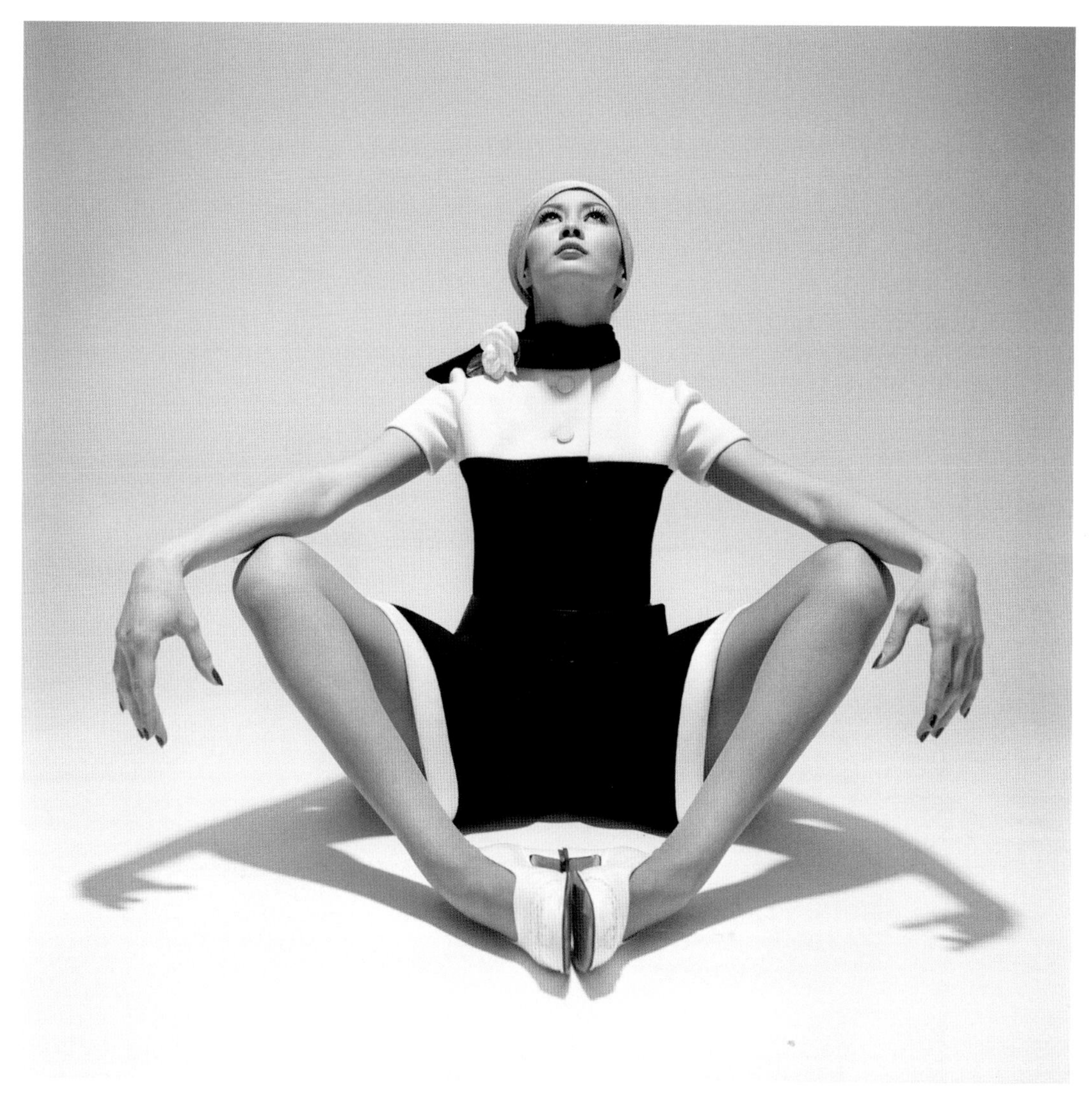

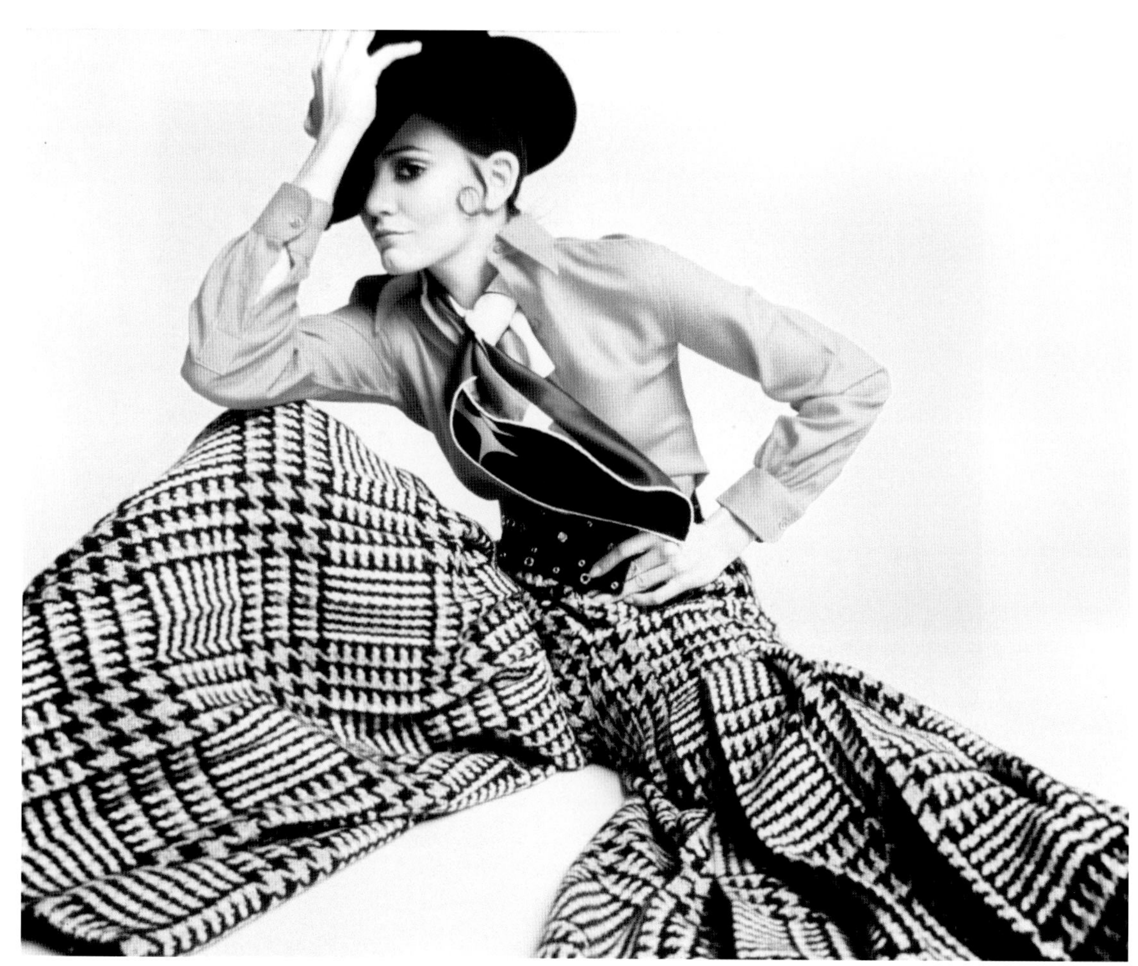

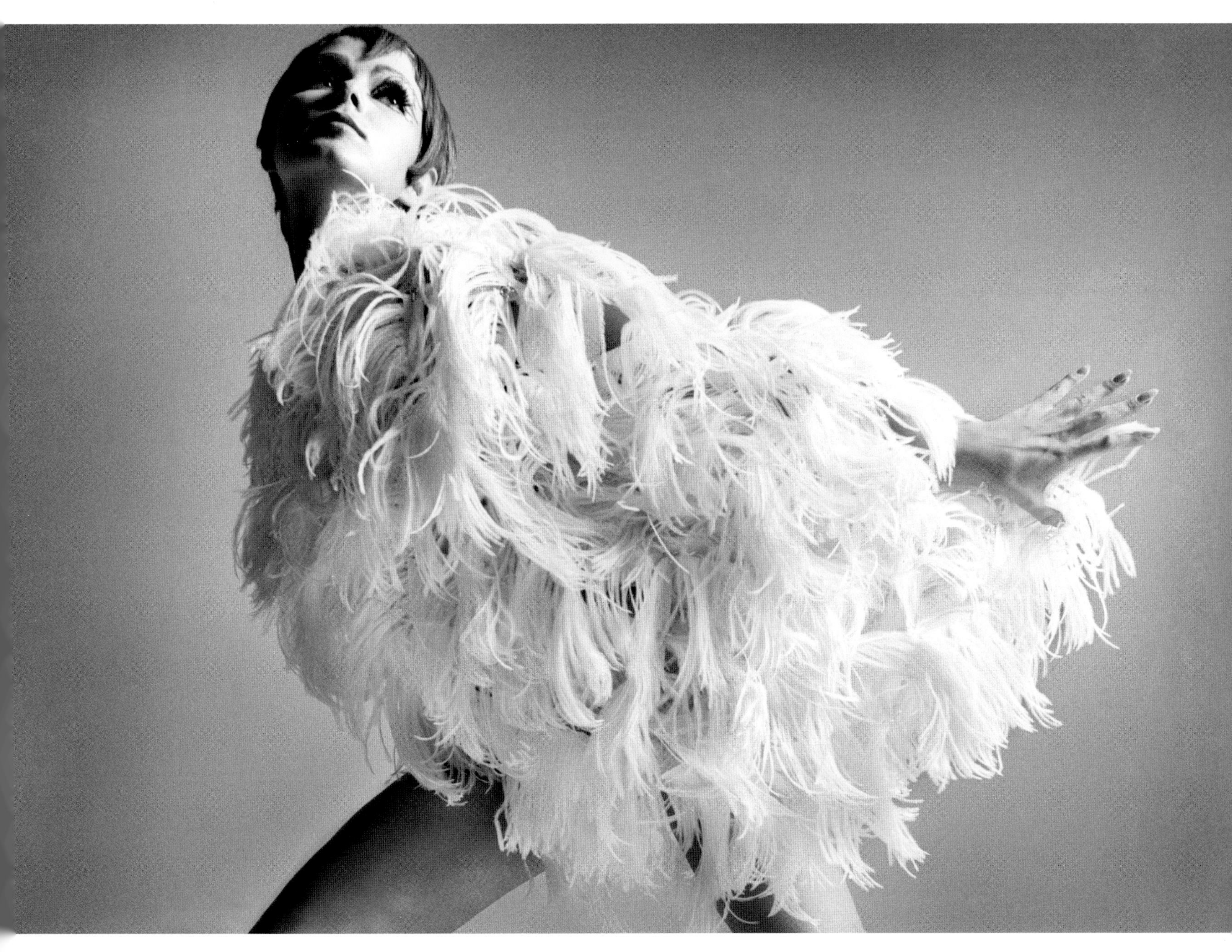

Paris, 1967

Paris, 1969

Daniella, Paris, 1967

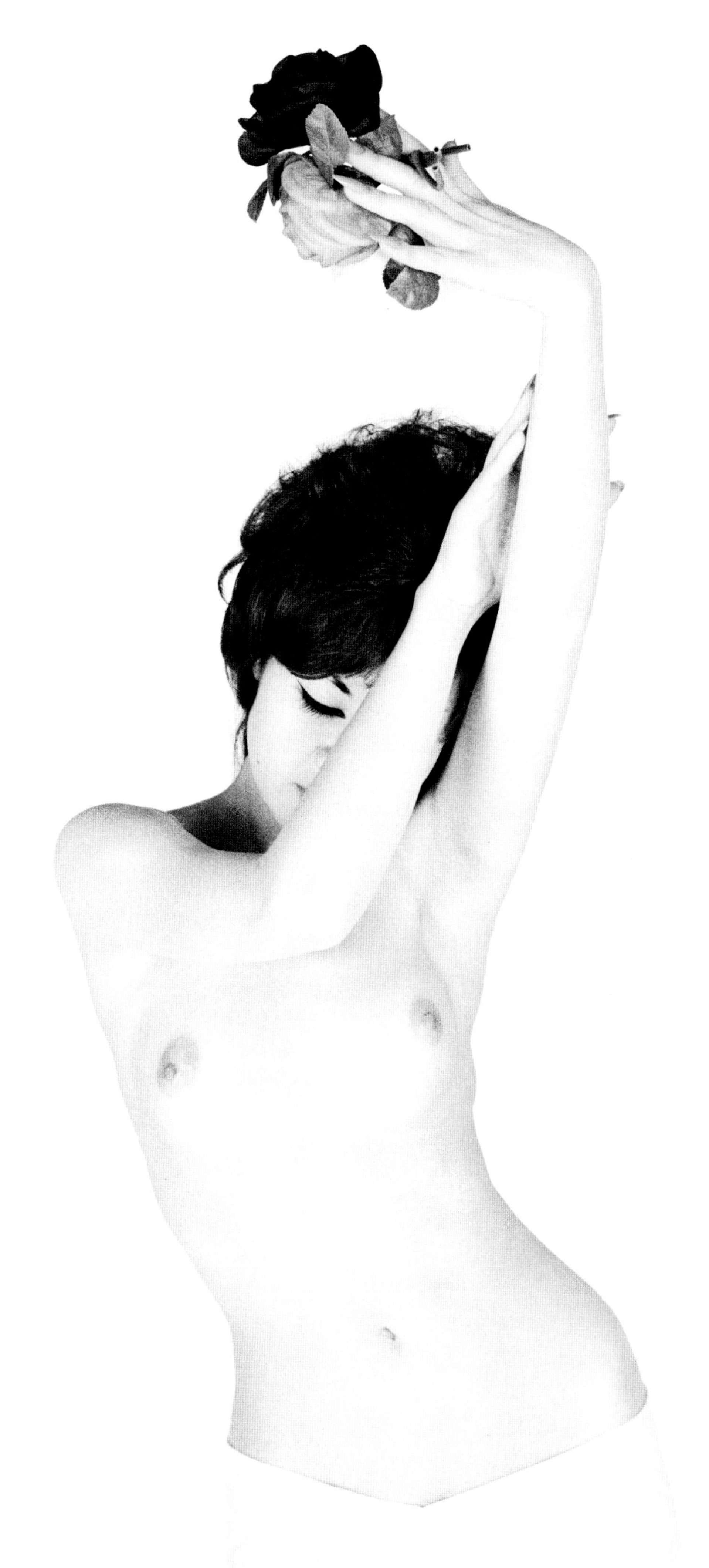

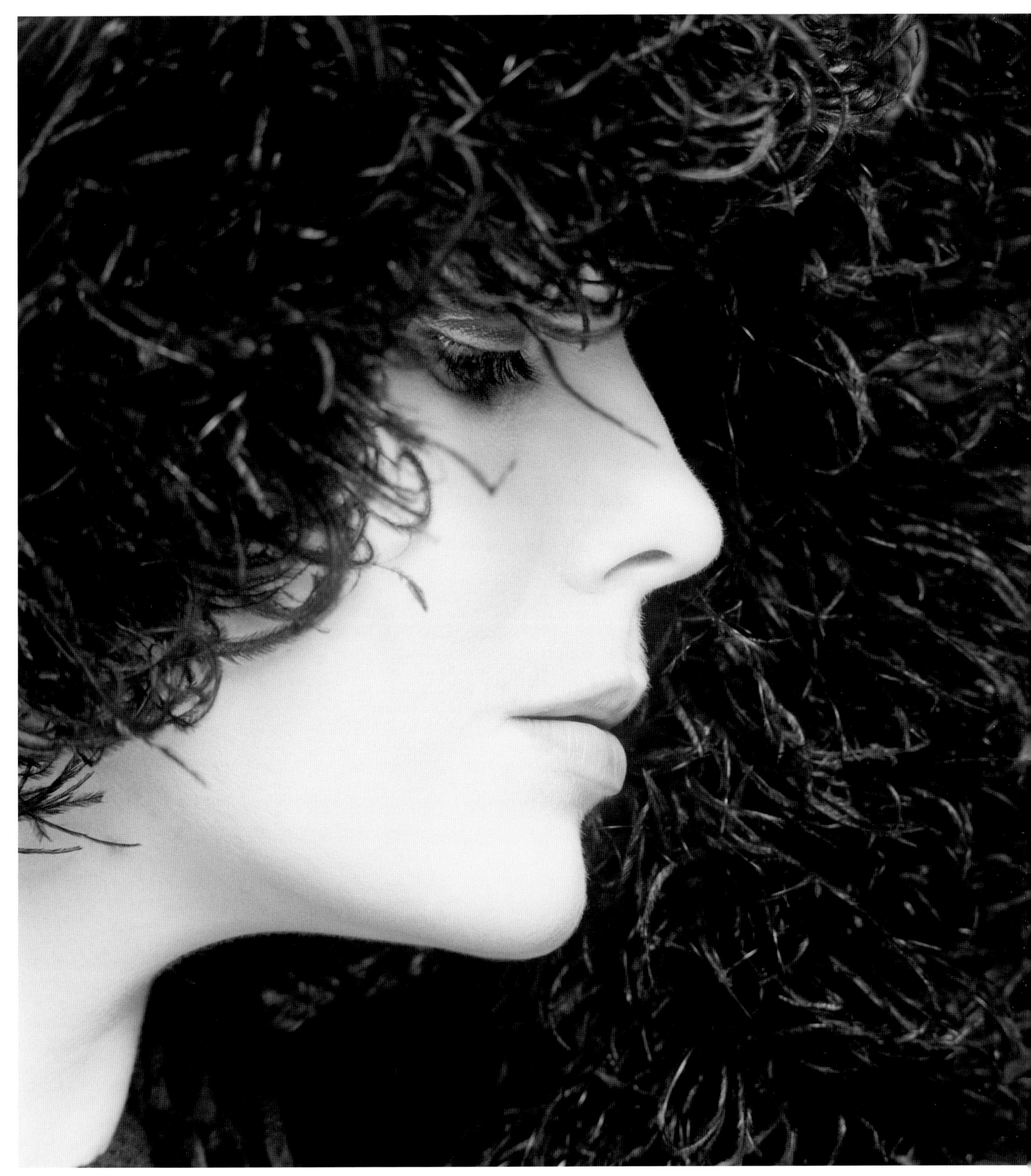

Paris, 1965

Juliette, Paris, 1960

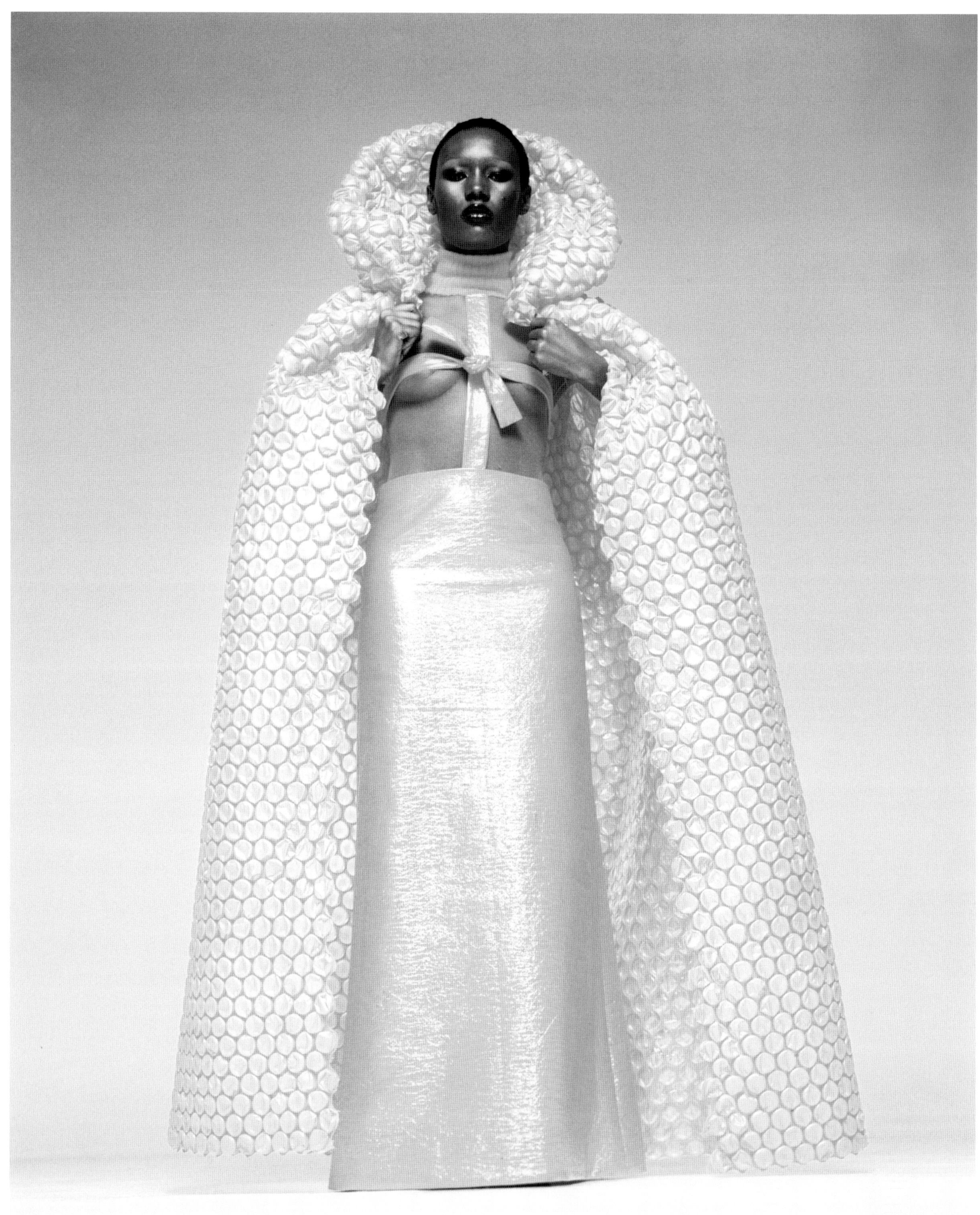

Grace Jones, Paris, 1969

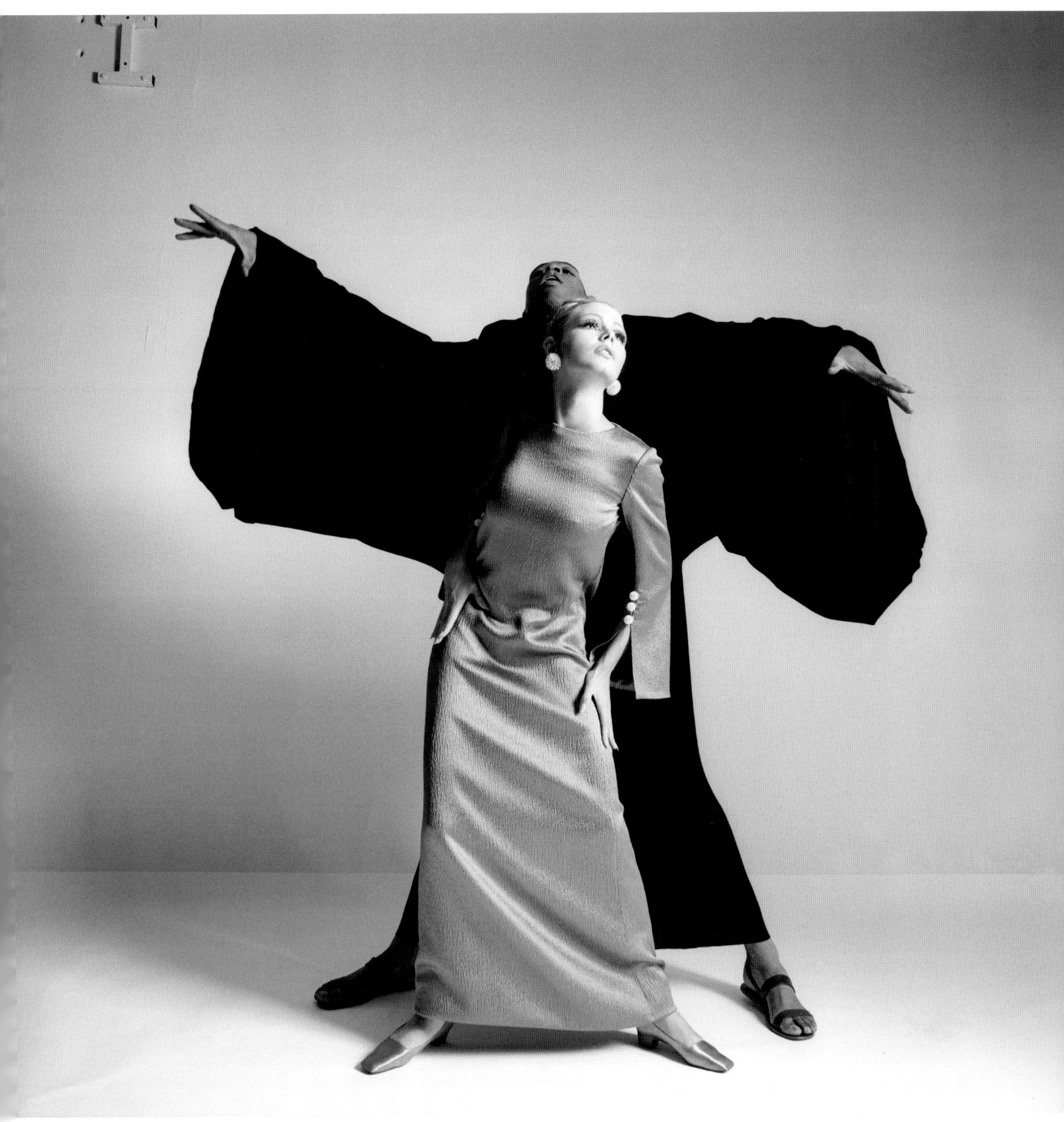

Geoffrey Holder and Danielle, Paris, 1968

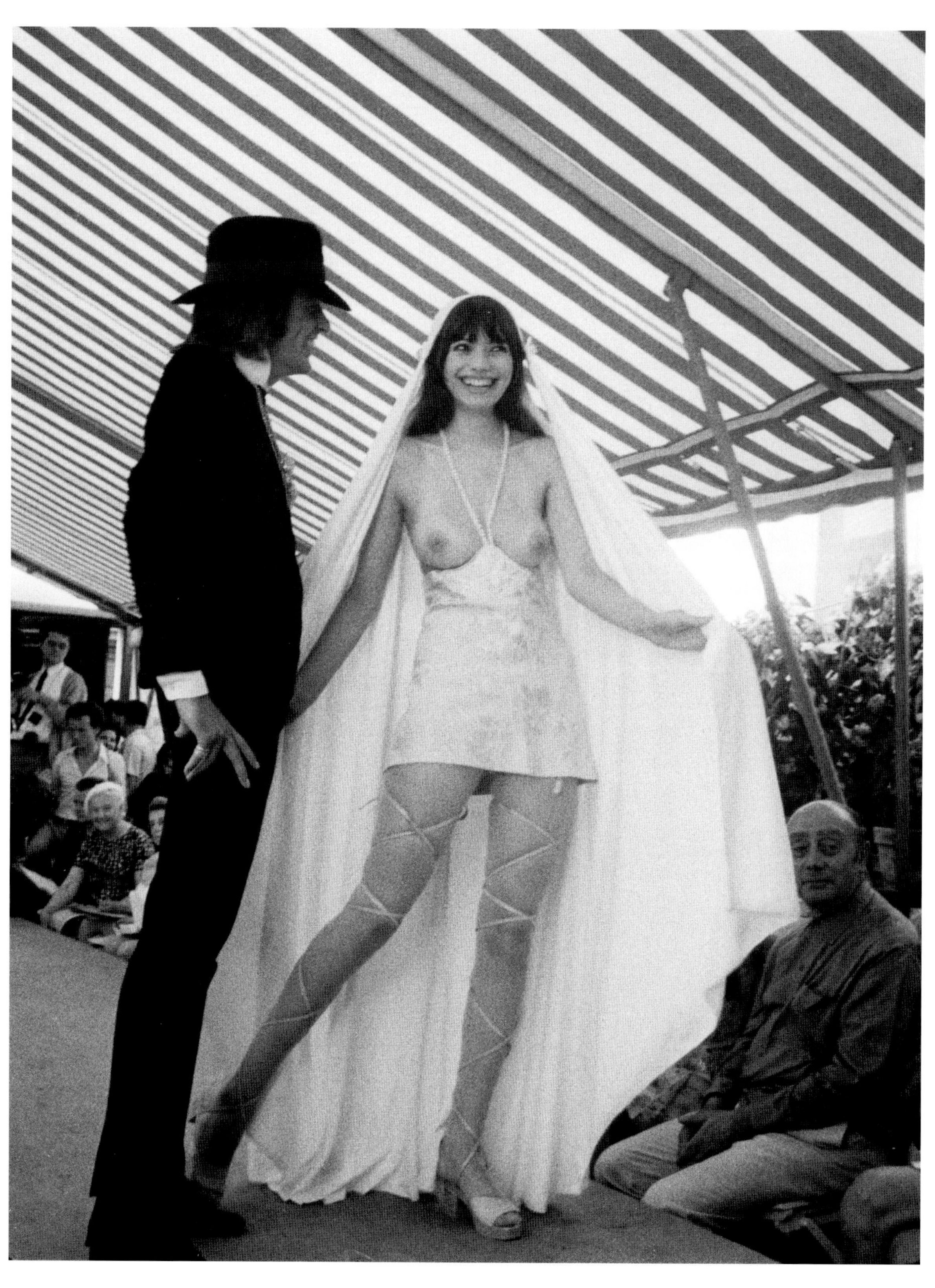

Paris, 1969

Veronica, New Orleans, 2005

Doc Cheatham, New Orleans, 1995 (overleaf)

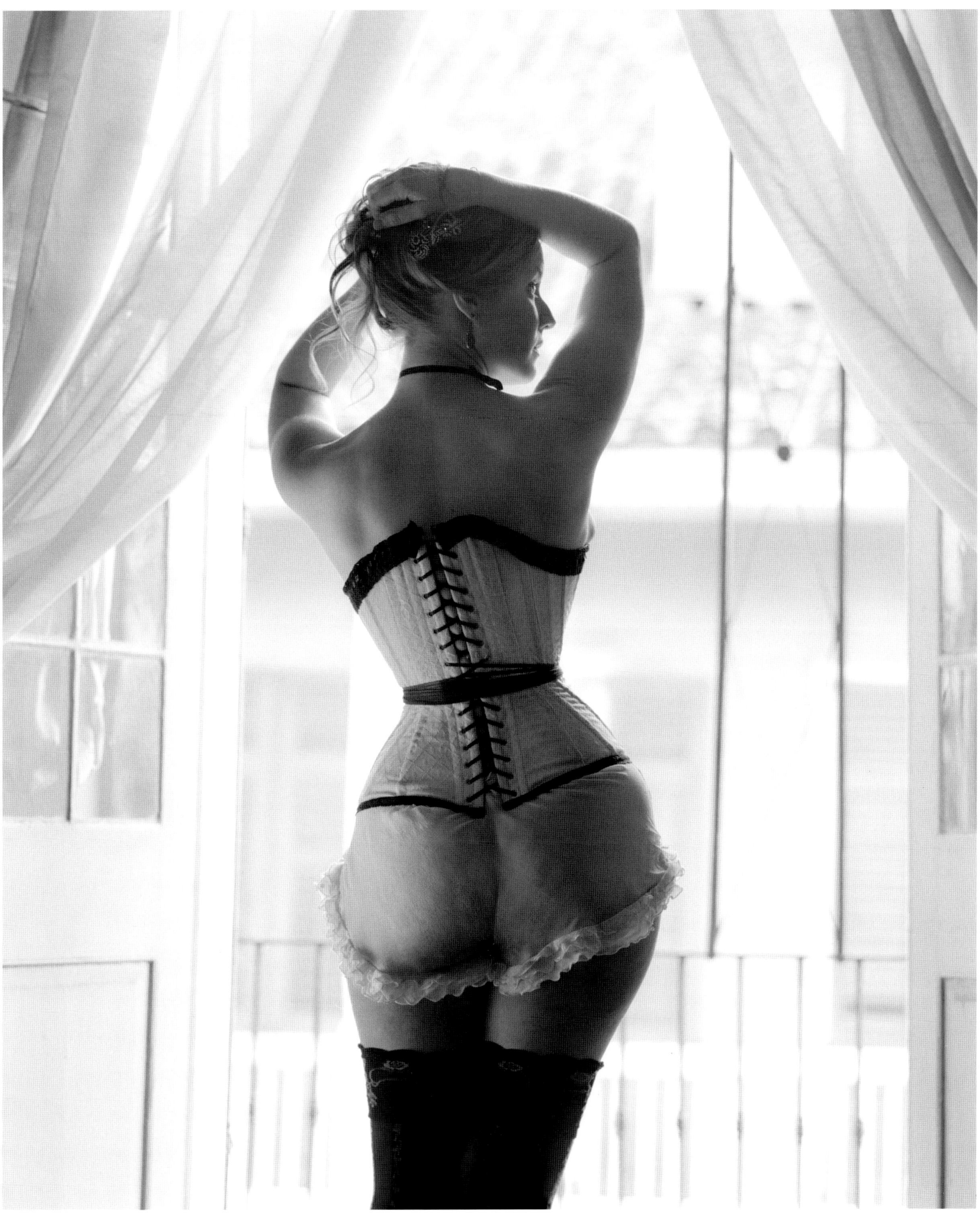

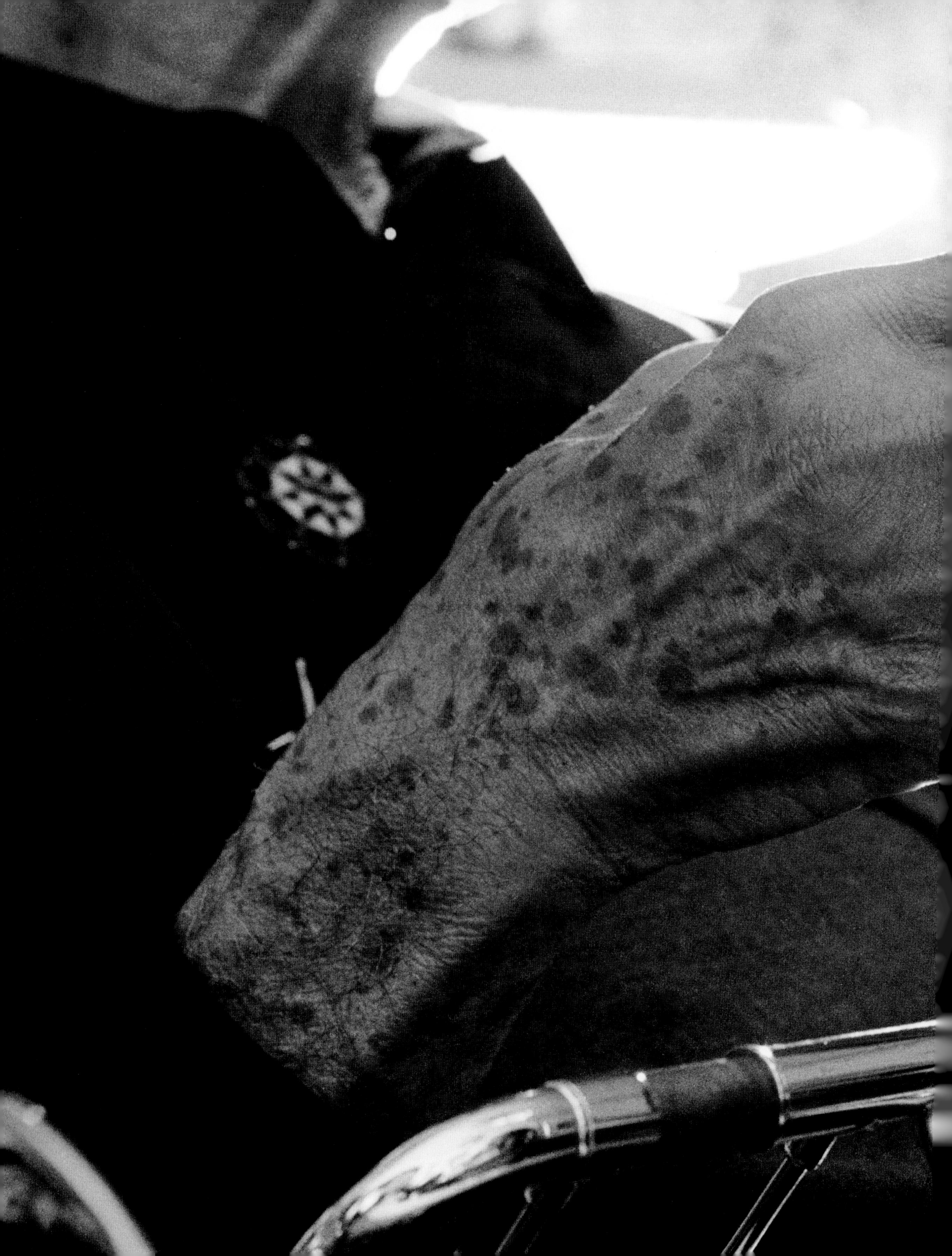

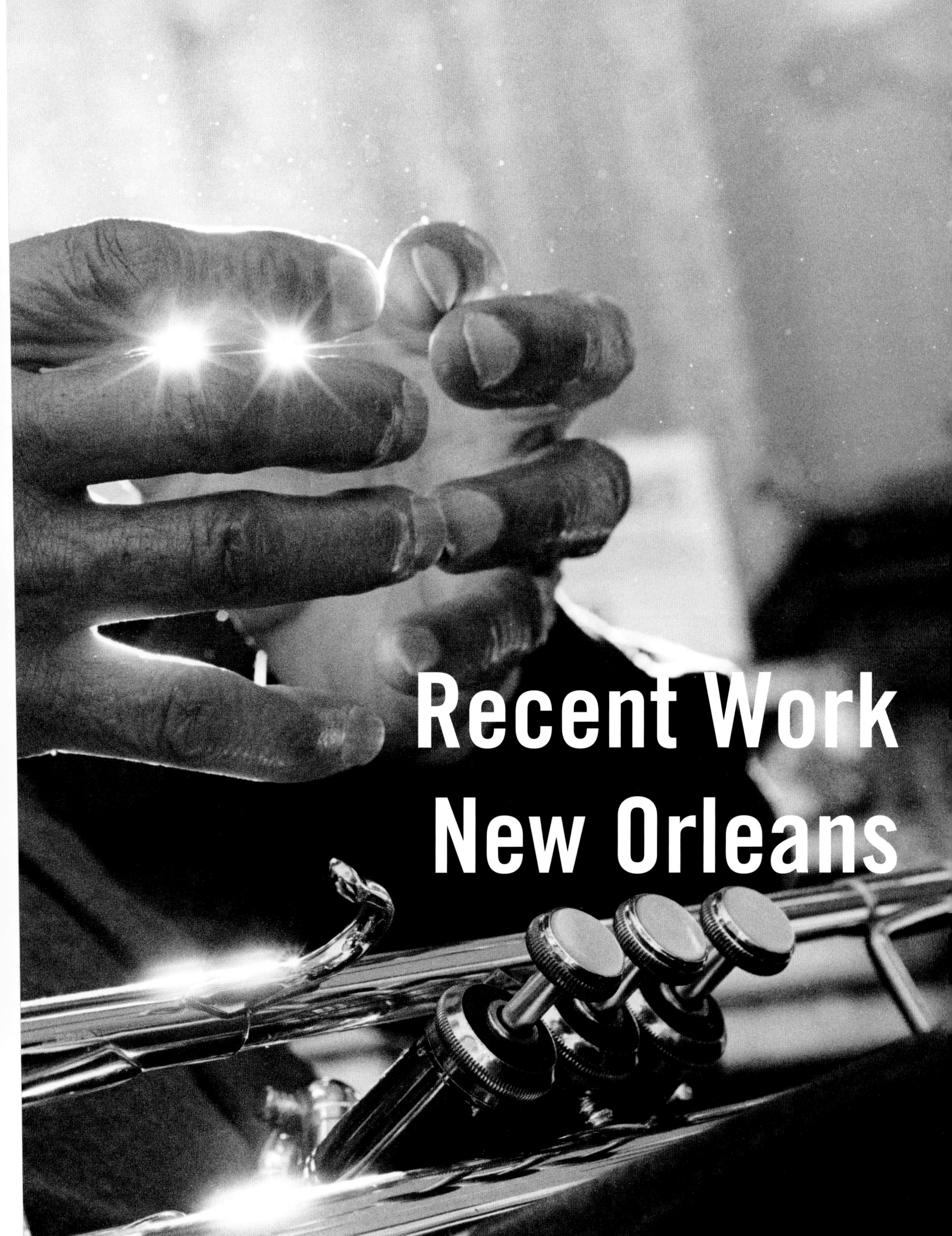

Recent Work New Orleans

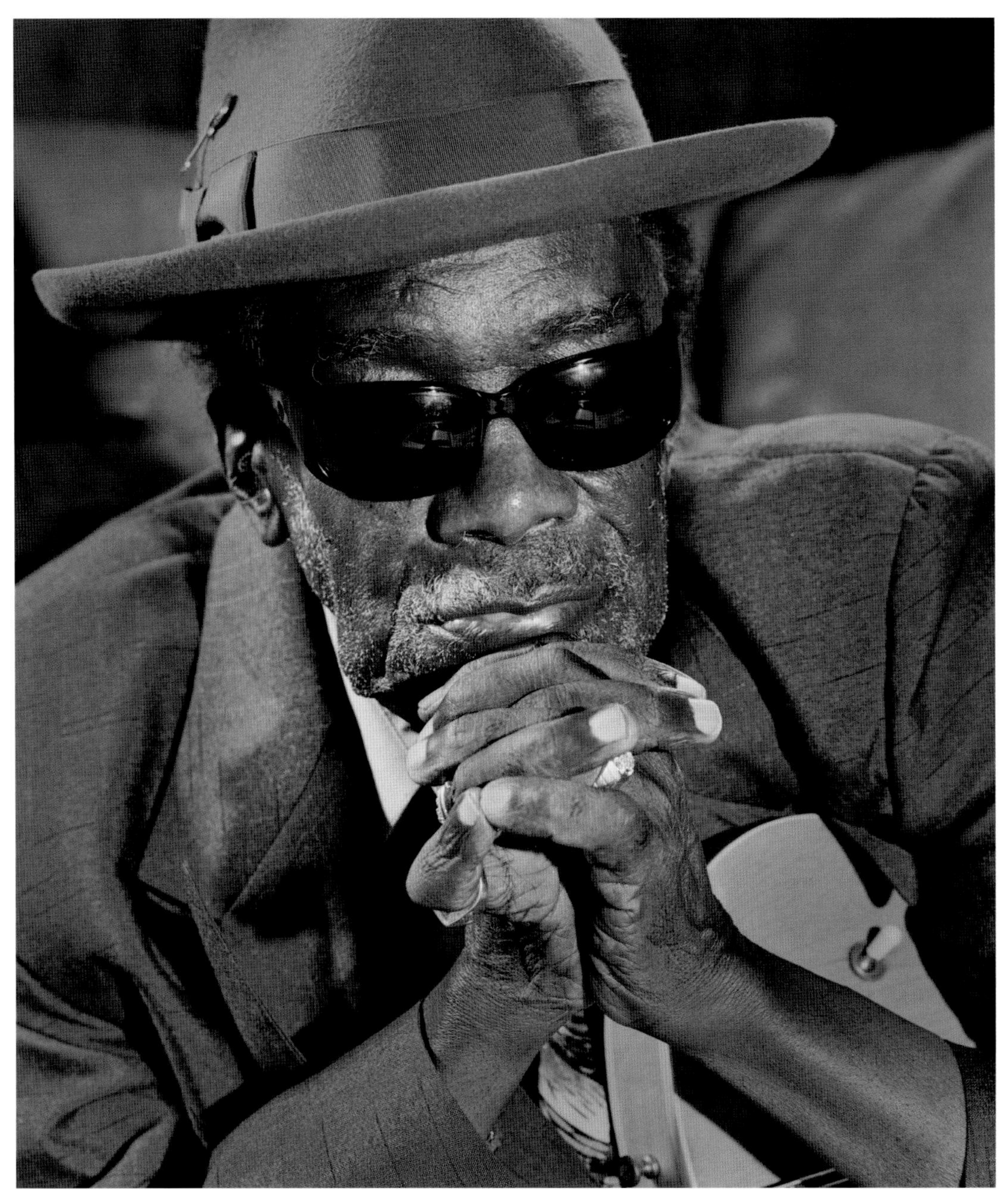

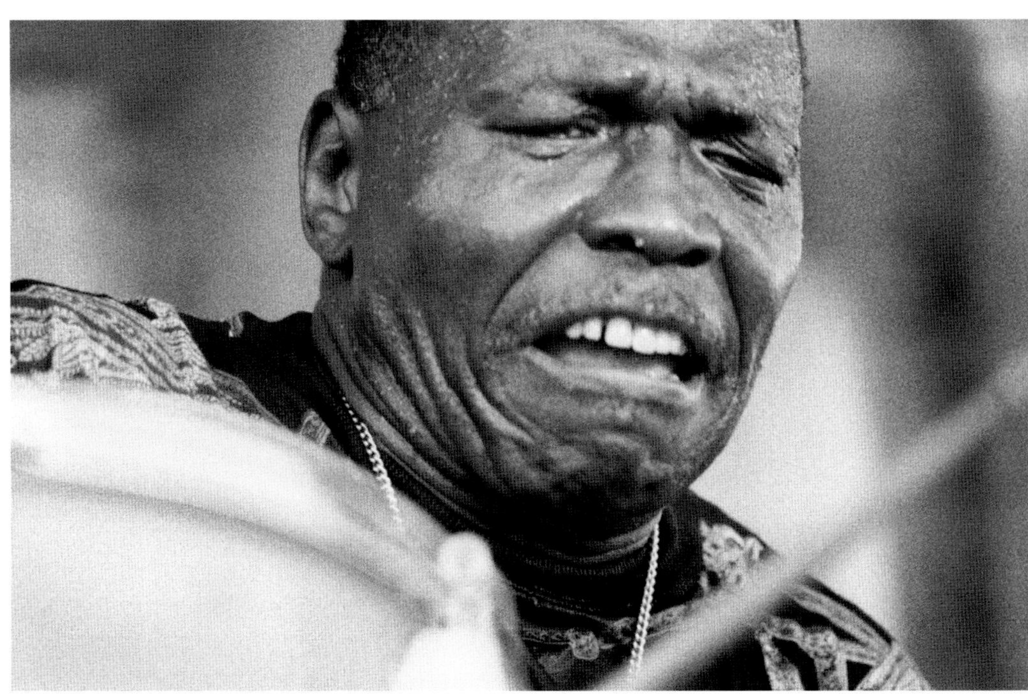

John Lee Hooker, San Francisco, 1998

Elvin Jones, Newport, 1990

Quincy Jones, Montreux, 1991

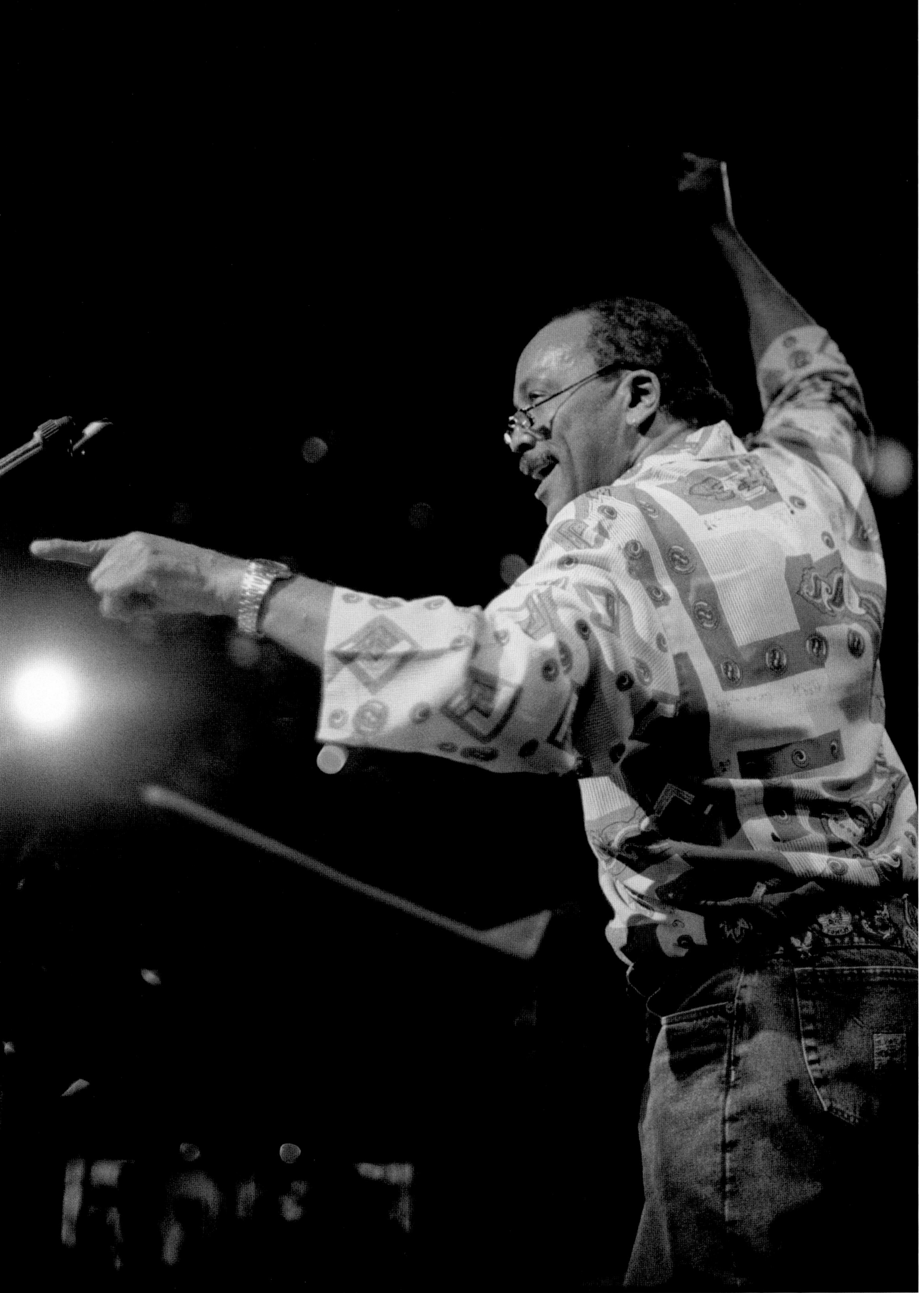

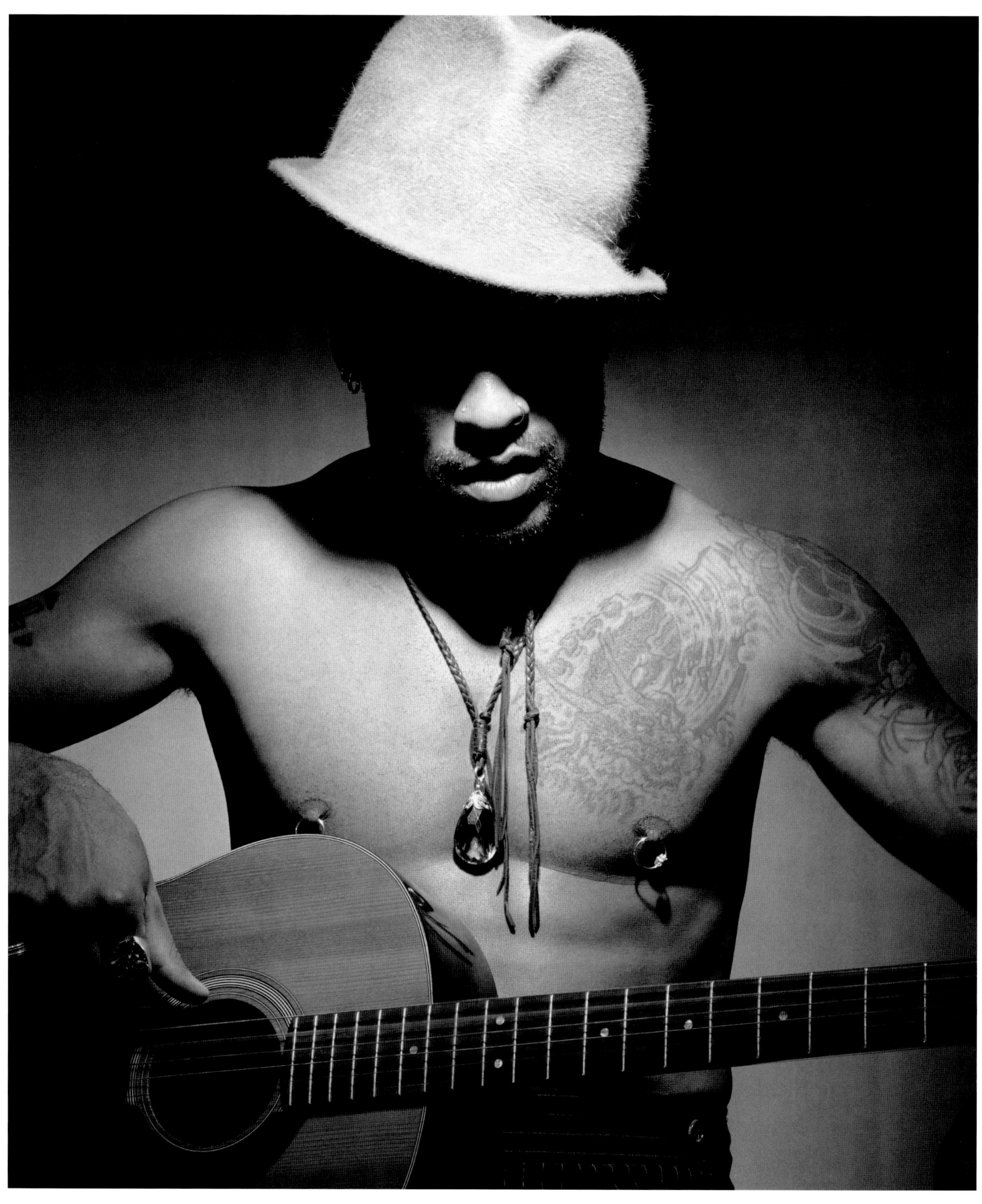

Lenny Kravitz, New Orleans, 2005

Lenny Kravitz, New Orleans, 1994

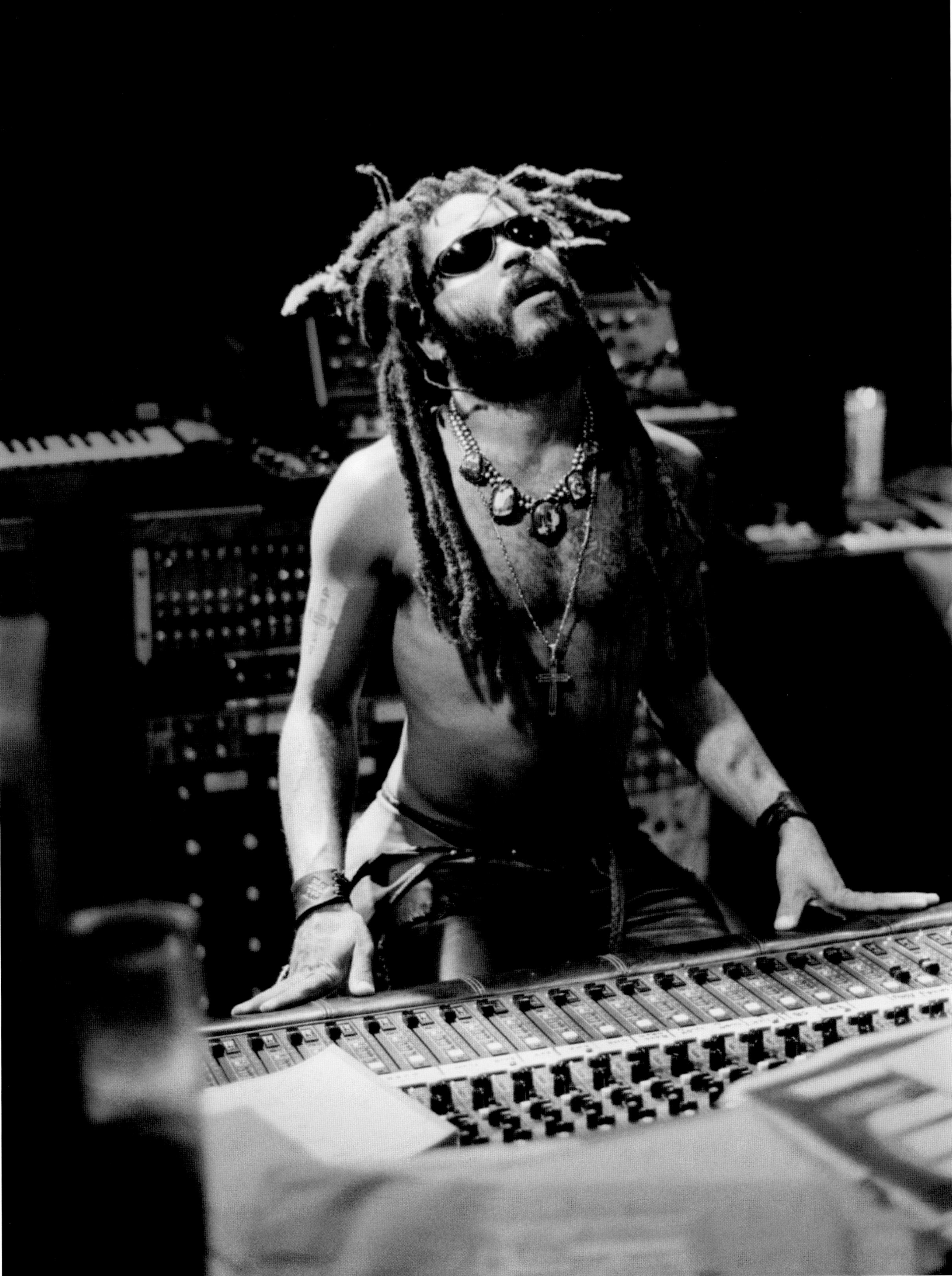

Michelle Gibson, New Orleans, 2001

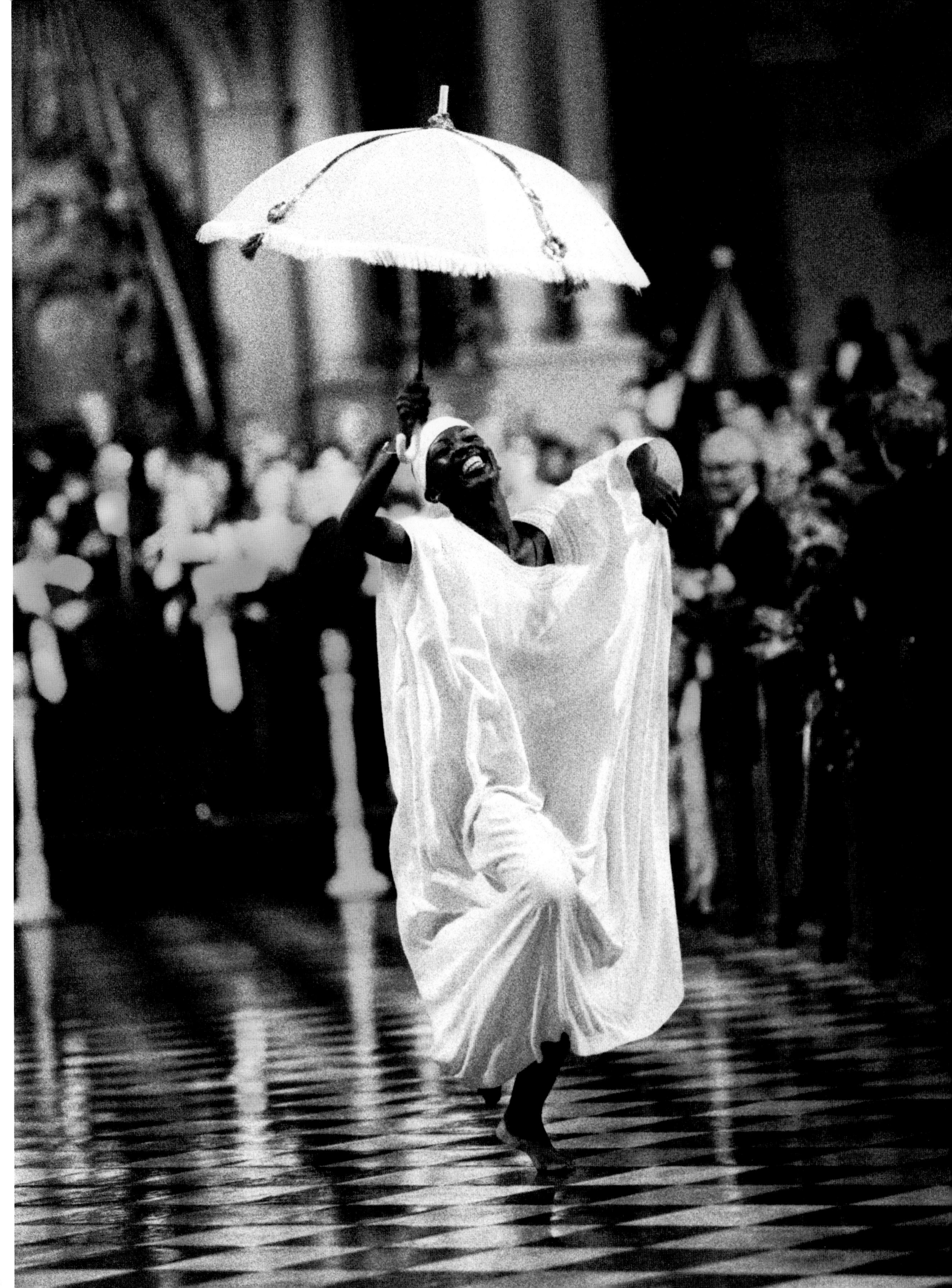

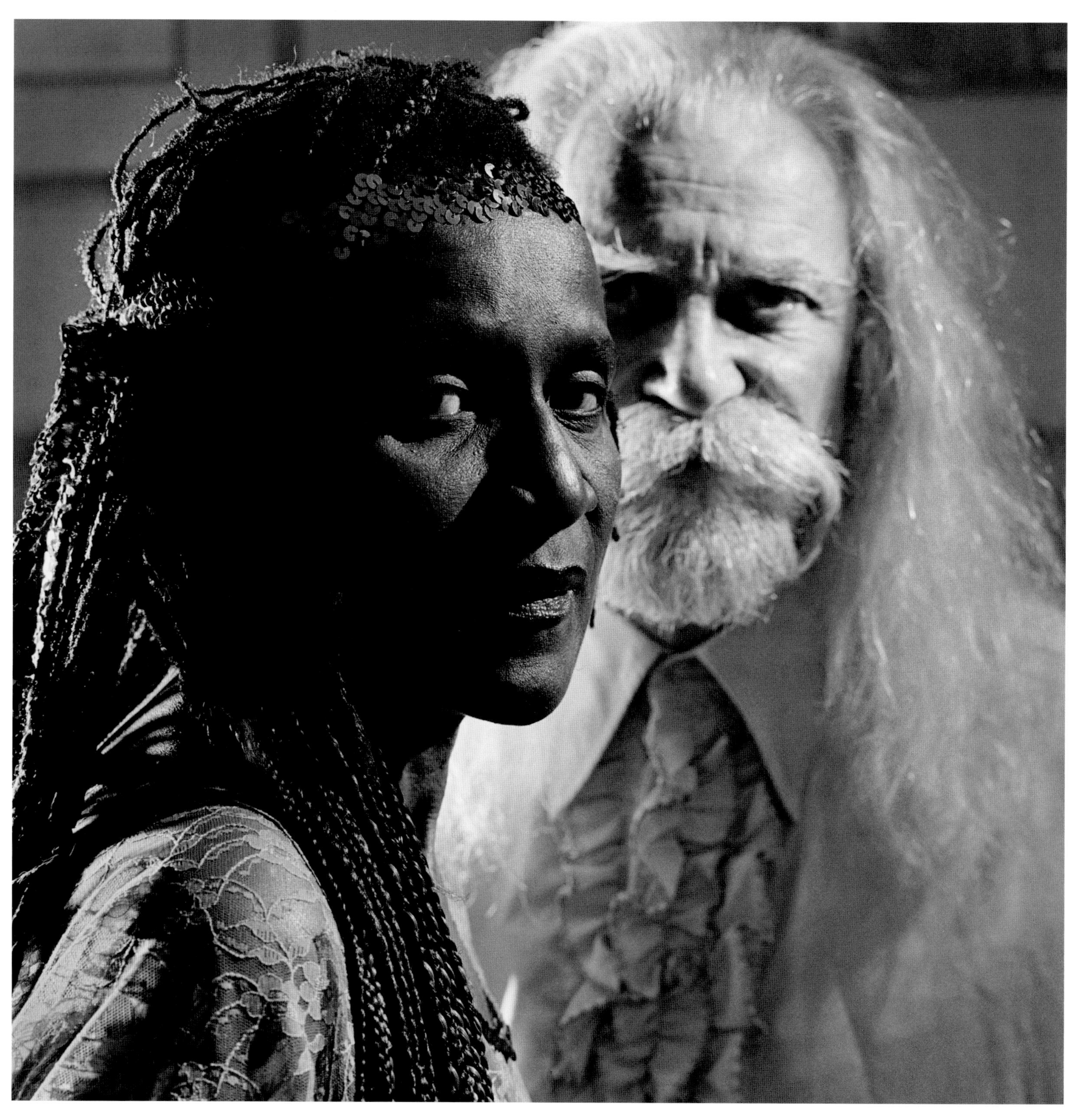

David Leonard and Roselyn Lionhart, New Orleans, 2000

Troy 'Trombone Shorty' Andrews, New Orleans, 1995

Terrylyn and family, New Orleans, 1995

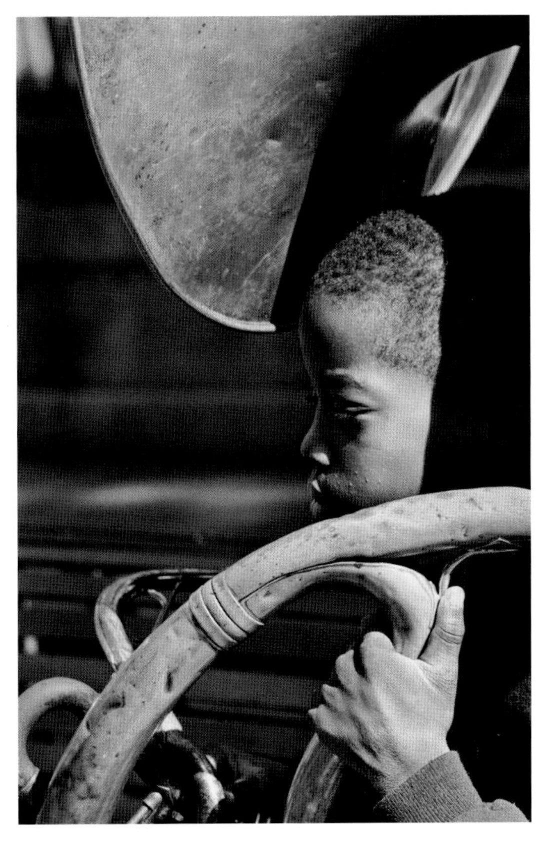

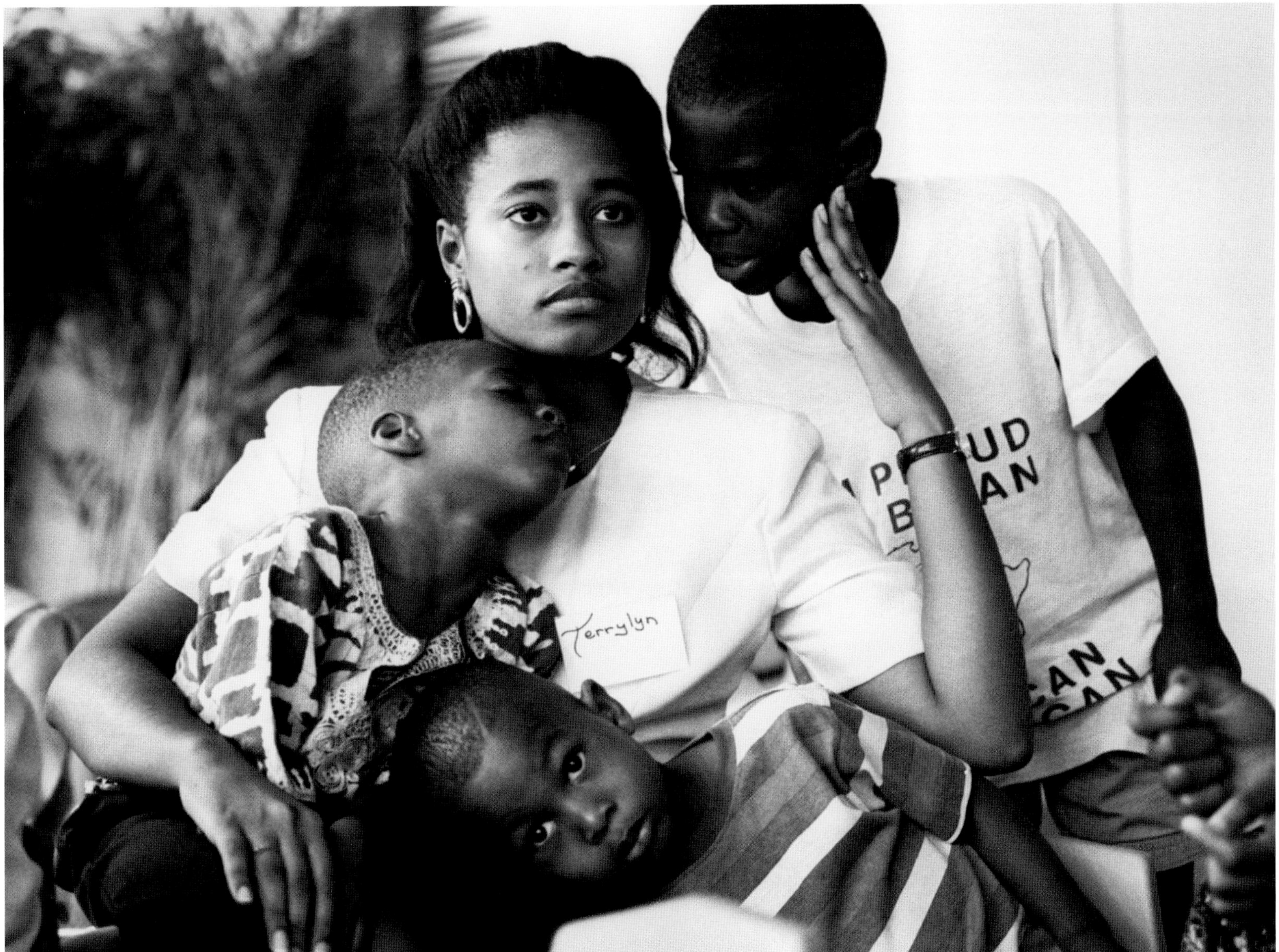

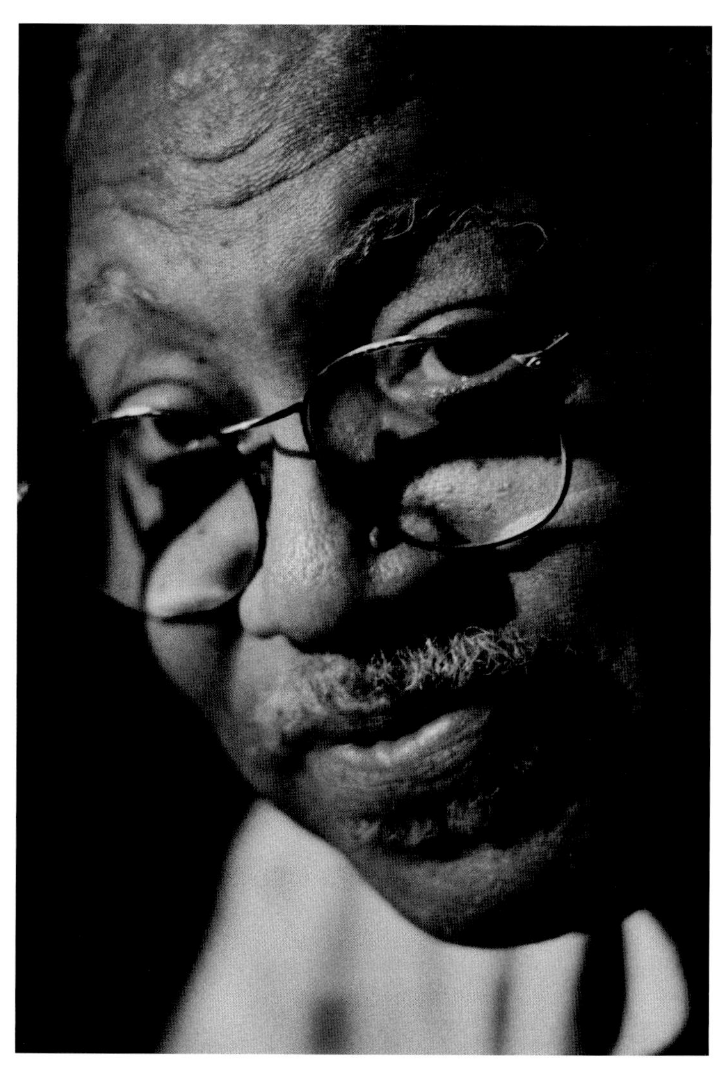

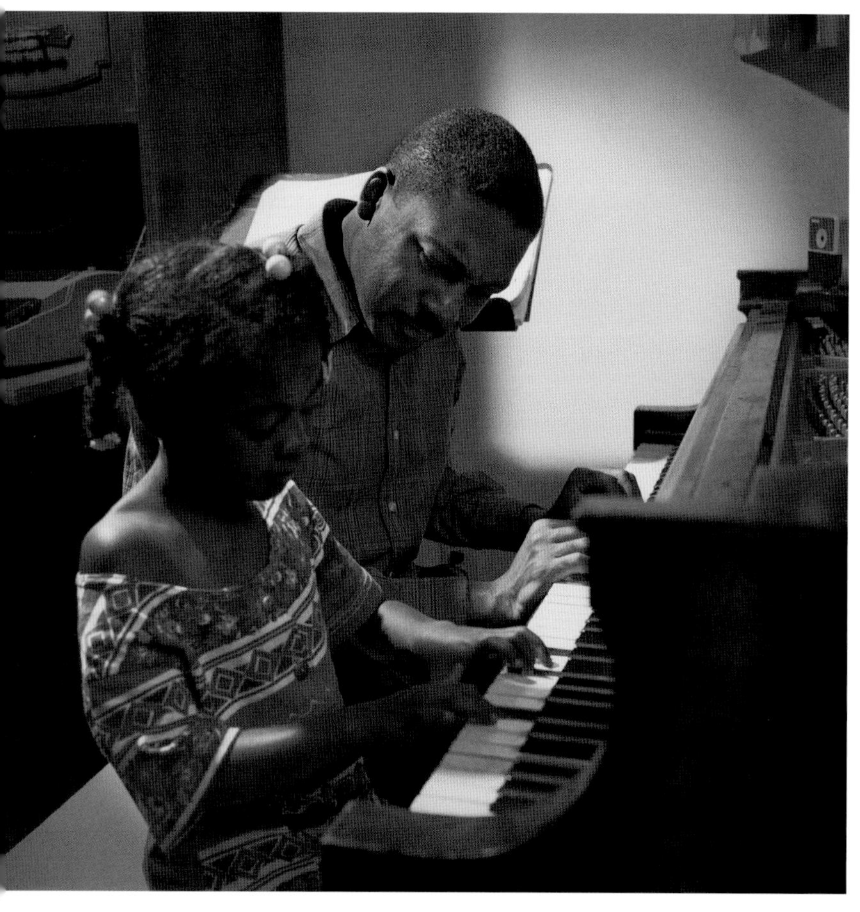

Wynton Marsalis and Colleen Annette McCarthy, New Orleans, 1993

Ellis Marsalis, New Orleans, 1997

Wynton Marsalis, New Orleans, 1993

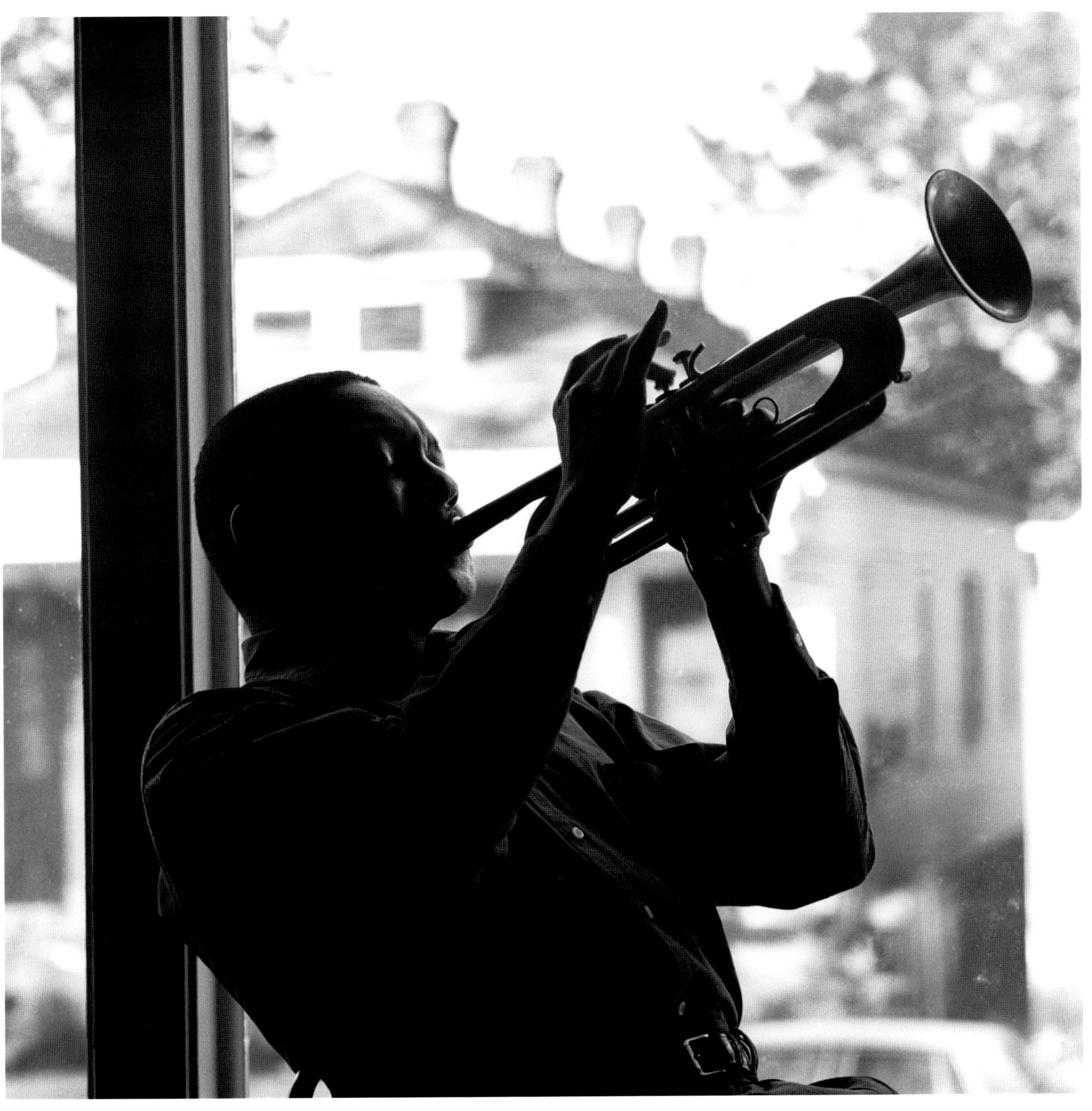

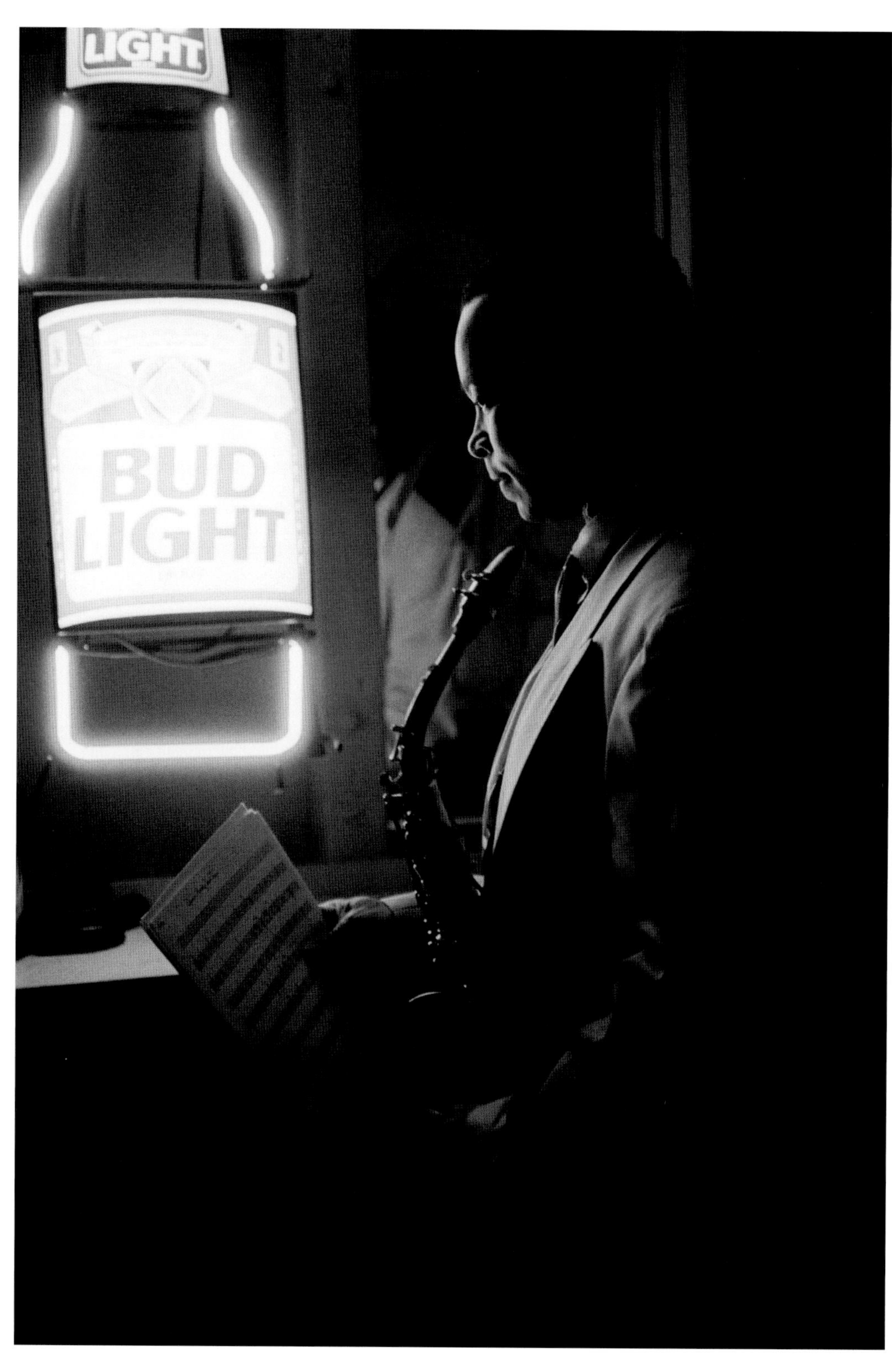

Victor Goines, New Orleans, 1996

Irvin Mayfield, New Orleans, 2000

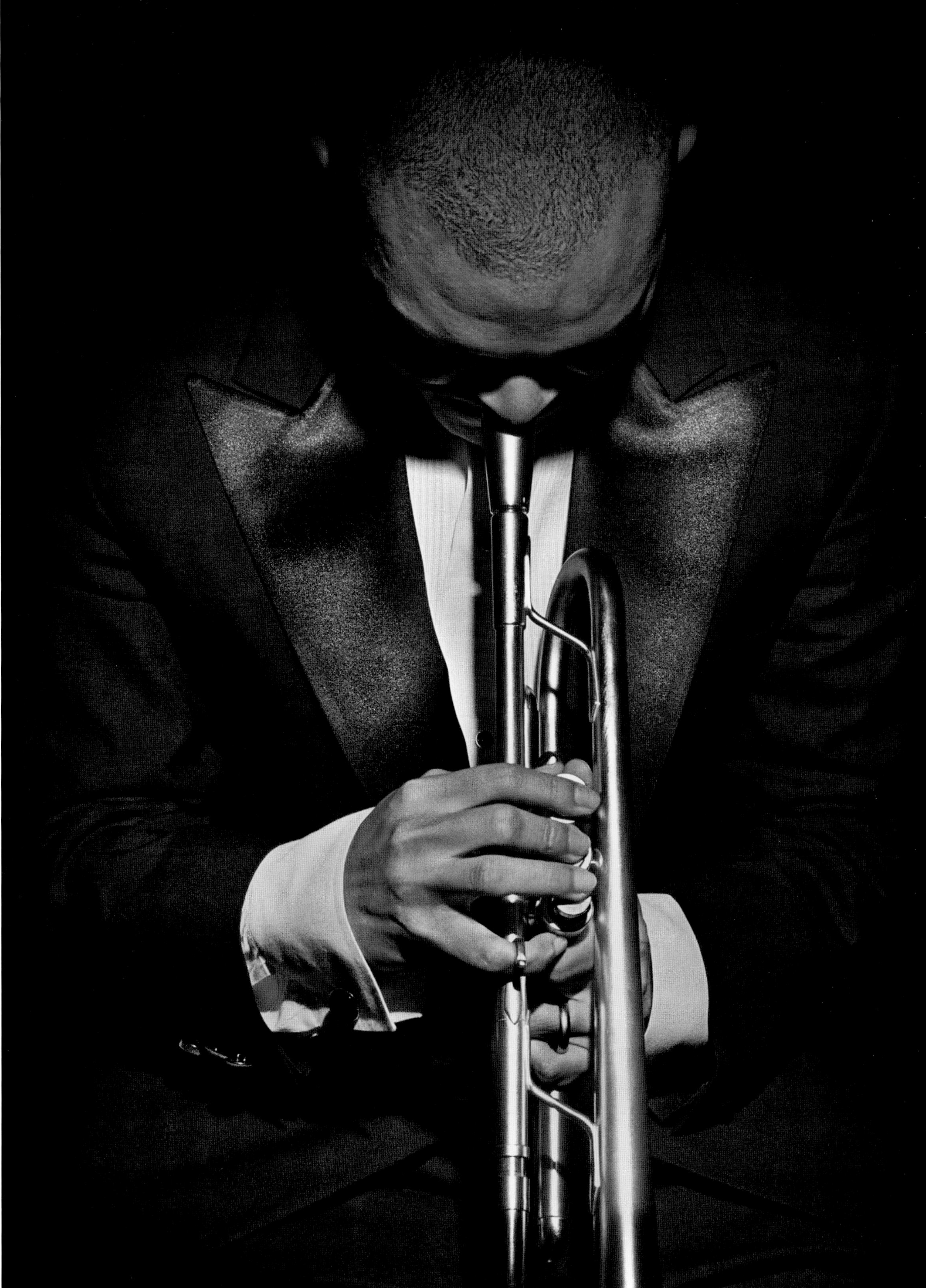

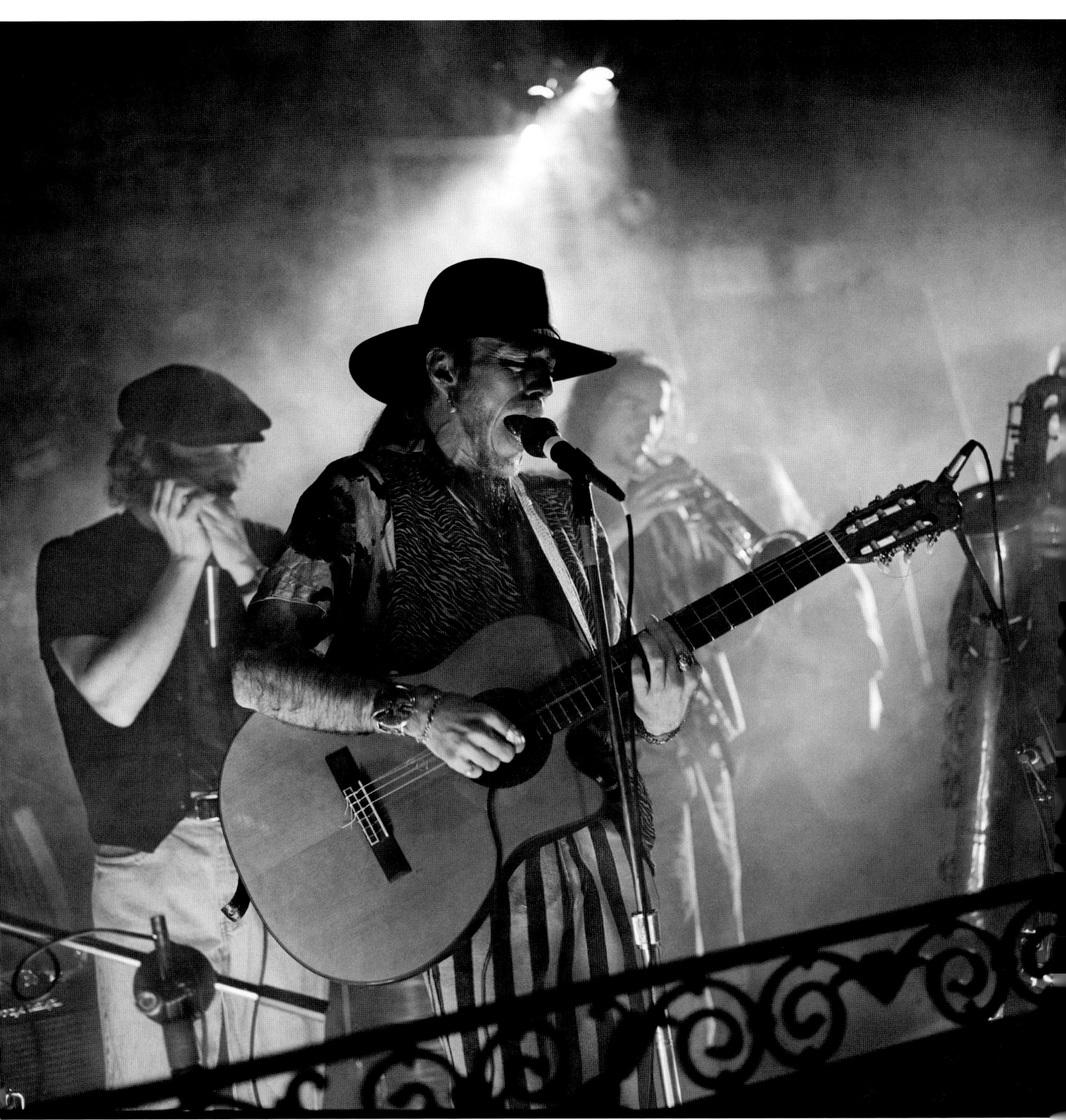

Coco Robicheaux, Checkpoint Charlie's, New Orleans, 1996

Henry Butler, New Orleans, 1999

John Vidacovich, New Orleans, 2002

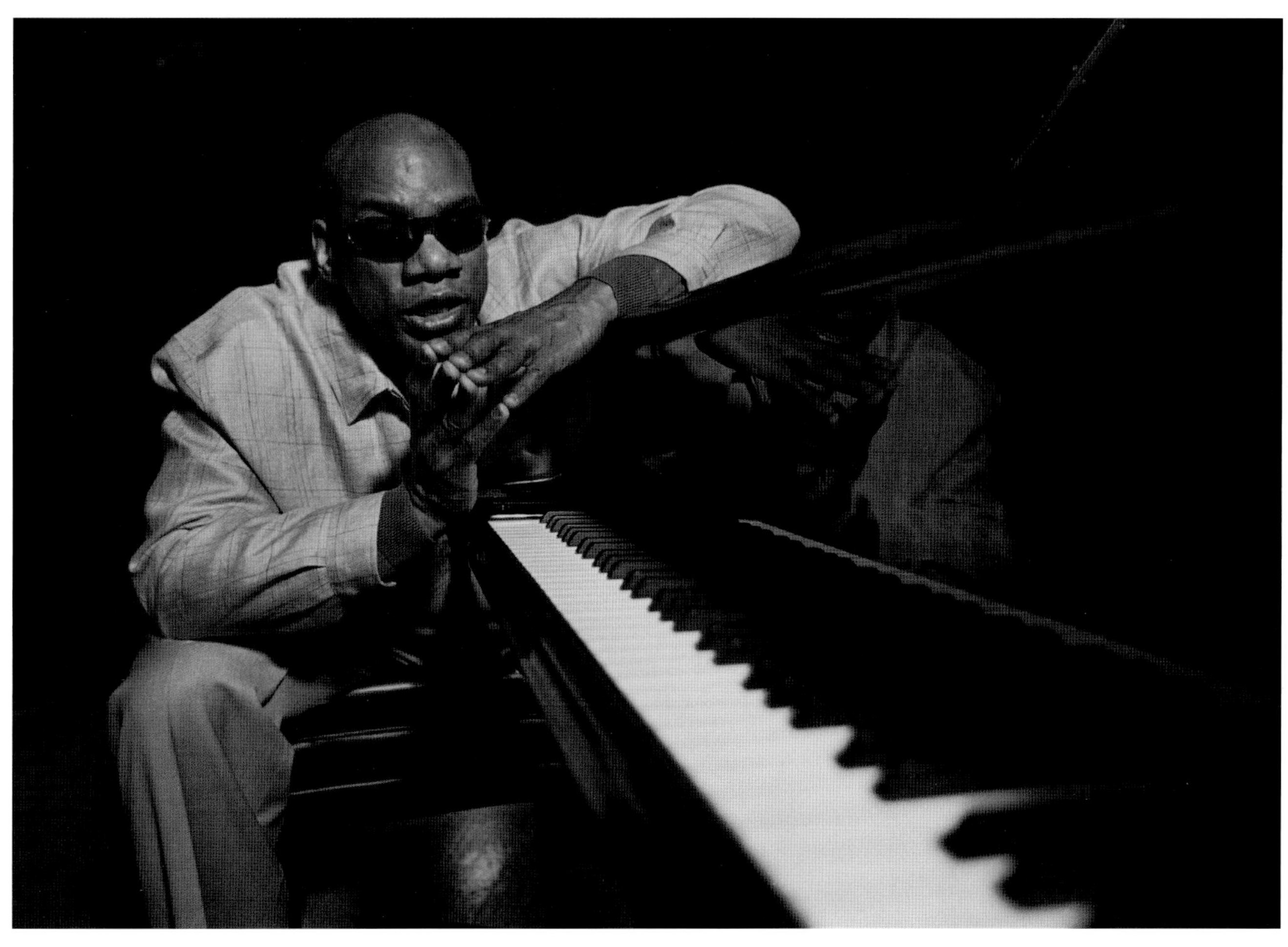

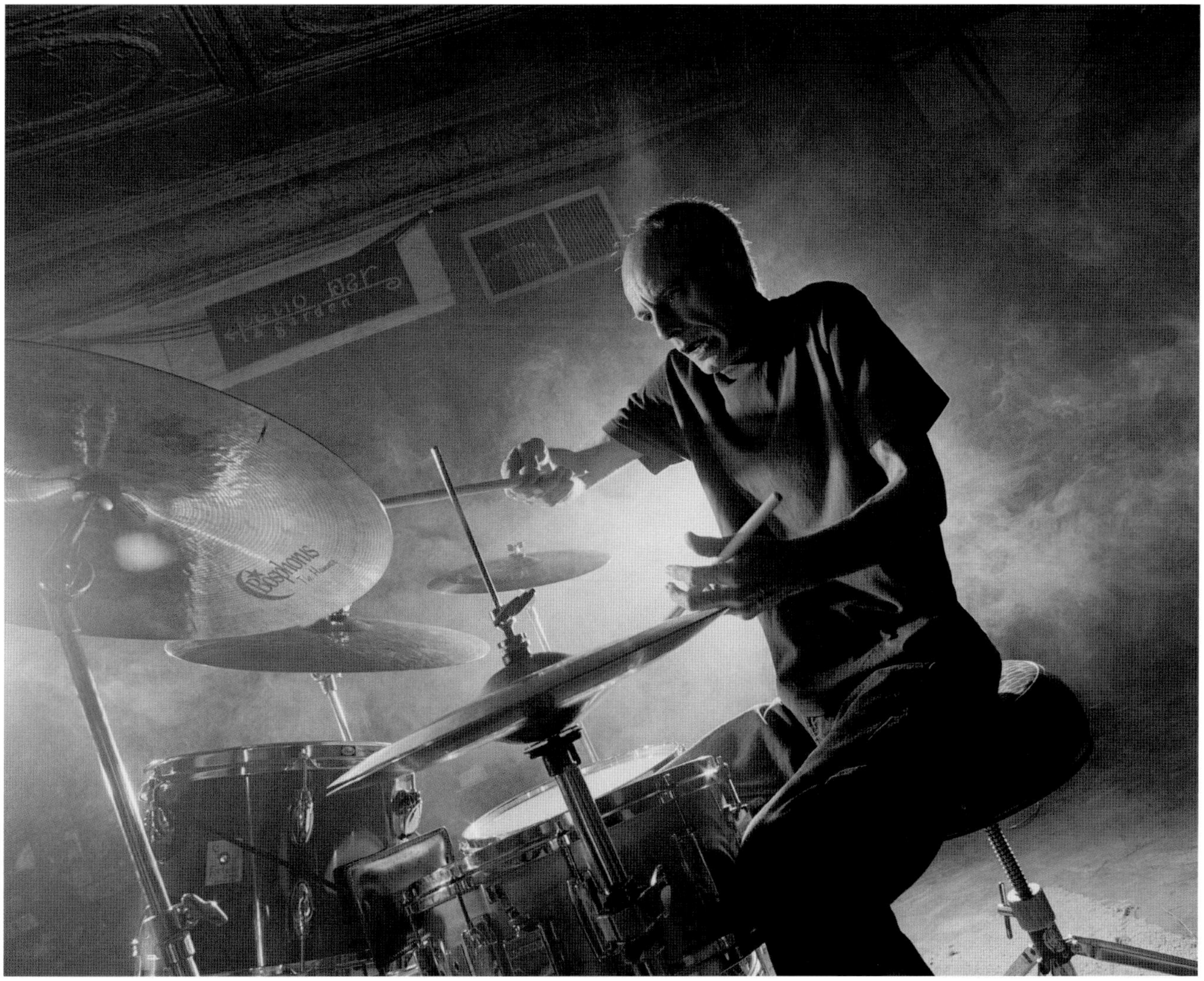

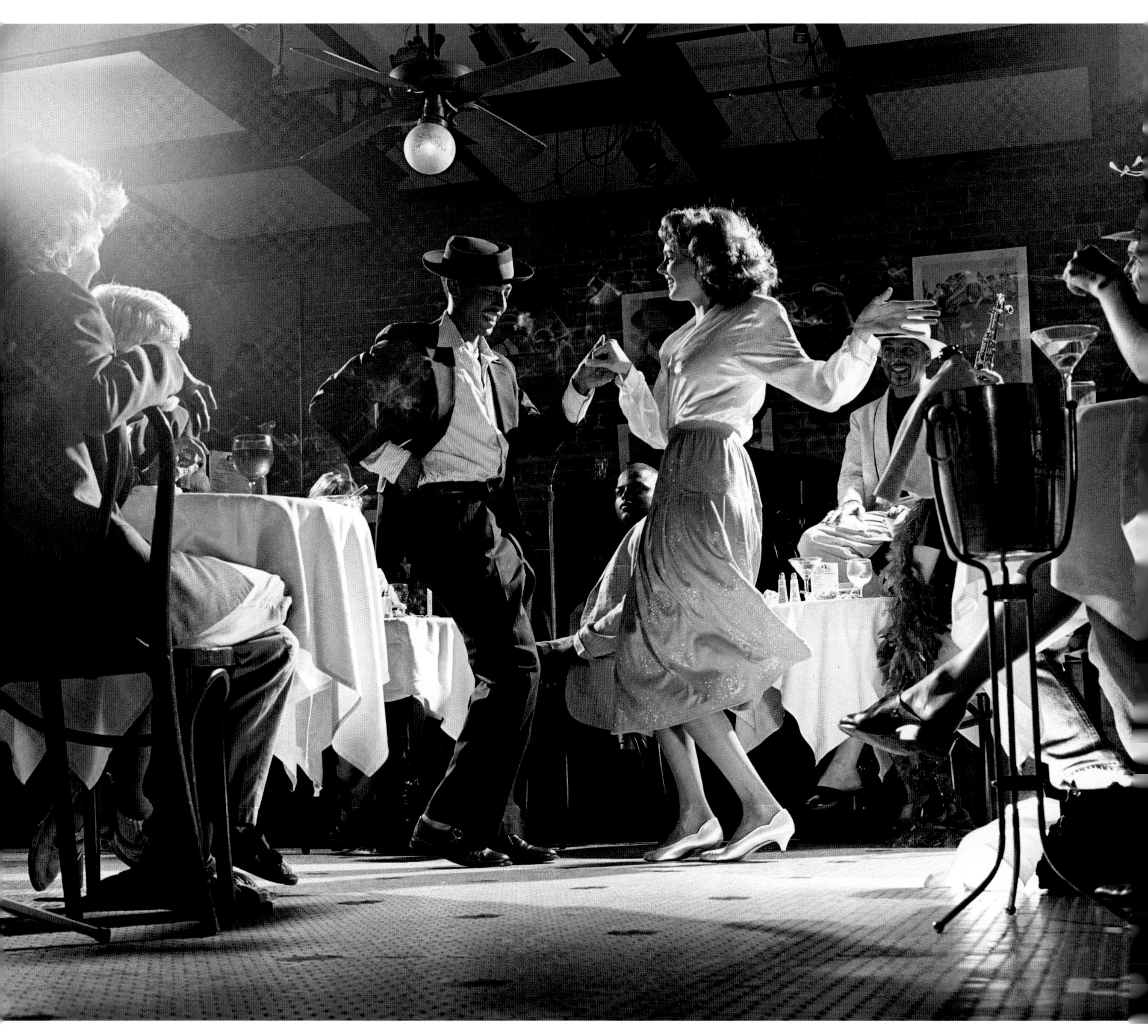

Palm Court Café, New Orleans, 1996

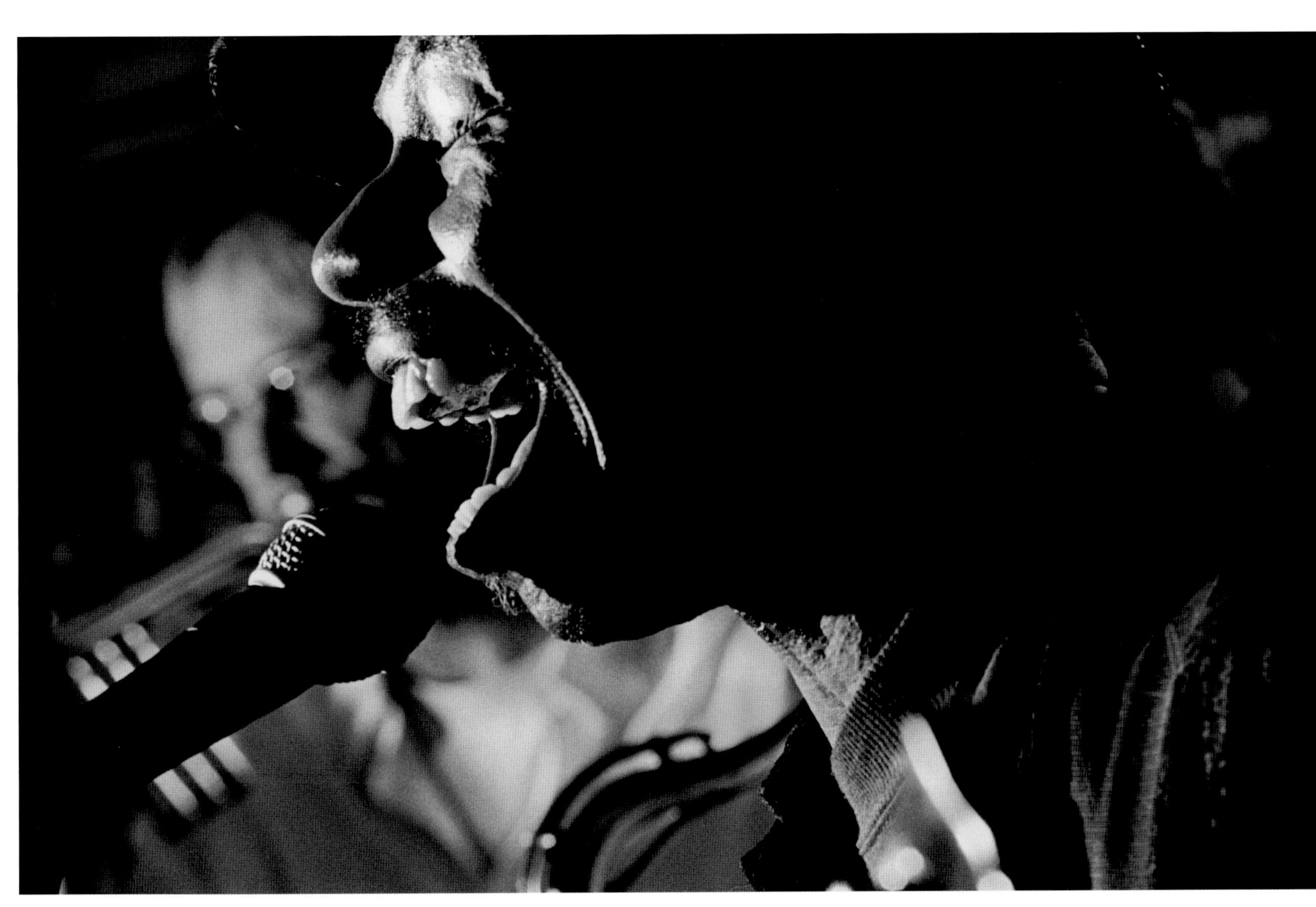

Walter 'Wolfman' Washington, New Orleans, 1997

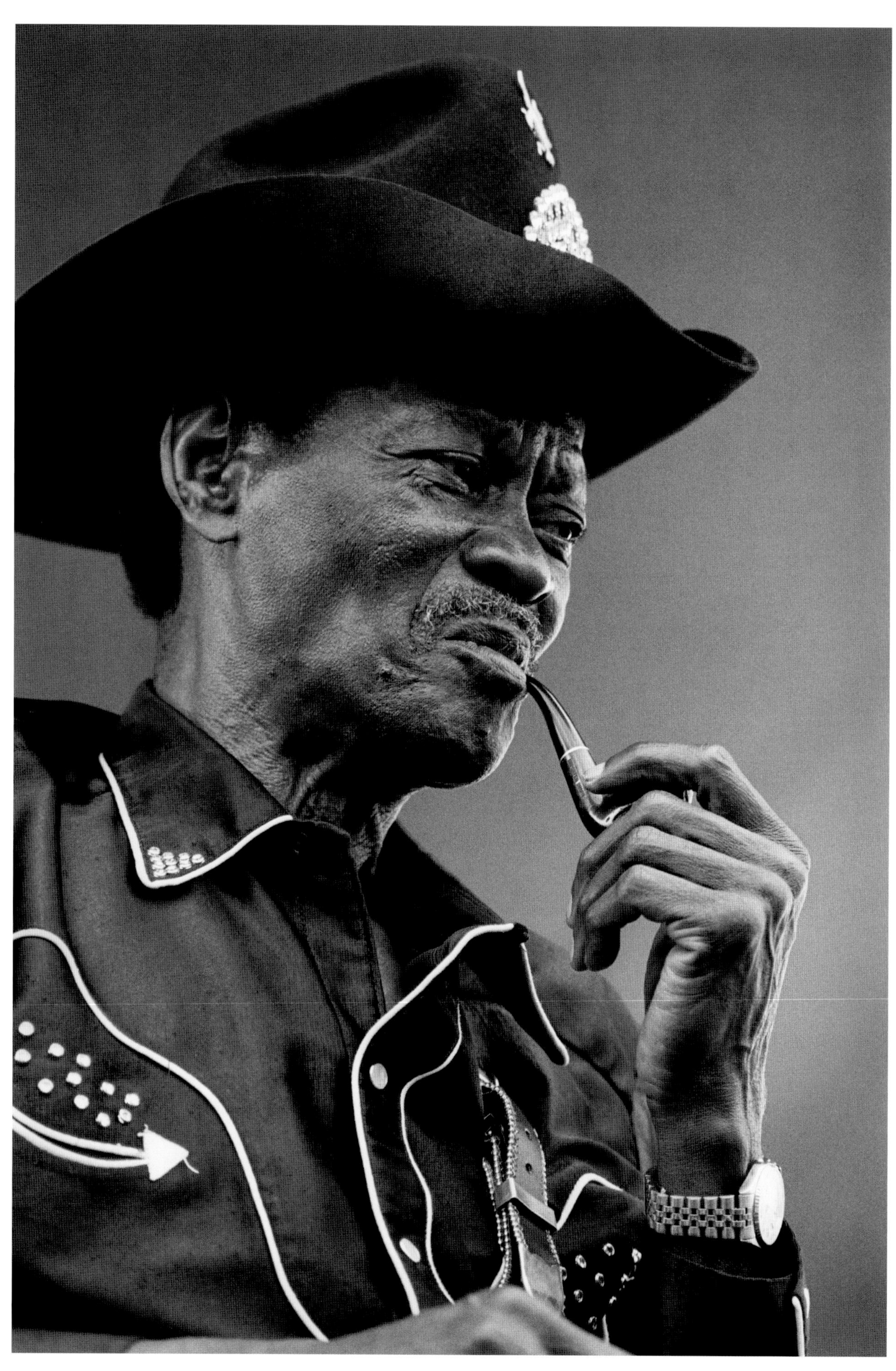

Clarence 'Gatemouth' Brown, New Orleans, 1993

Dr. John, San Francisco, 1992

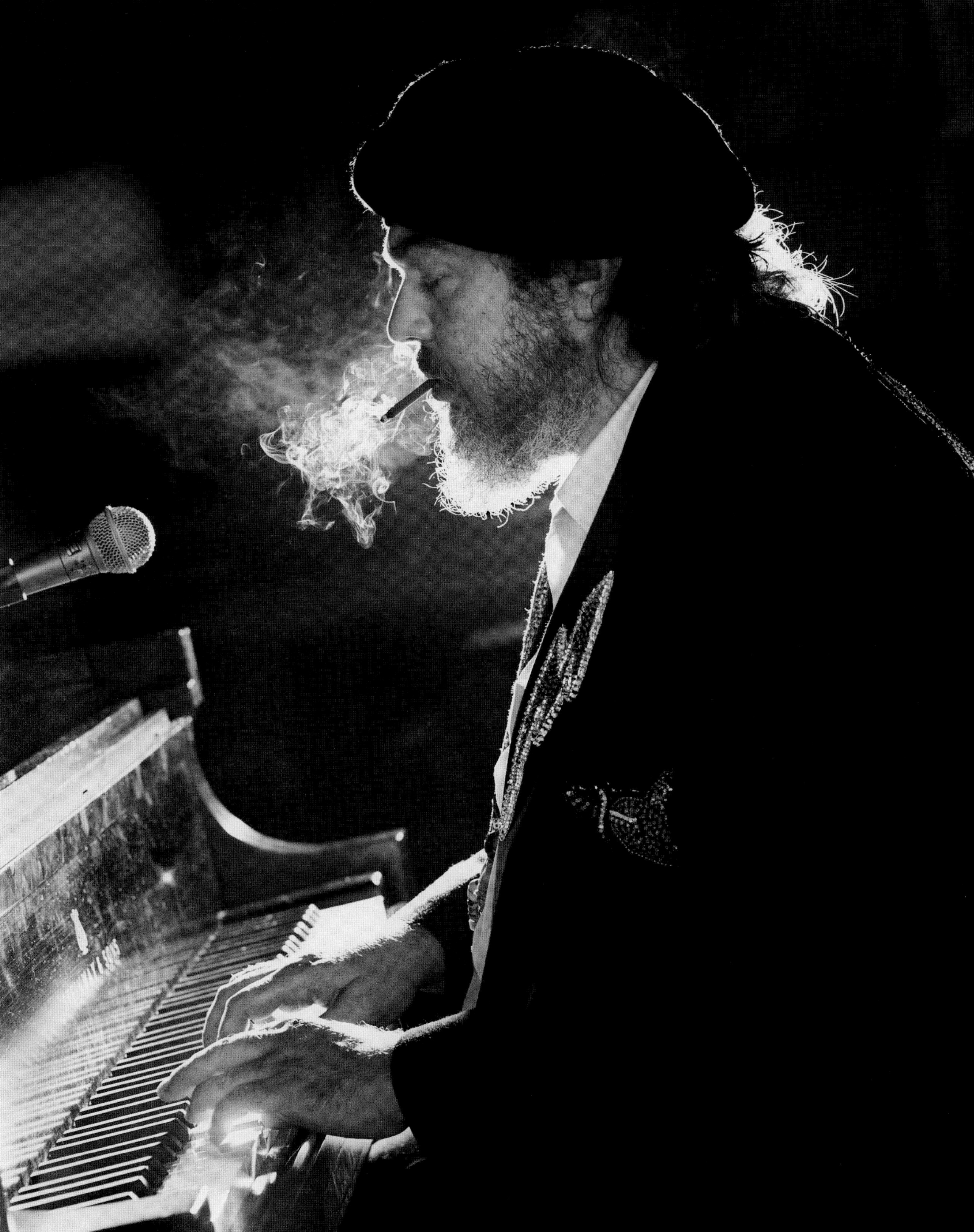

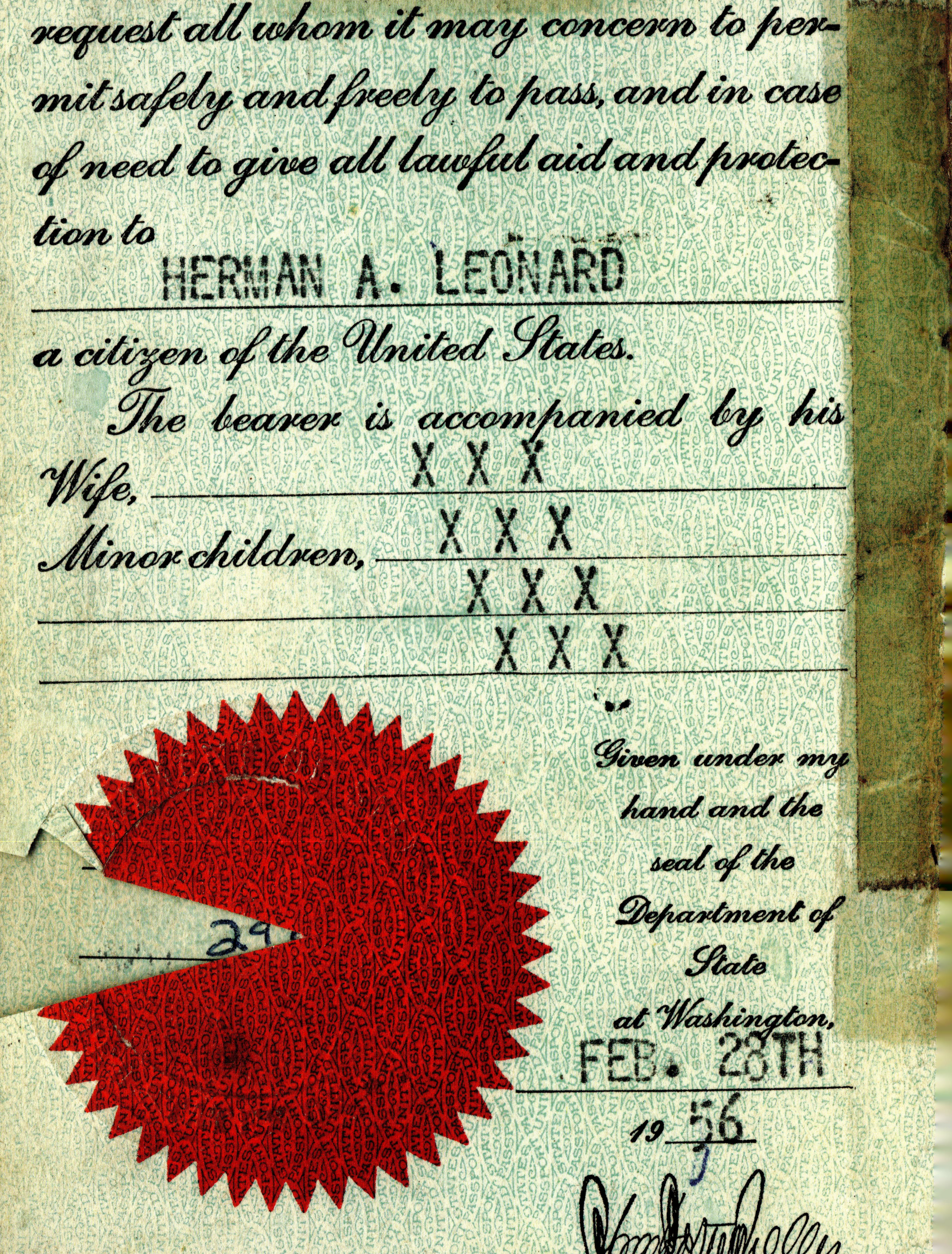

request all whom it may concern to permit safely and freely to pass, and in case of need to give all lawful aid and protection to

HERMAN A. LEONARD

a citizen of the United States.

The bearer is accompanied by his

Wife, XXX

Minor children, XXX

XXX

XXX

Given under my hand and the seal of the Department of State at Washington,

FEB. 28TH

19 56

Hair BROWN

Eyes BROWN

Distinguishing marks or features:

X X X

X X X

X X X

Place of birth ALLENTOWN,

PA.

Date of birth MAR. 6, 1923

Occupation PHOTOGRAPHER

X X X

X X X

Timeline
Exhibition History

Signature of bearer.

This passport is not valid unless signed by the person to whom it has been issued.

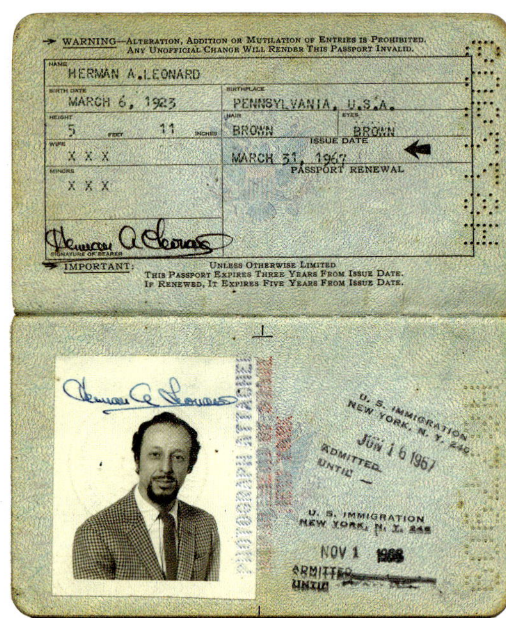

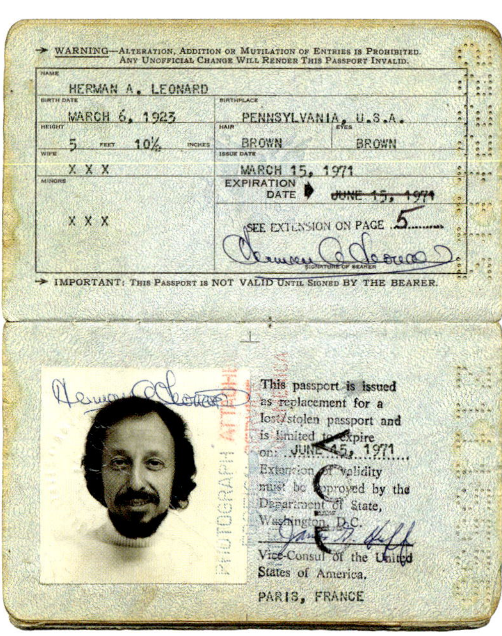

Photographs the movie sets of *Dr. No* and *Paris Blues* featuring American musicians including Louis Armstrong and Duke Ellington.
Marries Jacqueline Fauvreau.

1961
Shoots fashion in Morocco, Tunisia, Spain, Seychelles, Canary Islands, and Greece.

1962
Daughter, Valerie Leonard, born in Paris, to mother Jacqueline Leonard.

1964
Shoots *Playboy* features: *The Girls of Russia and the Iron Curtain Countries, The Girls of the Riviera*, and *The Prostitutes of Paris*.
Travels to Warsaw, Prague, Vienna, and London for *Playboy* shoots.

1965
Separates from Jacqueline Leonard, whom he divorces some years later.

1968
Meets Elisabeth Braunlich who becomes long-time partner.
Leonard and Braunlich travel to Tunisia, Morocco, and the Canary Islands.

1970–1973
Travels extensively, shooting for *ER* magazine: Hong Kong, Thailand, Indonesia, Bali, India, Kashmir, Afghanistan, Iran, Turkey, Ethiopia, Kenya, and Tanzania.

1971
Leonard and Braunlich move from Paris to London.

1972
Daughter, Shana Leonard, born in London, to mother Elisabeth Braunlich.

1974
Leonard and Braunlich move from London to Paris.

1977
Son, David Leonard, born in Paris, to mother Elisabeth Braunlich.

1980
Leonard and family move from Paris to the island of Ibiza, Spain.

1985
Publishes first monograph, *L'oeil du Jazz*, Editions Filipacchi, France.
Receives 'Music Book of the Year' award from the French Literary Society.

1987
Leonard and family move from Ibiza to London.
Braunlich and Leonard separate.

1988
First exhibition of Leonard's jazz photographs at the Special Photographers Company, London.

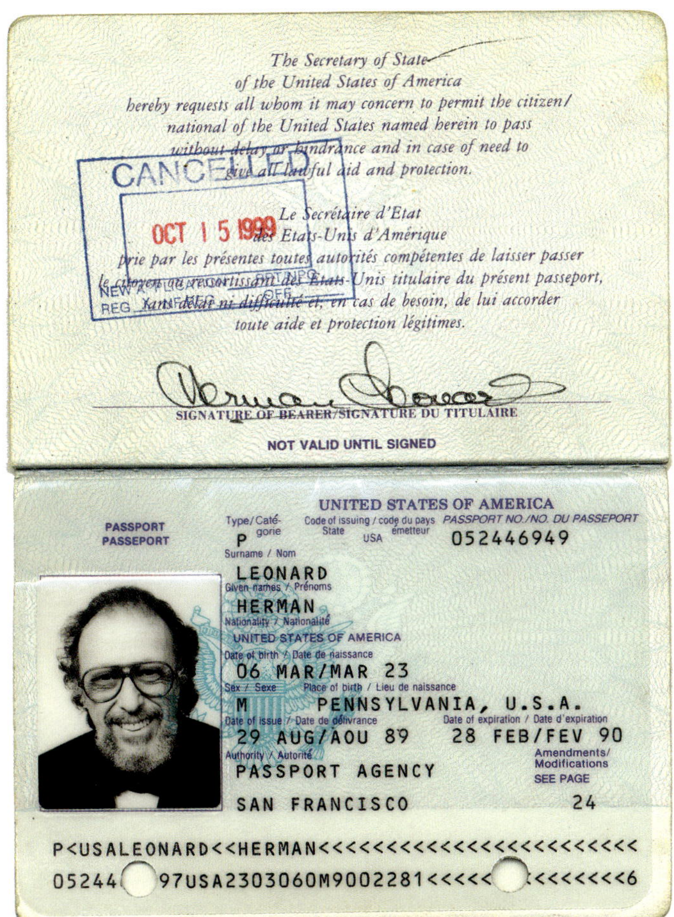
The Secretary of State
of the United States of America
hereby requests all whom it may concern to permit the citizen/
national of the United States named herein to pass
without delay or hindrance and in case of need to
give all lawful aid and protection.

CANCELLED
OCT 15 1999

Le Secrétaire d'Etat
des Etats-Unis d'Amérique
prie par les présentes toutes autorités compétentes de laisser passer
le citoyen ou ressortissant des Etats-Unis titulaire du présent passeport,
sans délai ni difficulté et, en cas de besoin, de lui accorder
toute aide et protection légitimes.

SIGNATURE OF BEARER/SIGNATURE DU TITULAIRE
NOT VALID UNTIL SIGNED

UNITED STATES OF AMERICA
PASSPORT
PASSEPORT
Type/Catégorie P
Code of issuing State / code du pays émetteur USA
PASSPORT NO./NO. DU PASSEPORT 052446949
Surname / Nom LEONARD
Given names / Prénoms HERMAN
Nationality / Nationalité UNITED STATES OF AMERICA
Date of birth / Date de naissance 06 MAR/MAR 23
Sex / Sexe M
Place of birth / Lieu de naissance PENNSYLVANIA, U.S.A.
Date of issue / Date de délivrance 29 AUG/AOU 89
Date of expiration / Date d'expiration 28 FEB/FEV 90
Authority / Autorité PASSPORT AGENCY SAN FRANCISCO
Amendments/ Modifications SEE PAGE 24

P<USALEONARD<<HERMAN<<<<<<<<<<<<<<<<<<<<<<<<<
05244 97USA2303060M9002281<<<<< <<<<<<<<6

1989
Moves from London to San Francisco, California.

1989
Publishes *The Eye of Jazz,* the English edition of *L'oeil du Jazz*, Viking Press.

1990
First United States exhibition tours major cities. First visit to New Orleans, Louisiana; attends opening at A Gallery for Fine Photography.

1991
Moves from San Francisco to New Orleans.
Extensive product line published by Graphique de France featuring jazz images.

1992–2006
Establishes a full service archive with images appearing in publications and exhibitions worldwide. Continues to shoot and expand his archive.

1995
Publishes *Jazz Memories*, Editions Filipacchi, France.
Receives Honorary Master of Science in Photography from The Brooks Institute of Photography, Santa Barbara, California.

1997
Premier of the film *Frame After Frame: The Images of Herman Leonard,* by Louisiana Public Broadcasting.

1999
Receives 'Milt Hinton Award for Excellence in Jazz Photography', Jazz Photographer's Association.

2000
Receives 'Excellence in Photography' award, Jazz Journalists Association.

2001
Extensive image use in *Jazz: A Film By Ken Burns* and the accompanying book and CD, *Jazz: A History of America's Music* and *Ken Burns JAZZ Collection,* respectively.

2002
January 5 decreed 'Herman Leonard Day' by New Orleans mayor, Marc Morial.
Publishes *Herman Leonard: Jazz Portraits,* Fotofolio.

2004
Receives 'Lifetime Achievement Award', *Downbeat* magazine.

2005
Exhibits *Passport: The Known and Unknown Photographs of Herman Leonard*, Ogden Museum of Southern Art, New Orleans.
New Orleans home and business destroyed during the flood after Hurricane Katrina.

2006
Moves from New Orleans to Studio City, California.

Exhibition History

1988
Special Photographers Company, London, England

1989
Southampton City Art Gallery, Southampton, England
The Museum of Transport, Glasgow, Scotland
Royal Festival Hall, London, England
The Concert Hall, Aarhus, Denmark

1989
Gallery of Photography, Dublin, Ireland
Triskel Arts Centre, Cork, Ireland
Galerie Lafrache, Cannes, France
Aberdeen Art Gallery, Aberdeen, Scotland
The Cornerhouse, Manchester, England

1990
G. Ray Hawkins Gallery, Santa Monica, California
Barbara Gillman Gallery, Miami, Florida
Fay Gold Gallery, Atlanta, Georgia
North Sea Jazz Festival, The Hague, Holland
Catherine Edelman Gallery, Chicago, Illinois
Jane Corkin Gallery, Toronto, Canada
Robert Klein Gallery, Boston, Massachusetts
Robert Koch Gallery, San Francisco, California
Addison/Ripley Gallery, Washington, D. C.
A Gallery for Fine Photography, New Orleans, Louisiana
Camera Obscura Gallery, Denver, Colorado
Brent Sikkema Gallery, New York, New York

1991
Central Cultural Caixa de Valencia, Valencia, Spain
Kimballs East, Emeryville, California
Morgan Gallery, Kansas City, Kansas
Special Photographers Company, London, England
Blitz Corporation, Tokyo, Japan
Morgan Gallery, Kansas City, Kansas

1992
A Gallery for Fine Photography, New Orleans, Louisiana
Robert Koch Gallery, San Francisco, California
G. Ray Hawkins Gallery, Santa Monica, California
Parco Galleries, Tokyo, Japan
Kirin Plaza, Osaka, Japan

1993
A Gallery for Fine Photography, New Orleans, Louisiana
Brooks Institute of Photography, Santa Barbara, California
Museum of American Art, Athens, Ohio
Nagoya Galleries, Nagoya, Japan

1994
Kirin Gallery, Kyoto, Japan
S. K. Josefsberg Gallery, Portland, Oregon
Special Photographers Company, London, England
Ven Norman Gallery, Covington, Louisiana

1996
Govinda Gallery, Washington, D. C.

1997
Louisiana State University, Baton Rouge, Louisiana
Tatar Alexander Gallery, Toronto, Canada
Ven Norman Gallery, Covington, Louisiana
S. K. Josefsberg Gallery, Portland, Oregon
Carla Sozzani Gallery, Milan, Italy
Fahey/Klein Gallery, Los Angeles, California
Visual Blues Jazz Galerie, Berlin, Germany

1998
Jackson Fine Art, Atlanta, Georgia
Austin Jazz Festival, Austin, Texas
Northwestern State University, Natchitoches, Louisiana
Ohio University, Athens, Ohio

1999
Hastings College, Hastings, Nebraska
Marshall Artist Series, Huntington, West Virginia
Etherton Gallery, Chicago, Illinois
New Zealand Jazz Festival, Wellington, New Zealand
S. K. Josefsberg Gallery, Portland, Oregon

2000
Creative Allies, Boston, Massachusetts
Louisiana Center for the Book, Baton Rouge, Louisiana
Stephen Bulger Gallery, Ontario, Canada
Jazz at Lincoln Center, New York, New York
High Museum of Art, Atlanta, Georgia

2001
Missouri History Museum, St. Louis, Missouri
Sandra Byron Gallery, Sydney, Australia
Monterey Jazz Festival, Monterey, California
Walnut Street Gallery, Fort Collins, Colorado

2002
Candace Perich Gallery, Katonoh, New York
Commune de Padova, Padova, Italy
We Always Swing Jazz Series, Colombia, Missouri

2003
Rupertinum Museum of Modern Art, Salzburg, Austria
Oswald Gallery, Austin, Texas
Andrew Smith Gallery, Sante Fe, New Mexico

2004
King-Tisdell Cottage Foundation, Atlanta, Georgia
North Sea Jazz Festival, Cape Town, South Africa
Duque Arts Center, New Orleans, Louisiana
New Orleans Jazz & Heritage Festival, New Orleans, Louisiana
Ven Norman Gallery, Covington, Louisiana
Gallery of the Auditorio Nacional of Mexico, Mexico City
Gallery 270, Jersey City, New Jersey
Holden Luntz Photography, Palm Beach, Florida

2005
Utah Museum of Fine Art, Salt Lake City, Utah
Ogden Museum of Southern Art, New Orleans, Louisiana
Catherine Edelman Gallery, Chicago, Illinois

2006
Gallery One, Dubai, United Arab Emirates
Polk Museum of Art, Lakeland, Florida

Selected Permanent Exhibitions

Smithsonian Institution National Museum of American History

SITES: Smithsonian Institution Traveling Exhibition Services, Washington, D. C.

Jazz at Lincoln Center, New York, New York

Ogden Museum of Southern Art, New Orleans, Louisiana

American Jazz Museum, Kansas City, Missouri

Lyman Allyn Art Museum, New London, Connecticut

Pensacola Museum of Art, Pensacola, Florida

Louisiana State Museum Traveling Exhibition, Baton Rouge, Louisiana

Kennedy Museum of Art, Ohio University, Athens, Ohio

Gershwin to Gillespie: Portraits in American Music, George Eastman House, Rochester, New York

One Hundred Photographs: a Collection by Bruce Bernard

Joshua Mann Pailet, A Gallery for Fine Photography, New Orleans, Louisiana

Miami Children's Museum, Miami, Florida